IF VOTING CHANGED
THEY'D ABOLIS.

KEN LIVINGSTONE

If Voting Changed Anything,
They'd Abolish It .

COLLINS
8 Grafton Street, London W1
1987

William Collins Sons & Co. Ltd
London · Glasgow · Sydney · Auckland
Toronto · Johannesburg

BRITISH LIBRARY CATALOGUING IN PUBLICATION DATA

Livingstone, Ken
If voting changed anything, they'd abolish it.
I. Livingstone, Ken 2. Politicians –
England – London – Biography
I. Title
942.1085′092′4   DA676.8.L5

ISBN 0-00-217770-6

First published 1987
Reprinted 1987
Second reprint 1987
Copyright © Ken Livingstone 1987

Photoset in Linotron Ehrhardt by
Rowland Phototypesetting Ltd
Bury St Edmunds, Suffolk
Made and printed in Great Britain by
Robert Hartnoll (1985) Ltd, Bodmin

*For Ethel, my mother and Bob, my father,
who ensured I grew up without fear of those
whose sex, race, religion or sexual orientation
led them along alternative paths to my own.*

CONTENTS

ACKNOWLEDGEMENTS

I have deliberately aimed this book at a general public audience because without the support of ordinary people the Labour GLC would have achieved nothing. It would be invidious to try to list all those to whom I am indebted: I would inevitably exclude many people who contributed an enormous amount to what we achieved. The few hundred activists who worked for years to win the GLC, the thousands of staff who turned the policies into reality, and many others who rallied to our support, all share the credit for this book. I thank them all.

There are also those who physically ensured that the book finally appeared. My thanks to Jane (Max) Davis, who did invaluable research in assembling documents and statistics before we left County Hall; to Sharon Trunell, Theresa Coates and Pam Roberts, who had the horrendous task of turning my illegible handwritten scrawl into a clean typescript; to my agent, Anne McDermid, the only agent who seems to understand socialist writers; to Helen Fraser, my commissioning editor at Collins, for her continuing calmness as the book slowly appeared in dribs and drabs; to my editor, Nadia Lawrence; and to Inigo Thomas, the copyeditor. Finally, to those close friends who tolerated my endless discussions about the book and still continued to share my company, my thanks and love.

1

Lambeth Lessons

When I joined the Labour Party in March 1969 at the age of 23, it was one of the few recorded instances of a rat climbing on board a sinking ship. I was swimming against a tide of disillusionment. All the high hopes of Labour's 1964 General Election victory had been squandered by the incompetence of Harold Wilson's first government. Not only were few joining the party, but many good socialists had resigned. Wilson's support for the American bombing of Vietnam, racist immigration legislation, a wage freeze, cuts in the National Health Service and housing programmes, as well as anti-trade union laws had triggered an exodus from the Labour Party. The International Socialists (now the Socialist Workers' Party), the Socialist Labour League (now the Workers' Revolutionary Party) and a whole range of single-issue groups such as the Campaign for Nuclear Disarmament, Shelter and the Child Poverty Action Group all gained from Labour's loss.

There were also those who, having worked so hard and been promised so much by Wilson, now believed the world could not be changed and turned their backs on political activity altogether. Politicians who raise the hopes and capture the imaginations of ordinary women and men only to betray that trust do more to undermine faith in democracy than any fascist could ever do.

Events on the international stage at that time had convinced many socialists that the real struggle had moved to the streets, the factories and the universities. In 1968 the world went through a series of traumas and shocks which rocked one country after another. In Vietnam, the Tet offensive shattered the whole basis of American propaganda, and made it politically impossible for the

US to keep escalating its troop numbers, thus signalling its eventual defeat.

In Czechoslovakia, the 'Prague Spring' saw the beginnings of a liberalization of the regime and the replacement of an autocratic Stalinist leadership following popular pressure. That situation was mirrored by similar events in France, where a general strike, supported by students, drove President De Gaulle from Paris to seek refuge with French troops stationed in West Germany. All of this was taking place against the background of increasingly confident demands from women and black people in many countries and almost worldwide student strikes and sit-ins. Often in 1968 it seemed possible that somewhere in the world an oppressive regime would be defeated and a genuinely democratic society formed in its place which would reflect the new concerns and hopes of the post-war generation.

It was a time when thousands of people in Britain became politically active for the first time, but the idea of joining the Labour Party did not even enter their minds. For them, boring labourism had quite simply died on its boring Wilsonian feet.

For me, 1968 was also a year of lessons. By its end, Robert Kennedy and Martin Luther King were dead and the attempt by the young radicals to capture the Democratic Party in the United States had failed amidst the brutality of Chicago's riot police. Richard Nixon was in the White House, and Henry Kissinger was planning the destruction of Cambodia. Russian tanks had brought an end to the hopes of the people of Prague, De Gaulle had restored order in Paris after a deal with the French generals. In Paris the students and strikers continued to occupy and march, but without any co-ordinating role from the Socialist Party, the events of May '68 petered out. Everywhere student militancy began to ebb and while most of the new radical journals survived for some years, their readership now comprised mainly a few committed activists.

The slide from hope to disappointment in just twelve months convinced me that activities on the streets were unlikely on their own to change a Western democracy unless the central state machine was on the point of collapse. Therefore those who wanted to see change could not ignore the traditional parties of the left which gave us access to the levers of power. Equally, we had to realize that control of these parties would not guarantee that the state would respond to socialist policies unless those parties had built considerable popular support.

Two things struck me as I sat in the back room of a party activist's house with a handful of members from my local ward Labour Party. The first was how small the meeting was, and secondly how delighted they all seemed to be that I had turned up. Apparently I was their first new member for two years. Jovially the chair of the meeting told everyone to 'make sure he doesn't get away'.

Shocked at I was by the size of the local Labour Party I had joined, Norwood was nevertheless twice the size of the neighbouring Streatham and Brixton parties and ten times the size of the fourth in the borough, Vauxhall, which had only 50 members on its books. So, in March 1969, after welcoming me with open arms at the first meeting I attended, the party did not take long to find a use for me.

By the time I went along to my second party meeting a month later, I had become chair and secretary of the Norwood Young Socialists (there was only one other member, who was treasurer), a member of the constituency's General Management and Executive Committees and I was also on the Local Government Committee which was preparing the manifesto for the next borough election. After four months, I was the only nomination for membership secretary. My arrival had been rather like taking a bottle of gin into a room full of alcoholics. I was immediately passed round and consumed. I was even invited along to some *Militant* readers' meetings, though the invites stopped once they noticed that I tended to fall asleep during the speaker's lecture.

Although I enjoyed every minute, I was left slightly bemused by the speed of events. My upbringing in an ordinary working-class household and my job for the last eight years as a low-grade technician in a cancer research laboratory had not prepared me for this. I was used to an environment where I was expected to do as

13

I was told. These positions to which I had been elected in the Labour Party were my first taste of unsupervised responsibility. It was a liberation. At school I had often been in trouble, and the hierarchical and élitist world of the medical profession left me frustrated, yearning to have some say in the running of my workplace. When the laboratory management started pushing for redundancies, I became involved in the struggle against them. The workforce was unorganized, so the first move was to set up a branch of ASTMS.

The mood of the times had affected me like thousands of others. I had joined a number of anti-Vietnam demonstrations, though not with any group or party. The issue had become relevant to me in 1967 when I met an American draft resister on a hitch-hiking holiday in the Sahara. In 1968 he had asked me to help him get into Britain and that had brought me into contact for the first time with my local Labour MP, John Fraser, whose firm and public opposition to racism impressed me very much, as it was exceptional amongst Labour MPs at the time.

It had been the promise of the early Wilson era that in 1963 first turned me against the working-class Tory traditions of my family. But I had not been active in the party in the early sixties so I had been spared the very personal sense of betrayal many socialists felt. Many of the socialists who came back into the party during the seventies were amazed that I had joined just after they had all left in disgust, but we had drawn different lessons from the upheavals of 1968.

Within a few weeks of joining the party I started picking up the news and gossip coming out of Lambeth Town Hall, now in its second year of Tory control. The Tories seemed set on a path of radical reform. Their leader Bernard Perkins, who was himself a local government officer, firmly controlled his Group. In alliance with some of the more intelligent and energetic chief officers, Perkins started to reshape the whole outdated structure of the Council and developed a five-year plan to expand services. Their election manifesto had been fairly reactionary, but once in power, they seemed open to persuasion. The Council's Director of Housing, Harry Simpson, forced a change of heart on their plans to cut the housing programme by taking councillors to see the shocking conditions in which black families were forced to live in central Brixton. Instead of making cuts, the Tories promptly quadrupled the programme they had inherited from Labour. This they followed up with a major crackdown on bad landlords. What became clear was that the Tory administration was turning out to be more progressive in its house-building schemes than any previous Labour majority.

Lambeth had for years been a quiet backwater of local government where the leadership was never challenged. Like many other inner-city Labour councils, a strong authoritarian, quite conservative Labour administration had been in power since the war, led by a handful of competent working-class men with strong roots in the area. These men ruled over a group of mediocre councillors who were treated as lobby fodder. Many were barely literate but if they did as they were told and did not cause any trouble, they might, after ten or fifteen years' loyal service, be rewarded with a year as mayor and enjoy all the job's little perks.

Under this regime the approach to the housing crisis had been to decide by how much they dared increase the rates each year and to work backwards from that figure to arrive at the number of houses it would allow them to build. Alderman Cotton, the last Labour Leader of the Council, had spent most of his time preparing plans for turning Brixton town centre into yet another concrete jungle. Just before the 1968 borough elections, however, the Labour Government refused to fund the scheme on the grounds that it would have consumed 10 per cent of the entire sum available for town centre redevelopment throughout Britain.

By 1969, many Labour activists were dismayed by the contrast between their own party's record and the Tories'; and it was not only their housing policy. When it became obvious that some of the younger Tory councillors, who had been unexpectedly elected in normally Labour seats, had more in common with the National Front (calling for the compulsory repatriation of black people), Bernard Perkins moved quickly to expel them from the Group. The Labour administration had lacked the courage to take any action against some of its own members who were quietly but obviously racist. It has to be remembered, of course, that this was

1969. I doubt that Bernard Perkins would get very far in Mrs Thatcher's new model Tory Party.

Fortunately for Labour, there remained some issues on which they were to the left of the Tories, who opposed the idea of free bus passes for pensioners and had slapped on a series of enormous council rent increases. But the differences in direction between the parties were so few, they seemed only to highlight the similarities.

The Tories' successes in Lambeth galvanized a group of us in the local Labour Party to make absolutely sure we did better next time. The driving force behind us was a man called Eddie Lopez. It was a stroke of good fortune that I joined the party in Norwood, where Eddie was party agent. Unlike most agents he was fairly leftwing, genuinely interested in radical issues and impressed me immediately with his inexhaustible capacity for work. The son of a refugee from the Spanish civil war, he was a committed life-long socialist. He carried everyone along with his dynamic enthusiasm. During elections he would have us stuffing envelopes till four or five in the morning. A born leader, he set a hectic pace. He did everything to push me forward as rapidly as possible and was the first person to suggest I should stand for Lambeth Council. Without his support I doubt I would have progressed so quickly in the party. Most other agents would have been busy discouraging me from rocking the boat.

Under his guidance the emerging left wing in Norwood started looking at ways we could stop the mistakes of the past being repeated. The old Labour Group had virtually disintegrated. The former Leader, Alderman Cotton, had died leaving just two members of the old guard, both of whom had lost their seats, with the ability to block the changes we wished to see: Jim Calder, the former deputy leader, and Ewan Carr, whose abrasive style had excluded him from the inner circle of the previous leadership. We knew that a really effective Labour Council would only be possible if Calder and Carr could both be prevented from becoming the Leader. They were tarnished with Labour's poor record in the borough and, given all that was at stake for the people of Lambeth, we intended to do everything in our power to ensure the election of a more radical and open administration.

I set about using my new-found positions in the party to widen the membership. The need for a broader base in the community seemed obvious if we were to reflect its needs. My first contacts were with a group of radical left school students in South London called the Schools' Action Union, which had been set up in the wake of the 1968 student occupations. Many of them joined the party, injecting it with radical fervour. We outraged local head teachers by voting them on to local school governing bodies where they argued for school students' rights. I also campaigned with the Brixton branch of the Black Panthers against local police racism. Luckily Eddie Lopez agreed the party needed to reach out to community groups. Most other South London Labour parties might not have been quite so keen on the new members I was recruiting.

Our campaign for a new-style Lambeth Labour Council was given a boost by the General Election in June 1970. A whole wave of younger new members joined the party and we immediately started encouraging them to consider standing in the following year's borough elections. Our strategy was to target the marginal seats on the Council, which were mainly in our Norwood constituency, because we knew that very few leftwingers were likely to be selected in the safe Labour seats to the north of the borough. Our hopes remained high as endless meetings of the Local Government Committee plodded through the task of drafting the manifesto. The left wing managed to win commitments on all the key points: an increased housing programme; a more open administration; tenant participation in housing management; the establishment of neighbourhood councils; and free travel for pensioners on London Transport.

It was during the drafting of the manifesto that Eddie Lopez realized (long before I did) that we might succeed in preventing Ewan Carr from becoming Leader. He was blunt to the point of rudeness to party members and prospective candidates who did not have his experience of local government finance and procedures. And he lost more support by opposing a firm commitment to introduce the free transport proposal as soon as we were elected. Clearly that policy would have the most immediate impact on the budget, but we were determined to see that the days of fudging were over. Provided the left won all the marginal wards and found a left candidate with some previous experience on the Council, Carr had ruined his chances of leading the Group.

The selection process went much as we expected. In the 30 safe Labour seats in the north of the borough few of the old guard got back and there was an influx of talented, university-educated, young rightwingers – many of whom were eventually to leave the party to join the SDP. In the south, in the 21 seats Labour had a chance of winning, all the candidates selected, bar one, were prepared to vote for a break with the old guard.

Just before the selections started, Pat Craven, a *Militant* supporter, urged me not to stand for the Council on the grounds that local government was a complete dead-end and I would be wasting energy which could be more valuably used elsewhere. His reaction took me aback as I was already looking forward to the changes we could achieve locally. When he realized I was not going to change my mind he threw his weight behind my selection in the Knights Hill Ward and, with a mixture of cajoling and arm twisting, drummed up all the support he could.

I was beginning to feel excited at the prospect of becoming a councillor for the area in which I had spent my whole life. Now at last, I could improve the things that I had wanted to change when I was growing up. After twenty-five years, I knew the area in detail. My local knowledge gave me a distinct advantage over some of the trendy young rightwingers who had moved to the north of the borough and started to take over the Labour Party there.

During my selection I had my first memorable meeting with a new party member called Ted Knight who had finally been allowed to rejoin sixteen years after his expulsion in one of Labour's regular bouts of witch-hunting. I was immediately captivated by his engaging style when, in reply to my thanks for his vote in the selection meeting, he looked me straight in the eye and said: 'Well quite frankly, Comrade, there wasn't anything better on offer.'

The 1971 local election campaign came at the best possible time for Labour. Edward Heath's government was only eleven months old but it had rapidly lost public support. Labour's double-figure lead in the opinion polls proved well founded. Labour had its best local government results since the immediate post-war period. Lambeth's left wing fought to win all the marginal seats and did, though by only 11 votes out of 5,078 cast in one ward.

Looking back on the period leading up to the 1971 borough elections and the following leadership struggles in Lambeth it is interesting to note that almost all the techniques and strategies the left would later successfully employ to take control of the GLC were there in some degree: a discredited Labour leadership which was further weakened during a period of opposition to a Tory administration; the left's determination not to let it happen again; a widened party involvement in drawing up a manifesto with firm election pledges; the drive to radicalize the party by bringing in elements who did not see any real relevance in the Labour Party; links with outside community groups; the selection of left candidates in the marginals rather than a series of exhausting public struggles to take over safer seats; and, finally, the Establishment's candidate for leader being unaware until the last moment that he faced defeat.

In Lambeth in 1971 the left wing lost in the end but I learned valuable lessons from our defeat. In the first place, the whole process had been far too rushed, with personal tensions and antagonisms blurring what should have been a much clearer left-right struggle. The final battle had been exclusively between the councillors, with no real involvement by the wider party membership. We had not offered a large enough share of the positions to that vital centre group of councillors who held the balance of power, so they did not have a large enough stake in defending our planned administration.

Most important was the absence of an obvious left candidate competent to do the leadership job. As we were to find out to our cost, you cannot work around a weak leader. Instead of our shoring him up, he was going to drag us down.

During the closing days of the election campaign, Eddie Lopez was approached by councillor Charles Dryland, the chief whip of the Labour Group, who asked for the support of the left in a bid to defeat the right wing's heir apparent, Ewan Carr, in the leadership contest that was to take place on the Sunday following the election. Dryland was in his early thirties, had been elected for the first time three years before and had become chief whip in the opposition

Labour Group of eight only by default. Not everyone was enthusiastic about the prospect of having him as Leader because it had never been clear just where he stood in the political spectrum although he had voted with the left during the drafting of the manifesto. However, as only a dozen of the 51 Labour councillors had been on Lambeth Council before and none of them had the dual quality of being on the left and even remotely competent to do the job, we were stuck with Dryland.

A simple deal was struck. In exchange for our support we gained firm promises that he would support left candidates in all the key posts, fully implement the manifesto and operate in an open, democratic way, involving the whole party. While we did not trust Dryland, we believed we could control him by filling all the other important positions.

On the Friday morning after the election, while Ewan Carr was at the Town Hall discussing with the chief executive the way in which he intended to run the Council, we began lobbying for the extra seven or eight votes we needed to get our candidates in. The original idea that I should be deputy leader was dropped in favour of another leftwinger who had been in the party considerably longer than my two years and two months. However, since most of the struggles were likely to be in the housing area, we dug in our heels on the demand that I should chair the Housing Committee. Ewan Carr and his young rightwing supporters did not wake up to the fact that we posed a serious threat to their plans until it was too late. They also made the fatal mistake of revealing that their candidates for Leader, deputy leader and chief whip would also chair the three most important committees. We were able to spread the word about such an unhealthy concentration of power and it swung the crucial few votes that gave us victory.

At the Sunday morning Group meeting we narrowly won the leadership and deputy leadership but lost the vital position of chief whip. Our opponents were stunned and their reaction was immediate and vicious. In the thirty-hour interval before the election of the committee chairs they decided not to accept any of the positions we had offered them. The prospect of such a split in the party shifted a crucial few centrist votes into their camp. They also brought the Labour Party Regional Organizer, John Keys, into the fight on their side. When the Group reassembled it was faced with a boycott of the new leadership by about 40 per cent of the Group and a stinging personal attack on the left by Keys, who warned that disciplinary action might be taken against Eddie Lopez by the National Labour Party because of his role in the coup. Faced with such an onslaught the centre collapsed. The handful of councillors whom we had won over for Sunday's meeting switched on Monday and the committee chairs went to the old guard and their rightwing supporters.

I was defeated by Ewan Carr as chair of Housing but was then elected unopposed as vice-chair. After the meeting we gathered in the Leader's room to plan tactics. It soon became obvious to those of us on the left that Dryland, who was now surrounded by rightwing committee chairs, would shift his position. However, we could not know then that within three years we would be completely defeated and isolated and that we had seven years of hard struggle ahead before a left leadership would be elected.

Those of us who had arrived in the Town Hall for the first time immediately began trying to carry out the manifesto. The Council's full-time officers – as is usually the case – threw themselves into their normal post-election work of sizing up the potential of the new members, looking to see which of them had influence in the new Group, and beginning the task of seducing the brightest with the prospect of operating the Council machine until they had safely come to share the ambitions of the bureaucracy itself.

For me it was a case of learning as I went along. The officer who set out to take me under his wing and educate me in the ways of local government in general, and housing in particular, was Harry Simpson, the Director of Housing who three years previously had educated the new Tory administration into accepting the need for an increased housing programme. Simpson was a dynamic officer whose ambitions to tackle the housing problems of Lambeth co-incided with the Labour Party programme. His style was relaxed and open and he took delight in poking fun at the bureaucratic pomposities of his fellow officers. Unlike many of his colleagues, he welcomed the new Council's commitment to public participation and was eager to push ahead with tenant co-operatives on our estates.

I had known nothing about the politics and economies of housing until I became involved in drawing up the Labour manifesto and active in supporting the local family squatting groups. Simpson bombarded me with textbooks on the subject and I was constantly in the housing department questioning officers not only about our policies but about their own ideas. Rapidly, I discovered there were so many studies, reports and surveys around that you could construct a seemingly unanswerable case to justify almost any policy initiative that you chose to support. As it dawned on me that the facts could be manipulated in this way by skilful officers, I came more and more to rely on trusting my own instincts even if the supposedly impartial facts offered contrary advice. This approach used to outrage some of the university-educated officers and members who had a greater respect for 'the facts', but I was right more often than I was wrong.

It was intoxicating to be at what seemed at the time the centre of events. We were pushing ahead with our schemes. We had honoured our pledge that pensioners should travel free on London Transport buses. We introduced the provision of free contraception for anyone who lived or worked in the borough. When Mrs Thatcher (then Education Secretary) made it illegal for Education Authorities to give children free school milk, Lambeth – which was not an education authority – stepped in to continue paying for the service.

The manifesto proposal to establish neighbourhood councils went ahead under Mike Petrou, the deputy leader of the Council, who even managed to get the Home Office to provide 30 per cent of the £30,000 cost of the scheme. Five staff were appointed to help set up and service six neighbourhood councils, each with the grand sum of £1,000 to spend. These councils were not directly elected but were federations of local community, tenants and church groups.

I was suddenly involved in key decisions about the nature, form and speed of our growing housing programme. What balance should be struck between redevelopment and rehabilitation? How rapidly could we decant the homeless families from our Dickensian halfway homes? How soon could we establish tenants' committees on our estates and improve the speed of housing repairs. And for how long would we be able to freeze the rents?

The Tories had planned to increase the rents; we cancelled the increase. The Tories had planned to build a cluster of the highest residential tower blocks in Europe; we stopped the project until it could be reviewed by a committee of councillors. Homelessness was not to be treated like a crime, so we instructed that newly homeless families were to be immediately rehoused. The council was already preparing plans to provide housing for young single people as the next step to solving Lambeth's housing problems. As Lambeth had been the first council to open a centre to provide a comprehensive housing service for all its residents, we also received a constant flow of delegations from other councils who were interested to see how this new system worked.

One of my first priorities was to do something to tackle the scandal of the number of empty houses awaiting redevelopment or modernization. I called a meeting between the squatting groups with whom I had been campaigning before the election, the Leader, the Housing chair and officers of the housing and legal departments. We agreed to pass over to the squatters all those empty houses which the council could not use immediately, while the squatters would form a Housing Association, register all their members on the Council's waiting list and pass the houses back when our builders were ready to tackle them. Those who did not yet qualify for rehousing when their homes were passed back would be accommodated in alternative short-life properties which the Council would continue to pass to the Housing Association.

Councillors are generally led to believe that they are at the centre of events and that their decisions are being translated into directives which flow through the bureaucracy to reach the world outside, where they change the lives of the borough's residents. However, this is an illusion and in Lambeth nowhere was the illusion as strong as in the housing department. The bureaucrats' response to Labour's policies was low-key. Our plans to end the halfway homes were bitterly resisted at all stages by the department and the neighbourhood councils were viewed with distrust. Most chief officers considered them an unacceptable interference in the proper relationship between the local council establishment and the people.

The management structure of Lambeth's Council had undergone dramatic changes during the three-year Tory administration. Until 1965, the boroughs had been very small, weak bodies with most of the services concentrated at County Hall under the London County Council (the predecessor to the GLC). With the reorganization in 1965 of London's local government the boroughs took over many of the LCC's key services – the most important being social services. The Labour councils were slow to wake up to the reality of this shift of power. When Labour had lost office in Lambeth in 1968, the Council was still being run as a loose collection of unco-ordinated services. Those members who returned to the Council in 1971 found it completely transformed.

The Council was being run like a medium-sized business – having adopted all the practices of corporate management introduced by major British firms in the 1960s. Many of the new rightwing councillors had come from business or professional backgrounds and words like information flows, systems theory, critical path analysis, and forward planning rationalization slipped easily from their lips.

Lambeth had put itself in the vanguard of corporate management with a chief executive replacing the town clerk and a powerful hierarchical board of departmental directors who oversaw all the work of the Council and prepared a five-year community plan intended to be a firm framework for the future development of Council policies. At the centre of this new empire sat the Management Services Directorate, which had quadrupled in size during this management revolution. The result of the changes was that the number of manual workers employed had stayed the same at 3,600 but the number of white-collar workers had doubled from 1,800 to 3,600 between 1967 and 1974. Many of the extra white-collar staff were in areas such as the Social Services Directorate, where new working practices encouraged social workers to model themselves on the professions with elaborate career structures and a detachment from their clients. This meant that much of the increase of staff was consumed in internal management systems and failed to lead to any improvement in the service provided to the public.

The new Council was soon persuaded to believe that these systems would give greater councillor control and make the whole system more flexible and responsive to the needs of the borough. The truth was quite different. This was shown by an excellent study of Lambeth Council during this period undertaken by Cynthia Cockburn and published under the title *The Local State*. She demonstrated that the pressure for the changes had come from a central government alarmed to see that local council spending had doubled during the 1950s and 1960s and was now responsible for nearly a third of all public spending in Britain. The 1964 Labour Government had given in to Treasury pressure to bring local government spending under central government control and had initiated a series of committees to investigate local councils and recommend internal management changes. The resulting reports (by Maud, Mallaby, Patterson and Bains) laid down guidelines for running local councils as though they were businesses rather than democratically run services. Lambeth had adopted their recommendations.

Contrary to all the promises, councillors found that their powers were reduced under the new system and many areas of policy and services disappeared into directorates where there ceased to be any councillor supervision. All reports had to go through the Board of Directors before being presented to a committee. This gave the councillors no more than one option, which was the majority view of the chief officers. Although theoretically a chief officer could dissent from a report, this was unlikely to happen in front of councillors, who were often perceived as the enemy.

To parallel the Board of Directors there was a Policy Committee chaired by the Leader and including the chairs of all other committees. This was designed to operate like a cabinet, but the chief officers tended to dominate the proceedings and it was often difficult to defeat these 'professionals' in debate. Tory and Labour backbenchers were barred from this committee and its reports were private until the Leader chose to bring them up at a Labour Group meeting. Members of the committee were bound by the doctrine of collective responsibility; it was therefore difficult for backbenchers to overturn decisions once they had been taken.

The leading councillors were rapidly absorbed into the system,

25

but there was growing frustration among others who felt impotent. I shared much of their frustration. Unlike many of the new, university-educated professional members, I had no training in these new management techniques and constantly struggled to keep up with the jargon of leading councillors and chief officers. Fortunately, at the time I had just become a student at a local teacher training college and as the course was less than demanding I was able to spend time educating myself in the ways of the Town Hall.

It was not just the council bureaucracy which stood in the way of the implementation of our policies. They were finally buried by a fatal blow from central government.

The Heath Government carried into law the 1972 Housing Finance Act, which had two main purposes. Firstly it would force a series of annual rent increases for council tenants until the rents became what a central-government-appointed board deemed 'fair'. Secondly, it introduced a breathtakingly generous system of housing subsidies to support programmes in those areas with the most acute problems: 90 per cent of the cost of the building, modernization or acquisition of housing in stress areas would be borne by the Government. (It was this provision which allowed boroughs like Islington, Camden and Lambeth to undertake major programmes of municipalization until 1975 when the Labour Government took further control, giving itself the right to set a maximum limit for each council's expenditure on housing. Thus is was a Labour government that started the collapse in the housing programme which was to accelerate under Thatcher.)

Failure to implement the 1972 Housing Finance Act and increase the rents could lead to councillors being surcharged and debarred from office (the fate of Liverpool and Lambeth councillors fourteen years later after another local government finance act). The 1972 Act also included a provision allowing the government to appoint a Housing Commissioner to step in and run the council's housing department if the councillors failed to agree the regular rent increase.

It was during the campaign against the Housing Finance Act

that Ted Knight and I started working closely together. Most of the General Management Committee delegates viewed him with distrust. He had been readmitted to the party a year before and as he had spent eight of his sixteen years in exile working for the Workers' Revolutionary Party, some suspected, quite wrongly, that he might still be a secret member. Sensing their suspicion, Ted tended to be over-abrasive in his dealings with them, especially with those who had voted for his expulsion. He had often been under surveillance by Special Branch while with the WRP, so not surprisingly was intensely secretive and always kept his personal life separate from his political work.

Ted Knight appeared considerably older than his 36 years and his formal manner and conservative style made him seem out of place in the midst of those younger members who were products of the more relaxed and liberated sixties. He took a fairly traditional leftwing approach and did not display much enthusiasm for some of the more radical elements I was recruiting to the party. Originally I misjudged Ted by assuming that he had tired of revolutionary politics and had come back into the Labour Party in search of a parliamentary career. I was rapidly disabused of this notion. During his first General Management Committee meetings, he took a series of uncompromising and divisive positions. Although we usually voted the same way, I felt his speeches often did more to alienate support than to win it over. But on two key issues he changed my mind. The first was the need to withdraw British troops from northern Ireland. Like most people, I had supported the decision to send troops to stop those rioting police who were burning down Catholic homes in August 1969. Ted argued that the troops would eventually be used by the Heath Government against the nationalist community and as events proved him right, I changed my mind.

The second issue was over how to respond to the Housing Finance Act. I was very worried about what the Tory-appointed commissioners would do to our housing programme if we did not comply and raise rents. It took several hours of discussion before Ted was able to convince me that if we could mobilize enough public support we might be able to get a dozen or more councils to stand firm against the Government and force them to back down.

Once we had reached this agreement I threw myself fully into the campaign and Ted and I started a political relationship which, despite a couple of bitter clashes, remained extremely useful to both of us until the rate-capping disaster thirteen years later. Few people could be quite as charming and supportive as Ted Knight when he was on your side, or quite so obstructive when he was not.

The campaign against the Housing Finance Act never really took off. Every time Labour councillors from different boroughs came together to plan a concerted response it was obvious that no one was confident of achieving unity on the issue. Each council gave in one by one. Without a national strategy opposing the new law the public was kept in the dark about its implications.

In my own ward, where Ted Knight was chair of the local branch, we had a large proportion of council tenants and so undertook an extensive programme of leafleting, building up to a main rally in the local secondary school hall with a seating capacity of 1,200. On the night of the meeting, Ted, who was chairing the rally, sat on the platform flanked by myself and the other two ward councillors. We waited. Eventually two local residents – who happened to be members of the local branch of the Communist Party – plus one dog arrived. Undeterred by the absence of a crowd and convinced of the rightness of our cause, we delivered a 90-minute harangue to our public who, luckily for us, were unable to sneak out unnoticed.

When the Council finally met to vote on the housing act on Wednesday 9 August 1972, there was uproar. The leadership had taken a block booking on all the seats in the public gallery so that tenants would be unable to watch the proceedings. Many members of the Labour Group who had initially agreed with the campaign of non-compliance had changed their minds at the preceding Group meeting. In the end only 18 Labour members voted against the rent increase; one of them told me he was only voting that way because he knew we were certain to lose the vote. He later joined the SDP.

Our defeat led to an immediate decline in the radicalism and confidence within the Group, the majority driven to the right by the pressures of the Government and its penalties. David Stimpson, one of the Labour aldermen who had served under the Cotton and Calder regime, emerged as the leadership candidate of the right.

He had to wait nine months for the next annual meeting of the Labour Group for his chance to unseat Dryland.

Stimpson held the key position of chair of the Staff Committee, which put him in daily contact with the management, and he was by far the most competent and hard-working member on the right of the Group. His beliefs were based on a strong ideology which enabled him to make decisions and act quickly and decisively as each new policy row arose. The newly emerged rightwing majority in the Group meant that he could operate the Policy Committee more democratically without the fear of defeat on policy issues. By making the committee more accountable to the Group he also diffused – for the time being – some of the doubts being expressed by the left about the concentration of power within the Council.

By the annual meeting in April 1973, the usual canvassing had revealed that Stimpson and Mike Petrou, the left's candidate, each had about 40 per cent of the vote. Dryland would be lucky to win 20 per cent and he approached both camps and said he was prepared to swing his share behind whichever faction would give him the chair of Housing. We on the left took the view that if we could not support Dryland for Leader it was wrong to impose him on the Housing Committee, giving him a job which required hard work, confidence and sensitivity to public needs. Stimpson had no such qualms and so was elected Leader.

Dryland defeated me for the chair of the Housing Committee. In retrospect, many people thought we should have done the Dryland deal, putting forward the argument that a left Leader would have taken the Group back to its initial radicalism. We could have got rid of Dryland the following year once the leadership had assembled a new majority – the very tactic Stimpson adopted to marshal the forces of the right. My commitment to our housing policies prevented me from supporting that view but the episode was a valuable lesson which I was to bear in mind in the run-up to the 1981 GLC election, at a time when the left was a crucial handful of votes short of a majority in the incoming Group.

The chief officers now saw their chance to cement an alliance with the new leadership in shared control of the management system and they moved ahead quickly. The new Director of Housing and the Director of Development had increasingly come under attack from both the neighbourhood councils and local action groups who were opposing the Council's wholesale redevelopment strategy.

The new Housing Director, Tony Collinson, did not poke fun at the pomposities of other chief officers like his predecessor Harry Simpson. Instead he expected to be treated with the respect he felt his position deserved. Unfortunately for him the neighbourhood councils and some half-dozen anti-redevelopment groups were coming into daily contact with Council departments and beginning to realize that the great new corporate management machine was incompetent, bureaucratic, unresponsive and often factually wrong.

Faced with an increasingly well-researched catalogue of council errors of policy and fact, the officer leadership had two options: either it could learn from public criticisms, correct its failings and then operate in a more participatory and efficient way; or it could seek to exclude and marginalize its critics. Like most bureacracies, Lambeth chose to take the latter course and David Stimpson went along with that decision.

Collinson caused uproar amongst the NCs and parts of the Labour Party by refusing to attend an NC meeting. When he and Ted Hollamby, the Director of Development, did finally attend the meeting, they further soured ꞏations by announcing that they intended to tape record the eꞏ nts. At the same time they and the other chief officers refused to include the NC programme in the annual revision of the five-year community plan. Later, in a report to the Policy Committee, they pointed out that the NCs' right to submit reports direct on to committee agendas meant that, unlike all other reports, they had not been vetted by the Directors' Board and were therefore 'often uninformed of the wider context of the relevant established programmes and priorities of the Council'. They also complained the NCs were creating too many demands on officers' time with requests for information, meetings and the circulation of minutes. (I had never noticed any great reluctance to circulate paper in the Town Hall before this.) The officers asked the politicians to restrict the access of members of the NCs to the Town Hall and suggested 8.45am to 10am and 2pm to 3pm as approved visiting hours!

The Policy Committee broadly endorsed the officers' position but watered it down. When the recommendations came to the Group, the right wing launched a full-scale attack. Many backbenchers complained that the NCs were replacing the councillors as the point of contact between the public and the Council. Some of the more traditional, orthodox leftwingers condemned them as 'middle-class dominated' and 'outside' the Labour movement. The result was that the Group voted to close down the co-ordinating neighbourhood councils' sub-committee and although the reports from NCs were still placed on committee agendas, officers openly treated them with contempt. The reports often disappeared into the bureaucracy for so long that they were irrelevant by the time officers eventually responded.

Slowly but surely, officers started to restore the normal protocol and respect for the formal hierarchy which had been subverted in the initial radicalism of the new Council. NCs were now prevented from dealing with middle-rank and junior officers; all contacts had to be through the directors. The next attempt to re-establish orthodoxy came in an attack on the Family Squatting Group. The scheme had worked very well in the two years since June 1971; there were now more than 300 people living in about a hundred houses. The pressures of homelessness were building up under a new wave of evictions by landlords eager to cash in on the house price boom triggered, in part, by the gentrification of a number of inner-city areas.

With Charles Dryland as chair of Housing and Tony Collinson as Director, I was rapidly frozen out of the decision-making process. Without consulting anyone else, they decided to stop passing short-life houses awaiting redevelopment to the family squatters; instead, Council workers were sent into newly vacated homes to smash the toilets and kitchens so as to make them uninhabitable.

At this time I was also working with private tenants' associations to prepare compulsory purchase orders for the Lambeth properties of one of the largest private landlords in London, the Gerson Berger empire. Press interest in the Berger family was heightened by their unusual lifestyle; the family lived as recluses in a very ordinary house in Hackney and used all the profits from their property empire to sustain an obscure religious sect based abroad.

Although many of the flats were kept empty, and repairs to the blocks were almost non-existent, Dryland and Collinson did not want to take over up to 1000 flats at a time when the housing department could barely cope with its own over-ambitious redevelopment programme.

To get around the obstruction I foresaw, I exercised my right under the Standing Orders of the Council to write my own report for the Housing Committee outlining the scandal of the Berger properties and recommending compulsory purchase orders. The housing officers clearly had no intention of opposing my proposals in public. Instead, they asked the chair to move that the debate be held after the press and public had been excluded from the meeting. I had anticipated this and had made sure large numbers of the tenants came to the meeting. With elections only ten months away and many voters who lived in the Berger properties watching from the public gallery, the councillors on the committee threw out the proposal for a secret debate and then passed my recommendations. The chief executive, who had come to the meeting to point out that there was no provision for this policy in the agreed five-year community plan, wisely said very little. That evening effectively marked the end of any working relationship between me and the bureaucracy.

Obstruction from the Housing chair and senior officers also dogged my attempts to get families moved out of the council's three remaining halfway homes. The housing department had for years been biased in favour of the 'respectable' working class so that new council housing was usually filled by white, skilled, working-class and lower middle-class families. A housing welfare worker would be sent to look at the family's current home and assess their 'home standards'. Only families with 'good home standards' got new housing; the middle-class welfare workers invariably decided that black people, single parents and the unemployed only deserved older re-let properties. I had failed to overturn this policy because the Housing Committee had been told that the GLC would not accept Lambeth families for rehousing on GLC estates unless they had been graded. However, when I eventually became vice-chair of Housing Management at the GLC in 1974, the GLC Housing Director reported that the policy had been continued only because the London boroughs demanded it! Although I proposed we should stop the practice, Labour rightwingers voted with the Tories to retain the policy, knowing exactly what a discriminatory system they were perpetuating.

Although it was Council policy gradually to empty the halfway homes, the housing department was eager to retain at least some as they could use the threat of eviction into these blocks against tenants who fell out of line. I could make no headway until I resigned as vice-chair of the committee in protest at the obstruction of the policy of the chair of Housing. Then, with the 1974 Borough Council election campaign about to begin, David Stimpson moved quickly to ensure that the bureaucracy carried out the policy and the process of rehousing began.

Two months after David Stimpson was elected as Leader in April 1973, the Labour Party Local Government Committee held its annual meeting to elect new officers and begin again the process of drawing up the manifesto and of overseeing the selection of candidates. By now, Ted Knight and I had formed a good working relationship. We had organized to get the maximum left vote present at the meeting in an attempt to replace the existing leadership in Lambeth. Although Stimpson, supported by the council officers, had rapidly established his predominance within the Labour Group, his administration was viewed with some suspicion by the borough Labour parties.

It came as a shock to the right wing when I was narrowly elected to chair the Local Government Committee. Using this position we were able to widen the manifesto preparation further than in 1970 with a series of open working parties dealing with each area of Council policy. A number of radical elements were drifting back into the party at the time. Many of those who had left six or seven years before were now returning and local women's and gay groups started to get involved with the party. There was also increased activity by tenants' and community groups, particularly those in the neighbourhood councils who now had no illusions left about the direction of the Council leadership.

Ted Knight and I concentrated our efforts on two key areas. First, we had to convince many good socialists that they should stand for the Council. This proved not as easy as we had hoped.

Many people were reluctant because they felt they had neither the time nor the ability to be a councillor. Most of the committee chairs on the Council went out of their way to demonstrate that the demands of their jobs required workaholic genius. Simple issues were made unintelligible and verbal reports were laced with jargon when local councillors reported back to the party. With some success we set out to demystify the role of the councillor.

The second key area was to include a review of the corporate management system as a part of our manifesto process. After two years on the Council I was convinced that the system just did not work. Councillors and chief officers lived in a world of endless meetings and the decisions they made were seldom successfully transmitted through the hierarchy to the day to day of the lives of the public. A prime example of this was the grand housing plans which were rapidly coming apart. Vast areas of the borough were now under compulsory purchase orders and due for demolition. But within those areas were hundreds of perfectly good homes side by side with slums. All were to be demolished, irrespective of condition. This approach was partly the result of the Government's housing grants which were much more generous for demolition than for modernization. But the programme was now out of control.

Shortages of key Council staff and problems in the building industry caused delays and massive cost over runs when building work finally did begin. On average, it took seven years from the moment the Council declared a compulsory purchase order and announced it was to redevelop an area to the completion of the development. Often it would take three or four years to rehouse everyone from an area before demolition could even begin, and then the builder sometimes blackmailed the Council into paying him extra money to finish the building work after long delays. If the Council refused to pay, the builder would simply go into liquidation and immediately start up with another company. It is not surprising that the demand of local action groups for rehabilitation began to attract support within the Labour Party.

In the end we on the left got a manifesto which was a logical development of the socialist policies in the 1971 manifesto and many new people came forward on to the panel of candidates. Where we failed was in the selections themselves. At the next

34

election Labour was not expecting to gain extra seats from the Tories as we had captured the marginals in 1971. Therefore the left had to try to deselect sitting members. As most councillors had been elected for the first time three years earlier, and few of the new party members were joining in the north of the borough, we did not expect to find this easy. And we were not disappointed. Ted Knight and I tried to gain selection in wards outside Norwood but were defeated. By the end of the selection process the left had made only three gains but so had the right wing. In the election itself the Tories won five Labour seats, three of which had been held by leftwingers and two by rightwingers.

When the new Group met for the first time it seemed to have polarized. The left–right split had not greatly changed but within each camp several people had been replaced with others who were more firmly committed one way or the other. As the right held the majority, we would have trouble winning policy arguments even if we had the better case. Stimpson had already made it clear that if he was challenged, he would exclude the left from all posts. Unchallenged he would allow me to become chair of Housing. Notwithstanding this, and perhaps to a degree because of it, the left formed a caucus which was open to anyone else to attend and decided that I should stand against Stimpson.

The left candidates for contested posts were soundly beaten but in deciding to exclude the left, Stimpson had to fill many important positions with incompetents. As a result he spent much of the next four years defending them from both public and party criticism. Had he included Ted Knight and me and others on the left in his administration he would have avoided that problem and possibly survived longer. Ted had anticipated this and argued unsuccessfully in the caucus that we should accept no posts in the administration unless I was elected Leader.

The ideological narrowness of Stimpson's administration meant that he often stumbled into a problem that a broader-based leadership team would have avoided. As party criticism of these blunders built up, he was forced to rely more and more on the chief officers so that increasingly he came to share their priorities and methods of operation.

Within six months most of us on the left had been formally

expelled from the Labour Group. We had voted against Group policy in open Council after the administration had reneged on a promise made before the election to lay out an old factory site as open space. We were readmitted to the Group after a Labour Party National Executive Committee of inquiry found in our favour and criticized the undemocratic procedures of the Labour Group. Given that during the period of our exclusion we had operated as a more effective opposition than the Tories, our return was not unwelcomed by Stimpson.

Unfortunately for him, the experience had welded the left dissidents together. We now enjoyed working as a team against an administration whose growing incompetence earned ridicule at meeting after meeting. We functioned as a disciplined group with each one of us allocated an issue to raise at each meeting. It was like an intensive personal development course and, out of the dozen or so who regularly attended the caucus, both Lesley Hammond and Paul Moore went on to join the 1981 Labour GLC administration. The meeting of the full Labour Group began to resemble Council meetings, with an administration defending and an opposition attacking and slowly grinding them down. Because of his comfortable majority, Stimpson invariably won the votes in the end.

There was considerable good humour at most Group meetings although one old rightwinger used to annoy Ted Knight by ostentatiously switching off his hearing aid whenever Ted made a speech. The meetings were kept calm thanks to the impeccable fairness of the chair, Elsie Horstead, although she was firmly in the Stimpson camp. However, the moods of good-humoured toleration began to be severely stretched as those of us on the left supported the campaigns of the community and squatting groups against the Council.

The major problem facing the Labour Group remained housing. A new crisis had arisen following Dryland's decision to stop passing properties to the Family Squatting Association. As more and more properties were left empty, large numbers of single Homeless people started to move in and squat them. Colin Blau, the third Housing chair in three years, and Dennis Yates, the third Housing Director, announced – without consulting the Labour Group – that instead of passing short-life properties to squatting groups or wrecking them to make them uninhabitable, the Council itself would carry out temporary repairs and use them for homeless families instead of bed and breakfast hotels. By this time, however, there were over 2,500 homes empty. But although the new policy was unmanageable, the Council continued to refuse to pass over the empty properties to the Family Squatting Association. Their campaign against the Council was supported by some of the neighbourhood councils – who were still furious over their exclusion from the Town Hall – and by the left of the party.

From 1973 onwards and throughout 1974, Housing Committee meetings often took place in a state of siege. The police were often called to keep several hundred outraged squatters at bay. Instead of reviving the previous agreement with the Family Squatting Association, which had clearly worked well, the bureaucracy was determined to re-establish orthodox control over the housing stock even though many middle- and lower- ranking staff in the department realized that the position was hopeless. With staff morale collapsing, the Housing chair issued increasingly extreme warnings about his determination to evict all illegal squatters. Meanwhile the number of empty properties crept upwards and more and more people occupied them. The problem was further complicated when Tony Crosland, the Secretary of State for the Environment, quite reasonably started rejecting Lambeth's over-ambitious programme of Compulsory Purchase Orders. This removed the leadership's last hope of demolishing all their properties and solving their squatting problem by a scorched earth policy.

With each passing month, the Council leadership became more and more isolated, with growing opposition throughout Lambeth from both the general public and the Labour Party. I continued to be amazed by their determination to work with the unpopular and incompetent Council bureaucracy rather than build an alliance with the forces outside the Council. But Stimpson knew that would have meant taking power away from the cosy officer–leadership coalition with the Town Hall and this he was not prepared to do. It was not only from outside that pressures were mounting. There was by now growing trade union dissatisfaction with a Labour leadership implementing without a fight cuts demanded by central government.

*

In 1976 I was adopted as the parliamentary candidate for Hampstead. This meant a move to North London. I only had eighteen months left to serve on Lambeth Council, a time filled with frustration at my inability to influence the direction of the Council's housing policy. Watching idiots screw up is never good for your blood pressure. After just two years as Housing chair, Colin Blau asked to be relieved.

Blau's replacement was Malcolm Noble, whom I had first met as a student at my teacher training college. He had not long been in office before I was approached by a junior council officer who informed me that there was evidence of systematic racism in the housing lettings section. He claimed that the lettings cards for newly built council housing had 'whites only' written across them in pencil. I promptly went to Noble and gave him the exact details of which properties were concerned, where the card index system was and the name of the officer responsible. Time passed and I heard nothing so I tackled him again. Noble replied that he had taken up the issue but had found no truth in the rumour. I sought out the officer who had approached me and he stood by his account of events. I pleaded again with Noble to investigate the matter, but he remained convinced the story was untrue. We gave the story to the *South London Press*, who blew it wide open and found the evidence.

The guilty officer was temporarily suspended pending an investigation. I was put on a sub-committee to look into the matter. Malcolm Noble had to admit that the extent of his investigation had been to report our conversation to the Director of Housing at one of their regular chats, only to be told that nothing like that could possibly be going on in his department. Although they had both been told exactly where to look for the evidence, neither had bothered to do so. The director even managed to bungle the suspension of the guilty officer so that by the time he was disciplined he was merely reprimanded for 'mismanagement'.

The sub-committee was packed with leadership supporters and achieved very little. Management was present and consistently stonewalled us. The trade union representatives seemed primarily interested in preventing any disciplinary action being taken against the guilty staff. By a strange coincidence, the NALGO representative on the sub-committee was Bill Pitt, who became the Liberal MP for Croydon North West in 1981 and ran a stridently anti-Ken Livingstone campaign. Perhaps some of his delight in attacking me during that campaign was a hold-over from the bitterness of our clashes on racism in the housing sub-committee. I was leading the demands for disciplinary action while he was waffling on about 'putting the past behind us', which was a lot easier to do if you were well housed and white rather than a member of a black family who had been denied the decent housing to which you were entitled.

That David Stimpson was getting low on allies to fill committee chairs was evident at the next annual meeting. He held on to the leadership of the Group by only five votes over Ted Knight's challenge and I came within one vote of defeating Malcolm Noble in his bid to be re-elected as chair of Housing. Even at this late stage it would have been possible for Stimpson to survive if he had been prepared to change tack and break away from the Town Hall machine, but the final year before the 1978 elections was a succession of disasters. A mass eviction of squatters in St Agnes Place by police was followed immediately by the vandalization of the emptied homes by the Council's workforce. For the first time during his leadership Stimpson had failed to cover himself by getting Group approval before acting on a major decision.

For the party this was the final straw. After the 1978 elections Stimpson did not seek any office and Ted Knight took over as leader. The Housing Director left shortly before the election and three years later Stimpson, Noble and many of those who had held office during his administration defected to the SDP.

2

Films and Fares

I had only been on Lambeth Council for a few months when preparations for the 1973 GLC election began. It was Eddie Lopez who first suggested I stand. I had been thinking about it, but wondered how to overcome the small problem of earning a living whilst serving on a council which met during the daytime. The selection meeting in June 1972 could not have come at a better time for me: it coincided with the Housing Finance Act campaign and followed a year of very favourable publicity in the local press for the various reforms I had been urging on the Housing Committee. This was the first GLC election to be fought on a constituency basis; previously they had been contested as multi-member borough-wide seats. The 1970 election had seen a split representation in Lambeth with the Tories winning three seats to just one for Labour, won by Anna Grieves. Although Anna was the Lambeth-wide representative, she was not particularly associated with Norwood and this meant that there was no sitting member to displace. The only other internal candidate was Ted Knight, who withdrew in my favour a few days before the final meeting. By the time of the selection Eddie Lopez had quietly sewn it up and I won a majority on the first ballot, with Richard Balfe as runner-up.

The question of how to survive financially was kindly solved by the generosity of the Secretary of State for the Environment, the Right Honourable Mr Peter Walker. As a good Tory who had been actively involved in the City in the 1960s, he did not believe in doing anything for nothing and he had introduced a system of paying councillors an attendance allowance, which was to take effect from April 1974. This news opened up the prospect of my serving as a full-time councillor. I was delighted. By this stage I had become fascinated by local government and totally absorbed in my work. The establishment of consultative committees so that tenants could have a say in the management of their estates; the ability compulsorily to purchase properties where landlords were harassing tenants; our initial success in humanizing the treatment of homeless families; the drive to get empty property back in use by the Family Squatting Association – all had convinced me that an imaginative approach to local government could have an immediate and direct impact on people's daily lives. I found the prospect of organizing change in concert with outside groups much more attractive than the idea of being a backbench MP, endlessly discussing legislation and making faces at Tories. (Indeed it was only in late 1975, when it became clear that the Labour Government was determined to cut local government spending so excessively as to effect a shift of power away from local councils, that I began for the first time to seek a parliamentary seat.)

No London-wide leftwing organizing took place in the run-up to the election. The Tories had been in office at the GLC for six years; the previous thirty-three years of continuous Labour rule were generally seen as effective, albeit rightwing administration which had delivered a very impressive range of social provision for London – without any of the corruption that had been a feature of Labour rule in South Wales and the North East. Equally important in avoiding any split between left and right wings was the manifesto which had been drawn up by the London Labour Party Executive. It promised the complete municipalization of the private rented sector, an extensive house-building programme, tenant participation in estate management and opposition to rent increases. I was convinced that Lambeth could not solve its housing problems without the help of the GLC. I was also a keen supporter of the rest of the manifesto, which pledged to scrap the proposals for three motorways to be built in London (and had been supported by Labour till the previous year) and introduce a low-fare scheme as a first step to fares abolition.

Labour's election campaign went like clockwork. It was a stroke of fortune for us that early in the campaign Edward Heath became caught in a traffic jam and phoned the Tory Leader of the GLC, Sir Desmond Plummer, to berate him for failing to solve London's transport problems. Unfortunately for Sir Desmond, he was on a local government junket to Japan at the time and news of the phone call was soon on the front pages of the London evening papers.

My own campaign in Norwood was greatly helped when the Tory GLC member made the mistake of voting in favour of a last-minute change in the motorway plans, which would have re-routed them through the middle of the constituency he was asking to return him to County Hall. Altogether, over five miles of motorway would have demolished 1,100 homes, blighted another 1,200, ploughed through Ruskin, Brockwell and Norwood parks and led to the re-housing of 2,800 people. By planning to re-route the motorway through Norwood, the Tory GLC no doubt saved many votes in Croydon and Bromley but sank their candidate without trace in Norwood. When the candidate denied the scheme's existence we published the plans. When he said he opposed them we published the GLC minutes which showed he had voted for them.

It is an indication of the rigid party discipline inside County Hall in those days that members were prepared to vote to devastate their own constituency rather than vote against the party whip. It is possible that this candidate just did not anticipate the scale of public anger against such a proposal and in this he was not alone. When the party agent, Ken Phipp (Eddie Lopez had moved to be the agent in Exeter), and I first said we wanted opposition to the motorways to be a key issue in the campaign, we were opposed by *Militant* and by Ted Knight, who said it was only of interest to 'middle-class environmentalists' and urged that we should concentrate instead on a class-based attack on the Heath Government. But when over 700 people turned up at our first two meetings Ted was quick to accept the importance of the issue. Three years later he and I were happily disrupting the Archway motorway inquiry in Hornsey where he was standing for Parliament.

Election day saw the Tories decisively defeated. Labour won 57 seats to 33 Tories and 2 Liberals. In Norwood a last-minute red scare campaign made no impact and Labour's vote of 11,622 gave me a 3,615 majority over the Tory and a comfortable 54 per cent of the vote. London-wide, Labour had won 47 per cent of the vote, the Tories 38 per cent, with the Liberals trailing at 12 per cent.

Tony Banks, who was a fellow councillor on Lambeth Council and had been on the GLC since the 1970 election, had organized a small meeting of the left before the selections started but had only mustered half a dozen people. Incredibly, one of those attending was Dr Stephen Haseler, a leading anti-marketeer who wrote for *Tribune*, the leftwing weekly paper. (Haseler went on to become a founder member of the SDP and a virulent red-baiter.) At the meeting we discussed how to get individuals selected who would ensure that the excellent manifesto was carried out. But without an organized, London-wide left, things were to remain largely unchanged, though almost all the incoming members paid lip service to the manifesto.

We met again in the St Stephens Tavern at lunchtime on the Saturday following the election for a short discussion before the Group's Annual General Meeting. I had already been introduced to Illtyd Harrington, who was the leading leftwing personality in the old Labour Group and the obvious candidate for deputy leader. Given the generally dreary and moth-eaten appearance of the outgoing leadership, we hoped that Harrington's flamboyant style, raucus charm and left politics would help to establish the GLC in the public mind. Illtyd's reputation on the left was based on the witch-hunt launched against him in the 1960s by George Brown and Sara Barker when they were deputy leader and national agent of the Labour Party respectively. He had been selected to fight the constituency of Dover at the 1964 General Election but on the recommendation of Brown and Barker the NEC had refused to endorse him as a candidate because of his commitment to CND and other left causes.

While at first sight this may just look like the sort of intolerance which regularly grips the Labour Party, the reality is rather more sinister. It now transpires that every new Labour candidate to be selected in the late 1950s and early 1960s was vetted by MI5, who then met Brown and Barker to report their findings. Brown and Barker invariably accepted these recommendations and would then drum up reasons to persuade the NEC not to endorse those candidates who were unacceptable to British Intelligence. The bulk of the NEC, like the rest of the Labour movement, were ignorant of this process at the time, but when people now ask why the Wilson

Governments were so bad they should think about whether any party whose members were considered acceptable by MI5 could be anything other than anti-socialist. Although this process of vetting stopped after the 1966 election it is important to remember that the Labour Party was dominated by people selected under this system until the creation of the SDP.

As the Group meeting got underway, Sir Reg Goodwin was re-elected unopposed as Leader, but Illtyd's election was a struggle: he finally won by 32 to 25 votes on the fourth ballot. The left should have realized at that stage that the Group was not going to be quite as radical as we had hoped. The same factors applied as in Lambeth: the right kept their heads down and paid lip service to the manifesto while doing everything possible behind the scenes to sabotage the emerging new policies.

After the AGM I found myself sitting next to Sir Reg in the ILEA Labour Group AGM. I was pleasantly surprised when he told me that he thought the older members did not yet fully understand that they would have to make way for the newcomers during the life of this administration. I felt sure it was a good omen that the Leader took such a realistic and sensible view rather than fighting to resist an inevitable change. What I did not realize was that he was only talking about the others and fully intended to hang on himself. Indeed he was still Leader seven years later at the age of 71 and had it not been for the advance of the left, would have been determined to continue until at least 1982.

Sir Reg, who by a strange coincidence had gone to the same primary school as I did, did not exhibit any of the usual characteristics of Labour leaders or even of politicians in general. He was quiet, undemonstrative and hated publicity, particularly television. His manner was polite in the extreme and he clearly detested the crudeness of politics and the private vulgarities of politicians. Whenever he joined the Labour lunch table in the members' restaurant people automatically stopped swearing and conversation died away until only polite generalities remained. It was rather as though one had been joined by a frail remnant of the Victorian era. One journalist of the time, who was undoubtedly tired of the political egomaniacs he usually had to deal with, used to go into raptures about Sir Reg being the Labour Party's greatest asset since

Clem Attlee. Unfortunately for us, though Sir Reg shared Attlee's loathing of publicity, he completely lacked his firm grasp of leadership and sense of direction. The problem was partly due to his inability to communicate with colleagues, which meant that everyone left his presence with the idea that Sir Reg agreed with whatever they were proposing.

On one occasion I was able to rally enough votes in the Group to block his proposal for a major cut in the housing construction programme. As I sat down, Ina Chaplin, who like Sir Reg had been at County Hall for over twenty-five years, whispered in my ear, 'You've really upset Reg. I've never seen him so furious,' but when I looked all I could see was his usual immobile, sphinx-like mask staring into the middle distance. How he had managed to survive in the rough world of Bermondsey politics for over forty years, many of them as leader of Bermondsey Council, I never began to understand but it might have had something to do with his relationship with his staff. In contrast to the gulf between Sir Reg and other members of the Labour Group, his personal staff and some of the Council's senior officers seemed to be remarkably close to him and younger officers served him with great loyalty and affection. In retrospect nothing could have been worse than to elect as his deputy someone who loved life as fully as Illtyd Harrington. Rather than coming together as a team, I suspect they both viewed the relationship as cruel and unnatural punishment. In fact I have no doubt at all that the only reason Sir Reg was ever elected Leader in the first place was that in 1967 the Labour Group was reduced to just 25 and he was the best of a very poor field.

It was not until November 1973 that he revealed his true colours when Reg Prentice, the Labour Shadow Cabinet Minister who was soon to defect to the Tory Party, made a speech condemning the 'sillier forms of militancy'. Dr Haseler and his close friend Douglas Eden, an equally rightwing GLC councillor, drafted a letter addressed to Harold Wilson, to which the first signatory was Sir Reg Goodwin. The letter supported Reg Prentice, condemned the decision of the 1973 Labour Party Conference to agree to remove all penalties from the surcharged Clay Cross councillors upon the election of a Labour Government and asked Wilson to dissociate himself from that decision. The flavour of the Haseler–Goodwin letter is best captured by the third paragraph.

> It is entirely fitting and proper to oppose, disagree with and promise to change acts of parliament, particularly when they are imposed by a callous and cynical Government. But it is quite another matter for members of a potential alternative government to give aid and comfort to and even promise indemnification to breakers of the law, no matter how sincere they may be. Decent people who break laws out of deeply felt conviction have always been prepared to bear the consequences themselves. Those who demand protection against such consequences from a potential future government are in effect challenging parliamentary democracy. How can an alternative government encourage law-breaking when in opposition and expect to enforce its own laws when it becomes the government?

Harold Wilson's reply to Goodwin, which was signed by his secretary reflected his displeasure with a directness that was refreshing.

> At a late hour last night an unsigned letter arrived in this office addressed to Mr Wilson and purporting to come from you. In order that he might see who the sender/ senders were he was referred to an annexure with a list of persons prominent in local government together with a small number of prospective parliamentary candidates.
>
> The purpose of the letter was to express support for Reg Prentice, and the whole argument was in reference to the Clay Cross debate at Party Conference.
>
> Mr Wilson well understands that you would have been concerned at this decision, though since it occurred nearly two months ago it is difficult to understand why it has not been raised with him earlier. He would have been glad at any time to discuss the matter with you and to arrange for the deputy leader, who replied to the debate on behalf of the National Executive Committee to explain the difficulties he personally was facing, and the precise implications of the carefully worded terms of his reply.

Mr Wilson noted that at the same time as you wrote to him, envelopes were handed in for all the members for the Shadow Cabinet.

I am asked to say that letters from you to Mr Wilson will be welcome at any time, by which he means letters, not a 'round robin' cooked-up by a number of people with little interest in Clay Cross and less in unity and success of the Party, obviously with the intention of publication.

A letter over your signature or together with Ashley Bramall, would carry far more authority than one in which your authority is devalued by association with some of the signatories in the annex to the letter he received last night.

Mr Wilson would, however, like you to know that should any members of your GLC Labour Group step out of line and should you feel it necessary to take action to ensure, so far as possible in a democratic Party, that all members are speaking with one voice and for one purpose, he will not write, either individually or as part of a consortium, a dissociatory letter with copies to all your colleagues. We would feel that such an eventuality would be a matter for you and your chief whip.

When I arrived at the GLC I was apparently already viewed as a potential problem in the eyes of the leadership. It was Paddy O'Connor, the deputy whip, who later told me that they had been warned that I was a 'troublesome little bastard'. I immediately confirmed that view by coming within a few votes of overturning Sir Reg's proposed new committee structure, which was in reality a plot to try and prevent Gladys Dimson becoming chair of the Housing Committee. She had been the opposition spokesperson on housing during the previous three years and had built up a high public profile as someone determined to carry through the municipalization and housing construction programmes. She had indicated her opposition to the Housing Finance Act and had taken a left position in the drafting of the manifesto and, in Sir Reg's eyes, was clearly unreliable.

The method of selecting the committee chairs at the GLC was

cumbersome. The Leader, deputy leader, chief whip, five assistant whips and four advisers, all of whom were elected at the annual meeting, met to decide a slate of nominees, which was then recommended to the Group to be endorsed en bloc. As there were 29 committees, each with a chair and vice-chair, it was possible to give nearly everybody something and therefore a large majority of the Group had a vested interest in agreeing the complete slate. This procedure had originally been drawn up to replace the less democratic system where the leader made all the appointments on his own.

It came as no surprise that when the twelve members of the Advisory Committee first met, they were rapidly able to agree that their own personal qualities fitted them to fill all the major posts available. As Gladys Dimson had not sought election to the committee, this gave Sir Reg his chance. Where previously housing management had been a sub-committee of the main Housing Committee, with Gladys leading for Labour on development and Marie Jenkins on management, he now proposed to split housing into two committees, management and development. It was obvious that development would have the glory of municipalizing and building its way around London whilst management would grind down its chair with the repairs and transfer problems of 200,000 council tenants. Instead of doing the obvious thing and giving both Dimson and Jenkins the chance to prove their worth in the two positions they had been shadowing for three years, Sir Reg switched them round, knowing full well that after such a public snub Gladys Dimson was likely to refuse to accept the consolation prize of housing management.

Sir Reg then planned that in the confusion that would inevitably follow Gladys Dimson's withdrawal he would propose switching Marie Jenkins to chair housing management and also propose that Ewan Carr, my old adversary from Lambeth, should chair housing development. Thus he would achieve by stealth that which he lacked the courage to propose openly to either the Advisory Committee or the Labour Group. Sir Reg did not tell Ewan Carr all the details of the plot, merely that he would be the new chair, but unfortunately for Sir Reg, Ewan mentioned his appointment to me while I was lobbying him to oppose the break-up of the Housing Committee.

After talking to Gladys and Sir Ashley Bramall (Leader of the ILEA 1970–81), it was suggested that I move the rejection of the housing reorganization proposal, with Sir Ashley seconding it. This we did, only to lose narrowly, but in the general confusion that followed, a proposal from the floor was carried which placed Gladys in development and Marie Jenkins in management.

Had Sir Reg honestly and openly opposed Gladys Dimson's appointment he may very well have carried the Group with him as his authority was untarnished at that time, but when leaders are not honest with their colleagues they often help to mobilize unlikely alliances against themselves. Most of the members present at that meeting had no idea of the real motives at work behind the dissembling nature of many of the speeches. It is also remarkable how often vital votes such as this are so close that the issue may be decided by who is absent on the day.

In the light of these events I did not expect the Leader's Advisory Committee to look upon me with favour when they had their second meeting to dish out the remaining unfilled minor posts, such as vice-chairs of sub-committees. I do not know if perhaps there was an element of punishment involved but they nominated me for the post of vice-chair of the Film Viewing Board. They did not bother to check if I was actually in favour of censoring films and, even worse, when they wrote offering me the post they sent the letter by mistake to the retired former Tory member for Lambeth, who happened to· be called Livingston. He wrote back accepting the post, the appointment was announced, and I immediately received complaints from members of Norwood Labour Party who pointed out that party policy was opposed to film censorship. Rather than cause further trouble by resigning I said I would see how it worked out – but that was the least of my problems in those early days.

In my first few weeks at the GLC I found it very difficult to pin down exactly what was happening and where it was happening. The building itself was a problem, a vast Edwardian monolith built to impress and intimidate, housing 7,000 staff along seven miles of corridor and with another 28,000 staff in various locations around London. In addition, there were another 60,000 staff at London

Transport and over 50,000 working for the Education Authority. The building had been designed and finished to specifications of the Tory-controlled administration which spanned the First World War and whose members had obviously believed that their considerable importance should be reflected in the grandeur of their head-quarters.

While the staff occupied very ordinary offices, the first floor, which was reserved for members, was opulent. Wood-panelled throughout with a Council chamber decorated with Italian marble, it sought to rival the Houses of Parliament in the comforts it provided to its members. Not only the building, with its members' terrace and members' restaurant, but the procedures that became part of the traditions of the GLC were copied from Parliament – indeed, when the London County Council was created in 1889 its powers were so extensive that many members of both Houses of Parliament sought (and gained) election. The staff were not treated like mere local government officers but were employed and organized on civil service lines and always paid slightly more than their equivalent grade in the borough councils. In retrospect it is not surprising that so many borough councils and councillors had little love for County Hall and all its pretensions.

I had trouble not only finding my way around the building but also trying to cut in on the existing political and officer relationships. At County Hall, chief officers worked to their committee chairs to the exclusion of mere committee members. Unless you were a member of a particular committee you could not even get a copy of the reports going to that committee without enormous time-wasting effort. The committee chairs all had separate offices, personal assistants, typists, chauffeur-driven cars, entertainment allowances and various other time-honoured perks such as access to the royal box at the Royal Festival Hall. The chief whip, Harvey Hinds, eventually managed to get even humble backbenchers a shared office and access to a typist, which left them better off than the average backbench MP.

It was all too easy for new Labour councillors to catch the infectious self-important air that pervaded the building and begin to think that just being there was an achievement in itself. After that it was easy to forget why you had been sent there in the first place. The Labour Group was littered with dead wood that had done precisely that. It led to unbelievable situations – as when some of the women Labour councillors complained when a decision was made to allow women members of staff to use the lady members' toilet. On one occasion security staff were summoned because a messenger had been seen smoking by one of the longer-serving members!

Part of the problem was the strong middle-class bias in the composition of the members. Too often working-class Labour members seemed to feel the need to mimic class attitudes that were not their own and some of them slipped into a pattern of intolerable behaviour towards typists, restaurant staff, chauffeurs and messengers. But at least they still lived amongst the people they represented. For many of the richer members, County Hall was a pastime in an otherwise leisured world – somewhere to visit during the week before returning to the country for a long weekend. Coming from Lambeth Council into an environment where members speculated upon who was the richest millionaire, how much of Manhattan Willy Bell owned and whether Lena Townsend really had a second houseboat on the Nile just for the family horses was a remarkable experience. I was amazed that such people still existed. Being a GLC councillor could easily become a very comfortable existence in a very unreal world.

Gradually, the new Labour members began to make an impact. We managed to get the Group to agree to treble the length of the meetings, which were held every three weeks before Council meetings. Although our proposal to refuse to comply with the Housing Finance Act 1973 rent increase was defeated, we had better luck on campaigns that did not carry with them the threat of surcharges on councillors. We defeated the old guard and the officers who wanted to keep major chunks of the London motorway system and call them something else, and threw out a proposal put forward by Dame Evelyn Dennington and Andrew McIntosh for a major road scheme at the Cambridge roundabout on the North Circular.

By the end of the first year much had been achieved in housing and transport. I had been loosely working with about fifteen other leftwing members. We usually voted together against the old guard and tended to win because almost all the newer members voted with us except on surcharge issues. But for all that, the building had not changed. It was still difficult to find out what was going on. The leadership was secretive and seldom gave away information to the Group. Already this was leading to discussion about who would succeed Sir Reg when he retired.

The leadership's move to isolate me in the backwater of film censorship did not work for two reasons. First, it left me with a lot of time to dig into other issues where I was able to make an impact and establish a reputation for competence within the Group. The second reason was Enid Wistrich, the member for Hampstead. Like me, she was unknown to the County Hall machine when elected for the first time in 1973 and the Advisory Committee had recommended her appointment to chair the Film Viewing Board presumably because they thought that someone from Hampstead would be able to separate the porn from the art. But they had failed to ask if Enid agreed with censorship. As she did not, it meant that the chair and vice-chair of the censorship committee were two committed anti-censors out of the classic 1960s libertarian stable.

My commitment in this area was little more than a slogan but fortunately Enid Wistrich knew exactly what she wanted to do and how to do it. She embarked on a series of meetings with all the affected groups – the British Film Institute, the Police, the British Board of Film Censors, the Arts Council, film critics, Churches, Unions, exhibitors, the Home Office, anti-censorship campaigners and even the Festival of Light. She persuaded the Council to pay for a public opinion survey, ensured we had the required legal and professional advice and access to reports of research into film censorship. This very full investigative programme took some time and it was not until January 1975 that we were able to report fully to the Council and propose that the GLC should cease to censor films for adults over the age of 18.

We could see no justification for the censorship of films in a society which censors neither the theatre nor literature. With the decline of the cinema as a provider of mass entertainment, a role now filled by television, it had become increasingly a specialized minority art form catering overwhelmingly to the 15 to 25 age group. By 1972 there were only 206 cinemas left in the GLC area, of which 32 per cent were concentrated in Camden and Westminster. We found no conclusive evidence linking criminal or violent acts to the viewing of sexually explicit or violent films though there was some evidence that the long-term effects of a diet of violence performed by the heroes in long-running western and crime television series might legitimize violence and lead to the acceptance of such behaviour as a norm which young men might then mimic. This seemed an argument for the censorship of television rather than the cinema: there is a television set in almost every home and it is often difficult to prevent children from watching certain programmes.

While this work was going on we had to view the films that came to the GLC Film Viewing Board. In the first instance all films were seen by the British Board of Film Censors (an independent body funded by the film industry) which recommended 'U', 'A', 'AA' and 'X' certificates accordingly. If the film distributor disagreed with the recommendation they could appeal to the GLC, whose decision was legally binding. Thus, instead of being paid £10 per session to watch the whole range of films, we were called upon to view only those with which the BBFC were unhappy. By the time we had sat through *The Porn-Brokers*, *Is there Sex after Death?*, *Sex Farm*, *Schoolgirls*, *Big Zapper*, *White Slavers*, *The Sex Adventures of the Three Musketeers*, *Heat*, *Toilet Talks*, *Oh Calcutta*, *Techniques of Love*, *Teenage Love*, *Prison Girls*, *Hamburg*, *City of Sin*, *More about the Language of Love* and *Snow White and the Seven Perverts*, I was convinced that we should replace the 'X' category with 'T' for tedium. The films were so boring that I was surprised that the dirty raincoat brigade never tried to sue the cinemas concerned under the Trades Description Act. The debates which followed in committee were usually much better entertainment.

It came as no surprise to discover that the Film Viewing Board was the largest committee of the Council. About 40 per cent of the membership (all Labour) were opposed to censorship in principle and 30 per cent (all Tory) were fanatical censors who would happily have set about removing any evidence of sex from all aspects of human life. The rest of the membership tended to make up their minds on a film-by-film basis. As it was such a large committee, and against convention to operate a whipping system, votes were often decided on the basis of who turned up on the day. This meant that there was no consistent pattern to our decisions; films were banned one week although the week before similar ones had been given an 'X' certificate.

The different attitudes of the members of the two main parties would have provided a sociologist, or perhaps a psychiatrist, with a lifetime's study. Basically, the Labour side liked the sex and loathed the violence whereas the Tories did not seem to notice the violence but hated the sex and became positively apopleptic about flatulence. In November 1973 we saw a French film about four men eating themselves to death called *Blow Out*, which was so boring that I slept through most of it and was awoken on several occasions by unrealistically loud sounds of flatulence from the screen characters. I anticipated no trouble at all with such a tedious film and was therefore stunned at the violence of the reactions from two Tory women from Bromley who went on at great length about how the film was the most disgusting thing they had ever seen. Resisting the temptation to tell them that they should get out and about more, the chair patiently had to remind them that we only viewed films for any evidence that the sex or violence depicted might 'tend to deprave or corrupt'; it was unlikely that Londoners would become depraved by a bit of flatulence on the screen. Another wonderful Tory character was Frank Smith, also from Bromley, who actually dressed for the viewings in a dirty raincoat and on some occasions even managed to see the same film twice.

I cannot claim to have been completely consistent myself. In July we had to view our first Kung Fu film, *Fist of Fury* (consisting almost exclusively of windpipe-smashing, head-crushing and groin-kicking, with an almost inaudible soundtrack of grunts and groans), which the BBFC had given an 'X' but which the distributor wanted reduced to category 'AA' so that children could see it. Most of us were unhappy with the idea of children watching even more violence than they were already getting on television but our decision was made when we were told that there were about a hundred similar 'X' certificate films whose distributors were complaining about their certificates. We realized that we might have to see them all if we set the precedent of reducing the certification on *Fist of Fury*.

The press gradually woke up to the fact that more films were being passed and Mary Whitehouse and others got in on the act with dire warnings about 'The End Of Civilization As We Know It' if the GLC stopped censoring films for adults. Frank Smith even started escorting Mary Whitehouse to see the films he had already seen as a member of the Board! *The Times* got particularly upset when we gave an 'X' certificate to a serious documentary about the murderer Charles Manson. They devoted a leading article to attacking the decision which, they warned, might lead some Londoners (who were clearly not as intelligent as *Times* leader writers) to mimic Manson's lifestyle.

By the time the report recommending the ending of film censorship for adults went to the full Council on 28 January 1975, the initial radical phase of the Group had passed and we were into a massive round of cuts and retrenchment. Had we pushed the liberalization through immediately after the election, the Labour Group might have backed it, but by 1975 the Group's nerve was broken and it was in full retreat on most issues. There was no question of any radical new initiative. 17 Labour members, including Sir Reg Goodwin, voted with the Tories and we lost. In retrospect I was not unhappy about this as by the mid-1970s the nature of the films we saw began to change from the harmless *Hot Nights in the Swedish Sauna* variety to a disturbing mixture of violence linked with the degradation of women.

I believe I was wrong on censorship in 1975 and when in 1985 the Women's Committee complained to the BBFC that they were not being tough enough in cutting the violence against women from the films they were certificating, I supported them. James Ferman, who ran the BBFC, had some fun reminding me that only nine years previously I had been attacking him for being too restrictive.

As my film viewing duties were rather light I was able to get involved in several housing issues and also came to the notice of my colleagues as a critic of the generally chaotic nature of the decision-making process in the Group. This was largely a result of Sir Reg Goodwin's ineffectual style of leadership. Group meetings were often confused and disorganized, with members becoming more and more frustrated, although most of our policies were being carried out. Another problem was that it was unclear where power lay within the Council bureaucracy. The Director-General of the GLC, Sir James Swaffield, had been appointed with bipartisan support shortly before the 1973 election. He had been a distinguished Secretary to the Association of Municipal Corporations and had exercised considerable influence on successive governments. He possessed the style and gravitas of a Cabinet Secretary and was head and shoulders above the normal range of local government chief executives, but whether he or anyone else had the ability to exercise control over the GLC bureaucracy was never clear. Organizations the size of the GLC develop their own momentum and styles of operation and those in control usually try to slip into the established governing structures rather than recast them to conform to their own way of working. In contrast to Lambeth and the borough councils in general, with their coherent range of local services, the GLC was a collection of powerful and practically autonomous departments, with an array of unrelated services which could not be economically delivered on a borough basis. Sir James Swaffield had around him a small number of Assistant Director-Generals, a Programme Office and the research facilities of the Council through which he attempted to pull together a more effective central administrative structure.

The other key officer in the building was Maurice Stonefrost, Comptroller of Financial Services, who had been appointed by Illtyd Harrington shortly after the 1973 election. Like the D-G, Maurice Stonefrost had had a distinguished local government career – he had come to the GLC from the public sector treasurers association, the Chartered Institute of Public Finance and Accountancy (CIPFA). Unlike the D-G, who had developed a reserved and professional manner, Stonefrost was intense and passionate while arguing his case and relaxed and charming outside the formality of meetings. Impressed by his brilliant grasp of all things financial and an obvious social concern, most members were immediately seduced by him and Labour members in particular felt him to be sympathetic to their cause.

The first Labour budget presented by Illtyd Harrington in February 1974, just a few days before the election of the second Wilson

Government, provided the funding for Labour's programme of municipalization, house building, fares subsidy and expansion of other services. On paper there was a rate increase of 46 per cent but in reality it represented an increase of 85 per cent because the Government had set up the new health and water authorities which absorbed many GLC functions, such as the ambulance service.

As the manifesto was being implemented there was no need for a left caucus to operate inside the GLC Labour Group, but Tony Banks, David White, myself and a few others kept loosely in touch and decided to try and improve the quality of Labour's front bench at the forthcoming Annual General Meeting of the Labour Group. Several of us stood for election to the Leader's Advisory Committee but I was the only leftwinger elected to one of the eight backbench places. When the committee met the next morning I was amazed at Sir Reg Goodwin's indecisive handling of the affair. He had reluctantly decided to purge the chair and vice-chair of Housing Management and when it was proposed that Tony Judge should be the chair and I the vice-chair this was agreed without dissent. There followed a few minor changes in the lower ranks and that was as far as the Leader wanted to go. I objected to this, saying that there was widespread dissatisfaction in the Group with the quality of the front bench and proposed that another three more chairs be sacked. After an hour's agonizing we prevailed on Sir Reg to accept two sackings but not the one I most wanted which was Dame Evelyn Dennington, the pro-motorway chair of the Transport Committee. As we left the committee Illtyd Harrington patted me on the back and said, 'We've needed a little Robespierre here for some time,' but we both knew that the left was very weakly placed. Although we now had me as vice-chair of Housing Management, David White as chair of the Planning Board for South London and Bill Simson as vice-chair of Thamesmead Committee, and had retained Robin Young as planning vice-chair for North East London, this was the sum total of leftwingers in an administration of fifty people.

A month before the annual jobs carve-up I was elected to the Executive Committee of the Greater London Labour Party and so, while things were definitely not going my way in Lambeth at that time, I began to look forward to being able to make an impact on our policies at the London-wide level and threw myself into reviewing many of our housing management policies.

It was easy to work with Tony Judge, the new chair of Housing Management. Although he was on the right of the party and his job as editor of the *Police Federation Journal* was not usually the abode of a closet Liberal, he was honest, unaffected and hard working. He and I shared the view that GLC tenants were getting a dreadful service and there needed to be radical change. We also agreed that the staff dealing with the tenants included some of the most reactionary bigots to be found anywhere in the GLC. A minority, but a substantial minority of Housing Management staff were arrogant and insensitive in their dealings with the public and there was considerable evidence of institutional and sometimes overt racism. It was noticeable that as soon as we computerized the allocation of GLC housing and removed officer discretion in this area black people suddenly started being allocated new council property.

Harry Simpson, the ex-Director of Housing in Lambeth, had just returned from working in Northern Ireland to take up the post of Controller of Housing, but on the whole he left housing management issues to Len Bennett, the Director of Housing Management. Len Bennett was a London Eastender who had worked his way up the GLC ladder but had insisted as a matter of pride on maintaining his basic Eastend attitudes. During my time as vice-chair we clashed repeatedly on issue after issue. I even had one Tory complain to me that he thought Len Bennett was a bit reactionary in some areas.

Before I could really get dug into the new post, Sir Reg Goodwin decided to make his break to the right. When I received my papers for the Labour Group meeting on Monday 10 June 1974, they included a report setting out various options for a future fares policy. At the meeting Sir Reg Goodwin handed round another paper which recommended a 12 per cent fare increase. He said that he deeply regretted this, but that he felt certain 'a thoughtful public would understand' it was necessary as inflation was rising faster than expected. Unfortunately for the Leader, the Labour

Group itself was not feeling too thoughtful and a confrontational mood rapidly developed in which one chair let slip, cryptically, that the rest of us would understand the need for the fare increase if only we had 'heard Maurice Stonefrost at Aldermaston'.

Under questioning Sir Reg revealed that all the chairs and some chief officers had spent a weekend in May at an hotel in Aldermaston to review whether or not we could continue the cost of carrying out our manifesto. The meeting had been organized in total secrecy without any backbench or Labour Party Executive members being invited, and the documents given to the Aldermaston group had not been passed to the rest of the party. The news of this little weekend annoyed everyone who had not been invited. It seemed a fair bet that Sir Reg and Maurice Stonefrost had decided that we could not continue to increase the rates to fund our programme. Getting the committee chairs away from Labour Party influences in order to persuade them to come back and reverse the main manifesto commitment on fares through an unwarned and unbriefed group might have seemed like a good idea when Sir Reg planned it, but it was too big a jump for the Group to take without time to think and consult local parties. It was proposed that the decision should be delayed for two weeks. Sir Reg opposed this in such a way as to leave people thinking that he would resign if he lost the issue. Given the calibre of leadership he was providing, I honestly felt that his resignation would be a valuable bonus to the Group's decision to reject a fares increase.

The following morning I asked him if he would request the Greater London Labour Party Regional Executive Committee to hold a special meeting to seek the party's advice. He said he would think about it and waited until about 8pm before telling me his answer was no. Contacting enough members to requisition a special meeting was not easy at such short notice but by phoning around I got enough names to support the demand. I then presented the list of names to John Keys (the same Labour Party officer who had attacked the left in Lambeth), who refused to accept it and demanded individually signed statements. When I relayed this information to some of the members of the Executive their anger led to a rapid rethink and Bob Mellish, the chair of the Greater London Labour Party, convened an emergency meeting. The

Regional Executive at that time still had a rightwing majority but the transport unions in particular found Sir Reg's explanations unconvincing and called on the Group to refuse the fare increase. David White, Tony Banks and I had been busy phoning, trying to get as many Labour Party and trade union branches as possible to submit motions to the GLC Labour Group rejecting the proposed increase.

When the Group met again on 24 June 1974, it had twelve motions opposing the fare increase on the agenda and Harvey Hinds read out three more, which did not help to create the climate Sir Reg might have liked. His argument rested on the size of the rate burden on ordinary families but he ignored the fact that the main beneficiaries of holding the rate down would be the commercial ratepayers, as they would have to contribute 62 per cent of any increase. If the fares were raised the whole burden would fall on the travelling public. Sir Reg put great emphasis on inflation, which had recently gone into double figures, but many of us recognized that as inflation eroded the real level of fares, this simply allowed us to move more rapidly towards the low flat fare which we had promised in the election. David White moved and I seconded an amendment to freeze fares throughout 1975 and call for a public consultation exercise to decide the best method of introducing flat fares. An important segment of the Group agreed with Sir Ashley Bramall, who said it would be damaging to decide an increase in the fares at that time, with the autumn General Election only three months away. We were helped particularly by a calm speech from Arthur Latham, the MP for Paddington, who explained the Regional Executive's view. In the end the amendment against a fares increase was carried by 31 votes to 25.

That should have been the end of the affair but, without warning, Dame Evelyn Dennington asked to make a report on 22 July 1974, when a Group meeting had been called to discuss the emerging budget strategy for the following financial year. Apparently a few days earlier she had been given new financial projections by London Transport, taking full account of inflation in both oil prices and wages. These meant an immediate 2p rate increase (£38 million pounds) was needed in the present financial year. Deferring it to the following year would mean that GLC support to London

Transport would leap from a 1.8p rate in 1974–75 to a 10p rate in 1975–76. Instead she asked the Labour Group to agree to a 20 per cent fare increase. I objected on the grounds that the leadership were once again trying to bounce the Group into a decision without adequate notice and that it was contrary to our Standing Orders to rescind a previous decision without fourteen days' clear notice. Dame Evelyn's proposal was therefore out of order.

Amazingly, the leadership seemed to have overlooked this point and so we went through the farce of their attempts to keep the debate going whilst trying to find a way around the problem. I knew that the only way the matter could be discussed was if two-thirds of the members of the Group voted to do so. I was fairly certain that the leadership did not have the support of two-thirds of those present and therefore kept demanding that they move to a vote. Eventually Paddy O'Connor proposed and Ellis Hillman seconded a motion to suspend Standing Orders to allow a debate on the 20 per cent fare increase. The low fares camp had declined dramatically and if another four members had switched, the leadership would have won, but they mustered only 30 votes to our 20, which deprived them of the necessary two-thirds majority. Politicians seldom lose with good grace, and I felt an almost physical wave of hatred break over me in the aftermath of the vote. As the meeting broke up I was subjected to obscene abuse and speculation about my motives. One Docklands member said the whole thing was an attempt to seize the leadership from Goodwin. (Given that I had been a member for only sixteen months, even *my* ego did not let me assume that I was either capable of or ready to cope with such a responsibility.) A less speculative assessment came from one Newham member who loudly announced that he would like to kick my arse 'all the way back to fucking Lambeth'. I was left in no doubt that my future in the administration was somewhat vulnerable.

During the summer break the leadership went to work to get their two-thirds majority. They were assisted by pressures from the Labour Government, who were arguing privately for both the fare increase and cuts in the projected GLC budget for the following year. Those who believe that the Labour Government cuts began after the wicked International Monetary Fund intervention in 1976 should know that Labour ministers had been alarmed by the size of the rate increases in early 1974 and were privately demanding cuts within six months of their taking office. With inflation heading towards 25 per cent, increased interest rates and increasing debt charges all making a prior call on many councils' finances, severe cuts for councils which, like the GLC, had huge debt burdens were inevitable unless the Government provided assistance.

Every effort was made to keep all the lobbying by Labour ministers out of the public eye because of the forthcoming General Election on 10 October. There was also a GLC by-election in Greenwich on 24 October so the Leader was determined to keep the rate cuts and fare increases under wraps until after polling day. When it met on 14 October the Group was told that there would be a special meeting called on 31 October, but no papers were released until after the Greenwich by-election. The whips were given the job of lobbying all but the ten solid leftwingers and each member of the group was told that Sir Reg Goodwin would resign unless what had now become a 36 per cent fare increase was agreed. The Leader had also decided that debate should be controlled; as we sat down at the start of the meeting, the suspension of Standing Orders was rapidly moved and seconded, someone moved that we vote immediately without debate and a forest of hands went up in support, followed moments later by the same number of hands to suspend Standing Orders. After just ninety minutes of debate the Labour Group voted to cut every committee budget and increase the fares by 36 per cent with 46 members in favour and 9 against. Through it all, Illtyd Harrington sat looking more dejected than I had ever seen him. He knew as well as the rest of us that the Group had had its radical year and that the next three years would be downhill all the way. Illtyd was caught between a leader who had decided to comply with the Labour Government's desire for cuts, and the most competent senior officer in the building, who was preparing the detail of that strategy. There was not a single leftwing committee chair or member of Sir Reg Goodwin's disorganized cabinet to provide support for an alternative strategy. Illtyd faced the choice of staying and trying to limit the damage or joining a small band of isolated leftwingers who at best might hope to replace the present leadership after the 1977 elections, which in any event were likely to produce a Tory administration. He chose not to resign and although this meant a growing rift between him and the left, we all made efforts to stay in touch and relations remained friendly. I have no doubt that his decision to stay imposed considerable strain on Illtyd and was a major factor in the collapse of his health a few months later.

One of the arguments put forward with particular vigour by Richard Balfe, the chair of the Thamesmead committee, was that an agreement on the fare increase would allow us to protect our housing programme. The same argument was used to justify another rent increase, although by this time the law had been changed and we were no longer legally obliged to increase rents. Taken altogether, the rent and fare increases and the general cuts across the whole range of services resulted in a 1975 rate of 16p (an 80 per cent increase), which meant that the average London householder was paying £40 a year to the GLC. If we had continued with our manifesto programme without any cuts, rent or fare increases, the rate would have been 22p (an increase of 137 per cent) and the average householder would have paid £55 a year. Therefore, to save the average householder 30p a week we increased London Transport fares for the householder's whole family by 35 per cent, took 50p a week extra rent from our 240,000 council tenancies and got rid of over 2,000 jobs at a time of rising unemployment.

It seemed to me a poor strategy in electoral terms. We could not have been condemned any more for a 137 per cent rate increase than we were for that of 80 per cent but with the higher rate we would have had something to show for the pain and would not have alienated millions of public transport users and all our tenants. Commercial ratepayers did, of course, do slightly better; our cuts saved a firm like Shell £240,000 a year on its South Bank building alone. However, the worst was still to come. So far, all the cuts had been justified on the grounds that they would allow us to protect the housing programme and also that Labour Government Ministers were privately requesting them because of the severe economic crisis faced by the nation. The dishonesty of this strategy was revealed in March 1975, when the Leader started warning of the increasing costs of the GLC housing programme.

Gladys Dimson had spent a hectic two years expanding the new building and municipalization programmes with considerable success. She had more difficulty persuading the London boroughs to agree a Strategic Housing Plan for the whole city. The predominantly Tory-controlled outer boroughs feared that a major council-housing drive in their areas would bring with it large numbers of Labour-voting, often black council tenants. However, the mainly Labour inner boroughs did support the Plan and, most important of all, it had the enthusiastic support of Tony Crosland, the Secretary of State at the Department of the Environment, who was prepared to make it legally binding on all the London boroughs.

As vice-chair of Housing Management I played only a small role in the development of the Strategic Housing Plan, but I had given support to Gladys Dimson when she was subjected to sniping by people who were keen to remove her from the post. It was known a few days before the April Labour Group Meeting that Sir Reg Goodwin was going to propose major cuts and so both sides lobbied intensively. Just before the meeting on 21 April I phoned David Lipsey, who was Political Adviser to Tony Crosland, to ask what Crosland's position was. I had heard that Lipsey had been lobbying senior Labour GLC members on Crosland's behalf in an attempt to save the Strategic Housing Plan. He confirmed that Crosland supported the Plan, believing that a major cuts package would render it obsolete. Lipsey also admitted that he had been trying to persuade senior members of the administration to defer any cuts until Crosland had had more time to persuade the Treasury to release the money required to fund our housing programme.

At the Group meeting, Sir Reg Goodwin started by getting the members to agree a further package of cuts in all the non-housing areas of the budget – even though the budget had only been in operation for three weeks – but his main target was housing. Although Tony Crosland had already got Treasury agreement for another £150 million loan to fund our capital programmes (at one per cent above market rates) the Leader still proposed a £50 million cut in the housing programme. The line he put to the Group was pure Maurice Stonefrost: 'If we try to borrow the full amount of money we need, then the markets will refuse to lend such sums and confidence in the financial standing of the GLC will collapse.' I did not believe that financial institutions at home or abroad would pass up the chance to make a profit out of a British local authority since we were under a legal obligation to repay our debts as a first call on our income. The GLC could not go into liquidation even if it wanted to. It was a 100 per cent safe investment for the banks, as are all British local authorities. Given that Liverpool City Council had no trouble raising money in much more difficult circumstances in the mid-1980s, I am certain that had we been able to point out the fundamental difference between the GLC and New York – which actually did face the prospect of default – we could have borrowed the money to fund our housing programme.

Unfortunately, Sir Reg also chose to misinterpret the wishes of the Government and indicated that his £50 million cuts package was backed by Labour ministers. When I rose to oppose his package I gave the details of my conversation with David Lipsey and relayed to the Group Crosland's call to reject the housing cut. As I was effectively calling the Leader a liar to his face in front of the whole Group, the atmosphere was difficult to say the least. The Group deferred the issue for a week so that Sir Reg could re-examine his case and come back with full details of the proposed cuts. As the meeting closed he made a bitter personal attack on me for going behind his back but confirmed in his speech that he had met with Tony Crosland to discuss the issue. This was an important admission as within a few days Sir Reg Goodwin's supporters were rewriting history in an attempt to explain away the discrepancy between the Leader's report to the Group and my information about Tony Crosland's views. 'The Leader had been dealing with Treasury Ministers' was the claim, but the Group minutes which were drawn up before the excuse came to mind accurately record that he and I were referring to the same Minister.

Deferring the discussion of the cuts package for a week meant that the decision on housing would be taken by the group which allocated committee chairs the day after the Annual General Meeting of the Labour Group. In the ensuing week the two issues became intertwined. Dr Stephen Haseler (chair of General Purposes Committee) and Douglas Eden (vice-chair of Housing Development) had drifted very far to the right and were supporting Reg Prentice, the divisive rightwing Cabinet Minister who had made several strident attacks on trade unionists involved in industrial struggles. Dr Haseler and Douglas Eden's criticism was that the aimless drift of the leadership now threatened the most important area of our policy, namely the housing programme. A majority of the Labour Group complained about the poor leadership, chaotic Group meetings and lack of strategy but could not agree on an alternative Leader, as at least ten members of the Group considered themselves heir apparent. Friends of Sir Ashley Bramall, who was currently Leader of the Inner London Education Authority, canvassed support for him but found that he would lose by about two to one, so his challenge never materialized. In fact, I was most probably the only person on the left who would have voted for Sir Ashley. I had been impressed with the competent, honest way in which he led the ILEA and although we had disagreements in many areas of policy it was because of his ability to lead decisively that the ILEA avoided the substantial cuts which devastated the entire GLC programme.

Sir Reg Goodwin and those around him made every effort to create an administration which excluded both the left and the social democratic right. They were almost completely successful. The only leftwinger to get elected to the Leader's Advisory Committee was Tony Banks, who had emerged as the leading critic of Dr Haseler's attacks on the trade union movement. Largely because the left had been abstaining or voting against the Group in Council as the rent and fare increases went through, we saw our votes drop dramatically. Following my clash with the Leader the previous week my vote was cut from 27 to 11, making it the worst decline suffered by any member on the left. The following afternoon Sir Reg told me that unless I would give an undertaking to support future spending cuts as well as rent and fare increases I could no longer continue as vice-chair of Housing Management. When I declined he said he was sorry to lose me from the administration. I told him not to worry because I recognized that there was a genuine political difference and I would not be prepared to have him in any administration I was Leader of, either. David White was sacked from his position of chair of the South London Area Planning Board, not only because of his opposition to spending cuts but also because he had offended the Southwark Council leadership by turning down their planning applications for enormous speculative office schemes. The 'Bermondsey Mafia', as it was known, also ran Sir Reg Goodwin's local party and he did not ignore their demands for David's head.

When it became obvious that Sir Reg was going to be re-elected, Dr Haseler and Douglas Eden, realizing that they would be sacked, decided on a pre-emptive strike and announced that they were no longer prepared to serve in his administration. This was the start of an increasingly bitter split. The venom with which Haseler and Eden attacked the Labour administration, from what often seemed a Tory perspective, led to their eventual expulsion from the Group. The small band of leftwingers voted against their expulsion for two reasons: first, because we were opposed to expulsions in principle and second, because Haseler and Eden were obviously keen to be expelled so that they could complain that they had been driven out of the party by extremists.

When the Group met on the evening of 29 April, the Leader proposed that Gladys Dimson be replaced by Richard Balfe. However, Sir Reg's line on why we needed a £50 million cut in the housing programme had completely changed. He now warned that to carry on building would increase the rates as interest charges went up. He put a paper to the Group which warned that unless more cuts were made the rate would rise from the present 16p level to 50p by the election in two years' time. Richard Balfe made an impassioned speech in which he said that as chair of Housing Development he would find a £50 million 'saving' without cuts. The Group, who by this time were so demoralized that they would believe anything, voted to sack Gladys Dimson by 27 votes to 24 and to cut the housing programmes by 37 votes to 17.

Sir Reg Goodwin's paper claimed, 'cuts made now will mean . . . less of a rate increase in the run-up to the GLC election. This could well mean the difference between Labour winning power in 1977 with a modified housing programme or Labour losing with a higher but unacceptably expensive housing programme.' In the two years following the Group's acceptance of this strategy there followed two more substantial fare increases and annual rent increases; plans were underway to raise both fares and rents further when Labour lost the 1977 GLC election. The landslide against us produced 64 Tory members and a Labour rump of only 28. Cuts in each area of the Council's work were so extensive that the rate of 16p which had been set in February 1975 remained unchanged up to the election in 1977.

London is such a marginal area politically and the Callaghan Government was so unpopular in 1977 that it is unlikely that any strategy could have kept Labour in control at County Hall. However I have no doubt that the alternative of expanding services and freezing fares and rents would have led to a closer election result and made it much more difficult for Sir Horace Cutler's Tory Administration to push through a further package of cuts. There would also have been a sense of achievement and pride in the London Labour Party instead of the contempt for the GLC Labour Group and its leadership that most party members felt.

As the split between the party and its councillors widened, the Labour Group became less tolerant of dissent. Motions were passed denying members the right to speak in Council meetings if they opposed Sir Reg Goodwin's policies. At one point Jim Daly, who had now become chair of the Transport Committee, actually proposed that 'Ken Livingstone should not be allowed to speak' and this became official party policy after a majority of the Group supported his proposal – although naturally I refused to accept the decision. I was amused when Jim Daly defected to the SDP in 1981 and gave as one of his reasons 'the undemocratic and intolerant nature' of the Labour Party.

One of the many exceptions to the intolerance which characterized the majority of the Labour Group was Tony Judge. As chair and vice-chair of the Housing Management Committee the year before we had developed a sound friendship. We both hated the pomposity that afflicted so many of our colleagues and although we had political differences and disagreed on many issues, we respected each other's honesty and hard work and maintained a sense of humour. Knowing that the loss of my position would leave me in financial difficulties, he worked to ensure that I was kept busy fulfilling functions on behalf of his committee so that I could continue to claim my attendance allowance. Without that support I might have been forced to get an outside job and cut my political work to the minimum, thus depriving the left of its only full-time organizer within the building.

The reason for this general intolerance within the Group was that the eight members who regularly opposed Sir Reg Goodwin's policies in the Council chamber were slowly winning support within the Labour Party. There was a narrow rightwing majority on the Greater London Labour Party Executive, which was chaired by Bob Mellish, the rightwing MP for Bermondsey. Power rested in the hands of the trade union representatives, of whom the most powerful was Bert Fry, the Regional Organizer of the Transport and General Workers' Union (TGWU). An undemonstrative right-winger with a fierce loyalty to the Labour Party, Fry controlled the TGWU block vote which determined which trade union's representatives would be elected to the Executive each year. This state of affairs did not exactly encourage those trade union representatives who wished to continue as members of the Executive to oppose the policies Fry supported.

I had been elected to the Executive at the March 1974 Annual Meeting of the GLLP and watched this exercise of raw power on the small number of occasions when an issue would unexpectedly arise during the course of an Executive meeting. In such cases the TU delegates would not have been warned how to vote beforehand and would often stumble into a debate unaware of TGWU policy. Irrespective of who had said what during the course of the debate the TU delegates would always wait to hear Bert Fry's view before voting. A few quiet sentences usually ending with '. . . so there is no way the trade unions could vote for this proposal', and sixteen loyal trade union arms would go up in unison. It was purely coincidental that they all pointed towards heaven, as it was the judgement of Bert Fry which really exercised their minds.

Bob Mellish and Bert Fry viewed with alarm the sudden rush of motions condemning the decision of the GLC to increase fares and so for the February meeting of the Executive John Keys produced a long statement formally supporting the GLC decision and giving notice to Londoners that we were withdrawing the commitment to low fares that we had made in the 1973 Manifesto. The statement had been drafted by the Leader's office staff at the GLC and, after receiving the blessing of Bert Fry, was carried. At the Annual Meeting of the GLLP in March 1975, the left won all the arguments against the GLC policies but we were crushed by the union block vote. It was immediately after this that Sir Reg Goodwin pushed the housing cuts through the Labour Group, along with cuts across all other committee budgets. The following month came a 25 per cent fare increase to take effect in November, just seven months after the increase of 35 per cent.

Bert Fry and the other trade unionists on the GLLP Executive had been prepared to help out the Goodwin administration on the fares issue because they were assured that it was the only way to save both the housing programme and jobs in the GLC and London Transport. Like most activists in the Labour movement they expected the people they dealt with to honour their word and it was not long before it became clear that the Goodwin administration had alienated a key section of trade union opinion by failing to deliver their side of the bargain. In particular the TGWU were outraged that Jim Daly started cutting bus services and therefore the jobs of bus drivers and conductors who were members of that union.

Tony Banks, David White and I realized that we had to start organizing to replace the existing Labour administration with a new one at the 1977 elections. On 10 June, when the Council agreed the Goodwin cuts package, we issued a statement with six other GLC members condemning the policy and refused to vote for the package in Council. At the same time as we were rebelling at the GLC, the Camden Council Labour Group, led by Frank Dobson (later the Labour MP for Holborn and St Pancras), decided to convene a London-wide meeting to oppose the new housing expenditure controls which had been imposed on all councils by the Labour Government. At the inaugural meeting it was agreed to form an organization called 'Labour Against the Housing Cuts', which eventually became Labour Against the Cuts as we widened our scope. Although we made links with organizations outside the Labour Party and won support for our demands from most local

Labour Parties, we failed to build any public support or seriously threaten the hold of the right in County Hall or the London Labour boroughs. However, by the time of the March 1976 GLLP Annual Meeting we had built up a small, loose network of leftwing contacts in CLPs and trade unions and were able to deliver an unexpected and therefore all the more nasty scare to the Goodwin administration.

A GLLP Annual Meeting is like a smaller version of the national conference. Over 700 delegates from CLPs, trade unions, co-ops and socialist societies crowd into a central London conference centre (usually Camden Town Hall) to debate and vote on the motions which have been submitted by the affiliated organizations. As with the national conference there are fringe meetings called by various campaigning groups and elections for a new Executive. Since 1961, the Tribunite left in the party had produced a regular 'Briefing' document for delegates telling them which motions to support and which candidates for the Executive to vote for. Run on a shoestring by just one person, John Spencer, an elderly but hyperactive European refugee, it was this organization which first supported my election to the Executive.

A rival left organization called 'The Chartist Group' also ran a briefing document giving similar advice but seldom agreeing on the same slate of candidates. I had developed good links with the Chartists when they took over the running of Norwood Labour Party Young Socialists. I had also arranged for Lambeth Council to lease them a shop in Brixton (on commercial terms) as a headquarters and they had supported me against the right when I was vice-chair of Housing in Lambeth. I was thus well placed to act as a go-between for these two rival left camps as well as the Labour Against the Cuts Group, which also produced a broadsheet for delegates itemizing the policy betrayals of the Goodwin administration.

Putting any large number of political and trade union activists together in a confined space for two days is rather like creating a human version of the atom bomb. It only takes a small movement to trigger a reaction leading to a critical mass and an explosion. Any group of more than two Labour Party members is inherently likely to be critical, let alone seven hundred, and the Goodwin administration's policies were more than adequate to act as a trigger. During those two days, one bitter speech after another rained down on the collective head of the GLC Labour Group, but whereas at the 1975 meeting the union block vote had come to Goodwin's rescue, this time many of the trade unions who had seen their members' jobs abolished by the GLC joined the critics. At the end of two days the GLLP had rejected the housing cuts and the fare increases and for good measure had also opposed the Labour Government's cuts policies. Even the ILEA who, by comparison with the GLC, had merely trimmed their budget, were condemned and the Executive was instructed to prepare the 1977 GLC election manifesto on the basis of a return to the 1973 manifesto policies.

The area of greatest concern to the Labour Group was that of their own careers and here the ever pliant John Keys had been busy. Considering their voting records, some Labour members would have had trouble being reselected, so John Keys had persuaded the Executive to accept a proposal that sitting members need not go through a full selection procedure. Instead, if the local CLP Executive Committee successfully proposed to the local General Management Committee a shortlist consisting of the sitting member alone, with no alternative, then that would be adequate. Given that the campaign for automatic reselection of MPs was coming to its climax, it was remarkable that the right wing thought they could get away with such a change, but they pushed it through the Executive with the assistance of Bob Mellish's unique brand of chairing techniques. They had then refused to report the change of procedure to the annual meeting for endorsement. In an effort to stop this, Norwood Labour Party submitted a motion reversing the Executive decision.

When the annual meeting opened it came as no surprise that the Norwood motion had been placed on the agenda at 4.30pm on Sunday to follow the debate on unemployment. Labour's conferences always run behind schedule and as the unions in particular would want a full debate on unemployment there was no chance of our motion being reached. As Saturday and Sunday wore on with one defeat after another for the Goodwin administration, Bob Mellish's chairing of the meeting became slower and slower. The Norwood delegates constantly complained about this and lobbied the union delegates to put them in the picture. By 4.45pm on Sunday there was still no sign of the debate so leftwing Lambeth councillor Len Hammond moved the suspension of Standing Orders to enable the Norwood motion to be debated immediately.

To everyone's surprise there was a clear majority for this; Bob Mellish made no attempt to conceal his anger when he said he would allow only one speech for our motion and then move to a vote after John Keys' reply. John Keys guaranteed a victory for the Norwood motion by beginning his speech: 'Well, Chairman, I have not prepared a reply because we weren't supposed to reach this motion.' The roar of laughter and cat-calls drowned out most of the rest of his speech and the motion had an enormous majority in favour.

Although it looked as though the left had swept all before it, we had failed to win a majority on the Executive. This would clearly mean a hard struggle ahead, but we had won the backing of the Annual Meeting which, by a series of card votes, had instructed the Executive to produce a radical manifesto for the 1977 GLC election. As the meeting broke up, the left departed in a state of near jubilation; after two years of setbacks and defeat we had finally won the votes. Dr Haseler and Douglas Eden immediately issued a press statement saying that they could not support such an extreme manifesto and therefore would not seek reselection. The impact of this ringing declaration of principle was muted largely because neither of them had the slightest chance of being reselected by their respective parties.

When the GLC Labour Group met the following evening, the atmosphere was one of total panic. On the left we watched bemused as individuals on the right launched vicious personal attacks on one another and on the GLLP. Dr Haseler and Douglas Eden had submitted an emergency motion rejecting the decisions of the weekend and refusing to carry them out. Although the majority of the Group privately intended to do the same, they planned to do so by stealth, behind closed doors and safely out of sight of their constituency parties. So it was with total cynicism that they voted to refuse even to discuss the Haseler/Eden motion. Things really disintegrated when Sir Ashley Bramall asked Jim Daly a perfectly reasonable question about free travel for the elderly and received a venomous personal attack in reply. This resulted in uproar and opened the way for even more abuse which climaxed with Stephen Hatch screaming that he had never seen such disgraceful behaviour and he was going home – which he did, almost taking the door off its hinges in the process. Listening to the hysteria one would have thought that the fare-paying masses were outside the door with tumbrils ready to take the Group to a well-deserved mass execution.

Sadly, Labour Party members are more loyal and forgiving than they are just and avenging and as the year wore on only three sitting members were deselected. A better indication of rank and file attitude can be gained where loyalty to a sitting member was not a factor. The post of alderman was to be abolished after the 1977 election, and of Labour's nine aldermen seven were seeking seats. The two leftwingers found winnable seats while four of the other five were either unsuccessful or only selected in seats which we had no hope of winning in what was obviously going to be a difficult election.

In the small left caucus we discussed the best tactics to follow during the selection process. It was decided that David White would stay in his Croydon Central seat, where he was also the parliamentary candidate, while Tony Banks and I should try to seek safe seats so that we could make way for other leftwingers in Norwood and Fulham. Thus, in the event of a Tory victory we would still be in the Labour Group, able to continue the left presence in opposition and begin preparing for a left victory at the 1981 election.

Tony Banks was easily selected to replace Douglas Eden at Feltham and after getting the agreement of my Norwood Party I was invited to Hackney North, where Dr David Pitt, the first black member of the GLC, was retiring. It was my old friends in the Chartist group who arranged to get me selected in Hackney North, where one of the most reactionary 'mafias' in London Labour politics had recently narrowly lost their majority on the General Management Committee.

Jim Daly, who along with Tony Judge had emerged as the most likely rightwing successor to Sir Reg Goodwin, was the member for highly marginal Brentford, which we were almost certain to lose to the Tories. The only way he could keep his leadership ambitions alive was to get a safe Labour seat but he was more closely identified with the fares increases than anyone else within the Group. Throughout the summer of 1976 we were treated to the spectacle of Jim Daly moving from one safe seat to another and losing time after time. We were able to ensure that the left in each local party he went to were well briefed on the full details of his voting record and in the end he was left back where he started, in Brentford.

Overall, there were 10 gains by the left in the selections but nowhere near enough to give us a majority. We did not have a sufficiently wide list of contacts and there were not even enough leftwingers on the panel of candidates. The left in 1976 simply did not consider the GLC a priority. Discussing this at the time with Tony Banks, I said that I felt the GLC was the single most important elective body in Britain after Parliament and that the left should see its potential. He disagreed. In his view, the impact of the Goodwin administration had ensured that the GLC had about as much prestige as a regional committee of the engineering workers' union. Knowing what could have been achieved in the previous four years, I felt nothing but contempt for the majority of the Labour Group who had thrown away the most important opportunity of their lives to achieve real and positive improvements for Londoners.

The left's lack of success in the selections did not prevent the press from pretending otherwise. Writing in the *Daily Telegraph* under the headline 'SHOCK WAVE OF MARXISM HITS GLC ELECTIONS', A. J. McIlroy warned:

> Formidable gains by the left in candidates for next spring's Greater London Council elections have split constituency organisations and sent a shock wave through the Labour Party.
>
> Coming on the heels of controversial attempts to oust a number of Labour MPs to make way for Marxist candidates . . . it has brought quiet jubilation to Marxist and other leftwing candidates who, in the words of their most forthright spokesman, Mr Kenneth Livingstone, 31, a teacher from Norwood, see 'a breakthrough ahead'.

With about half of Labour's candidates selected, the left has already made seven gains, hoping eventually to ensure an effective and substantial minority group able to pressure through the GLC left-orientated policies.

Years of groundwork and some infiltration by dedicated leftists, particularly Marxists, have given the left a growing and often decisive voice on the important constituency organisations for selecting candidates.

As we surveyed the prospect of a continuing rightwing-dominated GLC Labour Group, we wished the red scare stories were true.

On behalf of Sir Reg Goodwin, John Keys had tried to persuade the GLLP Executive to establish a small working party to draft the manifesto. This idea was rejected as most members on the Executive wanted to help make policy and were not prepared to leave it to the leadership. Five working parties were established and began drawing up the manifesto in September 1975. I went on the housing working party and spent a year resisting Richard Balfe's proposals to include in the manifesto a commitment to start building council houses for sale and introduce an equity sharing scheme (buying just part of your council house). As the Labour GLC was cutting its housing programme, Balfe's proposals were rejected; he then submitted a minority report to the one-day consultative conference called by the GLLP for September 1976, at which his proposals attracted even less support. It was not until a decade later, in 1986, that the Thatcher Government considered the introduction of equity sharing as the final stage in its council house sales policy. Had the GLC introduced such a scheme in 1977 it would only have made it more difficult for Labour councils with long waiting lists to resist the enforced sale of housing.

Between the one-day consultative conference in September and the GLLP Executive Meeting on 10 January 1977, the manifesto was to be prepared from the various working party reports. At the start of the January meeting, all members of the Executive were handed a draft manifesto and asked to read it before voting on its adoption. This draft was a simple justification of the previous four years and had obviously been written by the GLC Leader's support staff. Introducing it, Sir Reg Goodwin stated that 'it commits us to

76

nothing' – and he was right. The draft ignored all the decisions of the 1976 Annual Meeting which had instructed the Executive to produce a firmly socialist manifesto. The rightwing majority on the Executive supported the Goodwin line, rejecting all the left's amendments and also our plea that we were honour-bound to follow the decisions of the 1976 meeting. We all had to return our copies at the end of the meeting for fear of leaks to the press, although it was pointed out that as there was nothing in the document it would be unlikely to attract press attention.

With the 1977 Annual Meeting just eight weeks away, the left started lobbying to get emergency motions submitted which would amend the manifesto in line with party policy. When John Keys became aware of what we were doing he consulted Sir Reg Goodwin and Bob Mellish and they agreed to publish the manifesto immediately, thus laying a realistic claim to enter the *Guinness Book of Records* as the only British political party ever to publish its election manifesto three months before polling day and eight weeks before the start of the campaign.

We only heard about this interesting little plot the day before publication on 17 February. Eight candidates immediately issued a statement drawing attention to the discrepancies between the manifesto and party policy and calling for the launch to be delayed until after the GLLP Annual Meeting in two weeks' time. Along with David White, Tony Banks, Robin Young and myself our press statement was also signed by Michael Ward, who had become the candidate in Battersea South.

The vilification which rained down on our heads in the aftermath of our action was as bad as anything at the height of the fare increase splits. In particular there was much hypocritical cant from Goodwin and Keys that our actions had damaged party unity, which was a bit steep considering that it was their ridiculously early launching of the manifesto which had precipitated the row. At times I felt we came close to being physically assaulted by some of our critics (particularly when the bars were open at County Hall). I had the backing of my local party, who shared my publicly stated view that the manifesto was 'garbage . . . devoid of any socialist principle'. We decided to refuse to accept the centrally produced election address and instead write our own, based on party policy.

The final Executive Meeting before the Annual Meeting opened with bitter personal attacks on the left from Goodwin, Keys and Mellish but the union representatives did not seem keen to take sides. Without reaching a conclusion about who was most in the wrong they simply voted to end the debate and move on to the next item on the agenda. At the Annual Meeting the unions took the view that to change the manifesto would probably prompt Sir Reg Goodwin to disown it and give the press a field day, so the block vote was used to give a four to one majority against bringing the manifesto in line with GLLP policy. Although we lost that vote the Meeting took the decisive step of voting for the first ever leftwing majority on the Executive, thus opening the way to the 1981 GLC administration. Bob Mellish and Bert Fry had both decided to retire, and the left won the Treasurership, which was a walkover for Ron Todd (the new TGWU Regional Organizer), and also elected Arthur Latham as Executive chair by a two per cent majority. A purge of three rightwingers amongst the Constituency Labour Party (CLP) delegates gave the left 13 out of the 16 CLP seats on the Executive, which guaranteed an overall majority for the left, badly rattling the right.

As the weekend wore on, the mood became electric, with the right wing, unused to being in a minority, making increasingly dire predictions about the future and the left allowing its success temporarily to erode the normal conventions of behaviour towards those on the right.

With passions running high and many delegates able to remember the insufferable arrogance of some rightwingers in the past, few leftwingers now remembered Sir Winston Churchill's wise advice: 'In victory – magnanimity.' Too many seemed to be following the guiding principle which has always been attributed to the former General Secretary of the National Union of Railwaymen, Sid Weighell: 'Always kick a man when he is down.' Although many delegates genuinely believed that leading members of the GLC were a corrupt, spent force whose time was up, telling them so to their faces only led to several unpleasant and unnecessary scenes around the fringes of the conference.

In the very last hour on Sunday afternoon, the meeting finally reached the debate on the manifesto. We knew that the left would lose the vote but were consoled by our gains on the Executive. During the debate there was a series of mainly humorous speeches from the left, highlighting the differences between the 1973 and 1977 election manifestos. John Keys failed to realize that he could have got away with a response along the lines of 'an honest disagreement amongst comrades' but chose instead to put the boot in, which only provoked screams of abuse from the floor. This spilt over on to the platform when Jim Daly bore down on me, shouting that the left had lost. He then gave me his analysis of the abilities of the left in general and of me in particular. When he started waving his fist in my face Tony Hart (who became the GLC chair of Finance in 1981) came and sat down between us to try and calm things down. All this took place in full view of the delegates and only encouraged the shouting from the conference floor. It was almost impossible to hear John Keys. After the vote the meeting broke up. The Executive member representing the Fire Brigades' Union came over to apologize for the vote to support the manifesto but said that it had been too late to do anything else. However he added that the problem would not arise again; 'You've got your majority on the Executive now so you'll be able to do it differently in future.'

After all the unpleasantness at County Hall it was a relief to spend the weeks in the run-up to the May election in Hackney North. Since my selection in June the left had consolidated its hold on the party. For years, elections in the constituency had been fought simply by the haphazard distribution of an election address and the candidate driving around with loudspeakers. This time we used all available methods normally associated with fighting a marginal seat as the opinion polls were pointing to a Labour rout which, if it was as bad as in 1967, could well make Hackney North vulnerable.

Modernizing the methods was one thing, finding the activists to carry them out was another. Hackney North did not have a large membership, but fortunately it did have a retiring Labour MP and a list of over eighty aspiring hopefuls who had asked to be considered. The local party simply wrote to them all saying that they would be selecting their parliamentary candidate after the GLC election, enclosed a list of addresses for canvassing and pointed out that they felt sure they would benefit from getting to know the constituency better. To raise money for the campaign we organized a sponsored walk in Epping Forest. The response was gratifying. Voters could hardly move on the streets of Hackney North without being approached by aspiring MPs and the tramp of ambitious feet across Epping Forest was enough to cause severe erosion damage. (Needless to say the Labour Party finally selected as its candidate Ernie Roberts, who had absented himself from all these ritual acts of self-humiliation.) By the time election day came around we had made such an impact that the Tory candidate came into our offices to complain that the Labour Party had been campaigning during the election. He pointed out that this was unreasonable; if one party campaigned in Hackney North then they would all have to start doing it and that would mean unnecessary work for everyone!

When the first results were declared it was obvious that Labour was heading for disaster. Hackney North was the third lowest swing to the Tories in London's 92 constituencies. London-wide it was the worst result for Labour since 1931, apart from the all-time low of 1967. For Mrs Thatcher it was a night of jubilation: 'Of all our victories, the GLC is our greatest prize – the jewel in the crown.' At that stage she had still to discover that the GLC was 'an unnecessary tier of government that provided no real services at all'. If Mrs Thatcher was jubilant, Sir Reg Goodwin was totally crushed and even looked as though he might finally make way for a younger man. However, his preferred successors, Tony Judge, Jim Daly and Richard Balfe, had all lost their seats; on the left, Tony Banks and David White had been defeated. Simon Turney and I, at the age of 32, were the youngest members in a Group whose average age was 65, which no doubt explains why the main, if not the only emphasis of the Labour campaign had been the defence of the pensioners' bus pass from the wicked Tories.

There were only three new members in the Group and the political balance was now three leftwingers, 12 centrists and 13 rightwingers. With such a small group it was impossible for the leadership not to give me a role and at the Leader's Advisory Committee it was proposed that I should be spokesperson on public transport issues or Housing Management. Sir Reg Goodwin vetoed both proposals on the grounds that they would bring me into frequent contact with the public and provide a high-profile platform. In the end it was agreed that I should cover Housing Development.

Sir Reg Goodwin had not anticipated the Tories' plans to run down house building from the recent peak of 7,000 to just 35 per year, to destroy our direct labour department and to sell off virtually all available housing land, thus crippling any future Labour GLC plans to restart the housing programme. In the end, opposing these policies led to my playing a major role in the attack on the new Tory administration. Sir Horace Cutler's regime turned out to be much worse than expected and the ferocity of the Tory policies was an early indication of what a Thatcher Government would be like. The effect of this was to reunite the Labour Group, who were used to the more patrician style of Lord Plummer's 1967–73 Tory administration.

As Sir Horace Cutler's administration got underway, the prevailing view within the Labour Group was that Sir Reg Goodwin would continue as Leader for one or two years at the most and then hand over to someone who could lead us into the next election. No member of the Group had an obvious majority to succeed Sir Reg but the electorate had achieved at the ballot box two things which could not have been achieved by conspiracy. First, they had reduced the field of leftwing contenders to just one. Secondly, they had by accident created a Labour Group in which the left and centre together could muster 15 votes to the right's 13. When the contest came my only chance of winning would be to squeeze out any centre candidates. Those journalists who were so outraged by my election in 1981 could have done their homework and counted heads in 1977, but only one did. Three days after the election the *Observer*'s Tony Craig wrote:

> While the Tories are still celebrating, the Labour Party rump at County Hall is in disarray.
>
> The swing cost the group many of its ablest leaders, including the leftwing Mr Tony Banks, who was Chairman of the General Purposes Committee, Transport Chief Mr Jim Daly, blamed for the capital's traffic problems and for the failings of London Transport, and the

81

two housing leaders (who often disagreed with each other as much as with the Tories), Mr Tony Judge and Mr Richard Balfe.

The new group, which will have only 28 of the 92 council seats, is sadly lacking in obvious leadership potential if Sir Reg decides to go, and there may be a move in some London Labour parties to persuade the leading leftwinger, the young and thoughtful Mr Ken Livingstone, to seek the succession.

Those of my colleagues who had been on the receiving end of my occasionally intemperate tongue and pen were too busy laughing at the description of a thoughtful Ken Livingstone to sit down and work out the figures for themselves. Had they done so they would undoubtedly have put in the necessary effort to prevent such an outcome. It was my good fortune that so many of my Labour colleagues were completely amateurish in their approach to politics. However, their lack of professionalism was more than matched by those Fleet Street journalists who only woke up to what was happening four years after the event.

3

A Very Open Conspiracy

Nothing short of a miracle would have prevented the Tories winning the 1979 General Election. Any last minute hopes raised by the one opinion poll which showed the Tory lead down to just one per cent were quickly dispelled on election day itself when we saw the dramatically high turnout in the Tory areas of Hampstead, where I was the candidate. An hour before the close of poll I visited the polling stations in the traditional Labour areas of Kilburn only to have my worst fears confirmed. The turnout was still below 50 per cent in contrast to the Tory areas, which were well over 60 per cent. At ten o'clock the party activists gathered back at the local ward committee room in Kilburn to hear the ITN exit poll announce that the Tories had won a more than comfortable majority over Labour and all other parties combined.

In 1976 I had been selected to fight the next General Election as Labour's candidate in Hampstead. It came as a considerable shock to the rather wealthy, liberally inclined old guard who had been running Hampstead Labour Party when I defeated the self-confident Foreign Office diplomat who was their preferred candidate by 24 votes to 20. They complained that I lacked the style and background for a sophisticated area such as Hampstead. One party member actually wrote to the National Executive Committee (NEC) urging them to overturn my election.

> His education is sketchy. I understand he went to a College of Education and we all know how low the standard is at some such places which I think I would describe as schools for nannies. This is a great pity when one thinks that there were in the running for the

candidature two PhDs, a QC and several other graduates
of reputable universities such as Oxford. I am not suggesting that every Labour candidate should be a graduate:
merely that to win a constituency with as sophisticated an
electorate as Hampstead we need a candidate of clear
intellectual ability. . . . the attached article of mine shows
the disastrous result we had in both 1974 General Elections when we had a postman as candidate . . . this
selection has been a clear use of Ovid's line: "Video
meliora proboque, deteriora sequor" (I see the better
things and I approve, I follow the worse). If the NEC
refuse endorsement . . . we would then have to reselect
and there might be a chance of a leftwing candidate who
is not a fool being chosen, though perhaps that is over
optimistic.

A handful of members left the party because of my commitment
to a wealth tax which would have separated them from a substantial
proportion of their income, and there was some disquiet when at
my first Hampstead dinner party I made the mistake of chewing
my way through the bouquet garni, and then compounded the error
with the excuse that bouquet garnis were not standard fare in
Lambeth.

As the Hampstead Labour Party activists waited for the result of
the 1979 election in the Kilburn committee room, and as I prepared
to go off to the count, we spoke about the implications of Thatcher's
victory. The overwhelming view was that Mrs Thatcher would be
so reactionary and incompetent in government that Labour would
have a walkover at the next General Election. I was in a minority
of one in thinking that a clear and firm set of radical Tory convictions
plus the benefits of North Sea oil could pose a real danger of the
Tories winning a second term. Some of those present were taken
aback when I announced that Thatcher's victory meant that it was
now vital that we make the struggle for leftwing control of the GLC
Labour Group our immediate and urgent priority.

Only one person agreed that Thatcher's victory could lead to a
breakthrough for the left in London. Bill Bush knew exactly what
was going on in County Hall. Bill had been only 26 years old when

nine months earlier he was appointed to head the Labour Group's dozen-strong band of secretaries and policy advisers. He was already disillusioned with the Labour Group, its unimaginative, cautious policies and comatose style. That evening in Kilburn we spoke briefly about the implications of Thatcher's victory. Bill and I agreed that it meant a certain Labour win at the next GLC election exactly two years away and that with the leftwing majority on the London Labour Party Executive we should be able to get a radical manifesto.

We also knew how much weaker the position of the old guard was now at County Hall. The right had lost its majority on the Executive and Bob Mellish was no longer there to chair it in a way that protected them at County Hall. Most important of all, the demoralizing effect of their record in the 1973–77 Goodwin administration had so undermined their confidence that they completely lacked the energy to fight for the power they wanted. I anticipated the howls of outrage when they finally discovered that power was not going to fall into their laps as of right.

In the months that followed Bill Bush and I continued to see eye to eye. His personal radicalism, laid-back style and irreverent sense of humour left him quite unsuited to the task of servicing a Labour Group who often seemed more interested in the Queen's garden parties than the London Labour Party.

Within weeks of his appointment at County Hall, Bush and I became good friends. Although he continued to suffer from a soft spot for Sir Reg Goodwin and was always loyal to him, he did not take long to decide that when Goodwin finally stood down, he would prefer working with me than any of the other contenders. Some members of the London Labour Party Executive feared that Bill's team was not to be trusted in the preparation of the manifesto as his predecessor had used his team to produce an alternative one. This had caused a divisive row which split the GLLP conference in the run-up to the 1977 election. I was able to reassure them that Bill had agreed that his secretariat would work with the Party rather than against it.

Bill made sure that nothing moved within the leadership without my being aware of it and often stuck his neck out dangerously far in order to ensure that the manifesto reflected Labour Party policy.

I often wondered what on earth had prompted the old leadership to appoint him. The answer, I discovered, was simply that no one else of any ability had applied for the job.

Although the way was open for a transformation at County Hall, Labour activists had not yet woken up to the possibilities for change. Since its inception in 1965, the GLC had remained remote from the actual needs of Londoners. Apart from giving pensioners free travel, the Goodwin administration had made no lasting impact on Londoners or Labour activists. Although it seems amazing in retrospect, the media took very little interest in local government at this time; to them it was a great bore. Ted Knight had been leader of Lambeth Council for only twelve months and the new policies had not yet begun to force their way through the Lambeth bureaucracy. David Blunkett still had a year to wait before assuming the leadership of Sheffield, and Liverpool seemed to be unshakeable under Liberal/Tory control.

I had tried to awaken interest in the GLC with an article in *Socialist Organiser* – the campaign journal of the Socialist Campaign for Labour Victory (SCLV) – in March 1979, but it sank without trace. Throughout that summer my efforts to raise interest in the need for socialist policies for the next GLC election produced no response whatsoever. The final humiliation came at a *Socialist Organiser* conference in July 1979 where a discussion workshop I was supposed to lead on the topic of the forthcoming GLC elections had to be cancelled due to lack of interest.

Fortunately, things were going more favourably on the London Labour Party Executive. Although we had only a very narrow broad left majority of two, we were making all the running. The election of Arthur Latham, a Tribunite, ex-MP for Paddington with a lot of local government experience, in place of Bob Mellish meant that the Executive was being run in a much more open and democratic fashion. More importantly, Bert Fry, the regional organizer of the Transport and General Workers' Union, had retired and been replaced by Ron Todd, who had no intention of continuing his autocratic style. Other trade union representatives were allowed to express their views without constantly fearing that such action could lead to their removal from the Executive by the skilful use of the

TGWU block vote. Nor did Todd make any secret of the fact that his own views were firmly socialist.

It was also a good thing for the left that the chair of the local government sub-committee, which was responsible for overseeing the production of the manifesto, had fallen into the hands of David Nicholas, the deputy leader of the Labour Group on Wandsworth Council.

David Nicholas was without doubt one of the nicest men I have met in politics. He was so courteous, calm and genuinely attentive to those around him that it was difficult to imagine how he survived in the London Labour Party. I never recall him losing his temper or being rude to those who could not keep up with the logic of his argument. He never pushed himself forward and it was wholly in character that when he stood for Parliament in the 1982 Mitcham and Morden by-election it was in the constituency where he was a very popular primary school headmaster. He died tragically young of cancer in 1985 and at his funeral we paid tribute to the crucial role he had played in preparing the policies which we tried to carry out. In his calm way he had been a major influence in persuading the full executive to widen the manifesto consultation process and it was on his sub-committee that I caught the first glimpse of the excitement that the Labour GLC would eventually generate. For months, younger party members worked, with an enthusiasm that the Labour Party had not seen in decades, to fashion the GLC as an instrument for change in London.

Apart from David and me, we also had on the left Michael Ward, who chaired the industry and employment working party, and Jeremy Corbyn (later MP for Islington North), who chaired planning. We worked closely together to ensure that the widest range of talent was appointed to the manifesto working parties and had them all established within six weeks of the General Election.

Most members of the Executive expected me to chair the housing working party but I had no doubt our transport policy was more vital in the planning of a radical GLC. Controversy around what fare levels and rate subsidy to adopt was likely to produce the most damaging split in any future Labour Group. A firm policy could prevent a repetition of the backsliding of the Goodwin adminis- tration. If the manifesto left any room for doubt one could almost certainly guarantee there would be as many resignations and sack-ings as had plagued Sir Reg Goodwin. I also knew that if we could achieve a lasting compromise in this most divisive area it would greatly increase my influence within the next Labour Group and leave me well placed to take over the leadership when Sir Reg finally stood down, which I expected to happen a year or so after the 1981 election, by which time he would be 74 years old.

Unfortunately, but predictably, the old guard did not view such a scenario with any enthusiasm and immediately began organizing to block my appointment as chair of the transport working party, which was due to be decided at the July meeting of the regional executive.

With the shift of power to the left on the Executive and with Ron Todd's appointment signalling the similar shift on the London region of the TGWU, the leadership of the rightwing trade union-ists had passed to the electricians' representative, John Spellar, who always preferred to avoid charming his opponents if he thought he could win by beating them into a pulp. In the hot, stuffy, over-crowded meeting room of the London Labour Party headquarters grand debates about great issues could often degenerate into insults and mindless points of order. It was in such a mood that we met that July.

The right had mobilized their maximum support and it was clearly going to be a close vote. But even before we got to the question of who was to chair transport John Spellar had gone on the attack. His contention was over a point of order. The vote on a leftwing motion had split evenly and Spellar insisted that the chair, Arthur Latham, should not use his casting vote, which would have carried the motion. The next item on the agenda was whether I should chair the transport working party. Unfortunately for John Spellar, a move by the right to have my name deleted and replaced by Brian Nicholson (at that time the treasurer of the London Labour Party) also ended in a tied vote. Arthur Latham was quick to point out that on the precedent just set that motion too should fall. I turned to thank John Spellar for his help in getting me the chair of transport. His reply was drowned by laughter.

*

The late seventies was a period of realignment in the Labour Party. In Hampstead Town Hall, on 15 July 1978, various leftwing factions had joined together to form the Socialist Campaign for a Labour Victory (SCLV) – an alliance that was to work with the Labour Co-ordinating Committee and Tony Benn. They shared objectives for reform in the party such as the demands for the reselection of MPs, the election of the party leader by an electoral college, and unilateral nuclear disarmament. Through my contact with one of the founding groups, the Chartists, with whom I had worked in Lambeth, I was invited with Ted Knight to speak at the opening rally.

Sadly this new unity lasted barely a year. The Thatcher Government's cuts in local authority grants left councils with a bleak choice: either to cut jobs and services, or to increase the rates. That dilemma opened up major rifts in the SCLV. The Chartists and I took the view that as over half the rates came from industry and commerce it was better to defend services and keep rents and fares down by increasing the rates. A larger faction, led by John O'Mahony, alias Sean Matgamna, strongly disagreed. They argued that rate increases were paid for out of workers' pockets and therefore the only acceptable policy was 'no rate increase, no cuts'.

Relations between Ted Knight and me also went into deep freeze at this time. As leader of Lambeth Council, Ted was faced with the problem of how to balance the books following the Government's decision to claw back grant in the aftermath of Mrs Thatcher's 1979 election victory. In 1979 Ted had gone for a 39 per cent rate increase when he was being advised that 45 per cent was required to fund the council's plans. Following Mrs Thatcher's election he came under pressure from his officers to recommend a cut of £1.5 million in residential child care, under fives' provision, meals on wheels and housing maintenance. This strategy made little difference to domestic ratepayers, who 'saved' only 20p a week, while the Shell headquarters made savings of £200,000.

Although Lambeth rapidly reversed its cuts decision under pressure from the local Labour Parties, it had confused the rates versus services argument and allowed our opponents to discredit the rate increase option. It delivered control of the SCLV and *Socialist Organiser* into the hands of John O'Mahony, whose faction packed the July 1979 SCLV conference and took a majority on its organizing committee. I further alienated O'Mahony by refusing to publish an attack on Ted in *Socialist Organiser.*

With the GLC selections only ten months away and the *Socialist Organiser* firmly in the hands of O'Mahony, who opposed all I stood for, I was suddenly deprived of access to what had looked like becoming a good broad left organizing network. I had no alternative but to try and interest the Chartist group in leaving the *Socialist Organiser* and establishing a campaign aimed specifically at taking control of the GLC. Throughout the rates versus cuts dispute we had taken the same view and now they were the only rank and file group that shared my perspective about how much could be achieved through a radical socialist GLC. We met to lay our plans shortly before Christmas 1979 at the home of Keith Veness.

Some of the groundwork had been done a few months before. During the 1979 Labour Party conference I had gone round looking for any and every London-based leftwinger and tried to persuade them to come to a meeting to discuss how the left could gain control of the GLC and implement genuinely radical policies. Every constituency party and trade union in London was also sent an invitation. When John Keys, General Secretary of the GLLP, saw one he over-reacted and sent out a letter deploring my actions, which only served to stimulate interest in the meeting. When the GLLP Executive met they accepted my right to organize openly, at which point John Keys finally gave in and started looking forward to his impending retirement. After this I could not resist calling the October meeting the 'John Keys Annual Memorial Lecture'. His successor, George Page, took a completely neutral position in the internal power struggle, effectively depriving the established GLC Labour leadership of the organizational arm they had come to rely on.

Although it was still two years until the GLC election it was vital to start working at once to ensure that we had enough leftwingers on the panel of candidates, which was to be published in early 1980. The reputation of the 1981 administration was to be built on opening up the structures of the Council, giving Londoners the opportunity to participate in their tens and hundreds of thousands. Ironically the leftwing organization which made that administration possible involved fewer than a hundred people meeting once a month at County Hall to discuss the precise nature of the policies we wanted to follow and the mechanics of the selection process and of the drafting of the manifesto.

The left had several advantages at this time over the right wing. We had pushed through the changes that ensured a full reselection process for sitting members and the democratic involvement of the whole party in agreeing the manifesto. We had written new rules and knew how they should work. Even if the right wing had known their way around the new rules there was very little base left for them to build on within the London Labour parties. The local leadership of Reg Goodwin and the national leadership of Jim Callaghan were discredited. Their failure to deliver even the smallest reforms while in government meant that the right had lost confidence, were demoralized and had no real conviction that they could do better – even if the electorate could be conned into voting for them again. In London that process of demoralization was so complete that most of the small band of surviving rightwingers felt that they had to mouth left slogans in order to have any hope of keeping their positions.

The process of change in the London Labour parties was being reinforced by events in the national Labour Party. In the two years following the October 1979 conference, the broad left coalition which assembled around Tony Benn swept almost all before it and came within a handful of votes of transforming the party. The reasons for the failure and defeat of the Labour Government bore a remarkable similarity to the loss of control of the GLC. The struggle of the left for control of the Party in London was mirrored almost exactly on a national level.

Most important of all was the agenda being set for the Labour movement by Tony Benn himself. He had been the first Labour politician to direct the attention of the left towards the nature of democracy and the need to open up British society. This included reducing the powers of patronage of the Prime Minister and bringing the civil service and its powers into the open. He was also the first to highlight the need for a wider Labour movement actively encouraging the involvement of women and black people alongside the traditional white male trade unionists. It was Tony Benn who opened up all these new areas for debate while examining and reinvigorating the traditional shopping list of Labour's policies. In those exhilarating years Tony seemed to be everywhere: on radio and television, writing books and in crowded meeting halls all over Britain. Audiences of hundreds and often thousands listened as he analysed, examined, predicted and gave confidence that we could achieve socialism and, yes, it did involve the very people in that particular audience. Not only did every speech seem to produce a new idea or policy but each one was crafted with a care and a beauty the movement had not heard since the death of Nye Bevan nearly two decades before. After the windy rhetoric of the Wilson/Callaghan years, Benn's speeches stood out like the paintings of a great artist hung amidst a display of painting by numbers. With the confidence and excitement being generated around Benn, it was not surprising that those who remained wedded to the traditional rightwing values which had failed so often in the past increasingly came to believe that they no longer had a future within the Labour Party and began setting up the SDP.

Our campaign to win control of the GLC was assisted, although we did not realize it at the time, by the private decision of Sir Reg Goodwin to hang on to the GLC Labour leadership until after the 1981 election. He then planned to stand down and hand over the reins to Tony Judge, though Judge had warned him that pressure of work would make it almost impossible for him to take up the position. Had Sir Reg stepped down within a year of the 1977 defeat, a younger rightwing leader might very well have assembled a new centre right Group capable of surviving the surge to the left which seemed to be sweeping all before it. Instead, Sir Reg held on to the post but failed to do the work which was essential to ensure that he could pass on the leadership safely to his chosen successor.

The left's position was strengthened by two further factors. One was a decision taken by the left caucus that it would be open to any Labour Party member. No one was to be excluded because they had voted incorrectly in the past and no one was allowed to set themselves up as the judge of who was or was not a 'real' leftwinger. Whilst this meant that often rightwingers turned up (Ellis Hillman even had the nerve to appear after he had persuaded a leftwinger to switch his vote at an ILEA meeting, thus ensuring the passage of a 4.2 per cent cuts package), the very openness made it difficult to whip up the sort of press interest which would have been generated by 'secret plotting'. It also ensured that no one, feeling excluded, deserted to the opposing camp.

Also working in our favour was the decision by the Chartists to finance and publish a new leftwing journal that would be the vehicle for our campaigns. *London Labour Briefing* was born. In the years since it first appeared in February 1980 no leftwing journal has attracted so much media interest. There is no doubt at all that initially the interest was due to the journal's discussion of sexual politics. Leftwing journals come and go and mainly cover a fairly orthodox range of traditional socialist interests, such as the economy, defence, foreign affairs, the welfare state and the evil nature of whoever is currently Leader of the Labour Party. *Briefing* was different: those of us who produced it shared a common belief that the personal was political and politics affected every aspect of our daily lives. We wanted to produce a left paper which was not under the control of any faction or tendency and would keep London's leftwing activists briefed with the sort of information network that we had lacked at the time of the 1977 GLC elections. We also sought to raise the kind of issues affecting the individual which other left papers chose to avoid for fear not just of media ridicule but also of alienating more orthodox socialists. We therefore initiated an open editorial group, although the vast bulk of the work, including fundraising, was done by Graham Bash and Chris Knight.

The first two issues of the journal were exclusively devoted to the struggles in local government. However the third carried articles on Ireland, sexism, and the infiltration of a Hindu fascist group into the Brent Labour parties. Sales rapidly built up, including many to the press and Tory GLC members who had finally woken up to the fact that something was beginning to stir within the Labour Party. But it was the fifth issue in August 1980 which brought the paper well and truly into the public eye.

Chris Knight and Ann Bliss had published accounts of their relationship and tried to draw out lessons which revealed the relevance of personal experience to politics. For the first time a left journal was talking impotence, monogamy, the way in which men possess women as property, the impact of multiple relationships on an original relationship, a proposal for the separation of love and sex and the implications of collective living. *Briefing* reviewed these publications sensitively, but other reactions were less tolerant. During the next GLC meeting the Tory chair of the Council, Bernard Brook-Partridge, actually had to call Tory members of the Council to order because they were disrupting the meeting as they clustered around my desk asking to buy copies of *Briefing*. Several local papers in London reported the August edition with an offensively flippant approach, and although few took the issues raised seriously, *London Labour Briefing* became an established and recognized voice. Further serious features followed on women, race, disabilities, male violence, gay rights and alternatives to the family, but the final straw for the press was the October 1982 issue which carried an article on transvestism. This unleashed a wave of hysterical homophobia in the Sunday papers on the first day of the Labour Party conference. Linked to a wholly bogus story claiming that Peter Tatchell (Labour's candidate for the Bermondsey by-election) had attended a Gay Olympics in San Francisco, and reminding their readers of my support for lesbian and gay rights, the Sunday gutter press claimed that they had 'reliable' information that Michael Foot was personally shocked at the large number of 'perverts' now attending Labour Party conferences. The result of this attack was to ensure a full attendance at the Labour campaign for Lesbian and Gay Rights fringe meeting which voted to exclude reporters from the newspapers responsible. Tony Benn came along to the meeting simply to express his support for those under attack from the press. *London Labour Briefing* had come a very long way in two short years.

With Labour still facing three years of opposition at the GLC in 1978, I decided to stand for Camden Council. I was determined this time to try and put into practice the changes I had been prevented from carrying out in Lambeth.

The situation in Camden was considerably better than in Lambeth. Throughout the 1960s the Council had been run by progressive middle-class elements, who, with access to a higher rate income than other Labour boroughs, had decided to expand, with the result that services in Camden were of a higher standard and greater strides had been made in tackling the housing problem.

Between 1971 and 1975 first Millie Miller and then Frank Dobson had provided strong leadership with a clear sense of direction, but the Labour leadership had then passed into the hands of Roy Shaw, who had more in common with Sir Reg Goodwin. Under Shaw the central policy committee was weak and issues came to the Group in a haphazard, disorganized manner, often without warning. Roy Shaw seldom gave clear advice to the Group and most of the running was made by the deputy leader John Mills and the chief whip Andrew Bethell, both of whom were competent and decisive rightwingers. No leftwinger held a committee chair, which allowed Roy Shaw to 'run' the Council by holding regular lunches to which favoured chief officers and some committee chairs were invited in order to discuss the key issues facing the Council. No minutes were taken at these meetings, so they did not have to be reported to the Labour Group, most of whom did not even know they had taken place. No formal decisions were taken, but the chief officers would nevertheless act on the consensus which emerged from the meetings.

Later when I became chair of Housing I was invited to one of these lunches as the Council's housing programme was to be discussed. I was appalled to find that the Director of Housing had not been invited because he had displeased the leadership by giving unwelcome professional advice in the past. I objected to the whole process and, rather than face a row, Roy Shaw agreed to discontinue the practice and to try and breathe some life into the little-used policy committee. Years later I discovered that after the lunches were discontinued some councillors were invited to 'parties' at the chief executive's house. The same select little group of councillors and chief officers were invited. No formal decisions were taken, no leftwingers were invited and no report of the existence of this forum was ever made to the Labour Group.

I had not expected to be invited to chair a committee when the Leader's Advisory Committee reported to the Labour Group after the May borough elections. There had been a major split in the final drafting of the 1978 manifesto because of the leadership's determination to avoid a commitment to a rent freeze. I had played a central role in this split and had publicly attacked the way the Group was run.

On the eve of the Labour Group AGM, the left caucus decided that there was no chance of removing Roy Shaw as Leader but that we should make a symbolic challenge to the deputy leader and chief whip. Phil Turner and I were to make that challenge, and if defeated, were to stand for the chairs of Direct Labour and Housing – if necessary against the recommendations of the Leader's Advisory Committee.

During the election campaign many Labour councillors had been disturbed by the number of complaints they had received about the housing department. For this reason I felt that if both candidates for the chair of Housing had to make speeches outlining what they intended to do to improve the department's record, I would have a good chance of winning. This is precisely what happened. When my opponent made the fatal mistake of saying he thought the Group's housing policies were correct, while I was demanding changes, I was home and dry.

I was suddenly in the position of chairing the most powerful committee in a Council under a weak Leader. After all the years of frustration on Lambeth Council and the GLC, where I had been forced to act largely as an opposition, it was an exhilarating experience. I found myself rising earlier in the mornings, impatient to get into the Town Hall to work on the changes I wanted to see.

Camden was very backward in providing facilities for members as the middle-class slant of the Labour Group meant that most leading members either had their own private businesses or worked in the sort of firms where they could use their employers' facilities to carry out their council work. I insisted on having a proper office in the housing department and a personal assistant to help with the vast amount of paperwork and letters from dissatisfied tenants and waiting list cases.

I was lucky to have taken over just as the main flow of new council housing, which had been started in the early seventies, was becoming available for letting and a full year before Mrs Thatcher's election brought our housing programme to a halt. Camden had an ambitious housing programme. Most of the planned new building schemes were on difficult and expensive sites or involved new forms of design such as building over railway lines on concrete platforms. This was not a cost-effective way of tackling the housing problem as it tied up vast sums of money for years before we saw any new, lettable homes. I therefore persuaded the Labour Group to scrap the plans and switch resources to municipalization. This meant the Council would take over housing which was in the worst condition, often with tenants who were being harassed by crooked landlords, and at the same time council tenants would be more likely to be housed in traditional homes with gardens, which most of them preferred to the 'experimental' new estates. The properties were modernized in a third of the time needed for a new building scheme. I was warned that our brightest young architects would leave the Council as their work would not be stimulating enough. However, I took the view that we were in the business of rehousing the homeless and not of providing intellectual challenges to architects.

The previous housing committee had geared itself up to a huge rolling programme of modernization for all existing council property, starting with the oldest and involving massively expensive schemes which the tenants had not been involved in drawing up. I visited all the estates and after a considerable struggle persuaded the Council to drop those plans. I suggested that they deal with the estates in a new order of priority, based not on age but on the level of tenant dissatisfaction, which could be gauged by the proportion of tenants on each estate who had requested transfers. The age of a property tells you nothing about its quality; many estates built at the time of cutbacks in council expenditure were less well built and desirable than older ones into which tenants were clamouring to transfer. It turned out after consultation with the tenants that instead of a full-scale modernization programme that would leave the estate like a builder's yard for up to a decade, they wanted the immediate installation of central heating, modern bathrooms and kitchens, all outstanding repairs to be tackled and an environmental improvement scheme in the courtyard. When key officers took so long to draft the report giving effect to this change that it began to look like deliberate sabotage, I wrote my own report and took it through committee. I did not run into that particular form of obstruction again.

Previous chairs had used a weekly meeting with the Director of Housing as the means of influencing policy. I reduced the number of meetings with the Director and made contact with the third tier of officers, who actually took the day-to-day management decisions. The more intelligent and active officers at that level were keen to co-operate as it gave them a quick political response to their requests for guidance. In the past they might have had to wait six weeks for a housing committee meeting or make their own guess about what members' priorities might be. With this level of daily involvement and constant pressure I was able to humanize the treatment of homeless families and reduce the number in bed and breakfast to under twenty. The number of empty Council-owned homes was reduced from the scandalous to the manageable by passing those awaiting demolition or modernization to short-life housing associations and concentrating the resources of the housing and direct works departments on the rest. This enabled Camden to avoid the conflicts with squatting groups which had plagued Lambeth.

Changes in the way the Council's housing stock was managed were more difficult to achieve. The senior officer in this section was particularly resistant to what he saw as members interfering in his job and my attempts to retire him were blocked by Roy Shaw. A closer working relationship with the departmental trade union, which would have been one way of working around him, was closed off at my first meeting with the NALGO branch. Although I offered to consider any changes in the internal management and policies of the department which they wished to propose, the NALGO representatives stated that they did not consider it to be part of their job to propose changes and that they preferred the traditional system of responding to management.

Long-serving members of the Labour Group who resented the amount of publicity I was getting also proved a stumbling block. I had been lucky that in my two years as chair of Housing, many of Camden's housing schemes were completed. As many tenants could now be rehoused, we made real inroads into the waiting list. It also meant that some of our resources were freed from these major projects, so we could now work on other schemes. I thought it was time to tackle the problem of single homeless and young people. On three occasions I brought papers to the Labour Group proposing such schemes. Unfortunately Camden Labour Group contained many wealthy members who had come to the area as students and stayed. These members were particularly sensitive to accusations that the pressures of gentrification were squeezing the original inhabitants out of the borough and loudly condemned any and every scheme to assist the young single homeless whom they dismissed as dropouts and squatters at worst and simply less important than families at best.

Under Shaw's leadership the Council became involved in a series of damaging and unnecessary disputes with strategic staff such as typists and telephone operators who had been left behind in the general income advance of white-collar staff largely because their jobs were almost exclusively held by women. The combination of bureaucratic delay in filling posts and the dramatic slowdown in Council work during a typists' strike not only delayed policy changes but also reduced Council expenditure. Delays in making staff appointments generally presented Roy Shaw with a series of savings with which he could plan to reduce the following year's rate, and undoubtedly this was a reason behind the delay in settling the typists' strike.

The seeds were being sown for the inevitable collapse of the Labour Group's initial radical period. It was the aftermath of the 'winter of discontent' dispute in February 1979 that finally forced a full retreat to rightwing policies.

The Council's manual workers' union, NUPE, went on strike for a minimum wage of £60 for a 35-hour week. The impact was immediately felt by Camden's 70,000 council tenants, who saw their heating cut off, lifts unrepaired and refuse piling up all over the estates. The left caucus met to discuss the problem and discovered that we did not have the votes to get agreement to NUPE's claim. Some of the centrists in the Labour Group were not prepared to see the better-paid manual workers such as refuse collectors get such a large increase but felt ashamed that some other staff were earning only about £45 a week.

The left caucus decided that we might win in the Group if we proposed not an increase in basic rates of pay but an additional supplement to the wages of every worker who was earning less than

£60 per week in order to bring them up to that minimum figure. I was sent away to see the Director of Finance to work out a rough cost, which turned out to be much higher than the £1 million a year that the scheme eventually came to. This we proposed to the Labour Group and won by one vote after amending the motion so that the reduction in working hours to 35 a week would not lead to an increase in overtime but to the creation of new jobs. The strike was settled in Camden and I hoped this might start a flood of identical settlements in other Labour councils. Sadly, Ted Knight refused to take similar action in Lambeth.

With the dispute resolved, we thought that would be the end of the matter. But no. A few months later we were informed that the Government-appointed District Auditor, Mr I. Pickwell, was investigating our minimum wage decision to see if it was legal. Mr Pickwell also informally indicated that Camden had not increased the rents of its tenants to his satisfaction and that unless an increase was forthcoming he might need to look into any possible loss to the ratepayers. He felt that our minimum wage decision was unreasonably generous towards the Council's workforce at the expense of the ratepayers and threatened to take action to recover £1 million from the 31 Labour councillors. (Our decision had, in fact, cost the average domestic ratepayer 7p a week and directly benefited our poorest workers, most of whom were women.)

The effect of this news on the Labour Group was electrifying. There was an immediate decision to end the minimum wage scheme and it was quite obvious that a rent increase would be agreed by a similar majority. A combination of panic and bitterness swept through the Group and the leadership seized its chance to bring the post-election radical phase to a close. What was most impressive to me was not just the speed with which the will of the majority of the Group collapsed but the fact that their anger was directed against those leftwingers who had persuaded them to adopt radical policies rather than against the auditor. The bitterness seemed strongest from those richer members of the Labour Group; working-class councillors who had less to lose were much more forgiving.

At exactly the same time that the auditor decided to try to surcharge, bankrupt and bar from public office the 31 Labour councillors in Camden, he took a completely contrary decision about the 39 Tory councillors in neighbouring Westminster. Unlike every other council in London, Westminster made no charge to local businesses for the removal of refuse. This was in breach of the 1936 Public Health Act and was causing a loss of £1.5 million a year to the ratepayers. As some of the Tory councillors also ran local businesses and all were members of the local Conservative Associations which were dominated by local business owners, suggestions were made which – because of our restrictive libel laws – I will not expand on. After much delay the auditor quietly announced that in Westminster he did not have enough evidence to go to Court. While he may very well not have had any evidence that Tory councillors had been unduly influenced by local business owners, he had all the evidence of the Council's own accounts that it was illegally not making a charge for collecting the refuse.

I was not surprised by the partisan nature of the auditor's decisions as the history of local government is littered with them. As far back as 1912 the District Auditor had ruled that the old London County Council was exceeding its powers under the Education (Provision of Meals) Act by providing fruit, cod-liver oil and extract of malt to schoolchildren. The auditor did not believe these things were 'food' in the meaning of the Act and although he eventually agreed to allow fruit to be defined as such, he maintained his ban on malt and cod-liver oil. The GLC were given a vivid example that such thinking had not changed when in June 1978 Auditor Nicholson (who must have been the lineal descendant of the auditor of 1912) submitted a formal report attacking the GLC's Direct Labour Department which would have done the Monday Club proud. I had also come under investigation by the District Auditor when rightwingers on Lambeth Council alleged to him that I was overclaiming on my attendance allowance. Instead of interviewing me directly the auditor chose to ask a member of staff in the Director-General's department to sneak into my room and check my diary. The woman concerned became worried and told me what was happening. As I had not overclaimed a single penny I was not concerned, but I was outraged that the auditor had abused his position by getting a junior member of the GLC staff to risk her career by snooping on a member. I could not complain without exposing the member of staff concerned but although I took no action I was disgusted that a public official could behave in a manner that would not have been out of place in the Nixon White House.

Instead of leading a vigorous public relations campaign against the District Auditor's decision, which would have revealed the bias in the system, Roy Shaw used the fear of surcharge to push through rent increases, cuts in services and numerous job losses in Camden's Direct Labour Department. This was coupled with an attitude to the auditor along the lines of 'he is only doing his job'. Shaw obviously hoped that the cuts package might convince him that we had seen the error of our ways and could be let off on the understanding that we would 'behave' in future. None of this had any effect, of course. In early February 1981, the District Auditor formally published his report and sought leave in the High Court to surcharge personally the Camden Councillors for £1 million. It was to be over a year before the judges finally decided the outcome of the case, but I had little doubt that we would lose so that the judges could use us as an example to other Labour councils. No public campaign was organized – the Council leadership believed that a quiet and moderate appearance in court would cut more ice with the judges than a mass demonstration outside – but even if Camden had decided on a campaign it is unlikely that either the workforce who had seen their minimum wage removed or the tenants who had suffered a return to regular rent increases would have rushed to our defence.

It is hard to recapture the scale of the panic that seized the Labour Group when we heard the auditor was to go for £1 million surcharge. Roy Shaw had warned us so frequently that this might happen that we had come to view his warnings as crying wolf. When the letter finally came it produced an almost physical state of shock and left me quite subdued for several days. Rage that such a Victorian system still existed was combined with an awful awareness of how much was at stake. That no fewer than three post-war Labour Governments had not abolished the practice could only be explained by the fact that the surcharge system applied only to councillors and not to MPs.

Other councillors must have felt the same stress and it showed in their behaviour. When I proposed that we should reject the auditor's warning and refuse to increase the rents, Camden's Policy Committee exploded into screaming abuse and threats of resignation. We were coming up to the Labour Group AGM, which once again I was facing at somewhat below my normal level of popularity.

I and fellow leftwinger Phil Turner had completed two years as committee chairs a few weeks after the chief executive formally notified members of the District Auditor's investigation and likely charges. Camden Labour Group had a rule that no one could chair the same committee for more than two years. Given the collapse in confidence of the Group, we did not hold out much hope of further office. Nevertheless, when the left caucus met it was decided that we must have leftwingers to chair the Finance and Staffing committees so that Roy Shaw's ability to block reforms via the management system could be ended. Phil Turner and I were nominated. I was not surprised when the chief whip, Andrew Bethell, approached us to say the leadership wanted to keep us in the administration but not in those key positions where the central management control of the Council lay. I made it clear that we were not prepared to be used to put a left face on a rightwing administration in which our proposed reforms would get no further than the administrative committees from which we were excluded. At the Group meeting just before Easter 1980 we challenged the Leader's Advisory Committee's recommendation to give those key posts to Andrew Bethell and John Mills, but lost. Knowing we now faced two years of rearguard actions against a Labour Group in full retreat, I was more than ready to slip away to Italy for a couple of weeks' holiday.

The GLC had never been understood and loved by the public the way its predecessor, the London County Council, had. The constant changes of political control as well as the U-turns within each administration meant that none had succeeded in imposing a strategy to alleviate London's housing, planning and transport problems. Given the record of failure, there was constant discussion in all political parties about whether or not the GLC should be retained. Under Sir Horace Cutler the massive rent and fare increases coupled with cutbacks in other service areas had led to the worst of all possible worlds: a large, expensive bureaucracy providing such a low level of service that its continued existence was very hard to justify. By the midpoint of the Cutler administration I had reached the conclusion that unless there was a dramatic improvement in the impact of County Hall's services on the lives of ordinary Londoners it would be better to abolish the GLC and introduce a system similar to that in the Canadian city of Toronto whereby all the GLC services and resources would be put under the control of a joint committee of the London boroughs. The new Labour manifesto was very much a final attempt to make the GLC work. I had no doubt that if we failed the GLC would shortly be abolished. I did not expect that we would be abolished because we succeeded!

When our manifesto working parties completed their work and the 157-page consultation document was produced, we had created what amounted to a Labour party 'Royal Commission' review of the role and functions of the GLC through its sixteen-year history. The five working party reports were full of original ideas and their conclusions effectively set new tasks and goals for County Hall.

The main unresolved question in the manifesto was how much rate subsidy we should put into keeping fares down. Only about a third of the 19 members of the working party favoured free travel but because the right seldom, if ever, attended meetings, the left were usually in the majority. As the commitment to abolish fares was London Labour Party policy, it had to be the basis of whatever we put forward. However, it was also clear that all of the transport unions were opposed to the policy and it was unlikely that the October special conference called to amend and approve the manifesto working party reports would agree that fares could be abolished within the four years of a new Labour administration. The union position was based on wider considerations than the potentially huge loss of jobs which the abolition of tickets would entail. London Transport had been in continuous decline for over twenty-five years and since 1959 the number of buses on the capital's streets had halved. To abolish fares without a major build-up of the rolling stock would simply cause the system to collapse because of all the extra passengers free public transport would attract. There was no quick way of increasing rolling stock and bus purchases would require Government approval. The Tories would also have to agree to integrate British Rail's local London services into the scheme or there would be a large number of passengers switching from BR to LT. Finally there was the problem of recouping the cost of increased rate subsidy from tourists and the Thatcher Government was never going to let the GLC have an airport or hotel bed tax.

Andrew McIntosh favoured an immediate fares cut of 25 per cent followed by increases in line with inflation. This would mean 5p extra on the rates in 1981 rising to 8p in 1985 and would have taken us back to the policy and subsidy levels of Jim Daly. The 25 per cent cut followed by a freeze would mean 5p extra on the rates in 1981 rising to 17p by 1985. The abolition of fares would have increased the rates by 26.5p in 1981 rising with inflation to 39.6p in 1985. Each extra 1p on the rates would cost the average London householder £2.50 a year. All the above figures were drawn up before the Government's new legislation was implemented, which allowed them to claw back grant from councils who were spending outside Government guidelines. This measure could have added another 6p to each figure. If we were to avoid the problems that had torn the Goodwin administration apart, the party desperately needed to have all the facts and figures for a period of debate rather than being railroaded into accepting one fixed position. The working party proposed, and the Regional Executive agreed, to publish all the options whilst expressing a preference for the abolition of fares a year after an initial 25 per cent reduction. Instead of recognizing the value of an open debate before the election rather than four years of infighting afterwards, Sir Reg Goodwin stomped off after the Executive meeting claiming that our action had cost us the election.

In addition to Goodwin's defeat on the fares issue, the left on the Executive won on every other point of substance. Goodwin was extremely disturbed to see that the panel of aspiring candidates agreed by the Executive included more leftwingers than ever before. The open left caucus meetings at County Hall had by now become regular monthly events with a usual attendance of 40 to 50. This had come as a surprise to the old guard, who had retaliated by leaking red scare stories to the press. They did not anticipate that their action would only serve to advertise that something was beginning to stir, increasing attendance and interest from activists who began to hope that the red scare stories might be true. The press speculated that there would be a large influx of leftwingers into the next GLC Labour Group and that Sir Reg Goodwin's leadership could be challenged, although at that stage the London evening papers were suggesting that our candidate would be Ted Knight.

At the GLLP annual meeting in March 1980 all Sir Reg's fears were realized. The broad left alliance was now almost totally dominant. Jim Daly, the only surviving rightwinger in the 16 CLP places on the Executive, was finally defeated as leftwingers won 76 per cent of the CLP votes to the right's mere 19 per cent. The conference voted for British withdrawal from northern Ireland by ten to one on a card vote and endorsed the position of increasing rates to defend jobs and services. The largest fringe meeting ever at the GLLP was called by *Briefing* and took place under the heading, 'Can the left take over the GLC?' Writing in *Time Out*, Beatrix Cambell clearly analysed what was happening.

> Few of the Goodwin dynasty were present to challenge the Ted Knight–Ken Livingstone leftwing axis, which by dogged activity and organisation has consolidated a strong base and seized a deliberate initiative over the cuts. This has turned what used to be a municipal desert into a promised land for the left.

Fourteen months later Fleet Street launched its attack, describing the new GLC as the product of a secret conspiracy. The truth is that no change of control within a political party had ever been conducted so openly. If Fleet Street's reporters had spent less time in the bars of Westminster and more reporting the city they were based in, they would not have been so surprised in May 1981.

In the five weeks that followed the annual meeting of the GLLP one decision must have weighed particularly heavily on Sir Reg Goodwin's mind. The meeting had voted to change the rules so that in future the Leader of the GLC Labour Group would be elected at that meeting instead of by the Labour Group itself. He must have realized that although it was by no means certain that the NEC would agree to the change, the only chance of the right's retaining control was if he resigned immediately, allowing Andrew McIntosh to dig himself into the leadership in the year before the election. It would be inconceivable to overthrow a Leader who had just won an election, and with the usual powers of patronage at his disposal Andrew would have no trouble hanging on during the radical phase of the new group until the chance presented itself once again to isolate the left. Sir Reg discussed the problem with Andrew McIntosh but told no one else before he gave his resignation letter to Harvey Hinds who, as chief whip, distributed it to the Labour Group on 15 April. The morning of the 17th saw *The Times* report: 'Front runners for the leadership are likely to be Mr Illtyd Harrington, aged 48, deputy Labour leader, and Mr Andrew McIntosh, aged 47, transport spokesman.' Only the London evening papers acknowledged that there might be a leftwing candidate. The *Standard*'s Mike King informed his readers: 'The left wing of the party is almost certain to nominate Mr Ken Livingstone, 34.' Len Vigars in the soon-to-fold *News* reported:

> There is also a strong likelihood of a leftwing candidate
> – Ken Livingstone, 34, a full-time councillor on the GLC
> and Camden Council. If there is a leftwing 'takeover' of
> the GLC after next year's elections, as has been forecast
> in some quarters, the new Leader could be ousted when
> extremists come to power. The group elects a Leader
> each year.

The reason that Mike King and Len Vigars were not certain whether I would stand was because I was still happily hanging around the bar in the Italian hotel where I was on holiday. I arrived back in London late on the night of the 17th but not too late to get a phone call from Bill Bush telling me that Sir Reg Goodwin had gone and that it was already a two-horse race between Illtyd Harrington and Andrew McIntosh. I feared that I had missed a vital three days' arm-twisting and that by now people would have been pestered into fairly firm voting commitments that it would be difficult to break.

I arrived at County Hall early the next morning, just ten days before the Group AGM and got busy on the phone. It was immediately obvious that no one was doing any lobbying worth speaking of. Most people assumed Illtyd Harrington would win but did not intend to vote for him themselves. While a clear majority was determined to vote against Illtyd, people were unenthusiastic about Andrew McIntosh and only four intended to vote for me. Ashley Bramall, Leader of the ILEA, would almost certainly have won the position if he had been prepared to seek it. However the ILEA was under threat of abolition at that time and he felt that to give up the leadership would be a demoralizing sign to staff that he viewed the break-up of the authority as inevitable and was protecting his own political career. Although Bramall came under considerable pressure from the right, who preferred him to Andrew McIntosh, his sense of duty to the education service inevitably led him to stand aside from the contest.

By Monday I had a fairly clear picture of how the Group would vote. One third wanted a rightwinger and although their first preference was Sir Ashley Bramall they would settle for Andrew McIntosh. Another third would vote for Illtyd Harrington. This group consisted mainly of members representing East End docklands constituencies plus Illtyd's considerable and determined band of personal friends. The remaining third now comprised five for me and another four who did not want any of the three candidates on offer. These four were determined not to vote for Illtyd and would reluctantly back whichever of Andrew or myself survived into the second ballot against him. One interesting feature of the split in the group was the desire for clear and decisive leadership after the Goodwin years and as Illtyd was closely identified with Goodwin's administration he was damaged by association. Given that almost all the members making this criticism had supported the Goodwin administration against its leftwing critics, it seemed unfair that it should be Illtyd Harrington who was carrying the can when no action was ever taken to remove Goodwin while he was Leader. As Illtyd himself put it: 'I am a leftwinger and everyone knows where I stand. As deputy leader for seven years I have been a bit of a political prisoner.' Whether it was fair or not, the plain fact was that Illtyd could not win. Both the ideological wings of the

Group would have rather seen a candidate from the opposite wing win the leadership if it meant that we would avoid a repeat of the drift and confusion that had characterized the Goodwin administration. After years of frustration, left and right combined to smash the centre.

In order to emerge on the top of this very small pile I had first to win over the four who were opposed to Illtyd but undecided between Andrew and me. Then I had to convince as many of Illtyd's supporters as I could that as he was unelectable they should switch their vote to me to keep Andrew out. I also needed to spend some time in Lewisham West, where a Tory GLC member had resigned; the Labour candidate, Lewis Herbert, was almost certain to win and was likely to vote for me.

When I first saw Andrew at County Hall after Sir Reg's resignation I briefed him on the position. As he had no one working for him he was not fully aware of the interplay of politics and personalities in the leadership struggle. We kept in touch from then on and had great fun comparing our voting lists so that we could see which members had promised their vote to both of us. Lobbying in such a small group is difficult. In a larger one you could get others to do it on your behalf, but in a Group of just twenty-eight, most of whom have been working together for years if not decades, you need to do it yourself without ever directly asking for support. Conversation was limited to discussion about why the Goodwin administration had failed and the strengths and weaknesses of yourself and your rivals.

With five days to go I was certain that on the first ballot all three candidates would be within three votes of each other. At this stage I went to see Harvey Hinds, who was Illtyd Harrington's main backer and a crucial influence on the other dozen members in Illtyd's camp. As chief whip he had been responsible for interviewing me on the occasions that I had voted against the party line during the Goodwin administration, and although I had been a continuous problem to him we had a reasonable working relationship. Harvey had always been as tolerant of dissent as it was possible to be, given that he had to cope with a large and often outraged right wing who demanded firm disciplinary action against the leftwing rebels. In fact I had detected a deliberation in his manner of investigating rebellions which allowed passions to subside. The only members to be expelled from the Labour Group had been Dr Haseler and Douglas Eden, who had been determined to achieve that particular state of grace and had finally done so by voting with the Tories against a Labour nominee for alderman.

Harvey and I had not shared the same committee interests at the GLC so our day-to-day contacts were not very frequent. When I broke the news to him that Illtyd would lose and the choice was between Andrew and me he was unconvinced but finally agreed to check out the list of voting intentions I had given him. As I left his room I was wishing that I had spent more time getting to know Harvey over the previous seven years. Despite my reminder on Thursday, he waited until the weekend before starting to phone around. By late on Sunday he had confirmed that my view was correct but he had not left much time for action. There were now less than twenty-four hours till the vote.

I had sent a written statement to all members of the Group the previous week, assuming that both the other candidates would do likewise. I was amazed to discover that neither of them thought it worthwhile. Bill Bush and his deputy had helped with a first draft which I then discussed with my small band of supporters. I used the statement not just to deal with policies but also to outline the way I would wish to see the Labour Group operating. Although it failed to sway the majority in 1980, the approach it advocated formed the basis of the 1981 administration's method of operation.

> Many members of the Group are unhappy about the decision that faces them on Monday and in an attempt to move the debate away from personalities I am setting out my views as to what I believe is required in terms of policy and style from those of us who are contesting the position of Leader. Undoubtedly in the run-up to the election the major role of the Leader is to explain our policies in a cool logical way. We must relate those policies to the day-to-day experience of Londoners, avoiding jargon, gimmicks and trivia. We need a complete contrast with the style of Cutler and must avoid being drawn into the slanging match which the Council has now become.

I believe that in office we can build a reputation of competence and service which could bring credibility to both Labour and the GLC, as was the case under Morrison.

In the crucial role of defending the interests of Londoners from the Tory Government we must avoid creating the impression that we seek confrontation for its own sake.

The Leader of the Group must be seen to represent not just one section or wing of that group. The influx of new members after the next election is likely to produce a group with a wide range of views. The only way in which that group can be held together is for the leadership to be open and avoid being drawn into a caucus or inner circle. We must have a strong Policy Committee subject to the group but I reject the idea that members of that Policy Committee must be bound by its decisions when they are debated within the group. No Labour Group is so full of talent that the Leader can exclude from chairmanships those who hold differing views. The full group must have before it all options as it debates each issue. Openness in the group would help avoid a repeat of the frequent splits which typified our last administration.

The Leader also has a vital role in relation to the Labour Party and the need to galvanize the party into ensuring a Labour victory. Recent elections show that we cannot take victory for granted. The GLC is unpopular and we must not be seen as defending the bureaucratic status quo. We must be committed to shifting resources within the GLC into the provision of new services. We will be judged on the basis of how effectively we can deliver those services we are responsible for, not on the endless talk about Regional Government.

The manifesto discussion document is radical, socialist and will be acceptable to members of this group. The one area of contention remains fares and I believe we can end the endless and damaging debate on fares by accepting a compromise that we cut the level of fares by 25 per cent after the election (which will return fares to their 1976 level in real terms) and then hold them for the full four-year period. If inflation averaged 10 per cent a year over our period of office this would mean that the level of subsidy to London Transport would be the same as that for public transport in most Western European cities.

If elected Leader I will do the job on a fulltime basis. I think that the GLC has a massive potential which has not been developed and it is essential that we have firm control of the officers. The Leader needs to ensure that officers do not play members off one against another. Individual members other than chairmen must be given areas of responsibility to chase our policies through the Council machinery. Because of the demands that the leadership would make I will not seek a candidacy in the forthcoming parliamentary selections. Nor would I seek to continue as a member of Camden Council.

Many of you said, when I was selected as candidate for Hampstead, that the choice would split the local party and mean a disaster at the general election. Instead I united a party which represented all shades of opinion and achieved the third smallest swing to the Tories in the GLC area. I hope you will give me the chance to unite both this group and the party outside and thus avoid a repetition of the problems of 1973–1977.

Monday was a hive of activity at County Hall with centrists rushing backwards and forwards in a last-minute effort to draft Sir Ashley Bramall and thus avoid the choice of McIntosh or Livingstone. The four doubtful members of the Group finally confirmed that with some reluctance, and on the basis of my statement, they would be supporting me. The meeting began by welcoming Lewis Herbert, who had won the by-election in West Lewisham, thus adding another vote to my camp. The vote was by secret ballot and most people were stunned when it was announced that the result of the first ballot was Livingstone ten with McIntosh and Harrington at nine each. In the run-off my supporters split seven to three in favour of McIntoch, thus eliminating Harrington.

The deal between the two ideological wings of the Labour Group held, with all my leftwing supporters switching to McIntosh in exactly the same way that the hard right would have switched to me if the eliminating ballot had been between Livingstone and Harrington.

The first stage of the election had achieved the desired result of forcing the Group to choose between the candidates of the left and the right but in the final ballot Andrew McIntosh pulled ahead by 14 votes to 13. One unknown member of the group had abstained on each vote and on the final ballot that person was joined by Anna Grieves, a devoted supporter of Illtyd Harrington, who could not forgive me for the role I had played in forcing him out of the running. In the final ballot I had the support of only three of Illtyd's followers including Illtyd himself and Harvey Hinds. If there could have been a twenty-four-hour gap between the two ballots Harvey and Illtyd would have been able to work on switching another three of his supporters into my camp but most of them had not been prepared for his elimination and had not had time to think and talk through all the ramifications. Faced with just under two minutes between the ballots they plumped for safety rather than the unthinkable.

Many people, including John Carvel, writing in *Citizen Ken* of these events, were astonished that Harvey Hinds, the chief whip, who had suffered my endless rebellions, and Illtyd Harrington, who had been eliminated from the contest by my vote and those of my supporters, switched to support me in the final ballot and went on to support the removal of Andrew McIntosh the following year. For people not actively engaged in politics, who have to rely on the media's presentation of events – which usually reduces political movements to individual personality clashes – the behaviour of Harvey and Illtyd is inexplicable. However, the media, whether knowingly or not, is often wildly wrong. Personality clashes and the conflict of competing ambitions are a thin mask over the developing economic and social forces to which individual politicians respond. Harvey and Illtyd may well have supported Goodwin during his 1973–77 administration, but that was largely because loyalty to an existing leader is a very strong force in a system where parties compete for power and internal splits often open the way to defeat and removal from office. Their support did not necessarily mean that they thought the direction of his leadership was right, merely that there was no agreed alternative strategy or Leader capable of commanding a majority within the Labour Group at that time. In the brief period when a leadership changes, individuals are given their best and often their only chance to break free of political restraints and to try to change the direction in which a party is developing.

It would have been impossible for anything resembling the 1981 GLC administration to gain office at County Hall in the 1950s or 1960s but as the population of London and its workforce changed so it became possible for new coalitions of interests to be represented by a completely different form and style of leadership. In the London of the 1950s, with its predominantly white, skilled, relatively prosperous population, the 1981 administration's members would have been irrelevant figures at the fringes of the Labour Party – if we had even been allowed to join. In the late 1970s London had become a cosmopolitan city with a million black citizens, a place with over 160 mother-tongue languages. Many skilled manual jobs had been dispersed to new towns, taking the workforce with them; in their place came the unskilled, the poor and the unemployed. Lesbians and gay men had found in London a home of relative safety compared with less tolerant cities in other parts of Britain. But most important of all, London was the city where women had become a major economic factor. All these new social forces were having their impact within the London Labour Party at the same time that the party nationally was rejecting the Callaghan–Healey leadership in a substantial shift to the left. Harvey and Illtyd knew that the next Labour GLC would have to respond to the changes taking place in the world outside County Hall and realized that the process of adjustment might be less painful under my leadership. I am well aware that many people will find it easier to assume, as Andrew McIntosh was eventually to allege, that we simply did a deal in which I gained the support of Harvey and Illtyd in exchange for a commitment that I would support them in their respective positions. The reality was that I was in no position to give or deliver such a pledge.

As my constantly shifting political relationship with Ted Knight and various leftwing factions reveals, it is the pressures of political and economic forces which determine the alliances that are made between politicians, not whether or not they like each other. I have often thought that Mario Puzo's *The Godfather* is a much more honest account of how politicians operate than any of the self-justifying rubbish spewed out in political biographies and repeated in academic textbooks. One sentence in that book typifies the way most politicians deal with each other. Tessio, the longest-serving of the Corleone mob, has switched his allegiance and betrayed the family by setting up Michael Corleone for assassination. His treachery is uncovered, he is led away to his death, and as he goes he sends Michael Corleone a final message. 'Tell Mike it was only business,' he says; 'I always liked him.' Fortunately for politicians, if not the general public, politics are conducted by ballots rather than bullets in most of the United Kingdom.

As the Group started to disperse, Andrew invited everyone to an impromptu party in the Leader's room. Although I gained some small comfort from watching Harvey Hinds berate Anna Grieves for her abstention, I felt despondent to have come so close and lost. I kept running over and over again in my mind the various things that could have been done to win the extra votes. Worse still was the fact that both Harvey and I agreed that Andrew should have no trouble hanging on to the leadership for a decade or more as it was inconceivable that he would not be able to assemble a majority around himself in the next Group.

Just before I left the party to phone the details of the voting through to my colleagues in *Briefing*, Harvey took me to one side. He suggested that we should stay in touch in the future so as to keep tabs on the new Leader and try to control him as much as possible. Although I had no doubt that an influx of new members would make a repeat of the U-turns of the 1973–77 administration less likely, it was not enough to lift my depression. In contrast, however, *Briefing* activists were jubilant that we had come so close to winning. Knowing how short-lived the radical phase of a new Labour Group could be, I did not share their joy. I was particularly amazed when Keith Veness told me that it was the best possible outcome. 'If you had won this time, the press would have really gone for you right the way up to the next election. We will avoid all that and still get rid of McIntosh after the next election.' I thought he was wrong but the passage of time would show his prediction to be more accurate than I could have imagined – on both counts.

In the first flush of victory, Andrew seemed to believe that he was comfortably in place. He immediately moved to nominate me as his replacement as spokesperson on Planning and Transportation, which would clearly be a key high-profile position in the run-up to the election, and also indicated his acceptance of my compromise proposals on fares policy. He agreed to change Group Standing Orders so that in future all committee posts would be directly elected at the AGM, thus bringing to an end the infamous Leader's Advisory Committee with its lobbying and backstabbing. When he took his place on the Regional Executive he put on a leftish face. If he could not support the left he usually abstained, although given the overwhelming support for the manifesto proposals there were few disputes on the Executive in the summer of 1980. But for all his efforts, no one on the left was convinced that he had changed one jot from the rightwing, pro-motorway loyalist who had supported the Goodwin administration. The press certainly had no illusions and welcomed his election as the lesser of the three evils but their endorsement of Andrew served only to increase the suspicions of the left. Andrew's problems were further complicated by his own personality. In many ways he seemed rather better suited for the academic or business worlds where it is possible to restrict your circle of colleagues to those who more closely share your educational and social status. To a lesser degree, Andrew shared Sir Reg Goodwin's desire to keep at arm's length the cruder elements on the political scene and his shyness was often mistaken for aloofness by many of his colleagues. Because he had to put considerable work into his market research company he had a poor attendance record at the GLC. He was not well known to many members of the Labour Group nor to the Regional Executive, who did not like his habit of using flip charts at their meetings as though he was giving a market research presentation to a prospective client. For some reason this particularly offended the trade union delegates.

The draft manifesto was now available to the party and the public and along with other members of the Executive I was involved in many meetings at all levels of the party to explain the details of what we were proposing. It was at one of these meetings that I met Valerie Wise for the first time. As Political Education officer for the Westminster CLP she had invited me to speak to her local party and as we chatted in the pub afterwards I suggested that she stand for the GLC herself, which after some thought she agreed to do. Unlike in previous years, the left were now very interested in standing for GLC selection. I sent every leftwinger on the panel of candidates a list of the seats in order of winnability, indicating those in which the sitting member intended to resign, along with the address of the CLP Secretary and a map to show where each seat was. The monthly *Briefing* meetings devoted a lot of time to reporting on how the selections were doing and which type of candidate would be the strongest to run in each seat. I had to overcome the reluctance of many leftwingers who worried that simply writing to a CLP and asking to be considered seemed too much like personal ambition and careerism. Most eventually accepted that the right wing had no such qualms and that if the left was to win they would have to overcome their scruples and get their hands slightly dirty.

It was during June and July that several events sealed the fate of Andrew McIntosh and set the pattern of the 1981 administration. First of all, London Transport sank into its worst ever crisis. The Tory administration had forced the London Transport Executive to adopt a budget at the beginning of the year which, with a growing deficit of £34 million, meant that London Transport would be technically bankrupt before the end of the summer. Sir Horace initially denied that there was any crisis and then sacked Ralph Bennett, the chair of London Transport, whose only mistake had been to carry out Sir Horace's orders. As the crisis developed through the summer, with LT proposing to close three tube lines, terminate entire bus routes and increase fares by up to 43 per cent, Labour's manifesto proposals were pushed into the spotlight, and I, as the Group's spokesperson on the subject, received more media coverage than I had had in the previous nine years in local government. Eventually the Tories had to switch another £30 million from the rate fund to LT and agree a September fares increase as well as quietly removing two of Sir Horace Cutler's own personal appointments from the board of LT.

The second factor working against Andrew was his failure to win over Harvey Hinds and Illtyd Harrington. As his deputy leader and chief whip they expected to be involved in both his thinking and his meetings with key officers. Instead of establishing a strong Policy Committee and taking all the key personalities in the Group through the various problems as they arose, the Leader tended to deal with each issue on a one-to-one basis with the appropriate opposition spokesperson. Most members of the Group only discovered what was happening at the Group meeting before the full Council meeting. Andrew aroused all our suspicions by having a series of private meetings with key officers such as Maurice Stonefrost at which no other Labour member was present – even Bill Bush, the head of the Leader of the Opposition Office, was asked to leave. It began to look very much as though Andrew intended to run his administration as Sir Reg Goodwin had done. Because of my influence on the Regional Executive Andrew most probably spent more time discussing things with me than any other member of the Group but, nonetheless, even I felt he kept most of his thoughts from me. In contrast I spent a lot of time talking to Harvey and Illtyd about the problems that would face the next administration and how we should tackle them. I knew that I would have their support when I stood against Andrew for the leadership immediately after the election. At that stage the left did not expect to win, but our opposition would demonstrate our strength and help to keep pressure on the Leader, constraining his scope for independent action. I had made it quite clear to Andrew before the first leadership contest that any decision of the outgoing Group could not be binding on the dramatically transformed and much larger Group that would take office after the next election.

It was during the month of June that we had our first scent of victory. As the first results of the constituency selections started to come in it became obvious that the left was doing even better than we had dared hope. As the weeks went by, the leftwing gains mounted. Of the six safe Labour seats up for grabs, the left took five. In addition Ewan Carr, who had died shortly before the reselection process, was succeeded by a leftwinger. Of the 22 sitting members who sought reselection, only three were deselected; two for health reasons, the third for political ones. Ellis Hillman finally received his just deserts from Hackney Central for a track record of loyal support to every cuts package throughout the Goodwin administration. In the 30 seats which Labour had lost to the Tories in 1977 the change was staggering. Although several rightwingers tried for selection, the only one to succeed was Tony Judge, who was very much the acceptable face of the Labour right and totally loyal to the party. In the remaining seats, 17 leftwing candidates took seats which had been held by the right in 1973. Whether Labour won the 1981 election by a narrow or a large majority, the left would be only two or three votes short of an absolute majority in the next Group – almost a complete reversal of the position in 1973. Providing I could keep the working relationship with Harvey and Illtyd, nothing could now prevent the election of a radical socialist GLC in 1981 – except the electorate.

Five months earlier my Hackney North general management committee had agreed that I should move to another seat in order to prevent a rightwinger being selected there. While this was part of the left's overall strategy to win a majority in the next Group, it also suited me at this turning point in my political life. I was to stand in an extremely marginal seat which would only go Labour if we won control of the Council. I had decided that ten years in local government in constant opposition to the Tories and rightwing Labour leaderships was enough. If a radical socialist majority was not to be elected in 1981, I would rather leave the Council and look for work more productive than sitting making faces at the Tories. In those vital six months from February to July, the whole picture suddenly and dramatically changed. I was now to be given the chance to prove that the left could win and could make a difference. The only person who seemed unaware of what was happening was Andrew McIntosh.

4

Coup in London

As we entered the last few months before the election, there was a general acceptance in the London Labour Party that the changes in policy and leadership were settled. People began to plan on that basis. For me this was fortunate as my life was undergoing upheavals which would have made a new round of infighting a burden. Although the break-up of my seven-year marriage was relatively amicable, it was not easy to cope with and involved my moving into a bedsit. Close friends rallied round to keep me from depression, and the vast amount of work involved in preparing for the election kept me busy. As the winter wore on I found it relaxing to go back to my bedsit after tense meetings and practise snooker on the quarter-size table I had treated myself to at Christmas.

Some candidates were concerned about the public reaction to the principle, or apparent lack of it, of replacing Andrew McIntosh within twenty-four hours of the election. It was suggested that with the new Group 'we would be able to control him' and that we should let him continue as Leader for a year before replacing him. Remembering how impossible it had been to control Charles Dryland, I opposed this. I was only too aware that the balance of forces inside the next Group would leave the left still in a minority and that it would be possible for the new Group's initial radical phase to be cut short by an unforeseen crisis, giving Andrew the chance firmly to establish his leadership. Although I was opposed to the suggestion of leaving him as Leader for a year, I shared the view that it was unsatisfactory to replace a Leader who had just led the party to an election victory. I felt it had been completely wrong of Sir Reg Goodwin to present us with this dilemma by hanging on for three years and then timing his resignation to try to force the selection of a rightwing successor.

At the same time I was worried about the general thrust of Andrew's pre-election propaganda. He had had discussions with Maurice Stonefrost about the likely cost of Labour's four-year programme and had presented these projections to meetings of the Labour Group and the Regional Executive in September 1980. They were alarming. The rate precept we would inherit was 24p and Andrew's projections showed it reaching over 70p in the third year of our administration. However, instead of scaring us into cutting back on manifesto commitments, it had the effect of toughening our resolve to fight the Government, whose use of clawback penalties had so dramatically increased the cost of carrying out our programme. The Tories and the press had also taken up the cost of Labour's programme. '£720m on the rates – the price of Labour victory?' screamed the *Evening Standard* whilst *The Economist* sneered that 'Labour has no clear sense of what kind of animal the GLC is. But it believes that, whatever it is, it exists to spend money.'

Andrew was coming dangerously close to sounding as though our main manifesto promise was simply to double the rates. However much we talked about the Government's responsibility for recent rate increases, most polls at that time were showing that people felt rates and taxes were just too high, irrespective of whose fault it was. I would have preferred a different emphasis in our campaigning but any disagreement between Andrew and myself would rapidly have become public knowledge, used by the press and the Tories to damage our election prospects. Andrew was convinced that it was better to be honest about the cost of our programme and no one could disagree with that, but I was fairly certain that, like all early financial projections, the figures would come down dramatically by the time we reached our budget decisions.

In the run-up to the election I felt very torn. I had to accept that it would be damaging to the party to change Leaders immediately after an election, but I also feared the effects of leaving Andrew in office, with the two of us wasting our energies fighting throughout the vital first year of the new administration. Therefore I decided to spell out to Andrew the hopelessness of his position and ask him to stand down as Leader. We had a good natured-discussion but, as I had expected, he refused to believe I was right about the likely voting figures and clung to the hope that Harvey and Illtyd would lead the vital centre block of votes into his camp. During election campaigns candidates have to convince their supporters that they are going to win the election irrespective of what the polls say and the first step in that process is to convince themselves that the straws they clutch will carry them to victory. Andrew was doing the same.

As I became more and more convinced that I would replace Andrew as Leader very shortly after the election, in spite of his illusions, I felt I had to begin discussing with other candidates what kind of new administration we would like to see. The eight months before the May 1981 election were a vital time in which we could prepare for the transfer of power from Tory to Labour on the GLC and from right to left within the Labour Group. Remembering the failure of the left to hold the support of the centre in Lambeth in 1971, I knew we had to keep Harvey Hinds and Illtyd Harrington informed and involved at all stages. This required making it clear to a small number of the new candidates such as Ted Knight and Lesley Hammond that there could be no purge of the centre. Any attempt to construct an administration solely of the left would have risked driving the centre into the arms of Andrew McIntosh and giving him a majority at the Group AGM.

The Regional Executive formed a series of shadow committees in which groups of candidates discussed how we would implement the manifesto after the election. This was vital if we were to make a quick start in changing policies once we had won control of the Council. But there was a much more important reason. Having watched how brief the initial radical phase of a new Labour Group could be in Lambeth in 1971–72, Camden 1978–79 and at the GLC in 1973–74, I hoped that by bringing the future councillors together to discuss the administration and control of the Council without officers present we would help to set patterns of behaviour which ensured that councillors worked together to impose their will on the bureaucracy. Unless the councillors developed that sort of approach *before* the election, the new committee chairs would be met in their offices on day one by chief officers who had already worked out how to implement the manifesto in a way that would leave the bureaucracy virtually unchanged.

The existing GLC Labour Group also agreed to my proposal that the new candidates should be free to attend the Group Meetings as observers. This gave people a chance to get to know one another and begin to assess the particular capabilities of individuals. In a Labour Group where 60 per cent of the members would be serving on the GLC for the first time, this was vital if we were to avoid the problems we faced in 1973, when it took us months to find out who was really on the left. As well as bringing the candidates together, it was important to prevent any splits developing over the allocation of committee chairs. As it turned out, the large number of new members helped, as most of them wanted to wait a year or two before standing for key posts. The decision to abolish the Leader's Advisory Committee meant that the whole Labour Group would vote for each post in turn at its first meeting, thus removing the Leader's powers of patronage at a stroke, which was a good thing in itself and also had the advantage of protecting the Leader from the endless lobbying of the ambitious.

My experience of council leaders and their styles left me in no doubt of the way in which I wanted to operate as Leader. I had watched three vague, secretive, indecisive Leaders (Dryland on Lambeth Council, Goodwin at the GLC and Shaw on Camden Council) who seemed to lack any firm ideological framework and were therefore simply driven by events. In contrast were Stimpson on Lambeth Council and Bramall, Leader of the ILEA, who were firm, decisive and open and, most important of all, confident in their political beliefs. It was interesting that the two strong leaders had run their administrations through powerful policy committees which acted as 'cabinets' in the classic sense and were answerable to the whole Group, whereas the three weak leaders avoided a strong central policy committee, preferring to operate through informal structures which were comprised of different councillors assembled at the Leader's whim.

Under the 'cabinet' system of Bramall and Stimpson the Labour Groups usually had a full range of information about each topic on which they were to make decisions, and a clear recommendation from the leadership. Whether or not we agreed with the recommendations we could seldom complain that events were being determined behind closed doors. Their policy committees functioned in a way that shared information and allowed a clear strategy to emerge so that councillors knew where they were going.

Under Goodwin, Dryland and Shaw the restriction of information, together with a lack of strategy and the frequent absence of leadership recommendations on individual policy issues, meant that their Labour Groups often sank into bitterness and chaos. In contrast to the devastation of services and the waste that characterized the Goodwin and Shaw administrations, Bramall and Stimpson had delivered the bulk of our policies, services had remained intact and cutbacks had largely been directed against waste in the bureaucracy.

The defects of the Bramall and Stimpson administrations had lain in their failure to share information and power with those outside the bureaucracy, in the form of the party and the public. Both of them had also made the mistake of excluding their most competent critics from their administrations, thus creating an alternative leadership on their backbenches which eventually replaced them. Had either of them chosen to absorb their critics into their administrations, they might well have survived for considerably longer.

It is strange that at the same time as some local councils were adopting the concept of traditional cabinet governments, Mrs Thatcher was moving decisively away from it. Many key issues were not going to full cabinet but being decided instead by ad hoc sub-committees. If a traditional cabinet had still been in operation, including the full range of ability available to Mrs Thatcher instead of letting her competent opponents rot on the backbenches, then it is unlikely that some of the more damaging incidents of her 1983 administration – the string of banana skins like Westland and the Wright affair – would have happened.

The only recent example of a leftwing administration we could use as a guide was Lambeth under Ted Knight. Following his election as Leader in May 1978 Ted had abandoned the strong central policy committee and, like Mrs Thatcher, tended to rule through a series of ad hoc meetings with different combinations of members and officers. He also instituted daily meetings with the chief officers from which he directed the general and sometimes detailed thrust of Council business. This produced a system in which a strong, competent Leader developed a very close relationship with the Council bureaucracy and also controlled the flow of information to the rest of the Labour Group, although of course individual committee chairs knew what was going on in their own departments. As a system it was deeply unpopular with many councillors. Those who were not part of Ted's inner circle of political associates complained of exclusions from the decision-making process on the grounds that everything was cut and dried by the time it reached them for general discussion. Some committee chairs felt that their chief officers tended to work towards Ted Knight's objectives rather than their own chairs' plans. I had no doubt that Ted would never have made the mistake of proposing a package of cuts in July 1979 if he had operated a policy cabinet system. With a more open and wider consultation process he would have detected much sooner the scale of party opposition to his proposals.

I wanted to ensure that while we operated a strong cabinet system, the party and the public were involved in the consultation process. There had to be a genuine delegation of powers away from the Leader to the committee chairs and their members. Since Herbert Morrison became the first Labour Leader in 1934, County Hall had operated on the same basis as central government with an unhealthy concentration of power around the majority party leader. If he chose to do so, the Leader could work with the chief officers to control and undermine those members of his administration who were being too radical or spending too much.

I therefore argued for a strong central policy committee comprising all the committee chairs. Officers would be present during the first part of the meeting so that all members of the committee could have access to information. I decided against continuing the traditional practice of having a private meeting with the officers before each committee meeting: council officers would have assumed that I wanted to decide what information should be made available to the other councillors. I also proposed that this Policy Co-ordinating Committee (PCC as it became known) should be open to all Labour Group members. It was decided that the Regional Executive of the London Labour Party should have two places on the PCC so that they could keep an eye on our progress in implementing the manifesto.

The vital question, however, was the nature of the role I would play in the inevitable struggles between the bureaucracy and the Labour committee chairs. The history of Labour Governments has shown that Prime Ministers worked with the top layer of the civil service to constrain and contain those Labour ministers who seriously tried to carry out Labour Party policy in the face of civil service opposition. The behind-the-scenes activities of Harold Wilson to undermine Tony Benn and prevent his attempt to carry out Labour's 1974 manifesto commitment to establish planning agreements in each sector of British industry is only one of the best-known examples in a long history.

I decided to reverse traditional practice by dealing directly with the committee chairs instead of with chief officers. This forced the chief officers to work exclusively to their own committee chairs. With the exception of my own personal support staff, my only contact with council officers would now be at committee meetings or when the Director General, Chief Solicitor or Comptroller of Finance asked to see me. This system meant that power was genuinely delegated from the Leader to the committee chairs and it created the conditions which allowed so many major changes to take place during the 1981 administration. If I had continued the practice of my predecessors and insisted on a vast array of policy detail crossing my desk, it would have imposed a severe restriction on decision making, and inevitable delays would have dramatically reduced the volume of policy change we could have carried through.

The deluge of publicity which was to turn me into a household name, with every GLC policy reported in the press as 'Red Ken has . . .', could not have been further from the truth. I was to be the least powerful Leader within County Hall since the post was created in 1934. Often, the first I knew about a policy initiative was when I read about it in the papers, where it was invariably reported as something which I had decided, as though no other GLC councillor existed. The delegation of power may seem like an obvious step if we were to carry out our full programme, but some senior officers were appalled: they were accustomed to dealing with political leaders who opposed delegation, fearing it would reduce their own authority and status.

As the election campaign developed there was an obvious build-up of enthusiasm and excitement amongst everyone involved and no one felt that more than I. After all the frustrations of the previous ten years I was confident that I would now have the chance to apply what I had learnt without being blocked by a more cautious Leader. I was also aware that with the swing to the left inside the Labour Party the new GLC administration would be seen as an indication of how a radical socialist government led by Tony Benn would operate. If we were to fail it would be a blow to the whole of the British left.

The prospect of a leftwing administration was beginning to interest the national press. Following Beatrix Campbell's article in *Time Out* in March 1980, the *London Evening News* (22 May) carried a long piece by John Evans which looked at the manifesto proposals and concluded that Andrew McIntosh would survive the challenge of the left. It was this piece which set the tone for much future coverage, with its description of 'Ken Livingstone, an austere and hungry-looking leftwinger . . .', a theme which was to develop to the point where I was characterized as a puritan. Perhaps it is because Fleet Street is unaware of any radical British administration since Cromwell and the Roundheads that they assume that any leftwing figure is by definition an unhappy, celibate recluse who spends his or her evenings alone plotting revolution and only emerging to impose a drab, grey regime of conformity on everybody else.

By 12 August the *Guardian* had followed with a thoughtful analysis by Lindsay Mackie which suggested that Andrew could be replaced following the election. Those papers who complained after the event, as did the *Daily Telegraph* on 31 August 1981, that, 'Using the cover of the moderate appearance of . . . Andrew McIntosh, Mr Livingstone waited for the voters to return the sheep's clothing before he, the wolf, popped out and arranged the top job for himself', had all known for at least nine months that Andrew would lose. Indeed, they made it a major feature of their pre-election coverage just as the Tories made it a key part of their election campaign. On 30 April 1981, just seven days before the election, the *Daily Telegraph* warned 'If Labour is put in control at County Hall next week, it will almost certainly be led by Mr Ken Livingstone . . . the triumph of the left in London . . . will then be crowned in glory.'

To complain after that sort of coverage that Londoners were un-aware of the likelihood of Andrew's replacement before they voted is absurd. In reality, of course, the vast majority of Londoners were unaware of Andrew McIntosh or Ken Livingstone and voted either from traditional loyalty or because of a specific manifesto commit-ment that appealed to them. The minority who knew who we were must also have known the likely outcome of a Labour victory.

A further wave of press interest surrounded the Special London Labour Party Meeting that was held at Camden Town Hall on 17 and 18 October to agree any final changes to the manifesto. During the summer trade unions and CLPs had been discussing the manifesto and submitting amendments, almost all of which the Regional Executive had been happy to accept. The full meeting saw little real controversy except on the issues of property speculation – because some, such as the electricians' union, believed it created jobs – and London Transport fares. All the trade unions in the transport field had come out against the abolition of fares and it was overwhelmingly agreed by the Executive to recommend a 25 per cent fares cut followed by a four-year freeze whilst the GLC undertook a major study on how fares could be abolished. The study could be used if fares abolition became party policy after the 1985 GLC election. Any opposition to this compromise was expected to come from those leftwingers who were totally commit-ted to free transport. It therefore came as a complete surprise when TSSA (ticket collectors) and APEX (clerical workers) submitted an amendment to delete the proposal to cut fares by 25 per cent. As the conference got under way we were again shocked to discover that the TGWU intended to vote with APEX and TSSA. This meant that they already had two-thirds of the votes necessary to win. The fares reduction was the most dramatic of the manifesto plans; there was no other contender for the central plank in our manifesto with anything like the same appeal.

I explained the situation at the Saturday lunchtime *Briefing* fringe meeting and everyone went away to lobby against the APEX/TSSA amendment. During the afternoon tension built up around the feverish activity of the pro-fares cut delegates, who fortunately had the whole afternoon for lobbying as the vote on the APEX/TSSA amendment was due to be taken at the very end of the meeting. By the time I rose to speak on behalf of the Regional Executive the tension in the hall was electrifying. Our proposal to cut fares had almost become the yardstick by which we tested people's commitment to carry out the manifesto and avoid repeating the failures of the Goodwin administration. To those unions opposed the proposal seemed like a hostage to fortune, a pledge which might lose as many votes as it gained. They preferred simply to freeze fares and let inflation erode their value, thus taking two or three years longer to arrive at the same end result.

In my reply I argued that to end the decline in London Transport we needed to capture the imagination of Londoners in a way which would convince them that we intended to break with the past. Only something as dramatic as a fares cut would rouse the public consciousness and start the process of getting people out of their cars and back on to public transport. I also spelt out the financial facts: commercial ratepayers would be paying 62 per cent of the cost of the scheme and the large national and international companies which had their headquarters in central London would pay a third of the cost. Given that the primary function of the transport system was to bring their employees to work I believed that they should be making a larger contribution to the costs of the public transport system. When the vote came the APEX/TSSA amendment was defeated by 416,500 to 173,500.

Had we lost that vote the whole course of events at the GLC would have been transformed. No fares cut, no Lord Denning and the Law Lords, no popular campaign against the resulting fares increase – it is impossible to imagine how the 1981 administration would have developed. Perhaps, though it is unlikely, the GLC might not have been abolished. So those trade unions that backed the amendment could claim that had their more cautious view prevailed, Londoners could very well have been better served in the long run with slightly higher fares but continued democratic control of GLC and London Transport services.

As we are not blessed with foresight, such thoughts were not in our minds as we streamed away from Camden Town Hall to celebrate. I was certain that my decision 18 months previously to seek the position of chairing the Transport Working Party had been the right one. We had achieved a compromise on fares to which the party was totally committed and there could be no doubt that the policy would survive the full four years of the administration. As an added bonus it had also placed me in a very strong position to challenge for the leadership. The only other possible contender from the left was Ted Knight and he had already taken decisions which would prevent his ever getting elected to the GLC.

The crisis which was to sink Ted started in July 1980 when Michael Heseltine demanded immediate cuts in councils' budgets and set a target of a £5.6 million cut for Lambeth. When the council refused to make the cuts Heseltine threatened to withhold several million pounds of Government grant. Lambeth thus faced the choice of levying a mid-year supplementary rate increase or borrowing money to cover the gap and setting a higher rate the following year to repay the debt. With its tight budget and the grant cut, Lambeth was £11.6 million in debt. After prompting from the Government, the District Auditor warned the Council that it was illegal to borrow such a sum and threatened to surcharge them if they did. Lambeth therefore decided to levy the supplementary rate and blame it on Heseltine rather than make what would have been massive and devastating cuts.

The supplementary rate increase was equivalent to a 70 per cent increase in the average weekly rate bill and arrived on householders' doormats immediately after Christmas. The response was explosive and local Tories organized an effective campaign. In the Tory parts of the borough one house in ten displayed posters simply stating 'NO' and at many mass meetings the explanation that it was all the

Government's fault could scarcely be heard above the calls for the introduction of hanging for Lambeth councillors.

In spring 1981, when the Labour Group met to set its budget, Ted Knight suggested a way of achieving a 10 per cent (£11 million) cut to our budget. The right wing of the party were delighted with the proposals. 'But if only we'd done this earlier it would be less painful now,' they chorused. For the left, however, it marked a low point. Paul Moore, who was a Lambeth councillor as well as a candidate for the GLC, complained in the April issue of *Briefing*:

> Will Labour supporters remember Lambeth Council un-
> der Ted Knight as the one which raised rates by 37 per
> cent rather than 47 per cent? Or will they see it as
> one which – like so many others – allowed services to
> deteriorate while rates were still high?

For me this was a valuable lesson on the need for a clear financial strategy, and I prayed for a GLC majority big enough not to leave me dependent, as Ted had been, on the votes of rightwing Labour members in order to get budget decisions through Council. I was certain that the incoming Labour GLC should increase the rates by whatever amount was necessary to fund our manifesto and do it quickly in our first budget so that by the time we faced re-election the voters would have had the benefit of four years of improved services and rate increases only in line with inflation after the initial large increase. I was determined not to be caught with a series of increases big enough to hurt but not big enough to fulfil our manifesto promises.

Selections for the GLC were complete. I invited all candidates to an open broad left forum on 21 November. This was followed by two more in January. At these meetings we discussed the implementation of the manifesto and the way in which the Government might try to obstruct us. A majority of candidates in winnable seats attended, including Andrew McIntosh, who thought the idea so worthwhile that he proposed that the GLC Labour Group should reimburse me for the cost of postage in convening the meetings.

For the meeting on 11 January I circulated a 2,500-word report which was effectively my personal manifesto for the coming leadership contest. Once again I was surprised that Andrew did not take a similar initiative. My report (which is printed in full as an Appendix at the end of this book because, unlike the rest of the book, it details my thinking at that time without the benefit of hindsight) spelt out a strategy of winning public support by establishing all our major policies within the first three months and concentrating our resources on expanding services rather than the GLC bureaucracy. I recognized that this might lead the Government to withdraw all remaining grants to the GLC but as the impact of such action was much less than it would be for a borough council I proposed that we should be prepared to lose the grant and thus break free of the Government's penalties. I warned that in this event it was possible that the Tories would consider abolishing the GLC but that we could counter that.

The report was well received and seemed to reflect the thinking of the overwhelming majority of new candidates. The response at the meetings left little doubt about the outcome of the leadership vote. Not only did Andrew lack the support of many candidates but the Regional Labour Party officials who previously had given Sir Reg Goodwin their loyalty were being neutral. They had reconciled themselves to the forthcoming change and seemed quite happy at the prospect. The entire GLC Labour Group support staff were fervently praying for a change in the leadership. In fact, everything seemed to be going perfectly for me and the left except the election.

At the 1979 General Election, London had been the worst area of the country for Labour. In the following two years a steady flow of local council by-elections in London had revealed that Thatcher's Government was retaining its support in London more than in other parts of the country. Labour was not increasing its share of the vote and it gained mainly borough council seats where a shift of votes from the Tories to the Liberals let Labour in by default. During the run-up to the GLC election the detailed London figures from Gallup showed that Labour could win by the same sort of margin as in 1973 but that there was massive underlying support for the Social Democratic Party (SDP). At that stage, the new SDP was going through its protracted birth. The 'gang of four' had formed the Council for Social Democracy in the aftermath of Labour's Wembley Conference and were planning to form their new party at the start of the GLC election campaign. Andrew and I both feared that the level of support shown for the SDP in these opinion polls was such that if the party had fought as its first major test of electoral strength with someone like Shirley Williams as their Leader, they might well have won or at the least would have held the balance of power on the GLC. Lord George Brown joined with Dr Stephen Haseler, Douglas Eden and Jim Daly in a group called the Social Democratic Alliance which had operated as a rightwing faction within the Labour Party. On 6 March, Lord Brown announced that 'the nation's capital is threatened by a Trotskyist takeover and bankruptcy'. He said that the SDA would put up candidates against the main leftwingers. Jim Daly had already stated that he intended to stand against me in Paddington. He claimed there was widespread dissatisfaction with me inside Paddington CLP (although only eight out of 1,000 members defected to the SDP) and 'a great deal of fear'. I could not resist pointing out to Daly that it was only four years since he had voted to expel Haseler and Eden from the GLC Labour Group. I also reminded him of comments he had made on his return from a visit to the USSR. He had been full of praise for the fact that the Russians did not tolerate the sort of dissent he had had to put up with whenever he proposed a fare increase.

The Liberals, who had already selected all their candidates, did not regard this new intervention as helpful and this may have been why the SDP leadership instructed Jim Daly, who was a member of the Steering Committee, to withdraw from the contest. Eventually the SDA contested eight seats, with Jim Spillius (a good friend of the Tongan Royal family) taking Jim Daly's place in Paddington and Dr Haseler standing against Ted Knight in Norwood. Although the newly formed SDP did not endorse the eight candidates, all of them made extensive use of SDP material throughout their campaigns. The Paddington Labour Party realized it had a real fight on its hands and rose to the challenge with a campaign in which they did not put a foot wrong. All the detailed, painstaking, unglamorous work of canvassing each voter, delivering the leaflets and election addresses irrespective of the weather was carried out without a hitch. It was my good fortune that of the five areas where I had been a candidate, this was the most active and supportive. I was also blessed with an SDA opponent who rapidly discovered he had made a mistake in standing.

At the first public debate between the four main candidates I spoke first and outlined Labour's manifesto. I was followed by Jim Spillius who simply said, 'How can you follow that? I agree with every word Ken has said,' and promptly sat down. I tried not to gloat too visibly. The Liberal candidate decided that he too agreed with the points I had made and then droned on about how important it was to vote. After such a start the sitting Tory member, Patricia Kirwan, could hardly disagree with my policies and concentrated on her record in the constituency. As the meeting wore on, Jim Spillius whispered in my ear, 'I don't know what I'm doing here. This is all a terrible mistake.' I was still chuckling when I got back to the Labour HQ, where my account of the meeting was greeted by gales of laughter. It was certainly an easier ride than Jim Daly would have given me.

From that point on I was confident I would win and the attempts of the media nationally to run the usual red scare campaign had little impact in Paddington. First off the mark was, of course, the Tory Group under Sir Horace Cutler, who had announced on 29 December 1980 that the forthcoming Tory manifesto would 'stress the ugly face of Marxism'. When it finally appeared the manifesto mentioned Marxism seventeen times in sixteen pages. The *Daily Telegraph* took up the cry with a leading article on 9 February under the heading 'Will London be Marxified?'

> COULD THE DICTATORSHIP of the proletariat, so devoutly wished by KARL MARX, be imposed without a prior Communist revolution? An inkling of that possibility seems to inspire the Left wing of the Labour Opposition on the GLC. The Left is now poised to take over leadership of the Labour Group . . .
>
> The Livingstone method is to create self-perpetuating dependency. Borough staff, manual and non-manual, are increased in numbers and pay. Crippling rates, bad

services, compulsory purchase, redevelopment and council flats are used to drive out productive citizens and
businesses, and replace them by more dependants, whose
low incomes and high degree of social problems increase
the council's entitlement to Exchequer aid. If he were to
gain control, how far off would our capital's point of no
return be from a 'Livingstone death'?

Given the poor record of the Tory GLC it was inevitable
that they would concentrate in the campaign on attacking their
opponents. They also campaigned against 'violent crime . . . mug-
gers . . . drunks at discos . . . lurid displays of pornography' and
in favour of 'legislation to restore standards of decency', none of
which, of course, was under the control of the GLC. As the
campaign speeches of the Tories took off it began to seem as if
they believed Labour's manifesto was proposing *more* mugging,
drunks and pornography.

It was Lord Matthews, through Trafalgar House, which controlled the *Evening Standard*, who was to put the attacks on to a
more organized basis when he instructed that the *Standard* should
do everything possible to ensure the return of a Tory GLC. The
usual County Hall reporter, Mike King, was pushed to one side
and a bright young thing called Keith Dovkants was brought in to
do a hatchet job on what had happened to the Labour Party. Given
that everything had been conducted in the open it was not difficult
to fill the newspaper with several thousand words of warnings to
the voters in the weeks leading up to the election. On the eve of
the election itself the front page of the *Standard* was given over to
an explicit instruction to Londoners not to vote for the Labour Party.
Under the heading 'Why We Must Stop These Red Wreckers', the
Daily Express reported Sir Horace Cutler's warning that Labour
intended to 'establish a Marxist power-base . . . from which a
concerted effort can be made to unseat the Government of the day
– even Labour . . . if it puts nation before party.'

Press coverage was so over the top that when I was being
interviewed by the smaller leftwing journals I often had to emphasize
that the manifesto was no more than a package of radical reforms
and that the left would not have a majority in the next Group but

would need to work with the centre in order to govern. Several of the people conducting these interviews seemed quite disappointed that the 'Red Terror' stories were not true.

Because of the media obsession with personalities I was asked at every interview whether I would be standing against Andrew after the election. I always responded that the question was irrelevant – every candidate was committed to carrying out the manifesto – and that the media should concentrate on the policies and not the personalities.

Fortunately it was the Regional Executive and not the outgoing Labour Group which decided when the new Group should meet for the first time. Andrew was keen to have the meeting at nine o'clock on the morning (Friday) following the election. He knew that the left could not hold a caucus meeting before the election as we could not be certain who would be elected, and if word that we were convening a caucus leaked out it could be used by the press to damage Labour's election chances. The left-dominated Executive agreed to call the first meeting at 5pm on Friday. The rather weak justification for this was that we might face protracted recounts which could take most of Friday. The real reason was that it would allow me to convene a left caucus for 3pm. In the two days before polling I phoned everyone who had indicated that they might vote for me or was still undecided and invited them to the meeting. Nothing could be put in writing for fear of its being leaked to the papers. I found as I worked my way through the forty calls that I did not need to spend more than a minute in conversation with each candidate. No one was surprised or required persuading; we all knew what was at stake. If anyone was agitated, it was because I had left convening the caucus to the very last minute. Some people had been worried lest I had decided not to invite them.

Polling day itself went like a dream in Paddington. A well-oiled machine and a loyal Labour vote made it clear we were heading for an easy win. Paddington was the second result to declare and as I went up to the stage a radio journalist reported that Labour had gained Hornchurch. That result, coupled with the 13 per cent swing to Labour in Paddington, indicated a possible Labour majority on the GLC of at least 16. But as the results came through they confirmed the evidence of the 1979 General Election and subsequent London council by-elections. The Tory vote held up very well and the final vote showed Labour only 2 per cent ahead of the Tories at 42 to 40 per cent.

In many of the Tory marginals we won by only a few hundred votes and we failed to take three key marginals (Hampstead, Brentford and Croydon North West). Nothing prepared us for the shock of Lambeth. In Norwood, which had been won by the Tories in 1977, the Social Democratic Alliance candidate effectively defeated Ted Knight by taking 3,709 votes from Labour and letting the Tories hang on. The Tory vote was slightly up; they actually increased their majority over the 1977 result, which had been one of their best years ever. It was just as if the impossible had happened and the Tories had lost a seat like Kensington at the 1983 General Election.

The SDA did well in Vauxhall and in Lambeth Central, but the rock-solid Labour majorities in those constituencies were only dented. The Labour majority in Islington was big enough to take the SDA gains. The SDA failed badly in Paddington, Putney and at Walthamstow, where they had hoped for a white backlash against Paul Boateng, our only black candidate. But overall it was a grim warning to Labour. Without any official backing, in competition with the Liberals and with no real party machine, the SDA had won nearly 20,000 votes (almost twice the total of the Liberals) in the eight constituencies they fought. Suddenly the jokes about middle-class claret drinkers seemed a little hollow. There is little doubt that if they had had the courage to organize a proper SDP/Liberal campaign led by one of the gang of four, there could have been an Alliance majority on the GLC.

The early hours of the morning saw the final result: Labour 50 seats, the Tories 41 and the Liberals 1. I calculated that the balance of forces inside the new Labour Group was 22 left, 18 right and 10 centre. The value of working with Illtyd Harrington and Harvey Hinds now became clear to even the most strident left critics of my strategy. Our problem, however, was that we needed a left–centre alliance. The Labour right had enough seats to allow any of our policies to be defeated by the Tory opposition simply by abstaining in full Council meetings. Furthermore, I feared that the stunning SDP advance against the left in Lambeth might very well have shaken the confidence of some of the key centrist votes who might as a consequence change their minds and keep Andrew as Leader. I decided against going down to Labour's election party at County Hall as it would undoubtedly have been crawling with press reporters looking for a 'Labour Split' story. I later discovered that Michael Foot, who by then was the Leader of the Labour Party, had endorsed Andrew McIntosh as his choice for GLC Leader and had left a letter to that effect for GLLP General Secretary, George Page, to read out to the Labour Group before the leadership ballot the following day.

That night was the first time in nine months that I had real doubts about the outcome of the leadership vote; after so many years of planning I faced the possibility of defeat. But I need not have worried. At County Hall the next morning I soon became aware that the narrowness of our majority was being blamed on Andrew's emphasis on the cost of the Labour manifesto and his poor performance in the BBC television debate with Sir Horace Cutler. No one seemed to have analysed the results of the SDP candidates as anything other than a reaction against Lambeth's supplementary rate. Andrew's victory press conference broke up and he went off to start a series of radio interviews. Illtyd and Harvey waited until we were alone in the Leader's room. Harvey shut the door. Illtyd said to me, 'You've got it all sewn up. For God's sake don't do anything to blow it today.' They both volunteered to keep an eye on Andrew to make sure he did nothing of which we did not approve, whilst I finalized preparations for the afternoon caucus.

The invited candidates assembled at two o'clock in room 166. I gave an opening introduction. I proposed that we should discuss each post to be filled in the administration; if there was more than one nomination each nominee should give a short speech and answer questions, after which we would vote on whom to support. People continued to arrive as I was speaking and there was a visible boost in confidence around the table when I was able to announce that a clear majority of the Group was present. By the end of the meeting two-thirds of the Group had arrived, including a couple of people who came along to tell me why they could not support the removal of Andrew. Illtyd nominated me for Leader, and this was agreed without dissent. Harvey and Illtyd were nominated unopposed to continue as chief whip and deputy leader. Ted Knight had made it clear before the election that he wished to be Finance chair. I had advised against this for two reasons. I did not think that coming straight from Lambeth supplementary rate row into a similar issue at the GLC would do much to increase his popularity. Nor was I happy about his constantly shifting positions on the rates problem. However, I had been unable to dissuade him. As no one else had considered standing against Ted this left a gap which was filled by Tony Hart. Tony Banks had been expected to stand for Transport chair but had finally decided to go for Arts and Recreation, which opened the way for Dave Wetzel. Gladys Dimson was unopposed for Housing and Michael Ward likewise for Industry and Employment. The major tussles were over the position of Leader of the ILEA and chair of the Public Services and Fire Brigade Committee but there were many other contested posts among the junior Group officers and vice-chairs of committees. The meeting was exhausting and at the same time exhilarating to chair, and it ended with only fifteen minutes to spare before the Group AGM.

The emptiness of the County Hall corridors whilst the left caucus was in session must finally have caused Andrew grave concern. As the Group assembled at 5pm there was real worry on the faces of many of the right wing who could not be expected to adjust easily to being in a minority after forty-seven years of rightwing domination. As chair of the London Labour Party, Arthur Latham called the meeting to order. George Page, successor to John Keys, quite pointedly failed to read out Michael Foot's letter of endorsement and Lesley Hammond proposed that instead of a secret ballot, voting should be by a show of hands.

As I expected, we failed to get the necessary two-thirds majority and so we moved straight to a secret ballot for Leader. The votes were counted. I was very tense and felt as if I was watching myself from outside my own body. Other people's voices seemed very distant. Arthur Latham announced the results. Livingstone 30, McIntosh 20. The mood in the room was still too fraught for any jubilation so I simply made a short speech about the need to work together. Harvey and Illtyd were elected unopposed and then the right wing proposed to adjourn the meeting until Monday so that they could consider whom to nominate for chairs and vice-chairs. Since half the people in the room were eager to see if they were about to be elected and deeply suspicious about the motive behind an adjournment, this was rejected. We started to go through the positions one by one and each was elected unopposed.

Only then did it dawn on me that because Andrew had expected to be elected Leader, assuming that the Group would then adjourn to give him time to plan an administration, no one on the right had been briefed to nominate anyone for any position. Within the space of a few minutes all 25 positions were elected unopposed, which meant that not a single person who had voted for Andrew held a position in the new administration. That was a recipe for disaster. We managed to rectify it by appointing some rightwingers to posts in the ILEA, and leftwingers soon realized they had overstretched themselves. GLC posts became vacant again and this time were filled by members who had opposed me. However, it was not until the following year, when the Group had settled down, that it was possible to achieve a proper balance representing the various factions within the Group.

The meeting adjourned until the following Monday. I was rushed away by Bill Bush to begin a three-hour series of interviews, and walked through the door into a rugby scrum of shouting, microphone-waving reporters. It was my first experience of the media in pursuit of a story and in the following six months it was to become a regular part of my life. The antics of the press were incredible but nonetheless I felt a strange combination of elation and calmness. This came from knowing that I was not going to have to cope with the frustration of seeing my plans blocked or moderated by a rightwing Leader.

From that moment on everything seemed to move at a speed which was out of keeping with the leisurely traditions of County Hall. Press, radio and television interviews consumed the evening. The next day saw the AGM of the ILEA Labour Group and the left caucus that preceded it.

As soon as Bryn Davis was elected Leader of the ILEA we

discussed the allocation of committee chairs and vice-chairs so that those rightwingers who wished to remain in the Labour Party and have a role in carrying out the manifesto could be kept busy with useful work rather than being driven into the arms of the Social Democratic Party. Seven members of the Group were considered potential defectors to the SDP by the whips office, and throughout the first six months of the new administration occasional statements from Jim Daly that he was in negotiation with these un-named members fuelled press speculation. A combination of finding work for idle rightwing hands and running the Labour Group in an open and participatory fashion helped to avoid many of the internal party rows which could have triggered enough defections to lose our majority in the Council. One encouraging sign for me was that in the week following my election nearly half the councillors who had voted for Andrew approached me to pledge their loyalty. It showed very clearly how quickly politicians realign around a new leadership and just how much power that gives an incumbent.

The Policy Committee (comprised of the chairs and Group officers) met on Monday. They agreed with me that we should take decisions in a more democratic and open style than under previous administrations, and my recommendations were adopted by the Group meeting that Monday night. The Policy Committee planned to meet each Wednesday morning; the following Monday its decisions would be reported in writing to the whole Group. Collective responsibility would not operate; those councillors who had opposed a decision in the Policy Committee would be free to oppose it again in the Group meeting. The concept of collective responsibility is one of the most important ways by which the left have been neutralized during Labour Governments. It dramatically reduces internal party democracy whilst increasing the powers of the Leader and the bureaucracy. I believed that the wider and more open the decision-making processes were, the more likely we were to come to correct decisions.

We all knew that the new system of decision making might break down if instead of submitting a controversial decision to the Policy Committee, the committee chairs tried to bounce it without warning through the Labour Group or their own committee. The Group therefore gave the Leader and the other Group officers the power to instruct that any report we considered controversial should go direct to the Policy Committee. Items which had not been considered by the Policy Committee could not be included on the Group agenda without the permission of the chief whip or the Leader.

Since Council officers could not attend the Policy Committee (PC) (because it was a Labour Party meeting) we established the Policy Co-ordinating Committee (PCC), which was a full committee of the Council with identical membership. Meetings would be on Wednesday mornings at ten o'clock; the councillors would work their way through the agenda, questioning officers about their reports, after which the officers would leave. The councillors would then decide what recommendations to make to the Labour Group. Once the Labour Group had taken its decisions the chief whip would write to the Council officers with a list of instructions. Although this decision-making cycle took a week to work it dramatically reduced the number of rightwing rebellions against our policies. I am also sure that we made fewer mistakes than we would have done with a more leadership-orientated and secretive process.

The PC/PCC meeting immediately became the most important in County Hall, other than the Labour Group meeting itself. Many backbenchers and rightwingers who were not members would turn up to observe the proceedings, free to intervene in the debates if they wanted to do so. We also co-opted two representatives from the Greater London Labour Party (GLLP) executive (Ted Knight and Arthur Latham) so that the interests of the Labour Party in the implementation of the manifesto they had drafted could be directly represented.

I found the task of chairing PC/PCC considerably less of a strain than chairing Camden's Housing Committee. In Camden the committee had tended to run from 7pm to past midnight. There was always the obstructive opposition of the Tories trying to delay any controversial item and the danger of Labour rightwingers voting with the Tories to block the reforms we were trying to push through. The need to concentrate on every speech, to understand fully every report in a pile of papers several inches thick and cope with interruptions from the public as well as the councillors meant that

I often lost five or six pounds in weight during the course of a meeting. In contrast, the PC/PCC meetings were usually good humoured and positive. The overwhelming consensus in favour of carrying out the manifesto meant that most arguments were about the practicalities of implementing decisions and usually involved the councillors working together to draw the necessary information out of those officers who were less than helpful. Because of my determination to delegate to the committee chairs I seldom felt particularly partisan about the bulk of issues coming before the committee and it was therefore possible to reach a consensus or a compromise on the vast majority of issues.

One great advantage was the large influx of new councillors who were of a dramatically higher calibre than the previous two administrations I had known. In 1974 Tony Judge had said to me that 'the Labour Party shows its contempt for County Hall in the quality of the GLC candidates it selects'. He was right, but no one could make a similar charge against the 1981 administration. The enthusiasm and open-mindedness of the new intake swamped the traditional bureaucrats, who began to realize that we seriously intended to carry out what some of the chief officers had assumed to be simply election rhetoric.

I had originally wanted to introduce a new top administrative structure in which we would force early retirement on two-thirds of the chief officers and bring in a system where the chairs of committees would have a predominant role in the administration of departments. This would have removed at a stroke many obstructive chief officers, serving also as a valuable warning to middle management not to be difficult. The Director-General's department would have been replaced by a younger team of administrative highfliers answerable directly to the leadership and the departmental empires broken up into smaller more manageable units. Maurice Stonefrost, the Comptroller of Finance, and John Fitzpatrick, the Chief Legal Adviser, would have taken on some of the Director-General's work but the main shift of responsibilities would have been to the elected councillors.

Secrecy was of course essential to such a plan. Had any word of it leaked out before the election it could have been completely distorted by the press. I discussed parts of it with some of my closest colleagues but no one was given enough details to be able to work out the full extent of what I had in mind. Unfortunately the plan was effectively sunk by the voters when they failed to deliver the 15 to 20 seat majority I had been expecting. It only needed five rightwingers to vote with the Tories against such a wholesale reorganization for the scheme to be defeated and my authority as Leader to be undermined to the point of disintegration.

I sounded out both Harvey and Illtyd about the possibility of abolishing the post of Director-General on the Saturday and Monday following the election and immediately realized that there was no chance of carrying all the centre within the Group meeting, let alone the right wing in the Council meeting. I had no alternative but to drop the idea. Instead, I would have to proceed department by department over a period of years. I was able to achieve each batch of changes only as the relevant committee chair came to the conclusion that they wanted a new chief officer. To try and remove a chief officer (even by early retirement) in the face of opposition by the chair who was working with them would have been impossible. Most of the senior officers I was determined to get rid of – because of their simple inability to understand what we were about, their incompetence, racism or Tory sympathies – were gone within two years, but in the chaotic circumstances of the last half of the administration such reorganizations were impossible, and so some officers whom I had marked down for removal survived until the very end.

By the time the Group met on the Monday following the election I was able to report that I had had my first rather stilted meeting with Sir James Swaffield. I then laid down the firm rule that chief officers were to work to their committee chairs; they were not to try conspiring with me to block our policies. The Group agreed a series of changes to Council meeting procedures aimed at cutting out the silly pretensions of the GLC to mimic Parliament. The most important of these was the introduction of a guillotine for Council meetings at 10pm. Oppositions had always considered it a matter of pride to keep the Council meeting going well past midnight but given that the meeting started at 2.30pm and the bar opened at 5pm, by the time we reached 10pm too many members were either too tired or too drunk for any business to be dealt with seriously. As I had failed to persuade my colleagues to make County Hall an alcohol-free zone, we settled for a 10pm closure instead. The Tories and the papers ranted on about the end of democracy and the erosion of freedom of speech but most of the Tories privately assured me that they were as delighted as I to be able to get to bed at a reasonable hour.

The press soon forgot about this threat to the fundamental right of politicians to drone on drunkenly when a rightwinger in the Labour Group leaked the news that we had voted not to attend the wedding of the Prince and Princess of Wales.

The Group had not intended any personal snub and had unanimously voted to give the royal couple a painting which had been commissioned for that purpose by the outgoing Tory administration. But the new Group was determined to end the junketing, freeloading image that had mushroomed during the Cutler years. The manifesto had promised an end to the practices of an annual international holiday for the chair of the GLC paid for out of the rates and the extravagant receptions at which the London establishment and the diplomatic corps had been fed and watered for about £30 per head. We also did away with the chauffeur-driven car, equipped with telephone, on permanent loan to the Leader of the Council, thereby saving ratepayers over £20,000 a year by the simple expedient of my using the tube to get to work. We ended the nonsense of the chair of the Council dressing up in medieval clothes to deliver a medieval address of welcome to every Head of State that visited London. In the light of those decisions the last thing the Labour Group wanted to see was me swanning around amongst the great and the good at the Royal Wedding as though nothing had changed since the Cutler regime.

Some members had suggested raffling the tickets for charity or sending four London pensioners – but they were non-transferable. When our private request to the Lord Chamberlain not to be sent tickets was ignored, the Group voted without dissent to decline the invitation. The press were in full hue and cry and devoted ten times the coverage to this 'snub' than they were giving to our policies. I spent hours patiently explaining why we had declined. But it all fell on deaf ears. Soon television crews from around the world were descending on me and I decided that if I was to get any other work done I would have to decline further interviews on the subject.

The obsession was such that one television journalist offered to go to bed with me in exchange for an interview. At the time I thought the idea was very funny and declined the offer but it should have served as a warning about the media hysteria that was to build up around the GLC and 'Red Ken'.

Although the struggles to push our policies through the bureaucracy went largely unreported they occupied almost all of the time and energy of the new councillors. In the three months following the election we all seemed to be constantly exhausted and exhilarated. When the bureaucracy threw up obstacles to our policies we found ways around them. The officers knew that our commitment to cut the fares was so public and central to our manifesto that there was no chance of our backing down, and we also had the management of London Transport on our side.

After the sacking of Ralph Bennett as the chair of the London Transport Executive, the Tories had toyed with the idea of appointing Sir Freddie Laker but settled instead for Sir Peter Masefield, who was already a part-time member of the LTE Board with a long background in civil aviation. Like his predecessor, he firmly believed in public transport and looked forward to the fares cut as a way of ending the spiral of decline in which London Transport had been trapped for over twenty years. Sir Peter had also been prepared to deal privately with the Labour Opposition in the run-up to the GLC election, giving us access to his professional advice about how to implement our policies. It also ensured that plans to implement our manifesto would be available immediately after the election.

Sir Peter was a classic urbane patrician of the kind that used to dominate the upper levels of the British establishment but has been forced into decline with the advent of Mrs Thatcher's Government. He was a 66-year-old workaholic who had spent a lifetime manipulating and surviving politicians and had rapidly established control over the erratic Sir Horace Cutler. Some of Sir Horace's appointments to the Board of London Transport were unacceptable to Sir Peter, but they were soon removed after a simple 'They go or I do' threat from Sir Peter. Sir Horace's frequent public attacks on London Transport workers ceased after a public rebuke from Sir Peter on a local radio programme. A disgruntled ex-employee from London Transport Acton Works had written to Sir Horace claiming that staff only worked an average of fifteen hours a week. Instead of investigating the charge first, Sir Horace wrote to Sir Peter and issued the letter to the press, who ran the story as though it were true, without any attempt to check the facts. When questioned on local radio Sir Peter said the allegations were untrue and continued, 'I'm going to talk to Sir Horace about this when he comes back from his well-earned holiday abroad. These things, you know, are quoted quite irresponsibly . . . quite out of context, and I shall be delighted to shoot down nonsense of this sort . . .'

Sir Peter was able to be firmly independent and critical of his political master because Sir Horace's reputation for mishandling London Transport was widespread amongst the media and public. Sir Horace could not easily have survived in yet another open conflict with the Board. This dispute between Sir Peter and Sir Horace served to highlight the very real difference between the position of the Board members of London Transport and the controllers and directors of GLC departments. The 1969 London Transport Act had given considerable independence to the LT Board. Although they were appointed and could only be removed by the Council, once they took office the day-to-day management of London Transport was under their control and the GLC could only issue broad policy directions. Unlike GLC departments, where members could intervene in day-to-day management, the affairs of London Transport could only be dealt with through the LT Board. GLC councillors of all parties felt frustrated by the system. The public understandably blamed them for any inadequacy of London Transport service, yet they were legally barred from intervening to deal with the problem.

Successive chairs of the Board had firmly defended their legal right to manage London Transport without day-to-day intervention by GLC members. Some had made no secret of their contempt for the politicians at County Hall and would occasionally take unexpected decisions which publicly embarrassed the GLC.

It was our good fortune to have in Sir Peter the most sensitive and subtle chair of LT the Council had had to deal with. Because of his commitment to public transport, he had an immediate rapport with Dave Wetzel, the chair of the GLC Transport Committee, whose past experience as an LT bus driver gave him a real inside knowledge of the system and its deficiencies. Sir Peter's confident personality and ability to work without conflict with some of the most tiresome backbench councillors, coupled with Dave Wetzel's belief in the system, produced the most effective working relationship between LT and the GLC that any of us had known. Dave Wetzel's down-to-earth style came over well on television and radio and struck a real chord with Londoners.

Dave Wetzel and Paul Moore, his vice-chair, pushed ahead immediately with a public consultation exercise on the fares reduction and worked with Sir Peter to reverse the cuts in London Transport services that had been pushed through by the Cutler administration. Within three weeks of the election Dave Wetzel successfully proposed the introduction of free travel for pensioners on the tube, and we were able to push our first manifesto commitment through the Council.

Whereas Dave and Paul had the enthusiastic backing of London Transport's managers for our policies, other committee chairs were not so lucky. The most difficult resistance was encountered by Michael Ward and Valerie Wise, the chair and vice-chair of the Industry and Employment Committee. The GLC had only limited powers to intervene in the London economy to save and create jobs for the unemployed, but the manifesto working party on Industry and Employment, chaired by Mike Ward, had been very high-powered and had produced a detailed blueprint for our new policies. The working party had included Stuart Holland, one of the few Labour MPs in the 1979 Parliament with a real grasp of the alternative economic strategy which had emerged in opposition to the dire incompetence of the Wilson–Callaghan years. Nick Sharman, one of the radical, younger trade union officials who were the driving force behind the South East Region of the TUC, also played a major role. They and others drew up detailed plans for the establishment of an Industry and Employment Department within the GLC and a separate Greater London Enterprise Board

(GLEB) whose task would be to fund job creation in the private sector.

The first attempt of the officers to sink the policy came whilst Andrew McIntosh was still leader of the Opposition. The Director-General lobbied him to put the proposed Industry and Employment Department under the GLC's Controller of Operational Services, who was responsible for the fire brigade, refuse disposal, arts and parks. Buried at a low level within the bureaucracy there was little chance that the new department would have the status or clout to develop in the radical way we wished to see. Mike Ward and I had agreed before the election that we would reject the Director-General's advice and insist on an independent department reporting directly to the members and represented on the D-G's chief officers' Board.

As soon as I became Leader I made this position clear to the D-G. I told Mike Ward that he would have my full backing in overcoming any further resistance by the chief officers. We did not have long to wait. Their next move was to go to a barrister and get an opinion which broadly said that establishing GLEB was outside our legal powers. It took Mike Ward several months' work and many further legal opinions before we could overcome the first one, by which time the officers were well into their favourite tactic of delaying the recruitment of the officers for the new department by claiming there was no office space to house them and stirring up the Staff Association to be difficult about recruiting from outside the existing GLC workforce.

Unsympathetic barristers were also producing obstructive legal opinions to prevent the ILEA from reducing the price of school meals. Clearly this tactic was going to be used against us again and again. The problem lay not with John Fitzpatrick, the Head of the Legal Department, who always did his best to assist members, but in the mass of conservative-minded lawyers who made up the GLC Legal Department. When chief officers who wished to obstruct our policies asked them to prepare the case to put before a barrister they could also decide which barrister should be used. Within our first few weeks it became obvious that they used only those barristers who were known supporters of the Tory Party. The only thing we could do was change the rules of the game. We therefore added many new barristers' names to the list that the GLC used; in particular we included more women and the first few black barristers. We also decided that in any politically sensitive case no legal advice could be sought without agreement from the PC/PCC, and that in all such cases councillors would decide which barrister to use. The quality and usefulness of our legal advice instantly improved.

Although we had suffered some setbacks and delays, all our major policies were underway by the time the Council adjourned at the end of July. The right wing of the Labour Group had split between those who had accepted jobs in the GLC and ILEA administrations and were happy to work in carrying out the manifesto, and an embittered rump of half a dozen whose only success had been in voting with the Tories to defeat the Labour Group policy of switching resources in the arts budget from the Royal Opera House to community arts groups. There had been rumblings from Andrew McIntosh, who had voted against establishing GLEB and the Industry and Employment Department in the way that Michael Ward had proposed, but the most vicious attacks had been led by Mair Garside. She had been a devoted supporter of Ashley Bramall and was never going to forgive me for my part in his removal – and hers. She seemed unable to let a Group meeting pass without launching at least two poisonous personal attacks on me. In the first three months she frequently accused me of corruption, incompetence, dishonesty and laziness. She looked for any reason to oppose, even voting against establishing a small working party to distribute £1 million to voluntary organizations which were in dire straits.

Our Tory opponents in the Council provided no opposition worth speaking of. Sir Horace Cutler had decided to stay on as Leader in the hope that Labour defections to the SDP would allow him to form a Tory–SDP coalition. His decision to repeat Sir Reg Goodwin's mistake of hanging on meant that those who were ambitious to succeed him were constantly trying to upstage each other in the stridency of their attacks on our policies and my Leadership. This only served to increase press coverage and create the impression that something revolutionary was underway at County Hall.

What all our opponents found difficult to come to terms with was the change to a more collective leadership and the less tangible but equally important changes in style. The new committee chairs shared my embarrassment at the pompous traditions that pervaded the building. Dispensing with the Leader's car was easy but getting officers to drop the practice of standing when speaking at committee took longer. The porters and messengers were delighted when I told them that they should continue to call me Ken and no longer had to stand to attention when I walked by. But many of the senior officers liked the feeling of importance which went with the formality. Some of them continued to stride into my office booming out, 'Good morning leader,' as though we were at a Nuremberg rally. They also found it unnerving that individual members who were not committee chairs had been given powers to take decisions in particular areas; almost any member of the Labour Group might appear in the papers or on television announcing a new policy.

Our open-door policy, and the decision to let any non-racist London group meet free of charge in the committee rooms, which in the past had stood empty at weekends and in the evenings, meant that the corridors were often filled with ordinary Londoners in all their diversity. The members' restaurant, which had once had the air of a gentlemen's club, was suddenly bustling with women and black people who had come to raise issues and had been invited to stop for a meal. Sometimes it was a real pleasure just to sit back and enjoy the looks of distaste which flickered across many a Tory face.

The most dramatic blow against the staid tradition of County Hall came at the first formal meeting of the GLC on 28 May. At the same time as establishing our new committee structure and agreeing free tube travel for pensioners, we voted to welcome and entertain the People's March for Jobs. On 1 May, 500 unemployed people had set out from Liverpool, Huddersfield and Llanelli to march to London in protest at the doubling of unemployment in Mrs Thatcher's first two years of office. Carrying the original banner of the Jarrow marchers, they were already well on their way when I became Leader. I asked Valerie Wise to take control of planning for their reception and soon we had a package of events agreed.

On the morning of the 28th the marchers entered London. Along with most Labour Group members I went to the Harrow–Watford boundary to greet them. This was followed by a nerve-racking dash back across London to be in time for the GLC meeting, to vote through the costs involved in accommodating the marchers in the GLC building. Valerie had found the camp beds (which, in a triumph of hope over reality, were supposed to be used in the event of a nuclear attack on London) and the money to put on a proper reception as well as the daily cost of feeding the marchers. When finally they marched into County Hall two days later to a very emotional welcome the building was transformed. In the past, GLC receptions had been very respectable affairs for the great and the good and the press had never objected. When it was a matter of a reception for the unemployed, things were different. Journalists crawled all over the building looking for damage or signs of violence but all they found was the disapproval of some senior bureaucrats. The real change was something they could not see. It was as though the People's March had humanized the very building in which the GLC was housed. This episode rapidly and dramatically brought home to many people that we intended to conduct ourselves in a completely different manner to previous administrations.

Any doubts on this score were dispelled by our intervention to back a group of striking journalists who were setting up their own magazine in opposition to their former employer. *Time Out* was an entertainments listing magazine which had been started in the heyday of 'swinging London' and provided a mixture of 'what's on' with radical journalism. Tony Elliott, the owner, was a 1960s hippy who had mellowed to the point of supporting the SDP. He was now determined to end *Time Out*'s radical image and become respectable. He chose his ground well and launched his campaign by trying to end the system of pay parity for all staff. They promptly went on strike and occupied the building. When it became obvious that Elliott would win through the courts, Beatrix Campbell and other workers on the magazine turned up at the GLC to see if we could help. A long struggle began between Mike Ward and the finance and legal departments, who were horrified by the idea of making a loan to striking workers to set up a rival magazine. Part of the problem was culture shock. Respectable, white, middle-class, middle-aged male officers in immaculate suits had only just begun to adjust to the scruffy, bejeaned, loud new Labour members. Asking them to deal with a random sample of alternative journalists, some of whom were not obviously either male or female, was too much. Eventually Mike Ward overcame the opposition, a loan was made and *City Limits* was born. Five years later *City Limits* had repaid its loan and captured a third of *Time Out*'s market, while many of the officers who tried to sink the deal despaired and took early retirement.

Shortly after the *City Limits* deal one of our most senior officers decided he could no longer tolerate the new administration and left the building, never to return.

By the end of July the press hysteria had put us firmly on the map. Public interest was beginning to mount, although it was extremely critical interest. Inside the Labour Group there were some rumblings of discontent about the damaging publicity – which was concentrated on me – but it was generally assumed that as our policies started to have a direct impact on Londoners (starting with the fares reduction in the autumn) we would see a shift back in our favour in the opinion polls. In the last conversation I had with Valerie Wise before I went on holiday I remember confidently predicting that the left was now so firmly in control within the GLC Labour Group that a successful leadership challenge from the right wing was inconceivable. But I had not anticipated the scale of the attack that was to descend in the autumn and come so close to destroying me and overturning the whole Labour administration.

5

Under Fire

While the Labour Group busied itself with the task of implementing the manifesto our opponents were not idle. We knew that there was no way the British Establishment was going to sit back and let us carry out our election promises without a fight, but no one in the Labour Group anticipated the ferocity of the counterattack or the number of different directions from which it was to come.

There is nothing that happens to you at any stage in your life that can prepare you for the British Press in full hue and cry. As a socialist I started out with the lowest possible opinion of Fleet Street and was amazed to discover that they managed to sink even lower than I expected. After the event the world is filled with people who will calmly explain to you the mistakes you made, but that does not help as you are swept up in a screaming, shouting, pushing mob of fifty or a hundred reporters under pressure from their editor to get a 'better' story than anyone else. Other members of the Group and I would spend hours carefully explaining our policies only to open the paper the next morning and see instead a smear about my sex-life, alleged personality defects or some completely fictional account of a meeting or a split that never actually happened. You also have to contend with the nauseating experience of listening to the reporter whose by-line has appeared under yet another foul lie explain that it was not their fault because the editor changed the story that had been filed.

Looking back on my handling of the press in that period I am embarrassed by my naivety. Tony Banks, who had been close to Tony Benn throughout the previous ten years, had seen Fleet Street's methods at work in the attempt to destroy Benn and he argued from the beginning that we should simply refuse to have anything to do with the popular press. Those of us who had not been through that experience thought he was exaggerating. I believed that the constant calm reiteration of our policies would slowly get through to the readers, but soon realized that editors will only print the news that they think is fit to damage the Labour Party.

Having spent the previous ten years trying to drum up any national press interest I could in what was happening in local government, and seldom being able to get more than one story a year into the national press, I was astounded by the level of press interest. My experience of journalists, which began in my Lambeth days, had led me to believe that they were quite reasonable and fair in their reporting. As a Camden councillor and parliamentary candidate for Hampstead I had been even luckier to be in the circulation area of the *Hampstead and Highgate Express*, which is the best local paper in London and always had a good team of reporters who sought out real stories which were accurately reported and politically balanced.

It is an incredible indictment of Fleet Street that with all their resources there is not a single popular paper that can reach the standard set by a local paper such as the *Ham and High*. Shortly after my election as Leader, Gerald Isaman, the paper's editor, warned me that I should reply to every inaccurate or distorted statement in the press. It was impossible to act on his warning, however, as replying to each lie would have taken several hours each day, leaving little time for more important work.

The press started as they intended to continue. The day after my election, the headlines gave a taste of what was to come.

'EXTREMIST VOTED IN AS LONDON'S NEW BOSS', screamed the *Daily Mail*; 'NEW GLC LEADER PROMISES STORMS', claimed the *Sunday Telegraph*; 'RED KEN CROWNED KING OF LONDON – MODER-ATE CHIEF IS OUSTED IN COUP', warned the *Sun*; 'NEW LEFT THREATEN POLICE: WE ARE THE MASTERS NOW', said the *Sunday Express*. The *Daily Mail* followed up with an article headlined 'LITTLE STALINS', which quoted the boss of the electricians' union. The *Daily Telegraph* lead headline announced 'LABOUR GLC COUP BY LEFT', and reported Mrs Thatcher's warning that we intended to 'impose a tyranny which the peoples of Eastern Europe yearn to cast aside'. Londoners must have been surprised not to see Russian tanks occupying the city. No one would have thought that the papers had spent the previous three weeks predicting that I would become Leader if Labour won the election.

In the following week came a shift of emphasis towards my private life. As I left my flat on the Monday morning an *Evening Standard* photographer was hiding behind the dustbins to see who might be leaving the flat with me. The press became increasingly interested in the fact that my marriage had broken up the previous year and spent some time trying to find out if I was involved with anyone else. This included refusing to move from one GLC officer's doorstep until they had been allowed to search her house to see if I was in her bedroom. The discovery that I lived in a bedsit, kept salamanders, travelled to work on the tube, played snooker and read science fiction unleashed a spate of stories suggesting I was a strange eccentric who was unqualified to occupy such an important post.

The GLC Labour Group's reaction to this rather shallow and silly press coverage was mainly one of surprise. At that stage we could not understand why we were getting so much more coverage than Ted Knight had in Lambeth or David Blunkett did in Sheffield. Of course the GLC was the Council for the capital city but it controlled fewer services and had fewer powers than Sheffield or Lambeth. Perhaps it was simply easier for journalists to stagger over the bridge from the bars in Parliament to the bars at County Hall if they wanted to do a 'Red Terror' story rather than going all the way up to Sheffield and having to do serious research on local government in a city which was not as well blessed with wine bars as London.

This was also the time of major advances by the left within the Labour Party. Tony Benn's deputy leadership bid was coming to its climax. Many papers sought to portray the GLC as a grim warning of what would happen to Britain if a leftwing Government ever won an election, and exaggerated their coverage in order to confirm their own propaganda. When Tony Benn's illness took him out of the firing line, the policies of the GLC provided a substitute target for anti-socialist stories, without the risk of the sympathetic backlash which would have ensued had the press continued to abuse Tony while he was ill.

Initally, then, I misjudged the press campaign. I was to learn by painful experience that letting the press set the agenda could be extremely damaging. I did not deliberately plan the way in which I would raise controversial issues such as Ireland and lesbian and gay rights; I simply responded to requests from activist groups to speak at their meetings. The press were able to attend and take out of the context of my speech whichever sentences they could use to damage me most. Had I known how well planned the press campaign was I would have moved earlier to try and limit the damage but like most GLC councillors I assumed it was a fad that would soon pass. It was only years later that I was able to piece together, through the various indiscretions of journalists and the detailed research of Mark Hollingsworth in his book *The Press and Political Dissent*, the way the press attack was planned.

Without the obsessive interest of the editor of the *Daily Mail* the press might well have lapsed back into their traditional apathy about local government. This editor, Sir David English, who was knighted by Mrs Thatcher for his continuing efforts to ensure that the *Mail* remained a reliable vehicle for Tory Party propaganda, decided in the first flush of media hysteria to make the GLC and myself a prime target. One of the paper's best reporters, Richard Holliday, was brought back from covering the Middle East conflict and sent to County Hall with the instruction to file six anti-left stories a day. At each morning's editorial conference, Sir David would say, 'What are we doing on the GLC today?' He then decided which two or three of Holliday's stories best fitted the anti-left campaign for that day. Often the cartoonists were instructed to drop whatever else they had planned and devise a damaging cartoon to fit one of the 'Red Ken' stories.

The use of cartoons was vital to the whole exercise: they could be much more damaging than the printed word yet infinitely more difficult to sue for libel. Over the first six months *Daily Mail* cartoons created the impression that I supported the bombing and assassination of London residents by the IRA and even hinted that GLC funding was reaching the IRA. Had any of that appeared in the editorial or news columns I could have sued but legal advisors maintained that an action against a cartoon was almost unheard of and certain to fail.

The vast amount of GLC coverage in the *Mail* meant that other editors were demanding that their reporters file similar stories. Fleet Street became caught up in escalating editorial demands for yet more shocking GLC and 'Red Ken' stories. Richard Holliday was increasingly pushed by Sir David English to beat his rival reporters and he became a permanent shadow following me throughout my days' activities. The strain on him soon began to show. At first he looked merely under pressure but this rapidly developed into an obvious nervous tension, not assisted by my habit of pointing him out to the audience whenever I was speaking at a public meeting. The audience would almost always turn and hiss with a mixture of contempt and menace which would cause him to cringe over his notebook. As an individual he was engaging and pleasant and the quality of his writing was very good. He would have had no problems getting a job working for the *Financial Times* or the *Guardian*, but the *Mail*'s inflated rates of pay had long since trapped him and he could not afford to leave.

During the GLC election campaign, Labour Party headquarters had seconded to us one of their press officers, Veronica Crichton, to handle the media and she had impressed everyone at County Hall with her competence. I had particularly noted her refusal to fall into the usual media trait of flattering politicians in order to prop up their fragile egos. At one point in the campaign I had asked her what she thought of the leadership choice the new Group would face. She bluntly replied that she regretted that so important a post as GLC Leader had such a limited pool of talent to choose from!

On my first day as Leader I instructed the officers to create a new post of press officer to the Majority Party and I offered it to her. Unfortunately, she could not take up the post until after the Warrington by-election in July, and by the time she did arrive the press distortion had done enough damage to knock our position in the opinion polls down to rock bottom. Veronica had made it clear in accepting the job that while she would put over the best possible image to the media she was not prepared to lie on our behalf as that would compromise her professional reputation. That suited us fine as all we wanted was fair coverage in the press. Once the ground rules became known both the press and the politicians rapidly came to trust her. Her strategy was to concentrate on getting radio and television interviews which allowed the public to make up their own minds and meant we could reach beyond the newspapers to communicate directly with Londoners. She started rationing my time with newspaper journalists but this did not reduce coverage in the press.

Having all but exhausted genuine GLC stories the papers now turned to 'creative' work. The *Daily Mirror* phoned my father-in-law to ask his views about the break-up of my marriage and suitably embellished them. Richard Holliday and a *Mail* photographer travelled all the way up to Lincoln to try and get an interview with my mother. Her suspicions were aroused when she opened the door and Holliday said that he and his friend were doing 'a survey on what people think about the Humber Bridge'. When she replied that she thought it was a very good thing he followed up with the question, 'What does your Ken think about it?' She briefly replied with her views about the integrity of journalists, shut the door and left them to drive back to London without a story. The *Daily Mail* were prepared to use and damage others in their attempts to smear me and, on 20 August 1981, announced that three psychologists had decided my 'shocking' behaviour was 'due to a lack of parental attention as a child'. The psychologists quoted denied saying this and the President of the British Psychological Society wrote that the article 'falsely brought the profession of psychology into public disrepute', because of the 'irregular behaviour on the part of [*Daily Mail*] staff'.

The popular press's interest in my private life increased dramatically after they discovered my support for lesbian and gay rights. My decision not to discuss my private life or personal relationships only increased their interest. One way that clues to my private life could be found was in the weekly binful of rubbish that I used to put out the night before the refuse collectors called. I noticed that this invariably disappeared before the dustcart arrived in the morning. The knowledge that some highly paid journalist was picking his way through my rubbish merely ensured I threw away nothing that might interest them and made certain that the large number of old newspapers I threw out was well mixed up with vegetable peelings.

I had made the initial mistake of allowing Max Hastings and three television crews into my bedsit to conduct interviews. This had allowed the 'austere, bedsitter trot' stereotype to gain some credence and formed the basis of the Leninspart series in *Private Eye*. On Veronica's advice I decided to prevent any recurrence of this sort of coverage by insisting that all interviews took place at County Hall or in a studio. Most of my friends had stories of how they had been approached by journalists eager to purchase some gossip. None of them co-operated, so the *News of the World* sent an extremely attractive reporter to my flat one Saturday morning with a request that she be allowed to interview me at home. I sent her away saying that she could interview me any time at County Hall with Veronica Crichton present but neither the reporter nor the *News of the World* ever attempted to follow up the offer.

When the possibilities of 'creative' reporting were exhausted the popular press simply switched to straight invention. One particularly funny example was when my mother phoned to ask why I had had a vasectomy without telling her. When I protested that this was not true she referred to the *Sunday People*. There could have been no basis for the story as I had not been to any hospital for treatment since I was eight and I had been nowhere near a clinic since a motorcycle accident in 1976. The paper knew the story was a lie. They had made no effort to contact me for confirmation or a quote and I strongly suspect they simply invented it to fill a gap on the page. This did not stop other papers regularly repeating the story without making any effort to check it with me. The Princess of Wales has probably had more fictitious pregnancies than I have had vasectomies, but it is a close-run contest.

Every now and then some particularly nasty sexual smear would appear. The *Daily Mirror* alleged that I had enticed some unnamed reporter back to my flat and that she had to fight me off in order to escape with her innocence. The struggle was reported as being so violent that my hand had been bandaged for several days. The *Daily Mirror* did not know that I had stopped living in my bedsit and moved into the flat of a friend two years before their story appeared. Nor, as anyone who worked with me will confirm, did I ever have to wear any bandages at any time while I was Leader. This did not stop the paper repeating the story.

Eventually, as the strain built up, Richard Holliday was released from County Hall duties and replaced by Tony Doran, the 'home affairs' correspondent on the *Daily Mail*. My partner and I had been living together for nearly a year before somebody tipped Doran off. As we emerged from my partner's flat one Sunday morning on our way to visit friends, Doran was parked in his car outside looking like he had slept in it all night. He crept up beside us in his grubby, crumpled coat and said, 'What would you like to say about the new love in your life, Ken?' We ignored him and walked on. Not to be deprived of a good quote he then called on my wife and asked her opinion – although we had been living apart for nearly two years. My wife told me later that the *Mail* had offered her £10,000 for the inside story of our marriage and assured her that the task would not be difficult: she would just provide the details and a reporter would 'write it up' for her.

Rarely did any press story go so clearly over the borderline as to guarantee success in an expensive libel action – which I did not have the funds for – but eventually I had to act against *Private Eye* and a now defunct London entertainment guide. These two magazines alleged that Ted Knight and I had a numbered Swiss bank account into which Colonel Gaddafi had deposited $200,000. While I could ignore vague sexual smears, it was very damaging to have a rumour circulating that I was being privately funded by a foreign power that was in the habit of assassinating its opponents. The rumour appeared after Ted and I had launched *Labour Herald*. It was printed on the presses of the Workers' Revolutionary Party at commercial rates, although naturally the WRP would allow us a little more time to break even than a non-socialist printer would have done. What Fleet Street could not understand was how anyone could produce a leftwing weekly without massive subsidies. They overlooked the fact that we only employed one worker with every-body else writing for free and not demanding Fleet Street-style expense accounts. It was quite ironic that by the time we got to court the debts of *Labour Herald* had mounted to the point where we would have had to close if it had not been for the substantial out-of-court settlement we got from both magazines. These allowed us to clear our debts to the WRP and carry on publishing.

The fact that we were able to win on the Gaddafi smear does not however prove that libel actions work. We had to pay several thousand pounds towards the costs of the case during the two years it took to reach the courts and we could only take that risk because the libel was so specific we could not possibly lose. The fact that libel laws only exist to protect the wealthy was revealed shortly before we got to court, when *Private Eye* offered to settle for the bare minimum they thought they could get away with. Our lawyers pointed out the risk in not accepting the offer: if the jury eventually awarded damages lower than *Private Eye*'s final offer we would have to pay the entire costs of the case, which might very well have bankrupted both Ted and me. They also pointed out that *Private Eye* would argue that damages should be small because my reputation was so low in public esteem that it had not been damaged any further by this extra press libel. Thus the press can defend themselves in court by arguing that because they have destroyed your reputation with all their previous stories the one on which you finally sue does not really make any difference to your reputation at that stage! Of course, if you are a member of the Establishment you can expect perhaps ten times as much in damages.

Nor is the supposedly independent Press Council any real defence. With the exception of a couple of Labour movement appointees it is a solidly Establishment body which rushes in quickly to condemn any bad publicity on the Royal family but does everything possible to make it difficult for leftwing activists to get a hearing. When a member of the public complained about the *Daily Mail* story in which three psychologists had been misquoted about my mental state, the Press Council decided the story was correct – even though the psychologists denied it completely. When I referred the *Sun* to the Press Council for describing me as 'the most odious man in Britain' I soon realized from their generally unhelpful attitude that I would be wasting my time to proceed further.

It is all too easy to sit back now and say that because the Labour GLC and 'Red Ken' went on to overcome the press attacks of 1981, and by 1984 had built up a huge lead in the opinion polls, the press attacks did not matter. I believe that circumstances that allowed us to break through the press hostility were quite unique and that we were unbelievably lucky. Peter Tatchell in the Bermondsey by-election, Arthur Scargill and the striking miners, the women of Greenham Common and to a lesser degree Tony Benn, just did not have access to the financial and bureaucratic resources which we could mobilize in our fight back, nor did their opponents behave as incompetently as ours did. Fleet Street acts consistently to advance the interests of the Tory Party and their attacks on Haringey and Brent in 1986 were a carbon copy of the tactics used against the GLC in 1981. As Mark Hollingsworth details in *The Press and Political Dissent*, the Tory–Fleet Street campaign was carefully planned with an eye to the 1983 election in the same way that the attacks by Fleet Street and the Education Secretary, Kenneth Baker, on Brent Council in the autumn of 1986 were also part of Tory pre-election strategy.

In November and December 1982 Tory Central Office had a series of meetings at which it was decided to make abolition of the GLC an election issue. It was to be part of a general campaign theme: Scargill, Benn and Livingstone were the 'enemy within' that had to be defeated as the Argentinians had been defeated in the South Atlantic. A Tory Central Office press officer called Arthur Williamson was seconded to work with the Tory Group at County Hall, and through him Fleet Street journalists were fed a constant diet of stories to fill their pages.

The Central Office team had no scruples about spreading wholly fictitious stories about my private life. When they heard that *Sunday Mirror* women's editor Trudi Pacter was doing an in-depth interview for the issue of 6 March 1983 she was taken to lunch by a Tory official who informed her that 'we have reliable sources who claim that Livingstone was at a gay party where he was buggered by six men in succession'. Not concerned with maintaining consistency, they followed this up by circulating a rumour in Fleet Street that MI5 and Special Branch had amassed a file listing schoolgirls that I was alleged to be involved with.

About this time, I was leaving County Hall one day for an outside meeting when a reporter from the popular press came up to me and said that his newspaper had been approached by a man who claimed that I had attended a meeting of a paedophile group above an East London pub one Friday evening in February. Fortunately I was able to show him my diary, which recorded that I had been speaking at public meetings hundreds of miles from London every Friday evening during February. When he left to check the details I had given him I realized that I could have been in real trouble if I had spent one of those Fridays working alone at County Hall, as I often did in order to catch up with paperwork. What made me particularly vulnerable to that kind of set-up was that I and all other councillors had to submit a detailed account of all our activities to the Council in order to claim our attendance allowance. The account had to list every meeting, its location and every activity, with the time taken. This was then deposited for public inspection by any ratepayer. It would take someone no more than an hour or two to have worked out on which nights I was working alone. It would be almost impossible for me to disprove any allegation in which someone was prepared to pit their word against mine. Given the damage the press had done to my public image I thought it highly unlikely that I would convince a jury to accept my word against that of someone planning to frame me.

As Mark Hollingsworth makes clear in his book, many Tories were horrified by these tactics. In January 1983 George Tremlett, the Tory councillor for Twickenham, was invited by Arthur Williamson to meet reporters from the *Daily Mail* and *Daily Telegraph* who had 'come to get the dirt on Livingstone' as Tory Central Office was trying to trigger a censure debate in the Council against my leadership. The *Mail* journalist, Richard Holliday, took Tremlett to lunch at La Barca where he said, 'What we really want is something on his sex life. Is he queer? What about his women, who does he go out with? Is he a communist?' George Tremlett left without co-operating but was pestered again in March 1983 when Arthur Williamson wanted him to ask a question of me in the Council chamber which had 'been personally drafted by the Editor of the *Daily Mail*, Sir David English'. The *Mail* had launched a campaign against the GLC on the grounds of our alleged anti-semitism and the question was clearly devised to make the smear stick. When Tremlett refused, the *Mail* reporter, Tony Doran, approached a Jewish group and got them to make an attack on the GLC, which appeared on 18 March 1983.

The worst and most consistent press distortions were always reserved for those occasions when I or my colleagues spoke out about Britain's role in Ireland. The Labour administration was elected just two days after the death of Bobby Sands MP. His hunger strike had been in protest against the actions of successive British governments which had removed the political status of Republican prisoners as part of a policy of criminalization. It would have been impossible to ignore the issue at any time, but as the number of dead hunger strikers mounted and the IRA exploded bombs on London's streets I was not prepared to be silenced simply because the press would distort what I intended to say. Londoners' lives were at risk from bombing, young Londoners were sent to fight and die in Ireland, every London taxpayer was contributing towards the continuation of the war and I believed that our military involvement in Ireland led to actions which inevitably eroded civil rights and public morality throughout Britain. No one would have suggested that mayors in the USA should not have views and be prepared to express them during the war in Vietnam. The denigration that Fleet Street rained down on me was because of what I said, not because I had no right to speak on Ireland. If I had supported the Government's position, Fleet Street would have praised my courage but because I spoke for a united Ireland the Fleet Street editors – who never hesitate to express a view on everything although they have been elected by no one – denied my right to speak out for British withdrawal.

Although the policy I put forward had been adopted at the GLLP by a card vote of ten to one, opponents of British withdrawal represented a much larger proportion of the Labour Group. In addition, there was another group of members whose main concern was that the publicity surrounding issues such as Ireland and the Royal Wedding were distracting public attention from the manifesto policies of fares cuts and job creation. At the end of the Group Meeting on 27 July 1981, after many leftwingers had left, Ken Little (Edmonton) launched an attack saying that the publicity surrounding me was undermining the standing of the Labour Party in the opinion polls. Other rightwingers supported him and almost all the people I could have relied on to support me were absent from the meeting. Much more worrying was the intervention of Mike Ward, who made much the same point without adding the personal abuse with which some members had spiked their comments. Mike had invested two years' hard work in drawing up the Industry and Employment section of the manifesto and he was genuinely worried about the scale of unfavourable publicity building up. I replied saying that things should die down during the August recess and that attention would undoubtedly focus on the fares cut, which was due to be introduced after the summer break.

I was furious with those leftwingers who had left the meeting early, but recognized that I still had a lot to learn about how to handle the press – although I doubted that any of the others could have done better. Fortunately several people, such as the journalists on the *New Statesman* and individuals like Tariq Ali and my closest friends, kept urging me not to back down in the face of the press attack.

On my return from holiday I had a meeting with the whips and we agreed that committee chairs should take on more of the presentation of the PC/PCC report to the Group and also more of the general Council publicity so as to lower my public profile and reduce the press obsession with me. That evening (17 July) I went to speak to Harrow Gay Unity and made much the same speech about lesbian and gay rights that I had been making over the previous decade. I had not seen any reporter at the meeting but the following day the *Evening Standard* led off the hysteria which was taken up by the rest of the press the next day. The coverage of that speech rapidly entered folklore. It can be summed up by the comment of my nephew, Terry Booth, who rushed home from his paper round to show the front page to my mother, who was staying with his family at the time. My mother awoke as he pounded up the stairs excitedly yelling, 'Gran, Gran! The papers say Uncle Ken's a fairy!'

The worst was yet to come. An IRA nail bomb exploded on 10 October outside the Chelsea barracks, killing two civilians and injuring 22 soldiers and 16 civilians. Two days later I was speaking on reform of the rating system at Cambridge and one student asked my position on the bombing. I replied, 'Nobody supports what happened last Saturday in London. But what about stopping it happening? As long as we are in Ireland, people will be letting off bombs in London. I can see that we are a colonial power holding down a colony. For the rest of time, violence will recur again and again as long as we are in Ireland. People in northern Ireland see themselves as a subject people. If they were just criminals or psychopaths they could be crushed. But they have a motive force which they think is good.' I then went on to explain that as long as the IRA were driven by the force of nationalism they would be prepared to continue their military campaign, irrespective of the cost to themselves or others. That meant that British politicians had to be prepared to find a political solution in order to stop the killing. It was a theme I had reiterated on several occasions since the May election and in the context of the meeting (which was attended mainly by young Tories) was well received. Richard Holliday went back to the *Daily Mail* and wrote up the story without any particular emphasis on that part of my speech and the paper ran the story without giving it undue prominence.

But the other reporter present sold the story to the Press Association, and between the reporter and what was sent out on the wire from the Press Association to Fleet Street, the whole context of the speech was changed. So extensive was the change that the *Sun* was able to fill its front page with a photograph of me and a whole half-page headline: 'THIS DAMN FOOL SAYS THE BOMBERS AREN'T CRIMINALS!' Under the headline was a *Sun* leader.

> This morning the *Sun* presents the most odious man in Britain. Take a bow, Mr Livingstone, socialist Leader of the Greater London Council. In just a few months since he appeared on the national scene, he has quickly become a joke. Now no one can laugh at him any longer. The joke has turned sour, sick and obscene. For Mr Livingstone steps forward as the defender and the apologist of the criminal, murderous activities of the IRA.

All the other papers that purchased the Press Association's distorted account of my speech ran it in the same vein. *The Times* claimed that, 'as two men were being questioned ... about the

IRA nail bomb . . . Mr Ken Livingstone again took the side of the IRA'. The *Daily Express* headline stated, 'IRA BOMB GANG NOT CRIMINALS SAYS LIVINGSTONE', and called on the GLC Labour Group immediately to repudiate my remarks or to be branded as 'unworthy'. The *Daily Mail* rushed to catch up with the rest of Fleet Street by calling on the Labour Group to replace me immediately as leader. The *Sun* had actually sent a reporter to County Hall to show me the text of their story shortly before printing. The reporter eventually caught up with me as I was leaving that Monday night's Group meeting and asked me if I had said that bombers weren't criminals. I replied that I had not and furthermore I could not recognize the speech I had made from their account of it. None of the other papers even bothered to contact me to check if the story was true, though had they done so they would most probably have followed the behaviour of the *Sun*, ignoring my denial and running the story as they had originally intended.

The violence of the press coverage was stunning and shook the morale of many Labour councillors. The preceding five months had been bad enough and this latest assault could easily have been the final straw that brought together a coalition of forces in the Labour Group that was ready to replace me. Nothing had prepared the Labour Group for the scale of publicity we had received nor the effect that it had had on our standing in the polls. Audience Selection (a telephone polling firm) had published a poll during the summer, based on a thousand telephone interviews, which showed that since the election there had been a dramatic change in voting intentions in London. Labour were now third, behind the aggregated votes of the Liberals and the SDP. Asked, *'How would you vote in a new GLC election?'* the telephoned sample had replied as follows:

	May 81		August 81	
Labour	42%		27%	
Tory	40%		45%	
Liberal	14% }	17%	9% }	
SDP	3% }		13% }	28%
Alliance	–		6% }	

The poll also asked, '*Which of the words best sums up your feelings about the performance of Ken Livingstone as Leader of the GLC?*'

Splendid	2%	Bad	18%
Good	9%	Appalling	34%
OK	24%	Don't Know	12%

They then asked, '*Who would you prefer as Leader of the GLC, Andrew McIntosh or Ken Livingstone?*'

	All Londoners	Voters at the GLC election		
		Tory	Lab	Lib
Andrew McIntosh	38%	53%	41%	45%
Ken Livingstone	16%	5%	32%	5%
Neither	19%	25%	7%	17%
Don't Know	28%	16%	20%	32%

The poll claimed that of those who had voted Labour at the GLC election 38 per cent now regretted doing so and 48 per cent hoped that enough Labour councillors would defect to the SDP to deprive Labour of its majority on the Council. Even more worrying for some of my colleagues was the news that 77 per cent of the people phoned opposed increasing the rates to fund the fares cut; only 17 per cent supported the scheme. The only reasonably optimistic result in the whole poll was that 47 per cent supported job-creation schemes paid for out of the rates – but 48 per cent opposed even that policy.

Telephone polls have a built-in bias against the Labour Party, but even a traditional face-to-face poll carried out by the Opinion Research Centre for Thames Television in early September showed dreadful results.

Q) Is Ken Livingstone doing a good or a bad job?

Good job	20%
Bad job	47%
Neither	12%
Don't Know	20%

Q) Would you prefer London Transport fares

i.   to be lower and paid for by rate increases?   24%
ii.   increasing from time to time with no increase in rates? 64%
iii. Don't know   12%

The high public profile that the media had given me caused a deluge of letters from the public. Throughout that summer the letters I received were 50/50 for and against, but it was the sheer venom of some of the critical letters which worried my staff. Apart from those from fascists and racists which contained death threats and the odd razor blade and were usually anonymous, there were also signed letters of extreme bitterness. Relatively mild was this one from a retired army major who lived on the south coast:

Dear Sir

I listened to you on Radio 4 news this morning. What a slimy hypocrite you are.

Yours sincerely.

My favourite was quite elaborate:

The Rescue Mission
182 Elliott Street
Birmingham

Dear Mr Livingstone

Perhaps you have heard of me and my nationwide campaign in the cause of temperance. Each year, for the past fourteen, I have made a tour of Scotland and the North of England including Manchester, Liverpool and Glasgow and have delivered a series of lectures on the evils of drinking. On these tours I have been accompanied by a young friend and assistant, David Powell. David, a young man of good family and excellent background, is a pathetic example of a life ruined by excessive indulgence in whiskey and women.

David would appear with me at lectures and sit on the platform, wheezing and staring at the audience through bleary, bloodshot eyes, sweating profusely, picking his nose, passing wind and making obscene gestures, while I would point out that he was an example of what drink and women could do to a man.

Last summer, unfortunately, David died. A mutual friend has given me your name and I wonder if you would care to take David's place on my next tour.

Yours in anticipation

REV. DAVID KNIGHT

Mostly, however, they were filled with racism, homophobia and general invitations to 'go back to Russia'. One series came on the back of disused betting slips, which suggested that I was the recipient of the unsuccessful punters' anger each time they lost. Initially I pinned them up in my secretary's office to a wall nicknamed 'democracy wall', but gave up when I ran out of space. It was noticeable that the letters were almost always prompted by the latest attack in the press. My secretary would groan when the press went over the top as it always meant a day filled with obscene phone calls (including death threats) followed by a flood of letters of which many were signed and required patient replies.

As the press-orchestrated hatred built up, Bill Bush became increasingly worried about my personal safety and urged me to resurrect the Leader's car, but I was determined not to allow the campaign to have that effect. The Police Special Branch asked to meet the Head of Security at the GLC to warn him that my movements were being monitored by what they called 'extremist groups' and to point out that as I lived in a bedsit and travelled on public transport they could not hope to provide protection.

The press campaign finally had its desired effect in creating the climate of opinion which legitimized physical as well as verbal violence. I had decided to work at County Hall through the night of 29 July in order to clear paperwork before I went on holiday.

Shortly before midnight a gang of thugs chanting anti-Irish slogans and wielding iron bars attacked the main doors. A group of Irish men and women who had been conducting a silent vigil on the steps of County Hall in support of the hunger strike were beaten up but the security staff managed to keep the thugs out of the building until the police arrived. Not one newspaper or Tory member of the GLC was prepared to condemn the attack.

The *Sun*'s 'most odious man' headline also had its effect. On the following day I was due to speak at the City of London Junior Chamber of Commerce. The meeting had been widely advertised in the City. As I was walking up to the meeting hall's entrance I noticed two respectably dressed men who I assumed were waiting to escort me into the meeting. One stepped forward, saying, 'Good evening.' As we shook hands, his free hand swung up towards my face with an aerosol can. I was partially blinded by a painful spray but managed to grab the can and pull it to my chest. In the struggle he had slipped behind me. I threw myself back against the wall and rushed into the building as he dropped to the pavement. It was over so quickly that his friend who had been playing the role of look-out had no time to act. I went straight to the washroom and was relieved to see that the spray was only red paint. It washed off easily but my jacket looked as though I had been shot through the heart. By folding it inwards, I was able to appear at the meeting as though nothing had happened. I told no one about the attack as I assumed publicity would only encourage some weak-minded individuals to imitate the event. Twenty-four hours later a group calling itself the 'Friends of Ulster' claimed responsibility. None of the newspapers that reported the incident condemned the use of violence and I was left to wonder how they would have treated an incident in which a Tory MP was attacked by leftwing thugs.

The eight days that followed the *Sun*'s 'most odious man' headline saw County Hall under daily siege from the media. The Tories requested a special meeting of the Council for Wednesday 21 October to debate a motion of censure against me. Harvey Hinds convened a special Group meeting in order to agree Labour tactics in the debate. The media spent a week building up the tension with stories predicting that Labour rightwingers would abstain, allowing the motion to be carried and forcing my resignation as Leader. However, the sheer viciousness of the press that week made it impossible for any Labour councillor to vote in such a way as to allow the motion to carry. Frances Morrell provided a draft amendment which recorded a 'deep sense of outrage at terrorist acts of violence in London' and 'regretted that the Opposition and Tory newspapers had given exaggerated attention to the views of individual members in order to distract attention from the threat ... to London posed by Mrs Thatcher's disastrous economic policy . . .' After being hacked around in PC/PCC and the Labour Group, this gained unanimous support from all Labour councillors and it was agreed that I should move the amendment. In a Council chamber packed with reporters and television cameras it was carried by a majority of six votes. The press dutifully recorded the Tory attacks, which were even more violent in their imagery than usual.

Although we had won in the Council chamber there was no doubt that we had been badly damaged outside. That night after I had finished speaking at a public meeting for the Hampstead Labour Party about twenty of us went into the nearby Three Horseshoes pub for a quiet drink. As we were leaving, a gang of well-built, short-haired thugs started chanting 'commie bastard' and attacked our group. Quite a fight developed: one of my supporters was getting kicked in the head and a woman was thrown over the bar while my friends bundled me out to safety. The landlord's sympathies were obviously with his regular customers. Those newspapers that reported the incident failed to condemn the violence; one said it was understandable. Given the lies that those same papers had been churning out, they could hardly have said otherwise.

Not only had the press spent six months trying to turn me into a national hate figure, but, with their emphasis on 'Red Ken' stories, they had also been trying to drive a wedge between me and the rest of the Labour Group. There was a real danger that the Group would begin to see the rows around me as the main impediment to carrying out our manifesto. Fortunately the press campaign reached its peak of hysteria six months before I had to face re-election at the AGM of the Labour Group and to try and remove me in mid-term would have required a recorded vote. I might very well have been replaced as Leader if the AGM, with its secret ballots, had been due in October 1981 rather than April 1982. But those leftwingers who wanted to remove me could not preserve their left credentials if they were publicly seen to be working with the right. The other problem faced by my critics was that while undoubtedly a majority of the Labour Group would at that stage have preferred to see the back of me, there was no agreement on who would replace me. However, if I had shown any weakness under pressure during that week I could have been removed. I made it clear to the right wing that there was no question of my resigning even if the censure vote was carried. I told them I intended to remain as Leader unless an open vote of no confidence was carried in the Labour Group. It was vital that I projected confidence in order to carry as many of my supporters as possible; some of them were beginning to doubt my claim that if we stood firm under the media pressure we would come through and win an increased majority at the next GLC election. Even the knowledge that the election was over three years away did not reassure them.

My air of confidence was not wholly dishonest – I genuinely believed we could survive and go on to win – but I recognized that the odds were getting worse with each passing month. I never believed things were as bad as the polls indicated because of the feedback I was getting in my contact with the public. Every day people would stop me on the streets or in the tube, usually to say they supported what we were doing. I received countless letters or simply comments from passers-by along the lines of, 'Don't let the bastards grind you down.' I was also encouraged by the response at public meetings. Until I became Leader, like most politicians, I was used to addressing meetings of under a dozen people. The first indication that something had changed came when I was invited to speak to the Socialist Society at the London School of Economics. I had spoken to about twenty people at a GLC election meeting at the LSE a few days before polling and when I was asked to come back a few weeks after the election I expected an audience of much the same size. I knew that weeks of newspaper hysteria had had some effect when I was forced to climb over the people sitting in the aisles in order to get to the front. Since the election

I had been too busy to get out to public meetings and invitations were only just beginning to arrive in large numbers. By building me up into an 'IRA-loving, poof-loving Marxist', the popular press had not only guaranteed that I would get radio and television coverage, but had also ensured that the public would actually want to come and see me for themselves at public meetings.

The night before the censure vote I appeared on Thames Television's *Reporting London*. The programme had been planned in the summer when Alan Hargreaves had suggested a format in which a panel of editors of those newspapers which had been most critical would question me on live television, giving viewers the chance to make up their own minds about who was lying. My press officer, Veronica Crichton, and I jumped at the idea but as the date got nearer, one editor after another dropped out. By the final week every editor had withdrawn except for Max Hastings, who was representing the *Standard*. I thought it revealed the deep lack of confidence that the editors of the *Mail, Express* and *Sun* had in their own stories; not one of them was prepared to defend them in live debate in front of their readers. On the programme I explained my position on Ireland and made it clear that no one on the GLC supported the use of violence to achieve political ends. I emphasized that I believed that there had to be a political solution and that the Government's insistence on a military victory was simply prolonging the agony. As I came out of the studio Harvey Hinds phoned with congratulations and over the next few days I received a flood of supportive letters from viewers. I did not realize it at the time but from that point on the tide began to turn on the issue of my support for a united Ireland.

We immediately expanded our strategy to counter the press. As well as making radio and television appearances I also undertook a programme of up to 300 meetings a year. Two or three evenings and one or two lunchtimes a week I had public meetings, and I had sometimes four or five at weekends. We decided to target groups who were not normally Labour supporters. In particular, I concentrated on key influential groups such as City audiences who had influence with Government ministers. Over the life of the administration this strategy paid off. We were able to get respectable City institutions to support our claims for more resources for London and also, when the time came, to oppose abolition.

Although I was still optimistic about our chances of surviving through to the next election the general view of those outside the Labour Group was that I would not. In a rather florid speech to the Young Tories on 24 October, George Tremlett summed up the perception of many when he said:

> Although he may still be Leader in title of the GLC, Mr Livingstone is a prisoner of events. His days as Leader are numbered . . . In politics, the substance of power is actually a strange mysterious thing that few recognize when they hold it in their hands.
>
> 'Power is something that leading politicians acquire by commanding the respect of others by the force of their personality. By the way in which they exercise the authority of leadership, successful politicians holding important office can persuade others to make decisions which should be taken . . . Our system of government has developed . . . subtle checks and balances built into that system to prevent the abuse of power . . . And it is ignoring this feature of our system that is the fundamental error of Mr Livingstone and the little group of extremists who temporarily have control at County Hall.
>
> 'Mr Livingstone has been personally offensive to the Queen, to her children, to Members of Parliament and to the Metropolitan Police Commissioner. He has sought to undermine the work of the Police and the Government. And therein lies his downfall . . . By seeking to undermine the institutions of the State, Mr Livingstone has shown himself to be totally unfit to occupy the position he presently holds. His supporters are dwindling. Those who realize that he is no longer a credible figure, and they include his Front Bench colleagues and the Senior Officers of the Council, recognize that a discredited man is not someone to whom they can go for a decision in the belief that his recommendation will be endorsed by his Party. The power was in his hands. Now it has gone.

Temporarily there is a vacuum at County Hall . . . The moment comes when an elected leader, or in more ancient times a leader who seized power by other means, loses his authority. He may linger on, like some pathetic stag who has lost his potency, but one knows that the inevitability of history is that a younger stag or a more virile stag will destroy him and take over his herd. It always has been thus in the animal kingdom. It was always thus in the Middle Ages. You only have to read the writings of Machiavelli or the history of the Tudors and Plantagenets to realize that . . . Until London is rid of him and the Labour Party has shed itself of those people within its ranks who are seeking power in order to destroy the State and not serve its people, we shall never have a healthy society in London. Nor shall we have peace of mind within the State itself.

It would be nice to think that as the press attacks mounted we could have looked to the Parliamentary Labour Party (PLP) for support. But the reverse was the case. The more we were attacked the more the PLP dissociated itself from the Labour administration. Part of our problem was that several of London's Labour MPs were planning to defect to the SDP during the second half of 1981 and they therefore took every opportunity to join in the chorus of Tory-led abuse in the days before they defected. One particular problem was Ron Brown (MP for Hackney South), the younger brother of Lord George Brown. Until he defected to the SDP, Brown was the chair of the London Labour Group of MPs. He did everything possible to sour relations between Labour MPs and the GLC and acted as one of the main sources of unfavourable rumours about the Labour administration. Several times he told London Labour MPs that he had invited me to address their regular monthly meetings. Many of them made a special effort to attend but I failed to appear as Brown had never actually invited me. Nothing was more likely to annoy busy MPs, who not unreasonably felt that I was treating them in a cavalier fashion.

As the SDP surged ahead of Labour in the opinion polls it became convenient for rightwing Labour MPs to blame the cause of Labour's decline on the GLC. They managed to ignore the fact that polls conducted before the May election had shown massive potential support for the SDP and that the collapse of Labour support in London accurately mirrored what was happening elsewhere in the country.

Matters worsened dramatically during the Croydon North West by-election. When I heard in July that the local Tory MP had died I realized that the Tory whips would call the by-election on a date immediately after local ratepayers had received their supplementary rate demand to pay for the fares reduction. Having agreed the policy, there was nothing we could do to vary the time at which the rate demand went out as that was a matter for the local Tory-controlled Croydon Council. The by-election was called for 22 October and the local council helpfully arranged for the rate demand to be delivered at the beginning of the campaign. At the Labour Party Headquarters in Walworth Road it was decided that I should play no part in the campaign and I was discreetly informed that they would prefer it if I was not even seen canvassing in the area.

Only ten days before polling, Fleet Street were whipped into a frenzy by the *Sun*'s 'most odious man in Britain' reports of my remarks about the Chelsea barracks bombing. As luck would have it, the Liberal candidate in Croydon was none other than Bill Pitt, the NALGO representative with whom I had clashed so bitterly five years before on the issue of racism in Lambeth's Housing Department. He immediately pushed the issue of my remarks to the forefront of the campaign and announced that the Liberals were inviting me to their main election rally that weekend to justify my comments. Eddie Lopez was working for the Labour candidate and phoned me immediately, urging me to take up their offer as he believed I could defuse the issue. Acting on the belief that such a meeting could only be a success, I jumped at the idea and asked Eddie to clear it with the Labour Party. Their answer was that I should stay away. Although I thought they were wrong I respected their decision as it was up to Walworth Road to decide how the campaign should be run and lost.

Polling day followed the defeat of the Tory censure motion at the GLC. As expected, the Liberals won, and Bill Pitt provided the *Standard* with their headline: 'THANK YOU, MR LIVINGSTONE'. Michael Foot gave a confidential briefing to lobby journalists, saying that it was largely my fault. Roy Hattersley said it was a combination of my speech and the rate increase, and Ron Haywood, the General Secretary of the Labour Party, wished that I 'would concentrate on London more'. Predictably, the Fleet Street mob descended on me expecting a strident response to these attacks, but Veronica Crichton and I had agreed that the best thing to do was to play it down. As Michael Foot's only on-the-record comment was a mild 'I'm sure the GLC played its part in the disappointing result but that is not what I want to stress today', I could simply maintain that I did not believe he had blamed me. As the reporters were bound by the rules of lobby confidentiality they could not quote Michael directly. I dealt with Roy Hattersley's attack simply by pointing out that since 1964 Labour had won only one seat from the Tories at a by-election. I suggested that as he had been in Parliament since 1964 perhaps he might be prepared to accept part of the blame for this record rather than looking for a scapegoat elsewhere.

Labour's election record had been awful throughout the year. A month before the GLC election the Labour vote was down 11.7 per cent at the Glasgow Central by-election and in Warrington in July it was 13.3 per cent down. The 14.1 per cent decline in Croydon was not out of line with the general trend. Four weeks later the Labour vote declined by 15.9 per cent at the Crosby by-election. People could remember only too vividly the record of the last two Labour Governments and they were not persuaded that another one would do any better. This view was reinforced by the Labour Shadow Cabinet, who gave the impression that they had lost the will to govern and did not themselves believe in the policies which the Labour conference had adopted. One of them said to me, 'If I woke up tomorrow and found we had won an election I'd leave the country.' The air of defeatism that pervaded the PLP had communicated itself to the public, who now had an alternative opposition party to turn to. With the extensive media hype being organized around the SDP at that time, many people did precisely that.

A week after the Croydon North West by-election we suffered

a further blow when the SDP won St Pancras North in a GLC by-election, thus reducing our majority from eight to six. The by-election had been caused by Anne Sofer, who had defected to the SDP and resigned her seat to fight a parliamentary by-election under her new colours.

The left had originally voted to co-opt Anne Sofer on to the Education Committee before she was elected in her own right in 1977. As an active campaigner for parents' rights she usually voted with the left in her first few years at County Hall and when I nominated her as vice-chair of the Schools sub-committee she was opposed by both Sir Ashley Bramall and Mair Garside (Leader and deputy leader of the ILEA), who were worried that her support of parents' rights would alienate the leadership of the teachers' unions. Once she became chair of the sub-committee she soon developed a close working relationship with Sir Ashley and Mair and increasingly voted against the left. This process accelerated rapidly during 1980 as the shift to the left in the National and London Labour Parties led to an increasingly contemptuous attitude towards the Labour Party from Anne Sofer, Margaret Morgan and Mair Garside. Whereas Margaret and Mair often became quite bitter, Anne Sofer did not allow her political differences to change her generally friendly attitude.

When the left took control of the ILEA in May 1981, the left caucus decided as part of the policy of 'taking prisoners' (keeping the Labour majority intact by giving the right wing positions so that they would not be tempted to defect) to offer her the chair of the Development sub-committee in place of Schools, which was to be chaired by Frances Morrell, the new deputy leader of the ILEA. Because it would have meant displacing Margaret Morgan she refused and retired to the backbenches where, until her resignation, she specialized in irritating Frances Morrell. Only one thing had changed politically between her election as a Labour councillor (when she had known the contents of our manifesto and had been perfectly aware that the left would take over both the ILEA and GLC Labour Groups) and when she suddenly discovered that it was unacceptable to continue as a Labour councillor.

But that one change was crucial. In May, the SDP had officially decided to contest the elections and the 'unofficial' candidates had all lost. By October, they were more than happy to fight a by-election. George Page was particularly annoyed that Anne Sofer had tricked the Labour Party in this way but I felt that her decision to resign and contest a by-election mitigated the offence, even though she had waited until the Warrington by-election and the opinion polls gave her a fairly certain signal that she would be re-elected.

The St Pancras North result was exactly in line with Croydon North West and Crosby. Soon after, another Labour member defected. This new defection reduced our majority to four and further weakened the right wing within the Labour Group. I had known Paul Rossi for over a decade since he had become active in Lambeth – in fact, in 1976 he was one of the Labour counciliors who voted to expel Ted Knight and several others of us from the Labour Group. He had not made much of an impact at Lambeth, where he developed a weighty speaking style and started smoking a pipe in order to appear older, and he was no more successful at the GLC. His defection took some time as he changed his mind twice under constant lobbying by the right wing to stay and fight the left from inside the Labour Party. He had no intention of resigning his Lewisham East seat – unlike St Pancras North the SDP had no party organization there whatsoever and there was no certainty of winning.

On 6 November, a week after the St Pancras by-election, Michael Heseltine introduced into Parliament his much-heralded new legislation to control local council expenditure. Immediately after the GLC election he had announced that local councils were planning to spend £800 million more than the Government was prepared to allow and warned that unless councils cut back to the Government's target he intended to withhold £450 million of Government grant as a penalty. A full £102 million of that penalty was to be borne by the fourteen councils of which Labour had won control four weeks earlier. The budget we had inherited from Sir Horace Cutler after four years of savage cuts which had reduced GLC staff by 6,000 was £456 million but this was still £50 million above what the Government allowed. The penalty Heseltine was to impose on the

GLC was £5.6 million and to comply would have meant getting rid of another 800 jobs. The inherited budget was already based on 750 jobs being cut and to concede to the Government's demand would have meant going back on every pledge we had given the electorate.

A majority of councils gave in and offered up £196 million of cuts but the new Labour councils voted to carry out their election promises and increased their budgets by £211 million – more than half of that from County Hall alone. Heseltine's response was to announce that he would push new legislation through Parliament that would make it illegal for councils to spend more than the Government wanted. It was this threat which led Ted Knight, Matthew Warburton (his deputy in Lambeth) and I to set up the *Labour Herald*, a leftwing weekly paper whose main task was to try to co-ordinate the resistance to the new proposals. When the bill was introduced to Parliament it confirmed all our worst fears. The Government would tell each council how much it could spend and if a council wanted to exceed that limit it would have to win a referendum of all local voters. The catch was that commercial ratepayers would be protected so that the cost of the extra spending would fall on domestic ratepayers only. As commercial ratepayers were paying 62 per cent of the rate bill of the GLC this would make the cost to domestic ratepayers so large that there would be no chance of our winning such a referendum.

Had these proposals become law, local government would have been brought under central government control so effectively that there would have been no point in voting at local elections. There was no way that I could support the sort of cuts and fare increases which Heseltine would have demanded, nor did I believe it was right to try to increase the rates on a scale which would have placed an intolerable burden on ordinary ratepayers. My only alternatives were to resign, which would have been seen as leaving others to do the dirty work, or to refuse to carry out the new law and try to build public support for the inevitable legal and constitutional clash which would follow. We used the *Labour Herald* to campaign for the latter alternative and I presented a paper to the group along those lines proposing such a policy.

The debate inside the Labour Group and on the Regional

Executive was much the same as during the 1972 Housing Finance Act and 1984 ratecapping debates. Two-thirds of the Labour Group voted to endorse my paper and the press immediately complained that we were refusing to uphold the law. They were particularly upset with my proposal that MPs should 'take all measures necessary to delay and disrupt parliamentary business in order to prevent the passing of this legislation'. They seemed to feel that I was urging Michael Foot to perpetrate some outrage such as strangling the Speaker. Nor were they happy with my call for industrial action in defence of services, but I had no doubt that without such action we were doomed to defeat. In the initial meetings with trade unions we received very positive promises of support.

My worry was that with one-third of the Group opposed to the policy and the threat of surcharge hanging over us, we had little chance of getting the policy agreed in the Council chamber. Some members complained that as the Camden surcharge case was due to be heard in the spring and I was likely to be surcharged for the £60 a week minimum wage scheme, I had nothing to lose over a case involving the GLC. There was endless media speculation on various scenarios in which the Council voted to comply with the new rates act and the administration then disintegrated as the Labour Group split apart in Council meetings faced with each cut proposed by the officers. The truth is that the situation was so complicated that nobody knew what would happen.

Michael Heseltine was later forced to drop his bill after a Tory backbench revolt against the concept of referenda.

In the same week following the St Pancras by-election defeat we discovered that on 23 October a new organization called the 'Keep London Free Campaign' had been set up at a secret gathering of over forty-five top business directors and company secretaries. Led by Sir Charles Forte, who made a 'generous donation', the organization included representatives from Cadbury Schweppes, Taylor Woodrow, GEC, Blue Circle, Tate & Lyle, Sainsbury, Allied Breweries, Beechams, Lazards, Ladbrokes and De La Rue, and for some strange reason Kingsley Amis. In total, £200,000 was collected to establish two funds to be managed by Aims of Industry, a rightwing group influential in Tory business circles. Half was to be spent on legal actions against the GLC and the rest on a propaganda campaign to alert the public to the 'abuse of power' at County Hall and get the Government to 'look again' at the possibility of abolishing the GLC. Since many of the companies did business with the GLC, they remained anonymous behind a committee of Tory MPs, councillors and individuals such as Dr Roger Scruton, a rightwing philosopher, and Alfred Sherman, at the time a member of Mrs Thatcher's think-tank, the Centre for Policy Studies.

The idea of a group of private companies operating behind closed doors to block the policies of a democratically elected authority had a slightly sinister air about it, reminiscent of the moves against the Government of Dr Allende in Chile which opened the way to the 1973 coup. When we started enquiring about the names of the companies concerned, most of them put profit before principle and quietly withdrew from the fray. A publicity campaign appeared in the run-up to the borough council elections in May 1982, but once Tory-controlled Bromley, Kensington and Westminster Councils started using ratepayers' money to take legal action against the GLC there was no real need for big business to do so.

The final straw in that week following the by-election defeat came on Friday 6 November when Bill Bush presented me with his detailed analysis of the by-election. This showed that in a full GLC election the SDP and Liberals would win a huge majority of seats, reducing the size of both Labour and Tory Groups to barely double figures. My own marginal seat of Paddington would not have been one of the survivors and it was a fair assessment when Bill said, 'I doubt if there's a seat in London, except perhaps Brent South, where we could get you elected at the moment.'

That weekend one of my closest friends was taken into hospital for major surgery. I was worried enough without thinking about the future, but the sheer number of different directions from which we were under attack kept coming to mind. I did not doubt that the positions I had taken on the whole range of controversial issues had been right. They were the things I had believed in and fought for for years and I was certainly not going to let the owners of Fleet Street force me to back down. Had I done so, there would have been no further useful role for me to play in politics. Fleet Street would always be prepared to run their campaigns again; once you

184

had shown that you could be forced to back down on one issue, you effectively gave them a veto over all your future actions. Yet the cost of standing firm had been both high and painful. I seriously doubted whether we could pull back to get within striking distance of winning the next GLC election in 1985.

It had been right to raise the issues of racism, sexual politics and Ireland. It had been right to refuse to cut our spending programmes. But there was no certainty of victory ahead or even that we could survive our first budget meeting, which was only fifteen weeks away. The damage done to my public reputation by the press was clearly revealed by the opinion polls. It was so extensive that I realized that I might actually have reached a point where I was unelectable to anything in the future.

Fortunately the public support I did have was absolutely solid and so positive that it kept me going through all the abuse, but I had to face the prospect that the cost of my political beliefs might be very high: I could become a marginalized figure whose eventual defeat would overshadow and damage the issues I had tried to raise. However, I was certain that in October there was nowhere left to go but up. What I did not know was that during that weekend in November Lord Denning was making the final adjustments to what was to be the most controversial judgement of his career. A judgement which helped to lift us off the bottom of the polls and start us on an ascent which would turn the most unpopular GLC administration of all time into the most popular, all in the space of just three years.

With everybody else putting the boot into the GLC, the judges felt it was their turn next but with unbelievable stupidity they decided to attack us on the one issue where we occupied the high ground and enjoyed overwhelming public support: fares.

6

Here Comes the Judge

No one in the Labour Group believed that the vast majority of judges were anything other than a politically conscious arm of the establishment. We were confirmed in our view by Sir Robert Megarry's judgement in the High Court on 18 September on the issue of council house sales.

In the Labour manifesto we had spelt out our opposition to the sale of council housing. Most inner boroughs had about 10,000 families on their waiting lists and thousands more tenants were elderly people or families with children trapped in unsatisfactory high-rise accommodation. Each year about one per cent of London's housing stock in both the private and public sectors became so run down as to require complete modernization, and house prices in London had risen to the point where the majority of young families could no longer afford to buy in the private sector. The response of the Tory GLC between 1977 and 1981 had been to reduce the new house-building programme from 7,000 starts a year to 35. From the moment Mrs Thatcher won the 1979 election it was housing which suffered the greatest cuts, with new house-building reduced by about 80 per cent. Selling council houses in such a situation is little short of criminal. The Tory argument, that tenants might as well buy the homes they live in as no one else can move in, ignores the fact that between two and four per cent of council housing becomes vacant each year because tenants either die or move into the private sector. The GLC used to get 6,000 to 8,000 vacancies arising this way each year. Each sale reduces the pool of housing from which re-lets are available. It is usually the most desirable homes which are sold off so that councils are left with only their less desirable homes for those in need, accelerating the trend for council estates to become the ghettos of the poor.

I have no objection in principle to the sale of council houses in those areas where the waiting lists have been tackled. Indeed, in such areas I would have no objection to *giving* the homes to those sitting tenants who have paid for them through their rent over the years. But in an area with a housing crisis on the scale of that which London faces, I have opposed the sales policy at every stage. In drawing up the manifesto, however, we recognized that there was nothing we could do to stop the policy. Tenants had a legal right to buy the homes they lived in and it would have been wrong for the GLC to abuse its power in a way which penalized individual tenants instead of attacking the Government which was responsible for the situation.

Our problem was that the previous Tory GLC administration had gone way beyond simply letting tenants buy their own homes. Under George Tremlett's direction they had set out to liquidate the entire GLC housing department by any means at their disposal. Immediately after the 1977 election a nearly completed estate of 500 flats at Brentford Dock (in the constituency of Brentford and Isleworth, which the Tories had held by under one per cent at the previous election) was withdrawn from letting and passed over to an upmarket estate agent to sell. No preference was given to Londoners or those in housing need. Instead, because they worked on a percentage commission, the estate agents had an interest in forcing the prices up. They got the Tories to agree to keep most of the flats empty for up to four years on the grounds that if they were all sold at once it would depress the market and lower the price. The cost of a three-bedroom flat was now £70,000, which in 1977 effectively priced them out of the market for all but the higher income bracket. As the area was convenient for Wood Lane, the flats soon became attractive to BBC television executives, few of whom had ever been on a council waiting list. No newspaper complained about the moral aspect of leaving several hundred homes empty for up to four years in a city with over 100,000 families on waiting lists.

At first, George Tremlett concentrated the sale of empty council homes in marginal constituencies such as Brentford and Paddington, but later the policy spread to include sales in more rundown areas. With the 1981 election approaching, the Tories faced the dilemma that housing schemes which had started during the Goodwin administration would not be completed before the election. Their response was to establish a form of private company called Estmanco with which the council then entered into a contract, so that as estates became available for letting they were passed over to the company to be sold off.

By the time we won the election over 400 houses were involved. The bulk of these were in a politically vital ward in Hammersmith held by the Liberals, who were supporting a Tory administration on the hung council. Most of the rest were in my own marginal constituency of Paddington, which confirmed as far as the Labour Group were concerned that the Tories' motivation for their sales programme had more to do with the electoral chances of the local Tory party than the housing needs of Londoners.

We decided that where contracts for sale had been signed we would honour them but that the remaining 418 empty houses would be allocated to families from the waiting list. Those people who had already purchased homes decided to take us to court to force us to sell the rest: they did not wish to have council tenants living on their estate, fearing that this would reduce the value of their property.

We consulted Sir Frank Layfield, one of the most respected Establishment lawyers in Britain, who warned us that the courts might award damages against the GLC, although if we spelt out the desperate need for homes for rent in London he thought we would most likely win the right to let, forcing the few owner-occupiers to settle for financial compensation. In a smart move by our opponents, the first case to reach the court was that of Mrs Frances Cope, a 67-year-old widow who 'had bought the flat with her life's savings'.

It was outrageous enough that British judges would award compensation to people for the fact that they had to share an estate with council tenants, but Sir Robert Megarry went beyond that. Contemptuously dismissing our arguments and the needs of those on the waiting list, he made plain his own attitude towards the new GLC administration. In his judgement on 18 September he accused the Council of 'abusing its power' and went on:

Plainly, those who know that they are dealing with a trickster who will seek escape by any loophole, however dishonest, must seek to tie him up so tightly that escape is impossible.

'But these purchasers and their solicitors are dealing with the GLC, and doubtless they considered that they were dealing with a great body which would honourably carry out its agreements. It ill becomes a Council intent on not performing its contracts to taunt the victims with their failure to foresee its untrustworthiness. This is a shabby contention.

The same day Michael Heseltine announced that he was rejecting our plans to build 1,500 new homes. It began to seem as if the GLC role in tackling London's housing crisis was being wound up by a coalition of the Tory Government and the judiciary.

The one area where we were confident that the judges could not interfere in our policies was on the issue of the fares reduction. Since 1970, successive GLC administrations had increased and reduced the level of subsidy to London Transport fares as they believed right. The 1969 Transport (London) Act, which had transferred control of London Transport to the GLC, laid down that the GLC could 'direct the Executive to submit proposals for an alteration in the Executive's fare arrangements to achieve any object of general policy specified by the Council'. While the Act was being debated in Parliament in 1968, Richard Marsh, the Transport Minister, stated:

> The main powers that the GLC will have . . . will be to pay grant to the executive for any purpose it thinks fit . . . If the Council wishes the executive to do something that will cause it to fall short of its financial targets, it will itself have to take financial responsibility for it. The Council might wish . . . to keep fares down at a time when costs are rising and there is no scope for economies. It is free to do so.

The same point was made by Mrs Thatcher, who was Shadow Transport Minister at the time. She referred in her main speech to Mr Marsh's statement that 'if the council decided that the Executive had to operate services which would make it uneconomic, the Council would have to provide a subsidy from the rates'. She had no objections to that at all.

As the bill wound its way through committee, more and more Tories emphasized the freedom of the GLC (which was then under Tory control and likely to remain so for several years) to charge the ratepayers for fares subsidy. Michael Heseltine said, 'That would mean that the London Transport Executive would receive a grant from the GLC. That situation could easily arise, and many people would argue that would be right – that it would be better to subsidise those uneconomic services from the rates than to put up the fares for all the travellers.' In ten days in committee, and two more days in the House of Commons, not a single MP suggested that a fares subsidy from the rates would be contrary to the aim of the bill, which was passed without a division. The government ministers thanked Mrs Thatcher for her co-operation.

The transport working party which had prepared that section of our manifesto had spent six months studying the issue and throughout that time had had the private advice of the relevant GLC and LT officials as we devised the policy. There had then been six months of public debate before the fares policy was formally included in the manifesto, where it became the main issue of the election. Following our election victory in 1981, a very enthusiastic Sir Peter Masefield submitted a scheme for an overall 25 per cent fares reduction – which he had been planning for months – and the introduction of a simplified zonal fares system, which had also been promised in our manifesto. The first Masefield plan involved fare increases in several areas in order to bring in the zonal system. There is no doubt that many Londoners would have felt conned if, having voted for a fares reduction, they had seen their own fares rise and, moreover, most of the increases were in central London where it was most important to try and reduce car commuter traffic. We therefore asked Sir Peter to prepare the cheapest possible scheme in which no fare was increased but which still allowed us to introduce the simplified zonal fare system. Two schemes were put out to consultation at a series of public meetings conducted by Dave Wetzel and Paul Moore throughout London.

The Labour Group finally agreed an overall 32 per cent reduction, which came into effect on 4 October, increasing our subsidy of LT's total costs from 29 per cent to 56 per cent. In real terms, this returned fares to the level at which they had been at the end of the 1973–75 fares freeze under the Goodwin administration. It was also the level of fares in real terms which had been in operation when the Tory-controlled GLC inherited the system from the government in 1969. Sir Horace Cutler had planned to increase fares by 22 per cent immediately after the election, and there was therefore a £26 million gap in the budget which Sir Horace had not drawn attention to during the campaign. We had to finance this as well by increasing the rate.

The Government made life difficult for us in two ways. First of all Michael Heseltine imposed a £119 million clawback of government grant. Thus, on top of finding the £100 million to reduce fares, ratepayers had to cover the £26 million deficit left by Sir Horace and the £119 million fine imposed on them by Michael Heseltine as a punishment for voting for a Labour Party committed to reducing fares. Instead of having to pay the 25p a week that we had promised when the manifesto was published for public consultation in April 1980, the average domestic ratepayer now had to pay 65p a week. For the average family this was still a bargain as their weekly LT fares bill was reduced by many times that amount, depending on how many members of the family used LT and how far they travelled. Those who did not use LT did not wholly lose out: there were other benefits, such as reduced congestion, fewer accidents and less pollution as the number of private cars coming into London declined dramatically. Some pensioners felt aggrieved, but they had been enjoying the benefit of free travel on the tube since June 1981 and we had also lifted the restriction on the use of their travel passes during the afternoon rush hour. All Londoners were benefiting from the improved service as we recruited more staff and managed to get more buses back on the roads.

The second way in which the Government could make life more difficult was by forbidding British Rail to reduce its fares in line with those of LT. Because the tube barely serves South London we had made a commitment in our manifesto to subsidize all British

Rail suburban services within the GLC area to the same extent as the tube. To make travel simpler and more attractive we planned to introduce a common ticketing policy for tubes, buses and British Rail trains so that one ticket could be used on all three systems. I met with officials of BR before the election and put the plan to them. After consultations they came back to me with an agreement. However, they pointed out that the Government had a veto over how much money they could receive from external sources. This power had been introduced to prevent BR from borrowing more than Government policy allowed; it was never intended to be used to prevent a sensible policy of integrating fares.

As soon as he would grant us a meeting, Dave Wetzel and I went to see Norman Fowler, who was then Secretary of State for Transport. Fowler was by turns remote and kittenish; his attitude was that we were all 'men of the world'. Upper-class pleasantries over tea were followed by a pompous lecture about the necessity of cutting public spending and an anguished plea not to cut the fares. He admitted that there was nothing he could do to stop us as we were acting within the Council's legal powers, but made it clear that if we went ahead and gave a £20 million subsidy to British Rail he would reduce the Government's subsidy to BR by an equivalent £20 million. Fowler ended the meeting with yet another flood of pleasantries and begged us to come back and see him again.

Reporters were waiting outside and we delivered an impromptu denunciation, making it clear that we would not allow Fowler's blackmailing of British Rail to prevent us from going ahead with the fares cut on LT. Almost all of the papers ignored the story. The Government's decision would prevent a fares cut to hundreds of thousands of Londoners, the majority of whom were likely to be Tory voters, but the Tory papers decided this was not news their readers needed to know. The *Standard*, which always pretended to defend commuters, could have won massive popular support by opposing and campaigning against such an unfair decision, but chose instead to toe the party line, and after reporting that the meeting had taken place, let the issue drop.

We pressed ahead. Although Anne Sofer absented herself from the vote (so that she could oppose the supplementary rate during her October by-election campaign) and the Liberal Adrian Slade voted against us in the lobbies, the July Council meeting agreed the fares reduction.

During July, the Leader of Bromley Council, Dennis Barkway, persuaded his Tory Group to take the GLC to court on the grounds that the fares reduction was an unreasonable decision and that Bromley did not get the same benefit as those boroughs which were served by the tube system. He did not, of course, condemn the decision of Norman Fowler, which had deprived his mainly British Rail-using residents of the full benefit of our cheap fares policy. No one rushed to join Bromley in the court action as the other Tory borough leaders shared the view of Peter Bowness (Croydon) that the GLC was within its legal powers in cutting the fares. Similarly, not one of the Tory MPs who condemned our decision, including Mrs Thatcher, ever questioned our legal rights in the matter.

The case started in the High Court on 28 October, just over three weeks after the fares reduction, and was heard by Lord Justice Dunn and Mr Justice Phillips. Bromley's counsel was David Widdicombe QC, who was later to be used by the Government to conduct two inquiries into the policies and practices of the new radical leftwing Labour councils. The judges rejected Widdicombe's argument that London Transport should be run as a business venture but said that complete abolition of fares would be illegal. Mr Justice Phillips stated that the GLC's fare reduction was at the margin of what was lawful. The judges rejected all Bromley's other points and awarded costs to the GLC.

As the case progressed, John Fitzpatrick, our chief solicitor, would report to me each night about how things had gone. It became clear that this was proving to be a tougher case than we had anticipated. Mr Justice Phillips's judgement that there were legal limits to the extent of subsidy effectively changed the meaning of the 1969 Transport (London) Act and gave an opening for further challenges. On 3 November, John Fitzpatrick returned with good news of the judgement, but was worried that Bromley might go to the Court of Appeal, where the Master of the Rolls, Lord Denning, held sway in an increasingly idiosyncratic way. Lord

Denning had become well known for a series of rightwing decisions against trade unions that had been reversed by the Law Lords. Denning appeared to dislike all things socialist (although he claimed his pensioner's free travel pass from the GLC). Indeed, shortly after his attack on the GLC fares policy there was a public outcry about one of his books. Following this he announced his retirement. John Fitzpatrick predicted that if Bromley appealed, Denning would insist on taking the case himself and finding in their favour. The GLC would then have to appeal to the Law Lords, whom Fitzpatrick expected once again to overturn Denning. Bromley knew Denning's background as well as we did and immediately appealed. Instead of the usual months or years that such a matter can take, Denning decided to hear the case within a week. Exercising his right to decide which two judges should hear the case with him, he chose an honest conservative in the form of Lord Justice Oliver and an extreme reactionary, Lord Justice Watkins.

After the judgement was handed down John Fitzpatrick appeared in my office almost in a state of shock. As he recovered with a strong cup of coffee, he said, 'Can I be frank? It was like sitting through a party political broadcast!' I had developed a great deal of respect for John in the preceding weeks, but his problem was that he believed in the British judicial system. He found it shocking to see the legal system to which he had dedicated himself being used in a political way, whereas I had expected nothing else. It was only when the judgements were examined in the cold light of day that the extent of the damage became obvious.

Lord Justice Watkins had fully justified Denning's faith in him.

> I have no doubt whatsoever that the large reduction of fares . . . arose out of a hasty, ill-considered, unlawful and arbitrary use of power. As a result, 5 ½ million people who daily use buses and trains in London pay about 30 per cent less for the privilege of doing so . . . ratepayers of the great City, who are unlikely to gain anything from it – many of them will in fact be at a loss – will bear the cost of what seems to many to have been an astounding decision.
>
> Those who come newly to govern people and who act in

haste in wielding power to which they are unaccustomed would do well to heed the words of Gladstone. He knew a great deal about power, and in 1890 [nine years before Denning was born] he said of it: 'The true test of a man, the test of a class, the true test of a people is power. It is when power is given into their hands that the trial comes.'

The new Leader of the new Greater London Council had hardly been put to that test when he, on 12 May 1981, sought out the Chairman of the Executive and, as seems beyond question, told him that the Council intended to put into effect forthwith a promise contained in an election manifesto to reduce fares by 25 per cent.

Lord Denning was in his element slapping down 'the enemy within', but one part of his judgement suggests an element of political bias. During the 1974 Labour Government the Tories had won control of Tameside Council, just before a scheme agreed under the previous Labour Council to introduce comprehensive education was due to come into effect. When the Tories reversed the decision to introduce the scheme, the Labour Government took the Council to court. Rejecting the Government's case, Lord Denning pointed out that the Tories had promised in their election manifesto that if elected they would save the grammar schools by reversing the decision, and that many people had voted for this policy. In the intervening years, the noble Lord seemed to have changed his mind about the value of election manifestos. Now he said that a manifesto issued by a political party in order to get votes was 'not to be taken as gospel'.

It was Lord Justice Oliver's judgement which was the most important, however. Perhaps because he avoided gratuitous political comments he did not get into the headlines, but his was the opinion that went on to dominate debate amongst the Law Lords. Oliver had completely recast the meaning of the 1969 Transport (London) Act. He ruled that Section 7 (3), which states that LT has a duty to balance its books as far as practicable, meant *without* a subsidy from the GLC. Only when massive fare increases and service cuts had shown that it was impossible to balance the books could a subsidy be given by the GLC. He was saying in effect that public transport should be run as a business. He also ruled with the others that we had been procedurally wrong in not rethinking the whole scheme after the election; that we had approached the decision with closed minds. All the work that had gone into preparing the manifesto was dismissed by the judges as legally irrelevant.

Once again we were besieged by the press, most of whom could not conceal their glee. But the mood of the PC/PCC when it met the following morning was optimistic. The Court of Appeal decision was so extreme that it would devastate London's public transport system if it was carried out. We could not believe that the Law Lords could fail to reverse the Court of Appeal decision once they contemplated its likely consequences. We realized though that whilst the Law Lords enjoyed putting Denning in his place by overturning his judgements, they undoubtedly disliked the Labour GLC even more. Therefore we expected to win on the substantive issues but lose on a technicality about our decision-making process. This would allow all sides to claim victory and leave us free to rectify the technicality without changing the fares system and damaging London Transport. We were so certain the cheap fares policy would be retained that we decided not to waste money preparing a publicity campaign to use if we lost the case.

We retained Robert Alexander QC to present our case. One of the top half-dozen barristers in the country, he had a detailed knowledge of the foibles and idiosyncrasies of each of the Law Lords. I offered to appear in court and explain how much work had gone into the preparation of the manifesto, but as in the previous hearings my offer was politely declined on the grounds that my presence might be offensive and inflammatory to the judges, thus prejudicing them against our case. When the names of the five judges who were to hear the case were announced, our lawyers were delighted. With Lords Scarman, Wilberforce, Brandon, Diplock and Keith we were assured that it was the most 'liberal' panel possible. As the case proceeded, John Fitzpatrick reported back each night with growing confidence. We were in the fortunate position that initial monitoring figures were pointing to the fares policy being a great success. Half a million more people were using London transport each day. Traffic congestion had eased because commuter cars entering London were down by the crucial three to four per cent that made the difference between traffic running smoothly or clogging up. We would not have them in time for the case, but we were certain that road-accident figures would also be well down.

On the morning of Thursday 17 December, I was late getting to County Hall as I had joined a picket in my constituency at St Mary's Hospital, which the Government was trying to close. I arrived just as the Law Lords were delivering their judgement and went straight to the news tickertape machine in the members' library. I read the printout with growing disbelief. Not only had we lost but we had lost on every substantive point of law. In effect, they had taken the Oliver judgement from the Court of Appeal and built on that to overturn legislation which had been in use for 12 years.

The five separate judgements spelt out that London Transport should be run on 'ordinary business principles'. In future the GLC would not be able to make grants to achieve any social policy ends, only to cover unavoidable losses. Lord Wilberforce accepted that there 'has been for some years discussion at the political level as to what extent public transport should be regarded as a social service' but he was 'unable to see, however carefully I re-read the 1969 Act, that Parliament had in that year taken any clear stance on it'. This was news to the 630 MPs who took precisely that view – as the quotations earlier in this chapter show, in particular the clause which spells out the power of the GLC to set fare levels 'to achieve any object of general policy specified by the Council'. The judges had picked over the 1969 Act and cobbled together those bits and pieces which when taken out of context could be used to overturn the will and intention of Parliament when it drafted the act.

Even more damaging to the whole of British local government was the decision of the Law Lords to revive the concept of fiduciary duty. This is an imprecise judge-made concept the origins of which grow out of the administration of the Poor Law in the last century. At that time, some boards of guardians were deemed by the courts to have been too generous with the provision of food and shelter to the starving and homeless and, after successful court actions, were forced to reimburse the ratepayers from their own pockets to the amounts the courts considered had been overspent. The most famous case arose in 1925, when the Poplar councillors were found guilty of a breach of the fiduciary duty to their ratepayers because they had agreed to pay equal wages to women employees. Law Lord Atkinson had condemned them for 'the vanity of appearing as model employers of labour', and allowing themselves 'to be guided . . . by some eccentric principles of socialistic philanthropy, or by a feminist ambition to secure equality of the sexes'. This was the guiding legal principle that the Law Lords chose fifty-six years later to exhume and impose on the running of London's transport system.

The basis of fiduciary duty is that the primary responsibility of the councillor is to safeguard the monies of the ratepayer. In any decision between increasing the rates and improving services, the duty of the councillor was to hold the balance in favour of the ratepayer. Such a concept was unjust in 1925, and since all governments since 1945 have required councils to expand their services as part of the overall provision of the welfare state, fiduciary duty was allowed to wither away. In 1955 in the *Prescott* v. *Birmingham Corporation* case, the judges had revived the concept in their judgement against the council (which had provided free travel for pensioners) only to see the then Tory Government rush legislation through Parliament to reverse their decision.

It was now obvious that we faced a judicial attempt to defeat our administration. I was shocked and angry: there seemed no way in which we could hit back at the judges. But I soon realized that if the Labour GLC survived this assault, it would be a defeat for the judges, and so as calmly as possible I set about the work of assuring that our budget would be carried in mid-February.

There were only four days to go before the Christmas break and three things needed to be got underway. Later that day in a press conference I announced that we were launching a campaign to force the Government to rush through emergency legislation to reverse the Law Lords' decision. Dave Wetzel was given the job with Valerie Wise of organizing an immediate publicity campaign. Maurice Stonefrost and John Fitzpatrick were asked to produce a full analysis of the judgement and its consequences, to be reported in an emergency Labour Group meeting the following Monday. Finally, a series of meetings needed to be organized: with Labour

MPs, to see what help they could give in pushing the issue in the Commons; with the trade unions, to discover the mood of the workforce and what actions we could expect from them; with Sir Peter Masefield, who was as horrified by the decision as we were, to see what action he would take; and finally, with David Howell, who had succeeded Norman Fowler as Secretary of State for Transport.

The administration faced its most serious crisis yet. Fortunately, it was one in which the whole Group would be united in outrage at the Law Lords' decision, even if, as was almost certain, we would split once again on the issue of whether or not to comply with the law. I knew that the Labour Group faced the sort of defeat which could demoralize it, bringing to an end the radical post-election phase which had been so short-lived in the other three Labour Groups of which I had been a member. I therefore decided that the Group should take no decisions in the Monday meeting, when councillors would still be shell-shocked. I saw the D-G, Stonefrost and Fitzpatrick and asked them for how long we could delay having the Council meeting that would decide the issue. They accepted that members needed time to consider all the issues, and agreed to wait until 12 January for a decision.

By Monday's Group meeting the officers had been able to work out what the judgement entailed. As a planned subsidy was illegal, we would have to reach the point where either LT made a profit or fares became so high that each increase lost more income from passengers quitting the system than it brought in from fares. The estimate was that in order to reach this point and comply with the law we should increase fares by 200 per cent. We would also have to close down those bus routes which made the greatest losses and about ten per cent of the tube system. A quarter of LT's workforce would lose their jobs in what would be the biggest retrenchment of any public transport system in history. The officers advised that fares should be doubled immediately with a further 100 per cent increase during August. As the Law Lords had made any social subsidy illegal, free travel for pensioners and the disabled would also have to end.

It was Paul Boateng who pointed out that of all the judges

involved none was more open to a charge of hypocrisy than Lord Scarman. He had only just completed his inquiry into the Brixton disorders of April 1981 and had written movingly of the deprivation and poverty suffered by the people of the area. Yet the ink was barely dry on his report and he was doing more to worsen the quality of life of Londoners in general and the poor in particular than anyone but the Prime Minister herself.

Many such comments about the judges were made as the Group meeting wore on. I recognized only too well the same mood that had seized the Camden Labour Group during its surcharge crisis. One or two councillors were worried about surcharge but the Group accepted my advice that no decision was required before 12 January and so we agreed to meet again on the 11th finally to decide our policy. I went to work to assemble a majority for non-compliance with the Law Lords' decision. I was absolutely certain that there was no way that we could spend the coming six months voting through a series of cuts which would devastate transport services in London, especially since the Government would be only too happy to sit back and watch Londoners turn angrily on a GLC that carried out such a policy. As well as destroying LT it would tear open the Labour Party in London in an orgy of recrimination which could lead to the end of the administration. If the high-profile leftwing GLC was seen to collapse, it would be used against the left for years to come as an example to prove they could not govern. If instead the GLC refused to comply with the Law Lords' decision it would throw the ball firmly into the Government's court, making it impossible for them to resist our demand for emergency legislation to clarify the position.

Part of our problem was that LT's lawyers were advising Sir Peter Masefield that a fare increase of 150 per cent would conform to the judgement, while for the Government David Howell was claiming that 60 per cent was enough. Dave Wetzel and I met Sir Peter to go over the various scenarios. He must have thought we were mad when we said we intended to try for non-compliance, but he was too polite to show it. He explained that if the GLC rejected the fare increase, LT would be heading for a serious financial crisis. 'What would you do?' I asked Sir Peter. After a long pause he replied, 'I should have to continue to run the service until the Government steps in. I have the powers and if necessary we would borrow to cover the deficit.'

It was the answer Dave and I had wanted to hear. Sir Peter's response to GLC non-compliance would maximize pressure on the Government. Undoubtedly the media would go mad with condemnations of our lawlessness, but there was no way that the Government could allow themselves to be seen to be responsible for the devastation of LT. They would be forced to act.

After a very short Christmas break, Dave and I were back in the building lobbying other Labour councillors and preparing the publicity campaign to 'Keep Fares Fair'. The trade unions decided to start their campaign with a one-day strike and the prospect of an indefinite stoppage if the Government failed to intervene. We set aside £300,000 for campaign publicity and began working with trade unions, commuter, and other community groups to mobilize opposition to the Law Lords. The style and methods were a forerunner of the anti-abolition campaign. Politicians, workers and the travelling public formed an alliance. We shared control with the outside groups in the running of the campaign by the simple expedient of co-opting representatives of commuters and transport workers on to our campaign committee.

As the press woke up to the implications of the judgement, their initial pleasure at our defeat was replaced by a realization that the judges had gone so far over the top that there was bound to be a backlash. Londoners saw the new fare system at work and decided they wanted to keep it. The newspapers saw their readers marching off in a new pro-GLC direction and reluctantly decided they had better follow them or risk losing customers.

The judges also realized that they had miscalculated. Although all of them had applied for their pensioner's free travel pass, they seldom used them and had not been aware of how well the fares cut had been received. In contrast they did, of course, spend a considerable amount of time in the company of those business interests that owned the large office blocks of central London whose rates had contributed so much of the funding of the scheme. But that could not be the only reason that they had taken their decision to pervert completely the meaning of the 1969 Transport Act. In his book *The Politics of the Judiciary*, which has become the definitive and highly readable text on the subject, Professor John Griffiths examines the whole affair as one of the most revealing cases about the political role of judges within the system.

> It may be, of course, that the Court of Appeal and the Law Lords deliberately intervened to control the collectivist policies of the administration at County Hall because they disapproved of those policies. But in addition and perhaps more significantly, they seem not to have understood what they were doing, because they did not grasp the nature of the problem of London Transport . . . Administrators were stupefied and dismayed by what seemed to them to be arbitrary and wholly unrealistic sets of reasons advanced . . . for upsetting an attempt to solve the problems . . . of London Transport.
>
> The judgements . . . demonstrate how ill-suited is judicial review to the examination of administrative policies. They show how the narrow approach of the courts . . . leads to a misunderstanding of the purpose of legislation . . . combined with the application of a broad principle (fiduciary duty) to the examination of the exercise of administrative discretion, the mismatch becomes almost total. We do not know to what extent the members of the two courts sought to inform themselves of the recent developments in transport policy . . . By choosing to set the words of Section 7 (of the Transport Act 1969) dealing with financial accounting . . . over the policy provisions of sections 1 and 5 (the grants section) and by invoking the concept of fiduciary duty, the courts were able virtually to ignore social and economic factors which had produced the Act. Why did they make this choice?
>
> For the members of the Court of Appeal, one reason seems to have been their annoyance with the way the majority group implemented their manifesto commitment. In the House of Lords . . . the reason for the choice seems to have been primarily the Law Lords' strong

preference for the principles of the market economy with a dislike of heavy subsidization for social purposes. These decisions were in the tradition of individual rather than social, private rather than collective enterprise ... whether or not their Lordships were politically biased, their habits of thought determined their decision.

I have no doubt that the majority of judges found the Labour GLC and all its works so radical and offensive that they were determined to screw us into the ground whenever they could. It is impossible to read the judgements of McGarry, Denning, Watkins and the Law Lords without being aware of a distaste bordering on loathing for a form of politics which they would characterize as belonging to 'the enemy within'. They had no qualms about interpreting the law in order to defend the Establishment from a politics that they saw as challenging the privileges of their own class. But they had made a tactical error. In the past when judges have twisted the law in order to undermine trade unions, individual dissidents or the rights of black immigrants, their decisions have only affected a handful of people. In the fares case the judges' decision hit the pockets of millions of public transport users in the most dramatic way.

Press criticism began to mount as the full implications of the judgement sank in. Whatever happened, the Government was going to have to pass legislation of some kind to clarify the position, even if only to save the pensioners' free travel. Dave Wetzel's well-publicized jibe about 'vandals in ermine' was soon overtaken by dozens of jokes about stupid judges, Tory judges and vindictive judges. Thirty Londoners got extensive publicity by hiring and wearing judges' robes, hijacking a bus and forcing it to drive to the House of Lords with television coverage of every minute of the stunt.

The publicity campaign was off and running in early January as the network of community groups began organizing on the ground. An early indication of the public response came when I spoke to a 'Keep Fares Fair' public meeting on the borders of Dagenham and Hornchurch on 7 January. I arrived just in time to see the backs of a disappearing contingent of the National Front. Seeing the size of the crowd, they had decided that discretion was the better part of thuggery. The meeting of several hundred people was electric and angry; older political activists present claimed that it was the largest public meeting in the borough since the Second World War. Whereas in the previous few months I had been speaking to packed and supportive meetings of party sympathizers and students, this was the first meeting in which the audience was composed mainly of the general public and it was being held in an area which had registered the highest swing to the Tories anywhere in Britain in the 1979 General Election. For that reason the turnout was significant and gave a great boost to the confidence of the Group.

Travelling home that evening I was elated. There was no underestimating the importance of that meeting. The tide had turned with a vengeance and public opinion was now shifting decisively behind our policies. I had no doubt that we were still a long way from being certain of winning majority support in an election, but the initiative had been dropped in our hands by the judges and I did not intend to let it go. I was also pleased that introducing me, Alan Williams (the Labour GLC member for Hornchurch) had made clear his commitment to my continuing as Leader of the GLC. This was significant as Alan was the most influential member amongst the centrists in the Labour Group and without his support no one could mount an effective leadership challenge. It was the first firm indication that the centre and right in the Group had accepted that we had recovered sufficiently from the media battering (which had reached its peak only ten weeks before) for the question of my continuing as Leader to be removed from the agenda. But the aspect of the meeting that gave me particular satisfaction was the number of members of the general public who, in making their contribution to the fares issue, digressed to condemn the press campaign against me and unleashed waves of applause. As with the judges, Fleet Street's over-confidence that they could get away with whatever they chose to write had finally led them to overreach themselves, and a public reaction was now underway.

On Sunday 10 January I arrived at County Hall to meet with fifteen leftwingers who I knew would solidly support the tactic of non-compliance. We pooled our knowledge of who was wavering and decided which of us should work on each individual. The figures did not look good. Harvey and Illtyd had always made it clear that whilst I could expect their support on everything else, they were not prepared to vote to break the law. Even worse was the news that Tony Hart (deputy whip) and Mike Ward considered my proposal unrealistic and intended to oppose it. This left six leftwingers who were still doubtful and three who could not get to the caucus meeting but had promised their support. Even if all the six doubtfuls came down on our side we only had 24 votes out of a Group of 48. If the Labour Group rejected my advice it would put me and five committee chairs in the impossible position of having to vote against the policy of the Labour Group in Council. Andrew McIntosh saw the possibilities open to him in such a situation and started lobbying hard over the phone from his High-gate home. He was interviewed by *Time Out* journalist David Rose and openly admitted that he intended 'to use the fares issue to try and force Livingstone to resign'. McIntosh's plan was to get the Group to vote for a fares increase and follow that with a decision to impose a whip on the issue. 'If Ken goes against a whip, I will call a special meeting of the party and move a vote of no confidence in him.'

As usual, my opponents in the Group had not done an effective lobbying job and had assumed that the six doubtfuls would come down on their side. I took no chances. I spoke to and pleaded with five of them, stressing that their vote was essential for the survival of the administration. The sixth, Gerry Ross, was away on holiday and could not be reached, although he was expected to return for the votes. Dave Wetzel had already decided that if the Group voted to comply with the judges' decision he would resign, and there was increasing support among left activists in *Briefing* for Keith Veness's proposal that if the fares went up the whole administration should resign and go into opposition as a protest against the judges.

I persuaded the left caucus to agree to support the proposal for a free vote before the Labour Group took a decision on the fares issue itself. As no rightwinger would be bound by the decision if it went our way there was no point in imposing a whip; that would only strengthen Andrew's hand if I lost the vote on the fares increase.

One member of the Labour Group, Simon Turney, was in the USA studying ways in which American fire services overcame racial discrimination. As the left caucus ended I managed to get hold of Turney and, knowing his position to be the same as Harvey and Illtyd's, I asked him to stay in the USA instead of flying back to the meeting. As I expected, he had been getting phone calls from the right wing urging him to return at once, but he obviously did not wish to return if he could avoid it. He finally agreed to stay in the USA and miss both the Group and the Council. This gave us a possible maximum vote of 24 out of 47 but only if all six doubtfuls voted with the left. I spent hours chasing to ensure that all 24 were present and voting at the Group meeting. Three of them still had doubts about the strategy.

When the Group finally assembled, the public gallery was packed with observers from London Labour parties. It was announced that the Regional Executive had just voted by 25 to 7 to call on the Labour Group to refuse to increase the fares, but that good news was more than offset by the revelation that Gerry Ross had sent his apologies for absence. The maximum possible vote for non-compliance was therefore 23 out of the 46 present in the room and in the event of a tied vote the chair of the Group, John Ward, would use his casting vote. Unfortunately he was opposed to non-compliance. I began the meeting by proposing that there should be a free vote in the Council and after some restrictive amendments this was agreed by 22 votes to 20 with four abstentions.

After I had moved the PC/PCC proposal for non-compliance with the Law Lords' decision, Mike Ward moved an amendment which had the effect of reversing the recommendation on the issue of compliance while retaining the various campaigning proposals. The debate raged back and forth and tension built up as each of the five doubtfuls came down against compliance. We were heading towards a tied vote of 23 to 23, in which my proposal would lose on the casting vote of the chair. Then, suddenly, Arthur Edwards, a rightwinger, left to go to another meeting in Newham where he was the chief whip on the borough council. I could not believe my luck.

Since the right wing had assumed that most of the five doubtfuls would vote with them to give a comfortable majority for compliance, they had not made certain that all their side stayed until the final vote. As the roll call vote proceeded it became clear that my proposals had won by 23 to 22 and the meeting was thrown into uproar. Andrew McIntosh sat looking like a beached whale and Mair Garside, who had kept up a running commentary of derogatory remarks about each leftwing speaker, exploded with disbelief. I went off to join an impromptu party in John Carr's room.

The next day the Council chamber was packed with reporters and television cameras as I rose to propose the Labour Group policy of non-compliance. Mike Ward had decided to accept the majority decision and vote with us. This gave us 24 votes with 22 against and the prospect of victory if the Tories carried out their warnings not to vote for a fare increase greater than 60 per cent. Sir Horace had arrived at that figure on the basis that it would restore fares to the level they were at before the reduction. This was in line with David Howell's claim that 60 per cent was all that was necessary to comply with the law.

The meeting was transformed by the Tory amendment. It was moved by Sir Horace with all his traditional bluster but when Sir James Swaffield gave his legal advice the Tories were thrown into disarray. Not to vote for the 100 per cent fares increase 'could mean that the Council was in breach of its statutory duty and in contempt of court'. Tory councillors were every bit as vulnerable to surcharge as Labour councillors if they failed to vote for the fares increase. Sir Horace, who was determined that Labour alone should carry the odium of the increase, wanted his Group to vote for 60 per cent and then abstain. As this would give us the chance of victory I was more than happy to move that the Council adjourn so that the Tories could sort themselves out. It was an unbelievable turn-around in party fortunes that at a meeting in which the media should have been concentrating on Labour's split, suddenly all eyes were on the unfolding drama which was tearing the Tories apart. Both Labour and Tory benches were laden with lawyers, all of whom seemed to be prepared to venture conflicting opinions which did nothing to calm the panic so clearly visible on Tory faces. If they got it wrong they stood to lose every penny they owned. Several of them were millionaires or had assets worth hundreds of thousands of pounds and had no desire to put it all at risk just so Sir Horace could make a political point at the expense of the Labour Party.

By early evening Labour's benches had been restored to complete confidence as speaker after speaker poured scorn on the Tories. With Labour leftwingers urging Sir Horace to keep his troops in line and Labour rightwingers raising the awful spectre of bankruptcy, the Tories could not even find any comfort outside the chamber. As was usual on Council nights many of them had brought their spouses up for dinner and the corridors were crammed with intense family debates as wives and husbands suddenly realized that even their homes were at risk of confiscation if the Tories got it wrong.

During the adjournment Sir Horace managed to win support for his policy of abstention. As soon as I heard this I gave the news to the Labour councillors who were reassembling to resume the meeting. Suddenly there was a real chance of winning the vote and I looked to see if any of the left were changing their minds. With the exception of Neil Davies, who had gone a sickly green, no one looked likely to change their position. I asked a couple of colleagues to take Davies to the bar, keep his mind off the topic and under no circumstances let any rightwingers get to him.

When we finally reached the division, the Alliance cast their three votes with 21 Labour compliers, as 24 Labour non-compliers passed through the opposite voting lobby. The chair of the Council intended to use his vote for compliance, so I knew we had lost, but along with most Labour colleagues could not help laughing at the disorder on the Tory benches. Most of them looked sick as dogs, uncertain how the vote had gone, and sat in stony silence glaring at Sir Horace's back. Suddenly three jumped up, pushed past their colleagues and squeezed through the opposite lobby to join the Labour right and the Alliance to give a final vote of 27 to 24 in favour of increasing the fares by 100 per cent.

My immediate response to our defeat was to announce that we were stepping up the campaign to force the Government to pass emergency legislation. Douglas Jay, the MP for Battersea North, had given notice that he intended to introduce a private members' bill to restore the position to what we had all assumed it to be. As the councillors drifted out of the chamber I told the press that we were committed to mobilizing public support for the Jay bill.

In the days that followed, the campaign to 'Keep Fares Fair' took off in a big way. We started advertising in newspapers, including a cut-out coupon to send to MPs. All over London mass meetings showed the growing public backlash. By now, all of our opponents realized that the judges had made a major error in blocking us on the fares policy. We commissioned opinion polls, which showed rapidly increasing support for our policy. London MPs were deluged with hundreds and in some cases thousands of letters and the coupons from our newspaper adverts. Tory MPs with marginal seats began to worry, and when Douglas Jay's private members' bill was voted on, 25 London Tory MPs managed to be absent so as not to have to vote against it. As the vote was read out, MPs were stunned to discover that even after both Margaret Thatcher and Norman Tebbit had gone through the lobby to bolster flagging Tory morale, the bill had won its first stage by 205 to 177. We demanded that the Government pass the bill in forty-eight hours in the same way that they had been able to carry other emergency legislation, such as the Prevention of Terrorism Act. Instead, of course, the Tory whips organized behind the scenes to ensure that no further time was made available to progress the bill to law.

Not all Tory MPs were so easily intimidated by public pressure. Norman Tebbit responded to those who wrote to him, in the following terms:

Dear Constituent

Thank you for sending me a coupon clipped from one of Mr Livingstone's propaganda advertisements (paid for by your rates) about London Transport fares.

Don't be conned into thinking Mr Livingstone is trying to give you something for nothing. Not only did he cut the fares for Londoners, but he cut them for such people as foreign tourists and well-paid commuters from outside London. They don't pay London rates, so you had to pay their fares out of your rates. Until Livingstone and his weird friends took over the GLC, London Transport was becoming more efficient and sensible. Now he has messed it up we've got bigger increases than we need have had and a huge bill to pay for the money he has lost. You shouldn't be surprised. Livingstone is pouring your money down the drain in many ways. Did you know this year he has given your money to his friends in some very peculiar organisations?

For example, your money has gone to:
- the English Collective of Prostitutes
- Lesbian Line
- London Gay Teenage Group
- a series of leftwing propaganda sheets, including £500,000 spent on the extremist publication *The Londoner.*

And these are just a few of the items he is spending your money on. I suggest you write to Livingstone at County Hall, SE1, to ask him what benefit you get from giving money to these sorts of causes.

When I examined the division lists I was amused to see that Bill Pitt, who had made so much of his opposition to the supplementary rate demand which we had to impose to pay for the fares cut, had voted for Douglas Jay's bill. In contrast, those London Labour MPs who had defected to the SDP were still so consumed by hate for the Labour GLC that six of them, including John Cartwright and John Grant, did not support the bill.

The campaign was involving many non-political Londoners and the GLC was running rings around the hapless David Howell, who became more nervous with each encounter with us. But *Briefing* activists were becoming increasingly critical. Since the May elections they had shown more interest in our defeats on council home sales and fares than in the vast amount of work going into laying the foundations for the major expansion of services which would take place once we carried our first Labour budget in February 1982. There was also the problem that although Chris Knight and

Graham Bash remained my close friends and did what they could to cover my back, the composition of the *Briefing* group was changing. The Chartist group of Chris and Graham, with my support, had split away from *Socialist Organiser* in late 1979, following its takeover by John O'Mahony's faction. Since then he had watched with anger as *Briefing* rose to national prominence whilst *Socialist Organiser* declined into a sectarian journal which was merely a vehicle for the views of his own small and divisive group. Given the role I had played in encouraging others to quit *Socialist Organizer* for *Briefing*, I had no doubt that O'Mahony was unlikely to forget or forgive. *Socialist Organiser* had taken every opportunity since the election to attack the GLC for its failings while ignoring our successes, and this had produced a degree of bias in its coverage on a par with the *Daily Mail*.

When attending *Briefing* meetings towards the end of 1981 I had noticed increasing numbers of O'Mahony's group turning up. He was not stupid enough to attempt a straightforward takeover again, so he tended to send along effective operators like John Bloxham who, meeting by meeting, slowly chipped away at *Briefing*'s support for the GLC Labour Group.

An indication of how serious the problems with *Briefing* were came when my old friend Keith Veness (who had no time for O'Mahony) started to campaign for the Labour Group to resign and go into 'majority opposition'. Writing in *Briefing* he justified his position.

> The Group on the GLC have attempted to implement our manifesto and to support the policies we expect to be part of a socialist administration. In this sense *Briefing* remains the staunchest supporter of the Labour administration at County Hall. However, we have now reached the end of this particular road! The events of the last two or three months have put the GLC in danger of doing a U-turn and attacking those groups who have up to now been their most enthusiastic supporters. As a result of the judges, the GLC is now being forced to tear up the main plank of our manifesto and will be forced to dismiss hundreds of transport workers and cut services if it com-

plies. A slow, gnawing process of disillusion is being started that will result in a gradual wasting of our support. Only a clear refusal to shoulder the burden of office without power, or administration without control, can maintain our momentum. There is not sufficient reason to stay in office, despite the plans in employment and housing. These are little more than palliatives and will neither generate the enthusiasm we need nor make up for the failure to confront our enemies in the Government and the Law Courts. Given the setbacks in the courts and refusal of a large minority of Labour members to back any real fight, the only course now is one of majority opposition. At a certain agreed date we should simply withdraw from office and use our majority to defeat any proposals from the Tories and the SDP. This is no easy option. It means many committee chairs abandoning pet projects and it means losing all the subtle 'behind-the-scenes' help given to many groups of people. Nevertheless it spells out in a fairly dramatic fashion what the real situation is. It avoids the dilemma of office without power and means we do not carry out measures forced on us by the Tories and their 'stooges in ermine' in the Law Courts.

Majority opposition is now the only honourable course for the comrades at County Hall to follow. A decision to do anything else is the road to disaster. This is the acid test to distinguish socialists from social administrators. It cannot, and must not, be ducked.

For the Labour Administration to give up just when so many of the rest of our policies were about to take effect was ridiculous and I was determined to prevent the left falling for this defeatism. I spelt out the alternative.

The GLC Labour Group has received well over a thousand letters of support from both party members and the public. The overwhelming theme of these letters is support for a Labour Council which has fought to implement its manifesto in that continued fight. Not one single letter, CLP, ward or trade union branch has suggested that we should withdraw from office. Whilst Labour remains the administration at County Hall we will continue to implement each policy in our manifesto until the Government or the Courts defeat us.

Labour voters do not expect us to cling to office if we cannot implement our programme. But while we can continue to use our positions to expand and defend services and protect jobs we would never be forgiven or understood if we ran away from the tasks before us. Large areas of our manifesto relating to Industry and Employment, Arts and Recreation, voluntary group funding, the battle against discrimination against gays, women and blacks are at crucial stages. Defeat on the issue of fares does not make the unemployed, women, blacks, gays or our own workers feel that the issues that affect them can be forgotten. Again and again we find the same theme in letters of support. People who for years have given up on the Labour Party now look to the GLC as an indication that Labour can become a genuinely radical socialist party.

If we were to say that the setback on fares is an excuse to quit, then what chance for a Labour government committed to the policies of conference? Does anyone believe that such a government would not face total opposition from capital and would not be beaten on some issues? I would be the first to say we should not become a mask on the face of a Council which we no longer controlled. But that is not the position and we must not allow ourselves to be talked into surrender by those whose thinking has become fixated on the concept that Labour will always betray or be defeated.

It was while this debate was raging on the left that the whole Council descended into farce over a procedural point which, while it had no real significance, undermined our credibility and called into question our ability to carry the forthcoming budget. The

Council was due to meet on 26 January. Sir Peter Masefield had notified us of the new fares structure and asked us to agree to it. In the absence of a decision by the Council the Transport Act laid down the right of the LT executive to take their own decision. The Group officers met on Monday 25 January to decide what recommendations to make. John McDonnell, Valerie Wise and I were the only non-compliers present. I explained my fear that we could spend the entire meeting discussing these proposals without being able to reach any decision. Sir Peter had been instructed to double fares at the last meeting and would now do so whatever the Council decided, so the debate would be academic. However, as the fares would go up irrespective of the Council's decision, the Tories could vote with the left or the right of the Labour Group to defeat any proposal or amendment. In the light of that I suggested that we accept Sir Peter's proposals without debate and move on to the rest of the Council agenda. I looked at John, who did not dissent, but when I reported this recommendation to the Group meeting he led the attack, claiming that if we could defeat Sir Peter's proposals the fares increases would be illegal and could be overturned by a court challenge. The idea that we could go back to the Law Lords and get a reversal was an argument that I did not find convincing but there was nothing I could do to find a position around which the Group could unite.

The following day's Council meeting bore out all my worst fears. It was spent rejecting twelve separate amendments and resulted in no decision at all. Sir Peter charmingly indicated that nothing politicians did ever surprised him and got on with the task of raising the fares. But the damage had been done. Half the *Briefing* group suspected that I had been involved in some great betrayal. They demanded that the left combine with the Tories at the next meeting in order to reject the budget on the grounds that in voting for it councillors would in effect be accepting the Law Lords' decision. Amongst the senior Council bureaucrats the idea that we might fail to carry a budget opened up the prospect of an early end to the administration. Sir James Swaffield asked to see me the next day and baldly stated, 'If your party cannot carry a budget then I and my senior officers will have no alternative but to administer the Council as best we can until a new administration emerges.'

Harvey Hinds and many others felt it would be impossible to get Labour Group agreement on the budget because the right wing wanted a low rate and others were concerned that their left credentials might be damaged if they were seen to vote for a budget which did not include the 'fares fair' policy. Harvey's fears increased on Monday 1 February, when *Briefing* had its regular monthly meeting at County Hall. O'Mahony's troops were there in force and led a series of strident and vicious attacks on the Group and on me. As I tried to explain the fiasco of the previous GLC meeting, one activist turned towards me and loudly interrupted with, 'I smell a rat.' The debate on Keith Veness's proposal for majority opposition was a foregone conclusion. Graham Durham, a Brent East party member, later reported: 'The only speeches against were those of Ken Livingstone and Valerie Wise, who argued that other parts of Labour's budget were just as important. Neither of their arguments seemed particularly strong to the meeting.' The vote was overwhelming, with John McDonnell voting for the proposal to reject the budget. Dave Wetzel was the only other Labour councillor present to support the line put by Valerie and me.

I decided that the best way to fight back was to expose councillors to the views of the trade union activists who worked for London Transport and the GLC. With Dave Wetzel's help I convened a meeting of shop stewards and regional officials of the LT and GLC trade unions. All Labour councillors were invited. I opened the meeting by explaining that the budget we had prepared included an initial 10 per cent real growth in services with the certainty of more funds becoming available as the year wore on. After a short debate on the details I pointed out that on the left there was a strong body of opinion which felt that we should defeat the budget and go into majority opposition because our fares policy had been defeated.

In the uproar which followed, one of the most militant shop stewards could be heard booming, 'You must be joking, it's our jobs you're talking about.' Dave Wetzel and Valerie Wise then moved in for the kill and demolished the resignation arguments, so that when I asked if anyone wished to speak in favour of that option there was silence, except for John McDonnell who made a graceful little speech accepting the position of the trade unions.

From that point on, no leftwinger in the Group talked about resignation.

However, there was still a problem with the right. With our growth proposals and the cost of finding £125 million to write off the now illegal LT deficit, the early but very rough projections of the rate increase looked as though we would have to raise the rate to 46p from the 24p set by the Tories the previous year. I worked closely with Maurice Stonefrost and privately had no doubts that he would bring the final figure well below 40p. As I expected, Mair Garside and Andrew McIntosh started rumblings that they would not support any rate above 40p and I let them carry on so that they would be unable to block our budget when it finally came in at under that amount.

It was at this stage that David Howell finally came to life and announced the Government's response to the LT crisis by proposing to rush a bill through Parliament. He was not allowing us to 'Keep Fares Fair' but instead proposed to pass into law a scheme allowing the GLC to borrow the £125 million that we needed to cover LT's deficit. From an allegedly monetarist government it was a ridiculous proposal. Not only would we have to repay the sum with interest but we would lose Government grant each year on the interest payments. Ratepayers would therefore have to find almost double that sum to repay the loan. Had David Howell bothered to ask my opinion on such a deal he could have avoided wasting Parliament's time. His was an offer I could only too easily refuse. Maurice Stonefrost was as appalled as I at the terms and urged rejection of the offer. Although some Labour borough council leaders were attracted to the idea of taking the loan (therefore having a much smaller rate increase in what was their election year), with Ted Knight's vocal backing we got their support for rejection.

David Howell was also coming under pressure from Tory MPs who were wilting fast in the face of thousands of angry pensioners' demands for emergency legislation to save their free travel passes. With one million voting pensioners in London, he had no choice but to give in. Instead of acting quickly and taking the credit, he appeared only to have moved under the pressure of our campaign, enabling us to claim a victory. Howell was eventually reduced to introducing the bill to save the pensioners' passes with a speech in which he claimed that our publicity had been a great scare campaign and that the passes had never been in danger. Labour MPs had great fun asking why legislation was necessary if it was all a dishonest scare tactic.

As our campaign continued to build, Howell attempted to defuse it with a unique measure to answer our charge that the Law Lords' decision required a second huge fare increase within six months. It was suddenly announced that Sir Michael Havers, the Attorney-General, had ruled that no additional fare increases were necessary. There seemed to be no precedent for such an action anywhere in British law and the only similar mechanism was that of a papal dispensation. But whereas the doctrine of papal infallibility applied in the Church, no one had ever claimed such a doctrine for the Attorney-General, whose position is subordinate to that of the Law Lords. None of the Law Lords raised a peep as by now the judiciary had no doubt about the scale of their blunder. Our lawyers advised that the Attorney-General's decision would be a complete protection from any surcharge proceedings as it effectively served to warn off anyone who was thinking of a legal challenge.

Great Universal Stores (GUS) had launched a court case against Merseyside County Council's fares reduction. When this came to the High Court, Merseyside won the case as we had done in London and it was only to be expected that GUS would go to the Court of Appeal for another Denning judgement. By now, however, the public backlash was underway and GUS, which had close links with the Government in the form of Sir Geoffrey Finsberg MP, strangely let the matter rest.

I spent most of Monday 15 February with Maurice Stonefrost, finalizing the budget proposals to go before the Group that night and full Council the following day. As I expected, Maurice had worked several financial tricks at the Government's expense by exploiting the complications of their grant system, and had got the rate increase down to 35p, even including paying off the LT debt. Maurice was in favour of doing this because it made sound financial sense and I agreed with him, but I had another reason for accepting that view. Over the previous four years I had seen Ted Knight caught between the pressures of rate increases caused by Government grant penalties and the constant threat of his right wing to oppose too great an increase, as well as fierce reactions from Lambeth ratepapers. In paying off the debt we would raise the GLC rate to the sort of level required to fund the rest of our manifesto over the following three budgets. This one decision would remove any further problems with left or right wings or the ratepayers in setting future budgets. It would mean we could go into the next election after three budgets in which the rate increase would be roughly in line with inflation, while in 1982 the public would most probably blame it all on the Law Lords anyhow.

To everyone's surprise the Group agreed the rate after just a few questions following my presentation. The right could not complain, given that the figure was so far below the 40p limit they had made so much of, and the left accepted my reassurance that if the £40 million for real growth was inadequate more funds could be made available during the year as Maurice further exploited the complexities of the Government's grant system.

The following day's budget meeting had been the subject of considerable media interest as the Tories threatened to keep the Council meeting going through the night. Harvey Hinds drew up plans for members to sleep on camp beds and have breakfast laid on. After a bit of ritual bluster from Sir Horace, the Tories lost interest when it became obvious that there was no Labour split. The budget was carried and we were able to get home to our beds at a reasonable hour.

Three wholly beneficial developments arose from the fares and budget crisis. Firstly, Kensington and Chelsea Council used the concept of fiduciary duty to challenge our budget in the courts. We had anticipated such a challenge and worked closely with Roger Henderson QC (who had been recommended to us by Ted Knight) to avoid it. In his High Court judgement of 2 April, Mr Justice McNeill gave the decision which Denning and the Law Lords should have delivered on the fares issue. He not only rejected Kensington and Chelsea's case but took the opportunity narrowly to define the instances in which councils should be challenged under the concept of fiduciary duty. In his judgement Mr Justice McNeill stated that he had been reluctant to grant Kensington and Chelsea leave to bring the case.

> . . . It is now clear that the issue is one for the political hustings and not for the court. It is a matter of real concern that the court, exercising the power of judicial review, is increasingly, and particularly in this case, used for political purposes superficially dressed up as points of law. The proper remedy in such matters is the ballot box and not the court.
>
> If a rating or precepting authority over-rates or over-precepts, the remedy is in the hands of the electorate. It is only where illegality can be established – in the widest sense known to this court – that judicial review can be appropriately sought. The impropriety of coming to this court when, as I suspect to be the position in this case, political capital is sought to be made – even though here unsuccessfully – out of judicial review cannot be overstressed. It is perhaps even worse when public servants, as here, are, or feel, constrained to file affidavits, the contents of which demonstrate a political purpose.
>
> I regret to say that I found wholly unconvincing the affidavit of Mr Webber [Kensington and Chelsea's Town Clerk]. I may be unkind to him. It may be that the arguments which he put forward were not his, but those of the Party in political control of Kensington. There is, however, a marked and unmistakable difference between the balance of Mr Stonefrost's affidavit and the contentious nature of Mr Webber's affidavit.

This judgement pulled the judiciary back from the disastrous 'fares fair' decision and effectively warned off further legal challenges. It was not until the final death throes of the GLC that the Court of Appeal felt able again to intervene politically in its affairs.

Fortunately it was only twenty-seven days after the McNeill judgement that the Camden surcharge case brought by Ian Pickwell, the District Auditor, was resolved. Roger Henderson represented Camden Council and, fresh from his success in overturning our fares policy, Mr Widdicombe presented the Auditor's case that we should be bankrupted and barred from public office.

He relied heavily on the precedents laid down by Law Lord Atkinson in the Poplar councillors' case and was therefore dismayed when Mr Justice Forbes pointed out that 'looking back, as we do, over sixty years of progress in the field of social reform and industrial relations, some of their Lordship's observations may, with the benefit of hindsight, appear unsympathetic'. After stating that 'nothing in this judgement is intended as a criticism of Mr Pickwell personally', Lord Justice Ormrod then took his case to pieces, line by line. Nor did he spare the Law Lords, whose 'lengthy judgements [on the fares decision] are a mine of felicitous literary expressions'. Both Forbes and Ormrod built on the McNeill judgement and emphasized that it was their duty to ensure that the councillors had taken their decision correctly, not to substitute the judgement of the court for the decision of the councillors.

As I sat listening to the judgement I could not help speculating on what might have happened if this case had got to court before the fares issue. Although he had lost in the High Court, Pickwell would have known that Denning and the Law Lords would be much more likely to find in his favour. I have no doubt that had it been heard before the fares case we would have lost and I would have been removed from office. It was only the enormous public campaign which caused the judges to back off and leave the attack on radical Labour councils to the Government and press.

The second benefit to flow from the McNeill judgement was a 25 per cent fares cut twelve months later. On the same day in January that the left caucus met to discuss our tactics in the Council debate, I had had a meeting with Bob Lane, the senior planning officer from Camden. He was considering bringing a Camden-led legal case against the GLC if fares increased in line with the Law Lords' decision, as this would be so damaging to London's transport system. Camden would argue that the GLC had failed to take all relevant factors into account before increasing fares. After talking the issue through, we decided that the challenge would fail but that the scheme might provide the basis of another attempt to cut fares after a decent interval. I asked John Fitzpatrick to develop the idea with Roger Henderson, who was rapidly emerging as one of the leading local government specialists at the Bar. As soon as the budget was out of the way work started.

As the impact of the fares increase began to take its toll, with severe congestion and the number of accidents running at the rate of an extra 3,000 a year, John Fitzpatrick told me that based on his soundings in the legal world he did not expect that another fares reduction would be overturned as long as it was carried out in a different way from the last one. I pushed hard for a 36 per cent cut which would take us back to 'fares fair' levels, but Roger Henderson indicated that anything beyond 25 per cent was likely to fail.

Dave Wetzel and I agreed to go for the 25 per cent, and funded the establishment of a Public Transport campaign. This was run effectively by Jack Dromey, the TGWU official who had organized the support for the Grunwick strikers in Brent East. Dave launched an enormous public consultation exercise to show public support for the 25 per cent cut. We met monthly with Jack and his committee, which was chaired by Jimmy Knapp, who was subsequently to become the General Secretary of the NUR. At the GLC Dave put all the resources of the transport department into producing a detailed justification of another fares reduction. At all stages we had to appear open minded in order to satisfy the lawyers.

At this point David Howell awoke from his academic reveries to discover that we were serious, and announced that he was pushing a new bill through Parliament. This would give him the power to tell each council how much subsidy it could give to public transport; any councillors that gave more would be open to public challenge in the courts and surcharge if they lost the case. Throughout the autumn and spring of 1982–83, we worked with Roger Henderson to make the scheme judge-proof and Henderson pointed out a major flaw in the new bill. Howell had assumed that the risk of surcharge would be enough to prevent any council going beyond his subsidy limit but he had clearly not read or, if he had, he had not understood the full meaning of the McNeill, Forbes and Ormrod judgements. As long as we followed correct procedures the courts would not substitute their decision for ours on a matter such as the level of subsidy as long as the level remained 'reasonable'. We did nothing to alert Howell to this gap in his bill and I found it hard to believe that his civil servants had not drawn it to his attention.

We proposed our second fare reduction in late 1982, only to find that the LT executive refused to carry it out without a direction from the court. We took the executive to court, where they did not resist our case but awaited the judgements of Lord Justice Kerr, Mr Justice Glidewell and Mr Justice Nolan. On 27 January 1983, they ruled in our favour. I went to hear the decision as I was keen to see just how they would pick their way around the Denning and Law Lords' judgements. I was not disappointed and there was frequent laughter in the High Court as the judges quite transparently overturned the decision of the superior court.

> ... Apparently without legal advice the whole (fares) structure was radically changed as a matter of political policy. This was done on the basis of one of the statements in the election manifesto and without any regard to the powers of the Council under the 1969 Act and arbitrarily, without any regard to the interests of ratepayers but solely in the interests of passengers.
>
> This exercise of the Council's discretionary powers was accordingly set aside as clearly unlawful. There is no need to discuss it further other than to mention that the basis of the decision of the Court of Appeal and of the House of Lords was widely misunderstood, and, in many cases, obviously misrepresented. Some of the public comments gave the misleading impression that Lord Denning was sitting alone in the Court of Appeal and that the judgements at both levels were designed to thwart the wishes of the majority on the Council for political motives. Such reactions, whether based on ignorance or whatever, can only be described as total rubbish. If the Council succeeds in the present application it would be equally ignorant, or deliberately misleading, if the cry were to be: 'Judges slash fares' or – unfortunately more likely – 'Judges increase rates'. It is to be hoped that nothing like that will happen again.

Authorities invested with discretionary powers can only exercise such powers within the limits of the particular statute. So long as they do not transgress their statutory powers, their decisions are entirely a matter for them, and – in the case of local authorities – for the majority of the elected representatives, however, to one important proviso. This is – again to put it broadly – that they must not exercise their powers arbitrarily or so unreasonably that the exercise of the discretion is clearly unjustifiable. That is not to say that in operating their transport undertaking the defendants should be guided by considerations of profit to the exclusion of all other considerations.

The fares were reduced by 25 per cent, but because of the legal delays this now took place in May during the middle of the General Election campaign.

The final benefit to flow from the McNeill judgement was the emergence of Maurice Stonefrost as the obvious next Director-General of the GLC. Following his ham-fisted warning that he would administer the Council until a new administration could be formed if Labour failed to carry its budget, Sir James Swaffield came to see me to discuss his future. He indicated that if I wished him to, he was prepared to continue in office for another twenty-two months until his sixtieth birthday. It was tempting to ask him to resign immediately but Maurice Stonefrost had previously told me that he would not be involved in the early removal of Sir James. Also, new members of the Council were only just beginning to get clear in their own minds how they would wish to reform its structures and administration. I felt it would be a mistake to rush the process of reforming the structures and risk upheaval and change just as committees were concentrating on spending the extra 10 per cent growth in their budgets, so we agreed that Sir James would stay until his sixtieth birthday. In the meantime we established a working party to review the structures and administration of the central bureaucracy, with a remit that all changes should be in place by the end of 1983. Thus, in the unlikely event of a Labour Government being formed we would be ready to press ahead with major public works programmes.

It was a surprise to many that Maurice Stonefrost, whom I had identified as the evil genius behind the cuts of the Goodwin administration, should have emerged as the financial saviour of such a radically different administration. Since May 1981, Maurice seemed to have been genuinely enthusiastic about the changes of policy and style and it was almost as though his own personal and political development had become caught up in what we were doing. It had always been easy to be seduced by his charm and intelligence but as he rapidly emerged as a radical administrator we developed a relationship of trust in which neither of us felt the need to manoeuvre the other. A similar process seemed to be at work in my relationship with John Fitzpatrick. As the pressures of the judges and the budget had mounted, somewhere along the line the three of us passed a point where respect turned into friendship. Shortly after the budget was carried, I was at a staff party where I asked Maurice why he had gone so far out on a limb to help save the administration at a time when all the other senior officers except John Fitzpatrick were hanging back waiting to see if we would survive. 'I saw what "they" were trying to do to you and I thought it was wrong,' he replied. I did not need to ask who 'they' were.

Some of my colleagues, however, were not being quite so helpful. Much of the left was feeling frustrated by our defeat and did not share my optimism about the possibility of a future fares cut. John McDonnell sat down beside me during the meeting of the GLC on 26 January as we were sinking further into farce with the endless amendments to Sir Peter Masefield's proposals. He passed me a sheet of paper and told me, 'It will be in your own best interests to sign this.' 'This' was a plan to establish an additional fares campaign called 'Can't Pay, Won't Pay'. It would urge people to break the law by not paying the fare increase when it came in on 21 March. As an ex-anarchist, I found the idea of millions of Londoners defying an unjust law instantly appealing, although it was unlikely that such an idea would easily take root in a country without any anarchist traditions of struggle. When I realized that the trade unions had not been consulted, the answer had to be no, so I said I would want to discuss it with them before I agreed to sign. Ten members of the group did not feel a similar need to consult the trade unions and went ahead with a public launch two days later.

The campaign attracted major publicity but little support and only a few hundred people protested on the day. Despite my constant urging, the organizers refused to ask the London Labour Party Executive for support and the trade unions grew more alarmed when they heard nothing from the organizers. Bus and tube workers feared the campaign would put them in the firing line between protesting passengers and senior management. As 21 March approached, in each of LT's sixty-four garages the workers voted to call on the organizers to drop the campaign. Bitterness mounted when these calls were ignored, and in a handful of garages the workers passed motions of censure against those councillors who persisted in the campaign.

The only real support came from a few small leftwing groups and in particular *London Labour Briefing*. Although Chris Knight and Graham Bash remained good friends and continued to work with me up until and through the miners' strike, the rest of *Briefing* (in which *Socialist Organiser* now had a strong influence) had effectively severed links when I defeated their resignation option. Not supporting 'Can't Pay, Won't Pay' was the final straw. Writing in *Briefing* Paula Watson made her anger clear.

A vote passed by a large majority at the Target 82 meeting held on 1 February called on the Labour Group to vote against their own GLC budget rather than comply with the ruling of the Law Lords outlawing the cheap fares policy for London Transport. Such action would have brought the GLC to a standstill and placed those councillors who so acted outside the law, facing surcharge and possibly prison. The advice of the Target 82 meeting was not followed and the budget was duly passed. Canvassing in the last GLC election was a pleasure. For the first time, when the electors grumbled that politicians never kept their promises, one could reply that now it was different. There were Labour candidates of real courage and integrity who would stand fast by their manifesto promises. They would not betray their supporters. The canvassers were wrong. When faced with a real challenge from the capitalist establishment our representatives on the GLC surrendered, creating a crisis of credibility. What is left is the small print, tiny grants to the publishers of feminist and gay magazines and the establishment of committees on such matters as the rights of women and ethnic minorities. These are worthy causes but there is nothing specifically socialist about them. Any regime of pragmatic liberals could do as much.

A great deal has been heard of the 10 per cent growth promised in the budget, but 10 per cent of what? The actual figure appears to be about £40 million for the whole of London, the kind of sum that the Ministry of Defence probably spends on paper clips in a year. There remains the London Enterprise Board, but this is almost certain to be ruled illegal by the Tory Government and we know now that our councillors will accept that decision. A stand on principle by our Labour councillors would have produced electrifying results. Nothing would have been more conducive to creating the mass movement so often talked of than seeing our elected representatives actually prepared to fight and suffer in defence of local democracy and their manifesto commitments.

John O'Mahony of *Socialist Organiser* submitted an article.

You talk about doing better next time, in a different fight later. But if the GLC left will not fight for its major manifesto plank, what will it fight for? Comrades, the class struggle is always now. The struggle now is decisive for organizing and training a serious left that can secure the socialist future.

Chris Knight and Valerie Wise replied jointly:

When the budget vote was finally taken, the GLC Group remained united as it has rarely been before. In effect, we voted to keep within the law. There will be comrades who will feel deeply disturbed by this, and understandably. Are we not clinging to the trappings of office as all real power steadily drains from our hands? Is this not the pattern of all past Labour Governments, played out on a small scale within our own ranks – as if nothing had been learned at all? To such comrades, we would reply that they should not doubt us quite so much. We are not yielding ground to the Tories any more than we are being literally forced to. By staying in office, we can increase, rather than decrease, the scope for building that mass movement of resistance which we will need to take us along the road towards real power. Support from the GLC 'legitimizes' our struggles.

As the row continued Chris Knight replied again in the April issue.

It is not quite fair to describe Ken Livingstone's policy as 'protest against the fare rise but vote for it' (which is how you describe it in *Socialist Organiser*). When the crucial vote came up, Ken Livingstone and the GLC left voted almost unanimously against complying with the Lords. As the budget vote approached, however, there began to develop the most intense bitterness between those who had supported the 'Target 82' line on the one hand, and virtually the entire left of the GLC Labour Group on the other. Should we have pressed the division to the point of splitting the *Briefing* network irrevocably, with the Tories and the press able to exploit this split?

Had we been sure that 'disengagement' – i.e. the immediate resignation of the Labour GLC – was popular with the mass of London Labour Parties, with the trade union rank and file, and been sure that this would have strengthened, rather than weakened, our forces in relation to the Tories, we would have carried through the necessary split. But was this the case? Would *Briefing* have carried the bulk of London left activists with us in direct opposition to Ken Livingstone and the GLC? I don't think so. It is important that we are conscious of our own strength – not underestimating it, but not wildly over-estimating it either.

My view is that the mass of Londoners see the attempted doubling of fares on London Transport as being despite the efforts of Dave Wetzel, Ken Livingstone and the Labour GLC. They are not blaming us for these increases: they do see the Law Lords and the Tories as responsible. We have to choose between unsatisfactory alternatives. On the other hand, the fact that we do have to do this just shows that we are living and struggling in the real world, not just in a world of paper, propaganda and resolutions.

Whilst *Briefing* made the same charges against me that I had made against Wilson, Callaghan and Goodwin, I was trying to calm the stream of outraged transport trade unionists – rank and file as well as officials. In the end 'Can't Pay, Won't Pay' flopped, but being proved right annoyed *Briefing* activists even more. Slowly the suspicions widened to become a gulf. Whilst the Group pressed on with the work of our manifesto I became confident that we were building towards a re-election victory. But the criticisms of *Briefing* caused both pain and doubt. It was not how I had imagined the relationship between the GLC left and *Briefing* would be.

7

Working for London

Once our budget was carried, friends and enemies had to accept the fact that we were likely to complete our four-year term, and they would have to adjust their plans accordingly. Hopes of a return to office dashed, Sir Horace Cutler finally decided to resign as leader of the Opposition. We were surprised when he announced that he had decided to make use of the time on his hands to open a nude mixed-bathing sauna in my constituency of Paddington. He kindly invited me to the opening, but when I heard that the entrance fee was £50 a year for single men and £5 a year for single women I was worried that the club might attract men who were interested in more than swimming, and felt it wiser not to be associated with the project.

As the Labour Group AGM approached, John McDonnell told me that he was intending to stand for the powerful position of chair of the Finance Committee. He looked really shocked when I told him I would vote for him and I could see from his face that he thought I was lying. But I had several reasons for supporting John. First and most important was his competence and capacity for hard work, which was equalled by only two other members of the Group. Secondly, as I told him at the time, 'I'd rather have you using your talents to get control of the finance department than constantly rooting around looking for issues to strike holier-than-thou positions on.' Keeping John on the backbenches would have meant endless divisive rows splitting the Labour Group as he struggled to build his reputation on the left. Originally I had been concerned that his training as a supporter of the Militant tendency had made him less receptive to the issues of racial and sexual politics; and I felt even more doubtful when I saw the expression of disbelief on his face when he read an article in *Briefing* describing the pleasures of lesbianism. However, during his year as the first chair of our grants panel he had come into contact with many feminist and lesbian and gay groups, and after the initial culture shock had worked closely with the groups and learned a lot from them.

Another reason for supporting John was the strong possibility that Tony Banks, Paul Boateng and I might get elected to Parliament at the next election, which I expected to be in the autumn of 1983. If that happened, I would need to stand down as leader in time for someone else to establish themselves before the 1985 local elections. A strong contender would be Mike Ward, whom I had come to mistrust as a result of the role he had played at the Group meeting in July 1981 when I was attacked by the right. He had also created a lot of difficulties for me during the fares trauma in January 1982. I therefore wanted another candidate to support. If John McDonnell indicated the desire to hold together the broad left–centre coalition which was our power base within the Group, I would prefer him to be my successor. By the time I had to stand down the Group would have been in office nearly three years and it seemed to me that a successor from the far left might be the only way to extend the initial radical phase of the administration. I knew that the demanding post of Finance chair would soon reveal whether John was a democratic socialist or, as some of his critics suspected, a slightly Stalinist centralizer incapable of devolving and sharing power. At the AGM John won a majority on the first ballot; the only other changes of significance were the election of Valerie Wise to chair the newly established Women's committee and the unopposed election of Tony McBrearty (one of my most competent critics) to succeed Gladys Dimson as Housing chair.

Gradually, the bureaucracy within County Hall became less obstructive. We were able to move or retire some officers and recruit people from outside the County Hall service who understood what we were about. The press condemned every outside appointment as 'jobs for the boys' and 'abuse of patronage', though they made no such complaint about Mrs Thatcher, who had been doing exactly the same thing in national government since she was elected. The truth is that while many excellent officers in central and local government can work competently and loyally for whoever is elected (and such people are worth their weight in gold), there are others who become set in the ways they work and think and come to think of the proper method of working as a conservative one. It is much less painful for all concerned if these people can be retired as soon as possible, and those who are too young to retire be encouraged to seek employment with more traditional authorities.

The bureaucracy was also being transformed by the increasing number of points at which we opened the system to outside groups. An extreme example of this was our decision to cease co-operation with the Government on war preparations. The GLC was responsible for planning to deal with the consequences of a nuclear attack on London and a small team of officers had been assembled to draw up plans in co-operation with the Ministry of Defence and the Home Office. Unlike every other department, however, these officers did not make reports to the public or even to the Council on what they were doing. Most of the key figures in the department had come from the Ministry of Defence and made it quite clear that they considered the new administration to be quite mad and probably Russian agents.

I was convinced that William Whitelaw, the Home Secretrary, was exaggerating people's chances of surviving a nuclear war, but without access to the files we could not prove anything. The officers in the unit refused to give us free access, insisting that many of the documents were 'classified'. We vaguely knew that in the event of war becoming imminent it was intended that the Queen should sign an order suspending civilian government at local and national levels. At that stage the army supported by the police would take over the administration of the nation through a series of regional seats of government, each presided over by a junior minister. In each area the military command structure would be advised by three local councillors. This meant that as soon as a war looked likely I would select two other members of the GLC and together we would be whisked to safety in a massive bunker in Essex, which was also designated for use by the Cabinet and Royal family. The thought of spending my last days locked in a bunker with Mrs Thatcher's Cabinet while all my friends died held little appeal.

Whitelaw's big lie was to keep assuring the public that if they followed the Government's instructions, whitewashed their windows and waited a few days under the kitchen table they would have every chance of surviving. The Government booklet *Protect and Survive* included the immortal line, 'On hearing the all-clear you may emerge and resume normal activities.'

Without legal right of access we could not browse through GLC files until we found the damning documents and then publish them. GLC officers insisted that they would show us specific documents if we asked for them by number, but as we could not know the document numbers until we had seen the files, we were trapped in a perfect 'Catch 22' situation. In discussion with Simon Turney, whose Public Services and Fire Brigade Committee was normally responsible for this area of policy, we hit on the idea of creating a new post senior to everyone in the department and appointing Duncan Campbell to fill it. Duncan had an excellent track record of exposing unnecessary Government secrecy around defence issues. He had come to prominence as one of the defendants in the ABC secrets trial, when he was prosecuted along with Aubrey and Berry for writing about defence secrets. The prosecution was initiated by Dr David Owen in the bad old days before he decided to become a born-again freedom-of-information man and embrace the true faith of open government.

Our plans to appoint Duncan Campbell as head of the department were thwarted by the GLC Staff Association, which had an agreement with the GLC requiring us to seek their approval before making any outside appointment, except for the most senior posts. We got round this by co-opting Duncan to the Public Services Committee as 'Civil Defence Adviser' to the Council, which caused apoplexy among the Tories on the Committee when they finally realized who he was.

Within a few months we were getting all the information we needed to expose the lies behind *Protect and Survive*. The files showed that the Government knew that Britain could only support a much-reduced population in the aftermath of a nuclear war. They had decided that during the build-up of international tension which was likely to precede the outbreak of war, London and other large cities should be ringed by troops and police to prevent their populations fleeing to the countryside. The Government's projections were that six out of the seven million inhabitants of London would be dead from blast, radiation and disease within 12 weeks. Similar death rates in other main cities would wipe out the urban population and leave the rural areas closer to self-sufficiency. These plans did not take account of the 'nuclear winter' theory which was generally accepted a couple of years later.

The idea that the GLC should continue co-operating in the planned genocide of six million Londoners was hard to reconcile with our election manifesto, so we started working with CND and switched the Government funds we received for war preparations into the campaign for unilateral nuclear disarmament. Building on our experience with the 'Fares Fair' publicity campaign, we declared 1983 to be 'Peace Year' and organized a series of cultural events and posters throughout the city to reveal to Londoners the Government's secret plans for their sacrifice in the event of war. We refused to co-operate in any more war games and worked with other cities in the Nuclear Free Zones movement. The Government withdrew *Protect and Survive*, saying that it would be made available immediately before a war. Throughout the rest of our administration the Government found it impossible to organize any of their war-games exercises, and despite making repeated threats about court action and surcharge they were unable to move against us without revealing the truth about their plans.

Bringing CND into contact with our bureaucracy and involving them in decision making had an impact in one small part of the machine, but when we raised the question of racism the effects were felt across the whole of the Council's service. During the 1960s and 70s the Labour Party had failed to present an attractive anti-racist image to black Londoners. Few had joined the party, and the manifesto was drafted with very little input from black people. Mike Ward's working party on Industry and Employment had included a promise to introduce the TUC's recommended equal opportunities clause, which was a commitment to introduce 'positive policies to promote equal opportunities in employment'.

In the time between the adoption of the manifesto and the start of the campaign, working parties of candidates got together to discuss the implementation of policies after the election. The manifesto was strengthened at the final conference by an amendment from a local Labour Party which added the commitment to establish an Ethnic Minorities sub-committee to 'promote the welfare of Ethnic Minorities in London' and advocate the repeal 'of repressive and racially discriminatory immigration and nationality laws'.

The candidates' working party decided to upgrade the Ethnic Minorities sub-committee to a full committee. In order to avoid the committee being marginalized by the GLC bureaucracy, they insisted that it should be chaired by the Leader and that its officers should have direct access to members without interference by any senior officers. Following the election I therefore became chair, with Paul Boateng as vice-chair (doing most of the day-to-day supervision of the work of the Ethnic Minority Unit workers). John Carr, who was an experienced equal opportunities officer for Hackney Council, became chair of the Staff Committee, thus avoiding any conflicts between the objectives of the two committees. We had the good fortune to recruit Herman Ouseley, who had organized Lambeth Council's anti-racist policies, as the head of the Ethnic Minorities Unit (EMU).

That we faced a major problem with racism at County Hall could not be denied. Although computerization of housing allocations had ended the scandal of new estates being 98 per cent white, black Londoners were still being concentrated on the worst GLC estates in the most deprived boroughs. Although the GLC had claimed to be an 'Equal Opportunities Employer', for decades this had been merely a pious claim, with no efforts made to turn it into reality. The worst example was the fire brigade, which had over 6,500 staff, of whom only seven were black. The only way that could be explained in a city where 17 per cent of the population is black was by continuous and systematic racial discrimination by those responsible for recruitment.

Fortunately we had the active support of the Fire Brigades' Union in changing the situation. Both the national and London FBU leaderships were leftwing and strongly opposed to racism. Although it would have been easy for them to leave it as a paper commitment, they were prepared to go into the fire stations and argue for our policies in often heated debates. Sadly we did not have similar support from all trade union leaderships. John Carr discovered that amongst our own electricians only whites were being offered sought-after overtime. His proposals for changing the system were bitterly opposed by the electricians' union and no progress was made towards achieving an agreement. In the absence of any support from the trade union leadership he had no alternative but to impose change.

The key factor in exposing discrimination was information. We had to know how many black people and women existed at each level of responsibility in each department. Without that information we had nothing firm with which to justify recruitment and pro-motion policy changes. To achieve this John Carr spent two years in sterile, time-wasting debate with the GLC Staff Association (SA) at County Hall, in an attempt to change our systems.

In the early days of the former London County Council, the Staff Association was a radical pioneering body which had affiliated to the TUC decades before trade unionism became a force amongst white-collar council staff. Sadly it degenerated during the 1950s into a deeply conservative body that worked fist in glove with management to prevent any real trade union consciousness develop-ing among the staff. Always opposed to a rank-and-file shop steward system, it organized itself by mimicking the political structure of Council meetings. As a result attendance declined and large num-bers of the staff went unrepresented as many positions on the General Committee (a meaningless debating society) went uncon-tested.

The leadership of the SA was in the hands of three highly paid, older white men. John Hollocks, a founder member of the SDP; Arthur Capelin, the rightwing Labour leader of Greenwich, who had defeated his own local trade unions to push through cuts in services and staffing in that Authority; and finally, Charles Corco-ran, who had distinguished himself by explaining that he did not see the need to make sexual harassment a disciplinary offence as 'no one has ever sexually harassed me'.

I first clashed with the leadership back in 1976 when the SA privately asked Sir Reg Goodwin to prevent our small leftwing band of dissidents from opposing the cuts, claiming that this made it more difficult to get the staff to accept them. It was quite obvious that they did not approve of my replacing Andrew McIntosh as leader: it put them in the difficult position of resisting the progress-ive work practices being advocated by their employer instead of the usual situation where a reactionary employer resists progressive trade union demands. It often seemed to me that they considered the smaller and more radical branch of NALGO to be their main enemy rather than their employer.

It was with this motley crew that we wasted two years in debate. Most of our trade unions were prepared to accept a system of racial and sexual monitoring, but because the SA had a majority on the main white-collar negotiating committee they were able to block progress. They argued that they would support racial and sexual monitoring only if it was carried out by the staff themselves on a voluntary basis. Although all the evidence argued to the contrary, we had no choice but to try the SA suggestion. There was a widespread refusal to co-operate from many staff. Where they were most opposed to us politically, such as in the valuation and legal departments, barely half the staff returned the self-monitoring forms. After several wasted months the result was as we had expected and the SA could no longer oppose a proper monitoring exercise carried out by management. This exercise showed why the idea of monitoring had been so strongly resisted, providing a stunningly clear portrait of the racial and sexual make-up of our staff. Like a map of prejudice, it identified the way in which women and black people remained concentrated at the bottom of each department. The areas of systematic discrimination stood out starkly, for example, in Supplies, one of our biggest departments, where no women or black people had ever been promoted into middle management, even though they made up the bulk of staff recruited at the lower ranks.

The GLC staff were categorized into grades as rigidly as anything within the Civil Service. If you were recruited as a cleaner or clerical officer that was where you stayed, because you were barred from applying for promotion into the higher professional and technical grades. With the exception of directors of departments and their deputies, all vacancies within the bureaucracy were adver-tised and filled internally. Staff were recruited from school or university into a particular grade, and for anything up to the next fifty years they stayed there, gradually being promoted up the rungs

– if their face fitted. This meant that the middle and upper management of the GLC reflected the population of London as it had been thrity or forty years before. The great waves of immigrants who had made their homes in London over the years, as well as the unemployed, were barred from applying for jobs to which they contributed from their rates.

When John Carr and I highlighted the areas of greatest abuse, the SA's response was revealing. Rather than fight to change the attitudes of their members, as the leadership of the Fire Brigades' Union had done, they obstructed our proposals to change the situation. In the case of the Supplies department they even went through the preliminary stages of a libel action, letting the matter drop only when they saw that we were prepared to defend our accusations in court. As negotiations dragged on into 1983, it became clear that agreement would never be reached.

John Carr had the backing of Paul Boateng, Herman Ouseley and myself to demand three changes. First, that staff should be free to apply for any vacant post. Second, that vacancies could be advertised throughout London if councillors so decided and that councillors could designate any positions which had to be filled by councillor-level interview. The last condition was particularly important. The association had previously negotiated a deal in which only the most senior appointments should be made by councillors while all the rest were decided by Council officers. To tackle a problem as deep-seated as in the Supplies department was impossible without removing the power of promotion from the hands of those who had abused it so systematically for so long.

Having reached an impasse with the SA, John Carr proposed that we get an outside legal opinion to show that the effect of GLC recruitment and promotion policy was inherently discriminating against women and black people, and therefore illegal in the eyes of the anti-discrimination legislation of the 1974 Labour Government. Armed with this legal opinion, the Labour Group overwhelmingly backed the leadership's recommendation that after two years' prevarication by the SA it was time unilaterally to impose the required changes. The SA immediately took industrial action, but the trade unions on the GLLP Executive backed our decision, although one print worker expressed the reservation that our actions could have 'dangerous implications' for working practices in Fleet Street.

The SA's action was gradually undermined as their black and women members as well as younger staff recognized that the changes were in their interests. After six weeks they resumed normal working in exchange for a one per cent increase in wages to compensate for any loss of privilege caused to those staff who now faced greater competition for promotion.

As well as meeting internal opposition, our anti-racist policies had met with abuse from the popular press. In addition to distorting our policies, papers such as the *Daily Mail* invented new ones. A typical example was the story that we had forbidden staff to ask for black coffee, as this was racist. However many denials we issued, one paper after another ran the story without checking the facts. But if the papers disliked our anti-racist policies, they went positively bananas when we established a Women's Committee.

As the Ethnic Minorities Committee got underway with its programme of anti-racist activities and our Grants Committee started dealing with requests for funding from women's organizations, it became obvious that the reasons that justified the existence of a committee to advance the cause of ethnic minorities applied to women as well. Although they comprised over half the population of London, women were a small minority of the total number of councillors and MPs. Those women with paid work were getting only two-thirds the wages of men, and inadequate child-care facilities prevented most women achieving their full work potential. The threat of physical attacks and rape inhibited women from going out at night and there was no sign that the police considered the problem to be one of their priorities.

Within the GLC, women began to discuss the need for a Women's Committee. At the same time, Labour women in some of the London boroughs were trying to get commitments to establish committees included in the 1982 borough council manifesto. Outside London, however, the idea was greeted with disbelief. Valerie Wise announced our plans to establish a committee during a speech at Labour's Local Government Conference in Sheffield on 11

February 1982. Every council leader we spoke to treated the idea as a huge joke. There was a real struggle to get the proposal through the GLC Labour Group where some of the men had the same dismissive attitude. But the real opposition came from the three rightwing women in the Labour Group. Some of the men ridiculed the proposal and others felt threatened by it, but the really vicious attacks came from Margaret Morgan and Yvonne Sieve, ably led by Mair Garside. Opposition to each post created to staff the Women's Committee Support Unit and each financial proposal was coupled with a venomously dismissive attitude to Valerie Wise.

Valerie had shown an impressive capacity for work since her election. She had become one of my closest friends and advisers within the group. Only 24 years old when she was elected, her immediate appointment as vice-chair of Industry and Employment and her pivotal position as *Briefing*'s County Hall correspondent and joint secretary of the GLC *Briefing* Group caused some resentment. A relative newcomer to London, she was characterized by a directness and innocence bordering on the naive, which made her easy prey to those members of the Group who could not resist pulling her leg.

Valerie found that she could expect little support from most members of the Group as the press attacks mounted. I made it a priority to attend her committee whenever I could and to be as supportive as possible. Valerie had decided to start her committee with a punishing round of public consultations by subject area and by borough, so that women could define what they wanted from the GLC rather than have the Council announce a programme for them. Night after night, County Hall was filled with women talking, planning, debating and arguing. It was more than clear to even the dimmest sexist in the Group that the Women's Committee had touched a real need in half of London's population. Seeing the scale of public interest, members' attitudes began gradually to change.

Over the sustained objections of the Tories, the SDP and the Labour right, we opened the committee membership to women elected from the consultative structure we had established. As only one-third of the membership of a committee can legally be co-opted members, we created the posts of advisers who had speaking rights but no vote.

True to form, the Staff Association opposed the creation of the Women's Committee and did nothing to help in setting it up. Individual leading members of the SA actually leaked any damaging information that came into their hands to the *Daily Mail*. Sir David English at the *Mail* seemed to have developed an obsession about lesbians; anyone who depended on that paper for their news might have assumed that Valerie and her committee had made lesbianism compulsory for all London women between the ages of 6 and 106. When the workers in the Women's Committee Support Unit (WCSU) went on a residential weekend conference, they had to contend with a team of *Daily Mail* reporters who prowled around the hotel looking for any signs of what they called 'unnatural practices'. Walking along the beach the women were constantly spied on by photographers with telephoto lenses.

Given that at officer and at member level the vast majority of men who worked at the GLC had developed their careers at the expense of the women they lived with, they were hardly likely to be sympathetic to the work of the new committee. These were men whose wives or lovers had ironed their shirts, prepared their meals and raised their children. In many cases they had great difficulty in coming to terms with the proposals beginning to stream out of the Women's Committee. One notable exception was Maurice Stonefrost, who seemed genuinely interested in what was happening. Talking to him at a party I discovered that Maurice was familiar with the works of Andrea Dworkin, one of the most difficult feminists for most men (and many women) to come to terms with. There was no doubt that Maurice was the only senior local government officer anywhere in the country who had even heard of Dworkin, let alone read her books. It confirmed my view that Maurice would be the ideal replacement when Sir James Swaffield retired.

Most other officers continued to be obstructive. PC/PCC frequently had to impress on the more reactionary elements that we expected them to consult with the WCSU frequently, to ensure that any observations the women wished to make about a report would be heard early enough to affect subsequent decisions.

Since my speech to Harrow Gay Unity the year before, we had established a Lesbian and Gay Men's working party to discuss how the Council could assist in fighting prejudice against homosexuals. In previous years I had dealt with cases where gay men had been put under pressure to resign from the education service due to the ignorant assumption that every gay man is a child molester. In fact, during my thirteen years as a member of the ILEA, every case I had heard of where teachers had been molesting pupils involved male teachers and female pupils. The ILEA is the largest education authority in Britain, with over 1,000 schools, and one might have thought that would have been enough to calm parents' fears, but of course such information never appeared in the press. I therefore had no doubt about the existence of discrimination within County Hall.

Cyril Taylor, the Tory deputy leader, had once bragged in the members' bar that every 'queer-bashing speech I make is worth another 1,000 votes in Ruislip Northwood', his constituency. When we started to fund lesbian and gay groups, the press and several backbench Tory MPs kept up a constant stream of homophobic articles and speeches. A side effect of the press hysteria was that I received a constant trickle of letters from people who had been aware of their sexuality for years but felt unable to raise the subject with friends or relatives and did not know anyone else who was lesbian or gay. They all wanted me to put them in touch with organizations, which I did. I was depressed at the thought of how many isolated and lonely people were trapped because politicians, state services and the media constantly reinforced prejudice.

The worst press distortion came when we were asked by the Gay Teenage Group (GTG) to fund a research project into the needs of lesbians and gays up to the age of 21. Immediately, the Tory 'rent-a-quote' MPs were up in arms. 'You are encouraging it,' they screamed. But the GTG report painted a picture of such despair and anguish that no responsible central or local government agency could ignore it. In interviews with 416 young homosexuals, they found that half the sample had experienced problems at school, one in five had been beaten up because of their sexuality, one in ten had been evicted from their homes, and one in five had tried to commit suicide.

We pressed ahead with our policies, in particular the funding of voluntary organizations. Within two years we were funding over 2,000 groups in the community. Of these about 80 were controversial and usually came under the categories of peace, ethnic minority, women's or lesbian and gay groups.

The press continued to focus their coverage on these issues to the exclusion of others, and managed to create the impression that you could only get a grant if you were a disabled, black, lesbian peace-activist. To prove how irresonsible we were being with ratepayers' money, the *Daily Mail* created a phoney women's organ-ization to apply to us for a grant, but they never got beyond the first stages of the rigorous vetting procedure. Each group applying for a grant was investigated in detail by our finance and legal departments as well as by the service committee concerned, and people soon discovered that the GLC was no soft touch. The rigour of these vetting procedures meant that out of the final total of over 3,000 different bodies we funded, the number that ran into legal problems was in single figures.

Because of the image created by the press, people with all sorts of weird ideas wrote to me asking for grants. I even got letters from abroad. One gentleman living in the Manila Hilton in the Philippines requested a grant to cover the cost of an impending eye operation. Obviously his eyesight was still good enough to read Fleet Street's foreign editions. The strangest applicants of all were two women who turned up at my regular advice surgery in Paddington. After explaining that they had come about a grant they passed me a well-produced prospectus outlining their case. They had called their organization 'A Woman's Right To Leg Over'. It was intended to provide a commercially available listings guide to men, so that women could know before they went out on a date what the man was like as a lover as well as the quality and cleanliness of his accommodation. I was convinced that the application had been set up by one of the newspapers and was relieved that Bill Bush was present that evening at the surgery. I politely explained to the women that their proposed service would be outside our normal grant criteria. Later, when I checked them out, I discovered it had been a genuine application.

While we could understand the general public believing what they read in the papers, it was hard to accept some of the criticism we encountered within the Labour Party. In addition to the obvious and predictable complaints of rightwing MPs that the policy was losing us votes, some on the left condemned us for funding groups who were not part of the traditional Labour movement. These 'workerist' elements constantly referred to our grants policy as 'a diversion from the class struggle, comrade, which is confusing and upsetting ordinary working-class families'. What these leftwing critics never understood was that the working class was a lot wider than the traditional picture painted by Marx and Engels over a hundred years earlier. Part of the reason for the weakness of the Labour Party was that as more women and black people had become part of the workforce, the Labour and Trade Union movement had not adapted rapidly enough to the changing pattern: it had neither reformed its own internal structures to take account of these changes nor adopted policies to make the movement more attractive to these groups. Sadly, the Labour Party is still resisting the legitimate demands of women and black people for the right to self-organization. Each party conference sees renewed demands for black sections, and for the right of women to elect their section of the NEC instead of its being carved up by a half-dozen trade union general secretaries.

The policy seemed even more threatening for the Establishment than it did for some elements within the Labour Party. Britain is the most hierarchical, élitist, secretive and class-ridden of the Western industrial democracies. A policy recognizing the rights of groups which had been excluded from power and influence to have access to and influence upon the GLC ran counter to the traditional concept that Britain is safe in the hands of a small élite of the great and good who should be left to manage things without interference from all these uppity groups. Even more outrageous was the idea that these groups should be given public funds so that they could begin to respond to their own needs and develop the skills of management. Equally unacceptable was that they should retain power over their own ideas rather than see them incorporated into the local bureaucracy.

The trouble with the Establishment was that it did not recognize the diverse and cosmopolitan nature of the capital city. There was no longer the natural majority of decades earlier. London was now a collection of minorities and the only way it could work as a city was if each group tolerated the others. I never doubted that it was a major part of the responsibilities of the elected leaders of London to help people recognize the scale of that diversity and welcome it as an enriching experience. We needed in the first instance to listen to each of those groups so that we could understand their hopes and fears. Only then could we begin to educate people and remove the fears that created friction.

As we started to assemble this coalition of the dispossessed, other factors were moving our way in the struggle to neutralize our critics. Our relationship with London's Labour MPs began to improve once the worst of them (including Ron Brown) had defected to the SDP. The London Group of MPs elected Frank Dobson, Nigel Spearing and Jock Stallard to liaise with County Hall. They took a more enlightened approach to what we were doing and relationships immediately began to improve.

I was also getting more and more exposure on radio and television. Of particular importance were those programmes which were nationally networked instead of just being shown in the Thames and South East regions. The first real breakthrough came when I was invited to appear on *Any Questions*, the popular radio-panel discussion chaired by David Jacobs. Anne Lesley of the *Daily Mail* was on the same programme and made all the predictable attacks, to which I responded without losing my temper. The real benefits of taking part in the programme only became obvious the following week, when David Jacobs broadcast the listeners' response to the programme in *Any Answers*. A large number of listeners wrote in, amazed to find that I was not after all an unpleasant headbanger and that they actually agreed with me. Many of them made the point that I was completely different from what they had been led to expect after months of newspaper coverage.

Gradually the tensions within the Labour Group began to subside. In large measure this was due to Harvey Hinds's work as chief whip. Good chief whips are few and far between: people with the ability to do the job properly usually have ambitions to the leadership itself. Harvey had no such desire. He seemed to get all the satisfaction he needed from tending his 'little flock of sheep' and getting them through the right division lobby in sufficient numbers to defeat the Tories and the Alliance. No one had ever had to run the GLC without a comfortable majority before, and given that only a few of us worked there full time, Harvey often faced the problem of our majority disappearing through a combination of political rebellion, illness and bad timing. Perhaps it was because of his early training as a canon in the Church of England, or his subsequent job as a youth leader, that he was an excellent listener. One rightwinger after another would storm into his office to complain about the latest outrage, only to emerge after half an hour relatively pacified.

Harvey kept a watch on the health of Labour Group members and always had to cope with at least one person with a severe drink problem. It is true to say that we lost more votes because of drink than political rebellions. On one occasion, after losing a motion in Council by just one vote, Harvey asked me to help him find a councillor who had disappeared somewhere in the building, while Paul Boateng prolonged the debate until the next vote. Harvey checked the bar and toilets and I hurried to the members' room, to find the lost councillor lying on the floor in a drunken stupor. I literally had to carry him into the Council chamber and drop him in his seat, requesting the Labour member next to him to raise the councillor's hand when the vote was taken.

Two years of this pressure coming on top of fourteen previous years' service as chief whip in control and opposition was enough for anyone. Harvey decided to stand down and allow someone else to take over. It was typical that he timed his exit with perfection. He had stayed long enough to do what he wanted but not so long that people started to complain that it was time for him to go. The end result, of course, was that people constantly moaned, 'If only we could have Harvey back,' to the annoyance of his successor, John Wilson. After a year as chair of the Council, Harvey was not allowed to retire completely, and became the chair of Policy and Performance Review until abolition.

As we approached the mid-point of the administration everything seemed to be slowly moving our way. Things had definitely turned around; our standing in the polls was creeping up all the time. The only cloud on the horizon was the rumour that Mrs Thatcher was considering including a pledge to abolish the GLC in her election manifesto.

8

The Fight Against Abolition

The popular press consistently depicted the struggle over the abolition of the GLC and the six Metropolitan Counties as a personal conflict between Mrs Thatcher and me, sparked by her deep loathing of all that I represented. In fact, any personal element was dwarfed by the long-term political conflict between central and local government and, more immediately, the conflict of policies and ideology between the Tories and radical socialism. I have no doubt that the political leadership of the GLC reminded Mrs Thatcher of exactly the sort of people her parents had warned her not to talk to when she was a little girl, but personal loathing was not enough reason to waste two years of parliamentary time. Mrs Thatcher's Cabinet had always contained members she loathed and despised but with whom she continued to work. To suggest that the Prime Minister was prepared to spend such a large part of what should have been her crucially important second term trying to eradicate one political opponent ignores the reality of the last hundred years of local government history.

The creation of the old London County Council happened as a by-product of the struggle for independence in Ireland. The Government of 1835 had created municipal boroughs in every city but London, establishing local councils in much the same form as we would recognize today. Although Britain remained the most centralized state among the Western industrial democracies, it was finally recognized that the rapid growth of state services required some form of local control if central government was to avoid becoming nightmarishly huge. But having been excluded from the legislation, London had to wait another fifty years before it was finally given its own County Council. Part of the problem was the fear that a single powerful council representing the whole city could become a challenge to central government itself. As London's population rose from one million in 1800 to seven million in 1900, governments feared the revolutionary potential of such a seething mass of humankind, fears reinforced by the upheavals of the Paris Commune in 1871. At the same time, the vested interests of the City of London, which had been given its Charter in 1192, opposed any expansion of its boundaries to include the poorer areas; this would have given London's working class access to the enormous rateable wealth of the city corporation. Similar opposition came from other wealthy areas, such as Marylebone and Westminster. Together these vested interests defeated the first attempt to establish a County Council in 1837.

Over a decade later the issue was reopened in the aftermath of the 1848 cholera epidemic, which caused renewed demands for a local authority. After a Royal Commission's report in 1854, the Government proposed to replace the 170 parishes of London with seven large boroughs. With the city corporation each of these would nominate to a London-wide Metropolitan Board of Works, which would be responsible for strategic services. By 1855, however, opposition from the rich had forced the Government to drop the proposal for the seven boroughs while retaining the Board of Works. Things remained locked in this unsatisfactory position for the next thirty years. Progressives argued for a London-wide authority and conservatives for local boroughs. Gladstone came close to success in 1883 but failed when rightwing elements in the Cabinet baulked at giving the proposed London Council control over the metropolitan police. The right feared that this would make the new council too powerful, opening the way to a challenge to Parliament itself if radicals ever gained control.

When Gladstone proposed Home Rule for Ireland in 1886, Joseph Chamberlain led a breakaway group of Liberal 'Unionist' MPs across the floor of the House of Commons, thus removing Gladstone's Government and installing the Tories under the premiership of Lord Salisbury. Part of the deal to attract the Liberal Unionists into coalition with the Tories was a firm commitment to create local councils in London and those rural areas which still lacked local democracy.

Charles Ritchie, a Tory MP for East London, was given the task of piloting the creation of the London County Council through Parliament, a task made easier by the fact that the Board of Works had by now become notorious for corruption and inefficiency. The first elections for the LCC were held in 1889 and when the new Council met it had a majority of radical Liberals with a few trade unionists and independent socialists. These 73 members were opposed by only 45 Tories. The Council immediately set about tackling London's problems with a dynamic programme of public services. Lord Salisbury was horrified: he soon realized that he had given birth to a powerful instrument of change. By 1894 he was condemning the LCC in terms almost identical to those which would be used against the GLC over eighty years later: 'The place where collectivistic and socialistic experiments are tried . . . where a new revolutionary spirit finds its instruments and collects its arms.'

What particularly worried Lord Salisbury was the growing popularity of the LCC, which had started to campaign to take over the City of London and the police. Without consulting his Cabinet colleagues he proposed that boroughs should be created which would take over most of the Council's powers, leaving it a weak body dealing only with strategic issues. The Liberals on the LCC immediately launched a campaign to save it, winning a big swing in their favour at the 1898 elections. The Tories lost 11 seats, which *The Times* described as 'a crushing defeat'. Lord Salisbury was forced to water down his proposals and in 1899 he settled for establishing 28 virtually powerless local boroughs, leaving the LCC with its powers intact.

The LCC went from strength to strength and in 1904 took over responsibility for education by absorbing the old School Board. The last years of control by the radical Liberals were marked by the election of Tony Benn's grandfather as chair of the Council and his campaign to introduce 'cheap fares for working men'. He eventually went on to stand for Parliament in a by-election at Bermondsey but was defeated after a vicious campaign against him by a popular newspaper called the *Sun*. The declining popularity of the Liberal Government in 1907 opened the way for the Tories to win a majority of 79 to 37 on the LCC in the elections. Immediately the Tory demands to abolish or reduce the LCC faded away and the new administration set about creating the buildings on the south bank of the Thames which would provide them with imposing and comfortable accommodation to match their pretensions.

Thus things remained until 1934, when the London Labour Party led by Herbert Morrison unexpectedly won the election with 69 seats to the Tories' 55. Immediately Morrison launched a widespread expansion of services. The housing programme was restarted. The administration of the Poor Laws was humanized. Hospitals were reformed along lines which set the pattern for the National Health Service over a decade later. Not surprisingly the surge of popularity for the new administration alarmed the Tory Government who saw Morrison laying out the blueprint for how a Labour Government would reconstruct and reform Britain when finally it came to power. Morrison's Labour LCC represented a direct challenge to the ideological supremacy of the Tory Government and when Labour was overwhelmingly re-elected in 1937 not only were six Tory seats lost to Labour but 10 per cent more Londoners turned out to vote. Morrison was capturing the new middle-class vote and had co-opted many talented middle-class Liberals into his administration. In contrast to his bureaucratic successors he operated as leader in a very open way and delegated well to his committee chairs.

The Tories began planning to change matters but had not developed a strategy when war broke out in 1939. With Morrison in the War Cabinet the issue was dropped. It was not until the Tories were back in power in the 1950s that they could return to the problem. In 1957 Harold Macmillan's Government established a Royal Commission under Sir Edwin Herbert to consider the matter. As the majority of London's population now lived outside the LCC area there was an obvious case for creating a larger body along the lines of the GLC to deal with strategic issues such as transport and planning, with strong local boroughs handling all the direct personal services such as education, housing management and social services.

The Tories' primary motive was to break Labour's political hold on London, which after twenty-three years of continuous power was considered unshakeable. They worked throughout the period to lobby for a structure which would most benefit their electoral chances. The person appointed to direct this exercise was Roland Freeman, a rising star who had successfully planned the Tory takeover of the National Union of Students from the control of the Communist Party and had been the union's president a few years before. In 1983 he recalled that 'all our discussions turned on the fact that we couldn't win the LCC as then constituted. We wanted a GLC with the widest possible area so we would have permanent control.' After achieving most of the Tory objectives in the abolition of the LCC and its replacement by the GLC, he followed an impressive record as Tory leader of Wandsworth Council by getting elected to the GLC, where he became the chair of the Finance Committee when the Tories eventually won control for the first time in 1967.

With a Tory majority of 100 in the House of Commons, Labour's opposition was doomed to defeat and when the Macmillan Government introduced its legislation in 1962 it made major changes to the Herbert proposals which further strengthened the boroughs at the expense of the GLC. Many of the powers that Herbert recommended should go to the new GLC were either given to the boroughs or shared between them and the GLC. Those powers which Herbert believed should be devolved to the GLC largely stayed with central government. Thus, in the sixteen years from its first meeting in 1965 to 1981 the record of the GLC was on the whole one of failure. Contrary to all the Tories' plans Labour managed to win a majority at the first elections in 1964, but the predominance of old LCC members ensured that the Council tended to live in the past rather than examine its potential to break into new areas of policy and service. Political control was constantly shifting, with only one administration serving a second term. No party stayed in power long enough to establish new political priorities. By the time Labour was elected in 1981 the bureaucracy was demoralized by the failure to secure a proper role.

The 1981 manifesto was in a way Labour's own commission, reviewing the past and setting new tasks for the future. Our alternative to Mrs Thatcher's version of monetarism in all fields of policy became a challenge to Tory ideological predominance in much the same way as Morrison's LCC had done in the 1930s.

Immediately after the 1981 election, Michael Heseltine asked his civil servants at the Department of the Environment to examine the possibility of abolition. In their report they were adamant in their opposition to change. They advised that abolition would be a 'nightmare', with endless problems arising long after the abolition itself. Michael Heseltine wisely dropped the matter to concentrate on perfecting his financial powers over local councils. But the idea continued to hold attractions for the Prime Minister. During her time as Education Secretary in the 1970 Heath Government, Mrs Thatcher had been appalled by what she considered to be the financial excesses of the ILEA under Sir Ashley Bramall, and this had led her to block the original plans of the Heath Government to form the Metropolitan County Councils as education authorities along the same lines as the ILEA.

In the first four years of her premiership she watched as each attempt of the Government to cut back local council services was thwarted by the increasing number of Labour-controlled councils. The election of the Labour GLC and the Metropolitan County Councils led to greatly increased spending on fare subsidy and other services, which more than matched the cuts in services that were being made by Tory councils. We had every intention of proceeding with our election manifesto, which had received the endorsement of the electorate, and nothing in Mrs Thatcher's nature led her to accept that others might have a right to follow policies contrary to her own.

To add insult to injury there was also a huge gulf between the cultural values of the GLC Labour Group and everything that Mrs Thatcher considered right and proper. The loud, populist style of the GLC represented a challenge to a Prime Minister who had gained power by a rightwing populist appeal to working-class voters and racist and sexist prejudices. To fight racism while Mrs Thatcher assured white voters that she 'understood their fear of being swamped by an alien tide' was a direct challenge. To intervene in the economy to save and create jobs while the Government stood back and let market forces destroy 25 per cent of manufacturing industry showed that there was an alternative. Confidently to assert the rights of women and homosexuals while she preached Victorian family values was unacceptable. In our campaigning and in our refusal to pay lip service to the so-called impartiality of judges and civil servants we failed to accept the normal style and traditional courtesies of the Establishment. In our assertion that we believed Londoners had a right to information and a role in the administration of their city, we challenged the traditional establishment methods of administration by an élite. Mrs Thatcher droned on about 'the right of managers to manage'; we asserted that people should have a say in the day-to-day decisions which affected their lives both at their places of work and in the communities in which they lived.

Mrs Thatcher was also under pressure from big business, which had all but ceased paying tax to central government but could find no legal way to avoid paying their rates. The redistribution of wealth factor, which throughout the nineteenth century had led the richer parts of London to oppose establishing a London-wide authority, was still considered valid by the CBI. To make matters worse, the GLC had assembled on the public payroll the largest collection of radicals and socialists ever to work in central or local government and they were generating new ideas and services at an alarming rate. The GLC further infuriated the Government by developing a series of international contacts with socialist governments and liberation struggles in the developing world and initiating a very public dialogue with Sinn Fein. By the beginning of 1983 many political commentators were making the point that the GLC had become a much more effective opposition to the Government than any of the parties in the House of Commons.

With the election bearing down on her, Mrs Thatcher had made no progress on her 1974 pledge to abolish the rates and had no proposals for rating reform to put in her election manifesto. In January 1983, she switched Michael Heseltine to Defence and promoted Tom King from number two to Secretary of State at the DOE. Although King was against abolition because of the problems he foresaw arising from it, Mrs Thatcher asked the civil service to prepare option papers on abolition of the GLC and Metropolitan

Counties, and on rating reform. With the approach of the election this task was raised to 'priority'.

After extensive research amongst prominent Tories, Forrester, Lansley and Pauley described the internal development of abolition policy in *Beyond Our Ken.*

> Some of Mrs Thatcher's own colleagues were becoming uneasy about the extent to which her general view of local government and local democracy was becoming coloured by her deep-seated and almost obsessive objections to urban socialists, particularly Ken Livingstone . . . In March, the reports on rates reform and abolition had gone from officials to a committee of Cabinet ministers (Misc 79) chaired by Mr William Whitelaw, Deputy Prime Minister. Misc 79 had concluded that nothing could be done about the rates. But as a sop it had agreed 'in principle' to abolition. Many ministers, including Mr Whitelaw and Mr King, were confident that the sheer complexity of abolition would keep it out of policy in practice. Although they were not amused by the Livingstone style they did not rate him a major electoral threat. The real issue still seemed to be the rates. They reckoned, however, without Mrs Thatcher, who seemed to see Mr Livingstone as both a political and a personal threat. She set up a new committee of ministers and pronounced herself chairman. She firmly accepted the abolition plans and ordered civil servants to go away and do all their work on alternatives to the rates again. The end of April 1983 was their new deadline.
>
> Within weeks, in early May, the general election was announced. Suddenly the issue came to a head: 'What have we got for local government?'
>
> The real answer was nothing. The civil servants had finally convinced the Prime Minister that there were no alternatives to rating that would do.
>
> There was, however, a paper which Leon Brittain had concocted whilst Chief Secretary to the Treasury. This paper had been presented to Cabinet several times and

been rejected by all present. It argued for the Government to have the power to limit rates rises.

Mrs Thatcher immediately ordered it to be inserted in the manifesto. In spite of the caution previously expressed by other ministers about the dangers of abolition she ordered that in too, even though virtually no work had been done to examine the difficulties.

So there it was: some of the most far-reaching and unresearched proposals for local government for many years thrown into the manifesto at the last minute at the personal behest of Mrs Thatcher. They were proposals which many Cabinet ministers had opposed time and again.

Some Cabinet ministers claimed afterwards that they had no idea until the last second that they were in. Mr Heseltine was reported to be 'dismayed' and Mr King, when first told the news on a train in northern England, was said to be shaken and 'aghast'. But Mrs Thatcher was unconcerned.

Supreme in her thinking was the final realization of what had become a personal challenge: the removal of the power base which had enabled Ken Livingstone to taunt and defy her, to rival and, in some ways, even to better her. Even if he slipped into Parliament a repeat performance would be impossible. And if he did not she could and would wipe him off the national political map.

As Mr Heath said about the proposals during the abolition debate on 4 December 1984: 'They were put in nine days after the election was called, against the wishes of the Party Policy Committee. They were inserted without the general agreement of those who had been London Conservative members. The consequences are now apparent for all to see.'

They had also been inserted without anyone bothering to check whether they were popular. The usually efficient Tory machine did not commission any poll before the decision. Perhaps they remembered the GLC's very poor opinion poll ratings in 1981 – but that was not the same issue. The very first poll to be published in the *Standard* in October 1983 showed that 54 per cent of Londoners opposed abolition and only 22 per cent were in favour. Had the Tories bothered to check they would have seen that the poll ratings of the GLC had already risen well above the dreadful levels of 1981. A MORI poll published in the *Standard* on 20, 21 and 22 April 1983 showed that satisfaction with the GLC's running of London had crept up to 30 per cent with 49 per cent dissatisfied. By 45 per cent to 43 per cent Londoners supported our plans to increase the rates in order to introduce our second fares cut the following month. Although our grants policy 'to fringe and minority groups' was opposed by 52 per cent to 24 per cent, the position was reversed with our declaration of London as a nuclear-free zone. Not only was that supported by 51 per cent to 25 per cent, but we even had a lead of 41 per cent to 37 per cent amongst Tory voters on the issue.

My own ratings tended to fall somewhere between those of Mrs Thatcher and Michael Foot.

	Thatcher	*Livingstone*	*Foot*
Out of touch with ordinary people	47	32	17
More honest than most politicians	26	26	19
Rather inexperienced	6	23	14
Understands problems facing London/nation	35	22	25
Has a lot of personality	27	20	7
Down to earth	18	17	22
Rather narrow minded	19	17	21
Too inflexible	25	16	14
Talks down to people	43	15	8
A capable leader	44	15	11
Has sound judgement	24	8	10
Trustworthy	18	8	12
Good in a crisis	46	4	5

Given that the poll was taken when Mrs Thatcher's post-Falklands factor was still strong, and that I had only just returned from my visit to Belfast to meet Sinn Fein, the figures were as good as could be expected. This, then, was the background against which we started planning our anti-abolition campaign.

In my report to the broad left caucus of candidates in January 1981, I had anticipated that the Government might try to abolish the GLC if we seriously carried out our manifesto. Throughout the next two years, publicity to increase the level of public awareness of the GLC and its services was a constant consideration. On the other side of the equation, the 'Keep London Free Campaign' continued to lobby behind the scenes for abolition, and on 21 September 1982 the London Boroughs' Association (LBA) took the first steps towards calling for GLC abolition. The LBA was a voluntary association of the 32 London boroughs which, until that point, had worked on the basis of a consensus. Kensington and Sutton were the prime movers, and when later that year the LBA formally adopted an abolition policy most Labour boroughs withdrew to start the rival Association of London Authorities.

On 5 July 1982 I wrote to the D-G asking him to prepare a report,

> ... justifying the retention of the GLC, including details
> of our present functions, other functions we could take
> from central government, the redistribution role played
> by the GLC and spelling out differences between London
> and the rest of the UK where unitary local government
> could work.

This report was intended to form a basic statement of fact of the defects of the abolitionists' cause as well as providing a shopping list of demands in the unlikely event of a Labour Government's being elected the following year. While work was continuing on this project, leaks started appearing in the press about the Government committee chaired by Whitelaw to consider abolition, and these leaks became quite firm in December 1982 in the aftermath of our inviting Sinn Fein to visit London.

It was at about this time that the Director of Public Relations retired, giving us the chance to bring in Tony Wilson, head of Lambeth Council's public relations department since 1974. Wilson had impressed me while I was on Lambeth Council, and I had followed his work for Ted Knight's administration. A survivor of the battering that Lambeth's public image had taken would be ideal. He came with Ted's strong recommendation. Sir James Swaffield was still D-G at this stage and becoming increasingly unhappy with the sort of people we were appointing to key posts in the administration. The last thing the D-G wanted was for us to get real control of the PR department, so I was not surprised when after the post of Director had been advertised he recommended a short list which did not include Wilson. John Carr had to intervene to add his name to the list of candidates. In the event, he was so clearly the best choice that even the Tories, who were chronically suspicious of our appointments, had to vote for him.

Wilson immediately started work with opinion pollsters and advertising agencies to prepare our campaign. It was at this time that we discovered that the GLC's usual advertising agency had been taken over by a firm with substantial interests in South Africa, so we switched to the Boase Massimi Pollitt partnership, whose billings had grown from £800,000 in 1969 to £37 million in 1982. Although they were clearly not a socialist firm, they were far more lively, irreverent and imaginative than most advertising agencies. To work on the same campaign we hired the Smith-Bundy organization, which had been involved in several local government campaigns and had run the GLC welfare benefits campaign aimed at getting people to take up their social security benefits.

I had never shared the considerable suspicion about opinion polls that exists in the Labour Party. The GLC used opinion polls to investigate public opinion throughout the first two years of the Labour GLC. Although telephone polls are wildly inaccurate and biased against the Labour Party, traditional face-to-face polls based on random or quota samples of over a thousand people are accurate to within three per cent. Of course, polling questions can be slanted to elicit the required answer and about one poll in twenty is outside the three per cent margin of error. However, I know of no national political figure who does not privately accept the value of opinion polling, even though they have to issue ritual condemnations of the process whenever it shows their own party losing support.

I recognized that to get an effective advertising campaign going we needed to use opinion polls to discover and concentrate our attack on those areas where the Government's case was weak. All the polls showed rate increases to be unpopular, but there was no clear public opinion on who was to blame. So in the period before rate demands started arriving on Londoners' doormats that spring, we collaborated with the Labour boroughs in an advertising campaign emphasizing the Tory policy of switching £1,200 million of Rate Support Grant money away from London. At the same time, we needed to know where the GLC was vulnerable to attack from the Tories. A MORI poll for Southwark Council in 1980 had shown that only 60 per cent of those surveyed knew that the GLC was responsible for the buses and some Council housing, and about a third thought we ran local hospitals, rent and rate rebates and road maintenance. GLC parks had been used for years, but under half the population knew who ran them. Clearly, our campaign had to convey to the public precisely what the GLC did. So we started sticking GLC signs on all the services we provided. Thus began the 'GLC Awareness Campaign'.

When Mrs Thatcher called the election we were ready with a detailed report for Council on the future of the GLC and the consequences of abolition. Although we had been expecting an October election we were still able to get an issue of our free newspaper, the *Londoner*, distributed to each household and run a 'Keep the GLC' advert in the press before polling day.

The SDP came out in favour of abolition before Mrs Thatcher could overcome the reluctance of her Cabinet colleagues on the issue. We publicized a statement that Tom King had made on 24 February 1983 when James Wellbeloved, the SDP MP for Erith and Crayford, demanded abolition. King made it clear that there were 'no plans in the pipeline' and contented himself with an attack on GLC policies.

We also publicized the split in the GLC Tory Group. Alan Greengross, the new Tory Leader, had not been consulted or informed in advance about the policy on abolition and some of the more independent-minded members of his group had no intention of keeping quiet on the issue. The rather colourful and self-confident Bernard Brook-Partridge, who had chaired a GLC Tory working party on the future of the Council, had no doubt that the majority of GLC Tories opposed abolition.

> There are a number of us who will fight tooth and nail to prevent the present Government, or any other government, replacing the democratically elected GLC with a quango, or any other organization which is not directly elected. Some may think the electorate has already been divorced from too many decisions as it is, and by the Tory Party at that. Many of us would not want repeated in local government the costly nonsenses of certain water and health authorities.

He claimed abolition was only demanded by Tories who had little understanding or knowledge of the Council's work. As the campaign wore on his statements became increasingly sharp until they were quite specific attacks on the Government's ignorance.

I was certain some Tory MPs would refuse to vote for abolition when they became aware of the problems involved. If Labour gained enough seats from the Tories to leave them only a narrow majority, it seemed we might be able to defeat the legislation. It did not occur to me at the start of the election that Labour's campaign would turn out to be the most incompetent of any major political party in a Western democracy in the post-war world. Night after night when I got home from addressing election rallies, I would switch on BBC2's *Newsnight* and watch in disbelief the analysis of Labour's latest self-inflicted wound.

After the election I contemplated Mrs Thatcher's majority of 140 and knew that there was no chance of defeating the abolition proposals. Tom King had been replaced at the DOE by Patrick Jenkin, who would do whatever the Prime Minister wanted, anticipating the chancellorship as his reward for such loyalty. There seemed to be no chance of industrial action against the legislation by the trade unions at County Hall. The Staff Association would complain but do nothing. The Government would pretend to protect the fire brigade from real damage, thus avoiding a conflict with the FBU, the only disciplined trade union within the GLC. These two unions between them had over 60 per cent of the GLC staff. The rest were either not organized or in much smaller branches. The only other union of any size was NUPE, which was prepared to fight but did not have the numbers. GLC staff would reap a bitter harvest from the years of neglect of proper trade union work by the GLC Staff Association.

Although I had no illusions about our chances of winning, I was determined to do everything possible. Even if we were eventually defeated we could still waste a vast amount of the Government's time and delay the preparation of their privatization programme. We could mobilize public opinion against them, opening the way for Labour to gain control of more boroughs which could carry on the work of the GLC. We also needed proper commitments from the Labour Party leadership to reinstate the GLC under a future Labour Government, for this was by no means certain. Most Labour MPs thought that the GLC had been the cause of a huge loss of votes. One of the first to condemn us was Roy Hattersley. In an interview with David Rose published in *Time Out* just after the election, he singled out London as a particularly bad result which, he said, had let the party down nationally and was due to the leftwing stance of the GLC. This was not true. The swing to the Tories in the GLC area had been 3.8 per cent, in England as a whole it was 4.2 per cent and in Great Britain (excluding Northern Ireland) it was 5.2 per cent. But the lie was repeated by others and became part of the general propaganda against the left.

Facts count for less in politics than people's existing prejudices, and the GLC and I had largely been written off by the media. The rapid emergence of Neil Kinnock as the next Leader of the Labour Party only served to encourage the view that the Labour GLC had had its day and that the focus of attention in the Labour Party would now shift back to the House of Commons and the new team around Kinnock. John Carvel, who was at this time halfway through writing *Citizen Ken*, said that there was a sudden loss of interest in publishing the book.

Livingstone's brand of politics began to look out of place in the new atmosphere of studied harmony which descended on the Labour Party ... The word most often used about him by the young party *apparatchiks* who stay up too late in bars at party conferences was that he was 'marginalized', that he had become peripheral to issues of power in the party.

Fortunately, I take a long-term view of politics. I see it as a marathon rather than a sprint, and the pressures inside County Hall left me too tired to lie awake at nights worrying about my personal future. We would fight abolition as though we expected to win.

When the PPC/PC met to plan our campaign in the light of Mrs Thatcher's re-election there was no sign of defeatism. Michael Ward was keen that our campaign should not be merely defensive and wanted to continue new policy development. John McDonnell had already begun to think about how we would get the GLC's money out of the building and into the hands of those Labour councils and voluntary organizations which would carry on our work. He also saw the value of mobilizing not just the general public but what he called our 'client groups'. Paul Boateng put the case for a large and expensive public relations campaign. Lewis Herbert proposed getting around television and radio restrictions on political advertisements by advertising GLC services instead. George Nicholson pointed out that we were approaching the 100th anniversary of the LCC and should be able to make capital out of that. Nita Clarke, who had replaced Veronica Crichton as the Labour Group press officer, suggested that we should attend the TUC and Labour Party conferences to lobby for our cause. This might overcome the general distaste for the GLC in some areas of the Labour movement. She added, almost as an afterthought, that we should put on an exhibition at all the party conferences.

By 18 July, Tony Wilson was able to report that all the work was underway. Leaflets and academic papers to be used in the campaign were being written. A mid-term report on the achievements of the administration was underway. Display units and videos for our visits to all the conferences had been ordered. A team to respond to press inaccuracies had been set up. Detailed analysis of the damage to each borough from abolition was being prepared by Maurice Stonefrost. Local press and borough campaigns were being established to work with GLC funded voluntary organizations. Poster campaigns to increase publicity for GLC events such as Thames Day and Pensioners' Day were underway. A special effort to get across the benefits of our funding of voluntary organizations to counter press distortion was planned.

The very close working relationship that had developed between John McDonnell and myself now began to produce real benefits. Because of the level of trust that had been built up by my support of him during his first year as chair of the Finance Committee I could now delegate responsibility for large areas of the campaign to him knowing it would be effectively administered, and he responded without questioning when I needed the release of finance to fund the campaign. Working with John Carr the three of us established the Link Team, a group of bright young officers who could collect from the bureaucracy all the information we might need for our lobbying and campaign work. We knew that to mobilize pressure on the Government we would need community activists running petitions, marches, meetings and lobbies of Parliament, so we set up the Outreach Team. Unlike the Link Team, these were all outside appointments with a background of Labour movement and community campaigning. To supplement this work we got together a Local Press team from existing public relations staff.

Knowing the weakness of the trade unions within County Hall, we asked Mike Ward to co-ordinate our work in this field. Once again, John Carr had an interest in this area and helped smooth relations with the SA, who were recovering from their row with us over anti-racist and anti-sexist measures. This was not easy. The only way to build an effective trade union campaign was to bypass the SA-dominated formal committees and establish a rank-and-file committee. So while John Carr continued to placate the SA leadership, Mike Ward was busily establishing a committee of trade union activists who could be released from normal duties to begin building staff consciousness.

*

An absolutely vital role was that of parliamentary lobbyist. We needed someone with past lobbying experience (which ruled out GLC staff) and an excellent knowledge of local government (which ruled out existing lobbying organizations). I originally asked Chris Price, who had just lost his seat as MP for Lewisham West, but he had taken another job and did not wish to hang around the corridors of Westminster like a ghost.

The person I was certain could do the job well was Roland Freeman. But would he be acceptable to the Labour Party? Twenty years before, a bright young Tory, he had directed the campaign to abolish the old LCC. He knew all the details about the creation of the GLC. He had been chair of Finance to Sir Desmond Plummer, the first Tory GLC Leader. And he would certainly have been Plummer's successor if he had not missed a vital term on the GLC during which he sorted out his business, which had suffered as a result of his GLC commitments. Freeman had returned to the GLC during the Goodwin administration when a by-election in Finchley took place in 1975. Afraid that he might be a rival for the Tory leadership, Sir Horace Cutler never gave him a job, and Freeman remained a backbencher throughout Sir Horace's administration.

It was during the years of the collapse of the Goodwin administration, and then afterwards when I was the lone and isolated leftwinger during the Cutler years, that I came to respect Roland Freeman's intelligent judgement and share his contempt for the mediocrity of so many of his colleagues. He had joined the SDP, remarking, 'You know how rightwing I am and that should tell you a lot about the SDP', but in my view that was another reason why he would be an ideal parliamentary lobbyist: not only did he know the Tory Party inside out, but he was also likely to have considerable influence with the SDP in the coming struggle to get them to drop their pro-abolition policy. If we were trying to influence Tory and SDP opinion, Roland Freeman was likely to be much more successful than a Derek Hatton or a Ken Livingstone. In the end, the Labour Group were happy to agree to his appointment.

I returned from holiday in San Francisco (which inspired *Private Eye* to allege that I was importing exotic pills which changed the taste of human semen to strawberry flavour) to begin the autumn conference tour. It got off to an excellent start at the TUC, where support for our job creation policies was growing at a remarkable rate. During the debate of a motion opposing abolition, the new leader of the electricians' union, Eric Hammond, managed to unite the whole conference behind us by the sheer viciousness of his attack on the GLC. In a speech which even the *Daily Mail* would have admitted was biased, he accused us of being 'perverts and terrorist groupies'. It was much the most anti-GLC speech of the entire conference season, beating anything heard even at the Tory conference, and eventually it was drowned in a chorus of protests.

The SDP conference was bound to be very different, filled with people who had left the Labour Party because of people like me and who had just fought the election on a manifesto committed to abolition. We expected an uphill fight. The conference was at Salford University and our fringe meeting was booked into a lecture theatre. We had been given credentials to visit the conference and listen to the debate on local government the next morning. With TV covering every move, the strategy was highly risky: there were no ground rules or precedents for a politician from one party visiting the conference of another in order to try and change its policy. With so many old enemies formerly from the right of the Labour Party present, an ugly scene could easily develop. One mistake when you thought the cameras were off, or a slip of the tongue, could sink the whole campaign. The entire GLC leaders circus travelled up by train. Bill Bush and Nita Clarke fussed and bustled around as we speculated on what sort of reception to expect and how I should handle potential confrontations. A number of too loud jokes betrayed the tension we all felt. At Salford we were straight off the train and into the lecture theatre. Roland Freeman met us with the warning that as the main conference was overrunning we should not expect too many people in the audience yet, but as we entered, the room was already crowded. BBC TV cameras were ready to record a clip for the *Nine O'Clock News*. Tony Wilson's team had been busy and the GLC display provided an impressive backdrop. What was much more important was the fact that every delegate seemed to be clutching our GLC Fact Pack.

By the time the meeting started, people were sitting on the floor and others were squeezed into the corridor outside trying to hear. Obviously this was going to be the largest fringe meeting of the conference. Keith Sonnet of NALGO and Roland Freeman spoke before me, and then, after a brief introduction by John McDonnell, I delivered a speech which was a factual list of the problems abolition would produce for London, with a strong attack on the centralizing tendencies of Mrs Thatcher's Government. In the presence of so many former colleagues who knew all my faults, the only humour I dared to risk was self-deprecation. When the meeting finished I knew we had won the audience over, with the sole exception of Oliver Stutchbury, the former Labour GLC member from the Goodwin administration, who had resigned from the party to stand as an 'Abolish the GLC' candidate. The BBC reporter was clearly delighted with the TV footage: the mood in the meeting was almost news in itself. When the applause finally died down, it was obvious that the SDP delegates had received us every bit as favourably as those at the TUC, even without Eric Hammond's attack to help us along.

As the meeting broke up, it was difficult to get away from the sympathetic mob, but eventually we found our way to the main hotel bar. News of our reception had preceded us. I passed David Owen in the corridor.

'I hear you've been having fun with my delegates,' he said.

'If they carry on like this we might let them back into the Labour Party,' I replied.

There was a smile of disbelief on his face. 'If they carry on like that I might let you have them back!'

Later that night we celebrated in a local Greek restaurant. The owner showed us the Greek tradition of writing a wish on your plate and smashing it on the floor. We got through a lot of plates.

The next morning we heard that the BBC report had been excellent, and the reports that had made the London editions of the papers were all favourable. There was no formal vote to be taken at the conference session that morning, but the debate on local government turned into a review of SDP policy on abolition. Speaker after speaker went to the rostrum to oppose abolition and approvingly quote my speech. The old Labour Party hands on the platform looked aghast and rolled their eyes to heaven in disbelief.

During one particularly glowing reference I happened to catch David Owen's eye and we exchanged wry smiles. The speaker replying to the debate was John Cartwright. One of the six SDP MPs to hold their seat, and a strong proponent of abolition, he had caught the mood of his audience and was surprisingly noncommittal. Perhaps the best indication of our reception by the delegates came after I had left the hall to return to London. The GLC party was unaware that there was to be a surprise speaker from the Polish trade union, Solidarity; had we known, we would have stayed to listen, as the GLC had given full support to the struggles of the union. Seeing that I had left the conference, Bill Rodgers reverted to the old tricks that had earned him such a reputation in the Labour Party by launching a bitter attack on me for allegedly snubbing Solidarity. In the hours that followed he came under such pressure from delegates who deplored those sort of tactics that he was forced to withdraw his remarks.

From the SDP conference on we had the initiative; the Government became more and more defensive. The GLC Labour Group's morale soared. Even the *Daily Express* was critical of the abolition plans, and when finally they were published by Patrick Jenkin, David Owen condemned them. By the time we arrived at the Liberal conference in Harrogate the following week, the Young Liberals were wearing 'I'm Red Ken' badges and almost the entire conference turned up to our fringe meeting. The contrast between the sober, conservatively dressed SDP delegates and the radical individualist Liberals could not have been more marked, and their reception of what had now been nicknamed 'The GLC Roadshow' was, if anything, even more ecstatic. The Liberals had always been committed to devolution and local government and so had no trouble accepting the GLC's case. Even our controversial policies on racial and sexual equality were accepted by the vast majority present. Their position on Ireland was similar to mine. The only other thing that was required to establish complete rapport was to make a few jokes at David Owen's expense. The following day the Liberal conference voted by a large majority to oppose abolition.

The Labour conference was a foregone conclusion and lacked

the particular excitement of the Liberal and SDP conferences. The Labour Party was used to seeing the GLC contingent. However, the party bureaucracy was still trying to keep us at arm's length and we had more trouble getting exhibition space and visitors' tickets than at the Liberal and SDP conferences. The Labour Party machine was always the last organization in the country to hear what was going on or notice a trend and they still had not woken up to the increasing popularity of the GLC. The small team managing Neil Kinnock's leadership election campaign had decided that he should not be seen even talking to me at the TUC conference in case it associated him with the loony left or with losers who were due to be abolished. This led to the nonsense of Neil and I standing not fifteen feet apart in the foyer at the Winter Gardens with his minders steering him around me so that no photographer could get both of us in the same picture.

I had been aware from the start that the press would look for anything to damage our campaign and had laid down firm rules about expenses for the roadshow, which included staying in the cheapest hotels. This rule caused embarrassment for two prominent journalists at the Tory conference who had never been exactly favourable towards the GLC in their stories. One evening they were escorted back to our hotel by two prostitutes who used it for business purposes. The look on the reporters' faces as they drunkenly swayed into the bar draped over the prostitutes made up for all the discomforts of staying in one of the cheapest hotels in Blackpool.

George Tremlett had taken the courageous decision to speak on the same platform as me, even though he knew this was certain to alienate many members of his party. He was becoming more critical of the Government plans with each passing day and was the logical choice to join me on the platform. The flavour of Tremlett's attack on the Government is well illustrated by the article he published in *City Limits* at the close of the conference season. Under the heading 'Disgraceful, insulting and immoral' he wrote:

> My objections to the Government's proposals to abolish the Greater London Council are fundamental. I believe they are a disgrace to Parliament and bring shame upon the shoulders of the Conservative Party.

My feelings are that strong because I know that the Government is intent on forcing them through Parliament for reasons that are immoral and intellectually insulting. The responsibility for this lies with the Prime Minister.

She insisted upon a commitment to abolish the GLC being written into the General Election manifesto against the advice of senior ministers.

Her reasoning is banal. She believes 'Red Ken' can be abolished by wiping out the GLC. She believes the Labour Party can be crippled by destroying the metropolitan counties, their principal power base outside Parliament.

It is this that I find immoral since I believe in the two-party system and its inherent process of debate. If the people of London wish to vote for a Labour GLC, then I defend their right to do so (however much I may disagree with their decision).

Not so this Prime Minister. She tolerates no opposition ... ... The people of London would no longer have the right to determine a framework of local government for their city. They would no longer have the right to decide by what priorities their local rates should be spent. They would be taxed but unrepresented.

Yes, you would have a unitary state. But this is not our system of government.

That was the system Mussolini tried to force upon the Italians during the 1930s and which Hitler sought to impose upon Germany.

It is a system that always leads to absolute power and ends in corruption because it lacks the fundamental core of accountability to the people which the ballot box represents.

This issue is as fundamental as that because the Government intends transferring control ... to a motley rag-bag of non-elected boards and quangos.

The proposals would leave London the only major world city without its own elected city-wide local government.

The mood in 'The GLC Roadshow' as we travelled up to Blackpool for the Tory conference was very tense. The Tory Party had tried to block our attendance by refusing to rent space for our displays and when we had rented space in the local shopping centre pressure was applied to the management to cancel our contract. We promptly went to court and the judge said our booking must go ahead. No sooner had the exhibition been put up than it was attacked by a mob of young Tories. One of the vice-chairs of the Tory Party announced that my personal safety was at risk but was forced into a grovelling retraction when Tony Banks MP wrote asking why the party which claimed to support law and order had such people in its midst. Tony Wilson and Bill Bush had been sufficiently worried to bring six impressively built staff from our parks department to Blackpool. They remained out of sight of the press and public but it was good to know they were there.

These precautions were unnecessary. Our reception from the Tories was almost as good as at the other conferences. We encountered much goodwill, perhaps because a substantial proportion of the delegates were fairly non-political; just how non-political was indicated by the large number who when passed a leaflet inviting them to the meeting asked, 'What's the GLC?' or 'Who is Ken Livingstone?'

The meeting itself was slightly less enthusiastic than the others but a rowdy shouting demonstration by a couple of dozen young Tories at the back of the hall helped us to win sympathy from those who had actually come to listen. Most people were unaware that during the heckling meted out to George Tremlett, Nita Clarke had come up behind a man who was bent double outside the hall looking through a keyhole. When she asked if he wanted to come in, a very embarrassed Patrick Jenkin went bright red and rushed away. At the end of the meeting many people contributed to a collection to cover the costs, so that they would not 'add to the burden on London's ratepayers'.

That night in the bar I was approached by several Tories who wished the GLC success in its struggle. Most surprising of all were the two who took me to one side to say how much they supported all that I had done on the issue of Ireland. I was left with the idea that the Tory Party was an even broader church than Labour.

On the train to London the next day we discussed the remarkable turn-around in our fortunes in the four months since Mrs Thatcher's re-election. We had definitely seized the initiative with our conference tour, and all the other parts of our campaign were beginning to slot into place. Under Paul Walmsley the Outreach Team was helping to organize the first stirrings at grass roots level, with petitions and letters beginning to flood in to MPs. The information being assembled by the Link Team, with details of the problems abolition would bring, was starting to reach editors and professional bodies. Roland Freeman had put together his team of lobbyists and was beginning to find out which Tories were likely to rebel in Parliament and which were open to persuasion. For the first time it looked as though there might be an outside chance of defeating abolition.

We all agreed that our greatest asset was the Secretary of State for the Environment, the Right Hon. Patrick Jenkin. Although he was known to the public only for his stupid suggestion that people should brush their teeth in the dark in order to save electricity during the 1974 miners' strike, he had already had an impressive Cabinet career. Jenkin had just celebrated his 57th birthday and could look back on continuous service in Mrs Thatcher's Government, first as Secretary of State for Social Services and then at Industry. He also looked forward to promotion to Chancellor of the Exchequer as the reward for implementing the abolition pledge.

Patrick Jenkin was fairly typical of that great grey mass of place-men and time-servers found in all parties in Parliament. During Edward Heath's leadership he was a Heath loyalist. Under Mrs Thatcher's reign he was a Thatcher loyalist. On 1 August 1977 he had drafted evidence to the Marshall enquiry into the future of the GLC supporting its continuation and insisting that the principle of direct elections should apply to all layers of local government. In 1983 he was prepared to abolish the GLC and introduce unelected bodies running local government on a scale not seen since 1889, because that was the basis on which the job was offered. Tom King, who realized the problems of abolition, declined to give the undertakings Mrs Thatcher required and was demoted for the unspeakable crime of having a dissenting opinion in the Cabinet. Patrick Jenkin had no such qualms.

Jenkin spent his first year in office declining the offer of every radio and television political programme in Britain to join me in debate. What I had seen of his mediocre performance in that year was confirmed the following summer, when we finally met in a public debate set up by Alan Hargreaves for Capital Radio. Slow in debate, ponderous in speech, pompous in style, struggling to absorb the facts of the case in a breathtakingly unimpressive performance – in my contact with him I marvelled at the paucity of political talent and leadership that must exist in Britain in order for someone like Jenkin to have a chance of getting to the top. I am sure he was a very nice man who, as a neighbour, would feed your cat or water your garden while you were on holiday, but the idea that he had headed two of the most important state departments said everything we need to know about the decline of Britain. Caught between his senior civil servants with their opposition to abolition and the determination of the Prime Minister, if ever there was a case of *Yes, Minister* in real life it was Patrick Jenkin.

What we did not know as we travelled back in the train after the Tory conference was that Jenkin had already taken the decision which would lead to the humiliation of the Government in the Lords and end his own political career. Not surprisingly, it was the only decision he ever took which was against Mrs Thatcher's advice.

The problem the Tories faced was that it would take until 31 March 1986 to abolish the GLC. The GLC elections were due ten months before that date and the Tories were terrified that we would turn them into a referendum on the issue. In a confidential letter to the Prime Minister on 27 July 1983, Patrick Jenkin had proposed that legislation to 'pave the way' for abolition should include a clause deferring the elections so that the existing councillors would continue in office until abolition. The only other option was to cancel the elections and when our term of office expired to allow the London boroughs each to appoint one of their members to take over until abolition. Effectively, this would mean replacing

271

the Labour majority directly elected by Londoners with a Tory majority of two to one appointed by the London boroughs. Such a proposal would be controversial but under no conditions could the Tories live with the 1985 GLC elections. As Jenkin put it in another private letter to the Prime Minister:

> ... The 1985 elections cannot be allowed to go ahead: other objections apart, abolition would be a major issue in the elections, so that there would be a major public debate going on after the House of Commons had voted for the Second Reading of the Abolition Bill.

As it became known among Tory MPs that Jenkin had decided to 'give' the Labour administration another year in office, the extreme right went up the wall. During the summer he was endlessly lobbied by London Tory backbench MPs. Ever eager to please his supporters, Jenkin changed his mind. In another letter of 20 September to the Prime Minister, he reported that the committee he chaired was split on the issue.

> Some members argued that there were constitutional and political objections to substitution: in particular, that we should be accused of creating a new procedure in order to engineer a change in political control in the GLC area.
> A small majority of the Group, however, considered that both our own supporters and the wider public would find it incomprehensible that we should, in effect, extend the terms of office of the GLC and the MCCs. Moreover, to do so would provide those bodies with scope of obstruction at a time when this would be most damaging to our policies. They therefore favoured substitution.

Mr Jenkin described this decision as 'probably one of the most sensitive decisions we have to take'. He then recommended the substitution option to Mrs Thatcher and the Cabinet. Initially, Mrs Thatcher indicated her opposition to this strategy. In a letter from her private secretary, Michael Scholar, to Mr Jenkin's private secretary, John Ballard, it was stated that 'the Prime Minister prefers deferment of the May 1985 elections of the GLC to substitution'.

What happened between the Scholar letter to Jenkin and the publication of the White Paper on 7 October? We will not know until their memoirs appear, but Mrs Thatcher changed her mind and went along with the Jenkin decision to go for substitution.

Unbeknown to the Government, this exchange of letters, which contained a considerable amount of information about other matters including financial and staffing arrangements, had been passed to the GLC. I returned from my August holiday to find a copy of the Jenkin letter of 27 July on my desk. When I asked where it had come from, the story was even more interesting than the contents of the letter. It had apparently 'fallen out' of a man's briefcase while he was otherwise engaged in a brothel which specialized in sado-masochism and bondage. A copy had then been passed to a friend of a GLC councillor with instructions to see that it got into my hands. As the circulation of the original letter was only to the Cabinet, the Attorney-General, the Arts Minister, Jenkin's deputy and Sir Robert Armstrong (the Cabinet Secretary), there was intense speculation about whose briefcase had been left temporarily unattended.

Shortly after our return from Blackpool we received copies of the Jenkin letter of 20 September and the reply from Michael Scholar. The circulation list was the same, with the addition of Richard Hatfield in the Cabinet Office. The debate about whether it was a Cabinet minister involved or his private secretary continued.

Although we only received copies of the originals, I was worried that the documents might have been stolen, although it was unlikely that the owner would demand their return. I therefore asked the councillor concerned to make direct contact with the brothel keeper and offer her the temporary loan of a GLC photocopier. My colleague returned from the meeting to say that the woman who ran the brothel (and who had originally been a man) thought a photocopier would look out of place and might worry the clients. My colleague also brought the information that the second Jenkin letter had fallen into the brothel keeper's hands at Blackpool during the Tory Party conference. Apparently she always followed her clients to the Tory conference so as to continue her service. She also revealed to my colleague that the donor of the letter was actually tied to a bed when the letter 'fell out' of his briefcase and was therefore unlikely to have noticed what was happening.

Among the small group who knew of the existence of the letters and the circumstances of their route to us, there was a major dispute about the way we should use them. Given that the Tories were still reeling from the Parkinson affair, some were in favour of an immediate release. This I vetoed on several grounds. In the first place, we would not receive further information from the same source. Secondly, there was our responsibility towards the brothel keeper. Although attempts had been made to remove any identifying marks by which the owner of the documents could be identified, a handwritten marginal note on the second Jenkin letter had not been totally erased: fifteen words or parts of words remained visible. More than enough to lead to the identification of the owner. It would then be only a matter of time before the brothel keeper was identified.

I could still vividly remember the way the Establishment had hounded Dr Stephen Ward to death for his role in the exposure of the Profumo affair and had no doubt that if she was ever identified, the brothel keeper would be similarly hounded. There was also the question of the right to privacy of the man concerned. What he did in his sex life was entirely up to him. No one else had been damaged or harmed. Knowing what the impact of exposure, disgrace and a press witch-hunt would be on his immediate family, and remembering my disgust at press attempts to reach my family at the height of the campaign against me, I had no intention of being responsible for doing that to any other human being. Finally, there was the fact that as the brothel keeper had had a change of sex, there was every likelihood that public exposure of these events could trigger a wave of homophobia and sexual witch-hunting within Government and the civil service.

Although the flow of documents ceased, it was never clear whether this was because our offer of a photocopier had alarmed the brothel keeper or because the owner of the letters found attendance at the Cabinet a sufficiently humiliating experience. However, for the reasons outlined above we did not give the documents to the press. In March 1984, while I was away on the abolition campaign trail, it became obvious that the Government was about to publish its Paving Bill to scrap the elections. John McDonnell, on advice from Nita Clarke and Bill Bush, took the decision to give copies of the documents to John Carvel without indicating how they had come into our hands. When the story appeared in the *Guardian*, most people assumed that the leak had come from 10 Downing Street to give the Prime Minister the opportunity of distancing herself from the unpopular policy of changing the political control at County Hall without an election. Therefore no leak hysteria was unleashed. The final irony in all this is that John Carvel went on to win the Local Government Journalist of the Year Award for his exposure of the disagreement between Thatcher and Jenkin. I was asked to present the prizes. If ever there was a better example of the incestuous relationship between the press and politicians, I cannot think of it.

Between the party conferences and the introduction of the Paving Bill we worked closely with the Harris Polling Company (who also worked for the Tory Party) and Boase Massimi Pollitt to plan the first stage of our national publicity campaign. There has always been a tendency on the left to distrust advertising agencies for fear that they will dilute the purity of the socialist message. The truth is that Labour has seldom had much socialism in its message and too often relies on down-market unimaginative advertising campaigns as a substitute for firm socialist policies. At the GLC we had no hesitation in using modern business methods to get across our policies. We never allowed the advertising executives to dilute our policies but we were prepared to take advice about the best way of getting them across to the public.

The Harris research showed that the Tories were most vulnerable on the issue of the loss of democratic rights to Londoners. The majority of Labour members, however, would have preferred the campaign to focus on the issue of services, and I had major misgivings about how much impact a campaign around the constitutional issues would have. In the end we decided to concentrate on that issue during the time the Paving Bill would be before

Parliament and switch the emphasis to services during the time of the main Abolition Bill.

The second problem for Labour members was spending over £100,000 on a full-page advert in the national press and then only putting five or ten words in the message, such as 'Say No to No Say'. Left to our own devices we would have wanted to include references to policies on racism and sexism, job creation, service protection, nuclear-free zones, opposition to South African goods and support for Nicaragua. Instead of a clear message it would have ended up as a page of dense type, rather like one of those dreadful North Korean thoughts of Kim Il Sung adverts which regularly appear in the Western press.

Another problem was the cultural differences between the Labour councillors and the advertising executives. Behaviour, dress and jargon often grated on both sides, and after some rather pyrotechnic rows Tony Wilson decided to operate as the messenger between the sides, minimizing face-to-face contact.

Once we started to see proof of the vast shift in public opinion, complaints from councillors ceased. Just as our adverts first appeared on hoardings across London and in the national press, the opinion polls started to swing from the 54 per cent opposed to abolition in October 1983 to 62 per cent in March 1984, peaking at 74 per cent in September 1984. Support for abolition declined from 22 per cent in October 1983 to 16 per cent in September 1984.

When the Paving Bill was finally published on 30 March 1984 it aroused a storm of protest. Edward Heath delivered a critical broadside during the Commons' debate on the second reading, describing the bill as a 'bad bill, and paving the way for a worse bill'.

> ... It is bad because it is a negation of democracy ... Worst of all is the imposition by parliamentary diktat of a change of responsible party in London government. There cannot be any justification for that. It immediately lays the Conservative Party open to the charge of the greatest gerrymandering in the last 150 years of British history.

Mr Heath was joined in this rebellion by ex-Cabinet ministers Francis Pym, Ian Gilmore and Geoffrey Rippon.

Even the press was worried. The *Daily Express* warned on 13 June 1984, after the debate in the Lords:

> Once again the House of Lords demonstrates its value as the place for second thoughts.
>
> By giving the Government a tiny majority of 20 on the bill to abolish Greater London Council elections next year it sends a warning signal to No. 10: be very careful about tampering with the democratic process.
>
> The argument for doing away with the useless, costly GLC and the other metropolitan dinosaurs is overwhelming.
>
> But the case for abandoning a scheduled election is much less clear-cut.

Under the headline 'Abolish this Bad Abolition Bill' the *Mail on Sunday* of 17 June 1984 said:

> . . . What worries Mrs Thatcher is that if she allows the election to go ahead it will be used by the Labour Party as a referendum on the whole abolition issue. Worse still, they would use vast amounts of ratepayers' money to propagandize their cause.
>
> There can be no doubt that this is what would happen and it would be very undesirable. But the alternative route which is being taken by the Government is even worse.
>
> What an appalling precedent is being established for the future. Here is a moderate democratic government abolishing an election because it happens to be inconvenient. What will a more malign force do with that one in the years to come?
>
> There is still time for wiser heads to prevail. This is a bad bill – and ministers know that very well.

The *Daily Mirror* put it more bluntly.

> Defenders of the House of Lords say it exists to prevent the House of Commons getting too big for its boots.

Those who want to abolish it say it is the last bunker of the Conservative Party.

Today, we have the chance to find out who is right.

The Lords are due to debate a bill, sent to them by the Commons, whose purpose is to scrap next year's elections for the Greater London Council.

Instead, the GLC, for the last year of its life, would be run by the local councillors, chosen from London boroughs. Overnight, control of the GLC will switch from Labour to Tory.

All without an election.

This is a blatant piece of political gerrymandering born of the Government's hatred for Ken Livingstone . . .

The vote in the House of Commons was a majority of 93 for the Government. Eighteen Tories voted against the bill, but while it was only a small rebellion it was a rebellion of quality. Led by the traditional 'one nation' group of Tories who had considerable influence in the Lords, it was exactly what we needed.

The bill arrived in the Lords for its second reading and first vote on 11 June. We had spent the previous weeks flooding the place with information and working hard with the metropolitan counties (who were running a separate but complementary campaign to ours) to persuade the Labour and Alliance peers to support the same amendment. Roland Freeman and others had been successful but the price of getting Alliance support was a rather weak amendment which would have embarrassed the Government but not defeated the bill.

The calm leisurely pace of life in the Lords began to change with the vigour of our lobbying. Reg Race (the former Labour MP for Wood Green whom we had appointed to the number three position at County Hall) and Maurice Stonefrost were getting more directly involved in the campaign, drafting briefing notes and speeches and providing the resources to mobilize the maximum number of peers. On paper the Tories had 450 peers, Labour 110, Alliance 80 and there were 200 independents, the so-called crossbenchers. However, the attendance record of the Tories was worse than the others and it would be possible to win if we captured the bulk of the crossbenchers.

Working with the opposition whips we contacted everyone and planned a fleet of cars to get them to and from the Lords. We hired rooms in the Lords in which food and drink would be continually available on the day so that none of them had any excuse to slip out of our sight. Every foible was pandered to and it eventually paid off. On the day of the first Lords debate I sat watching from the corner of the chamber in the visitors' area. There had been much grumbling on the part of those Tory peers who did not like to be handled quite so firmly by Bertie Denham, the Tory chief whip, and Willie Whitelaw, the Tory leader of the Lords. The house was packed, and when the vote came we knew the result was on a knife-edge. All depended on how many Tory peers had refused to be dragged in to vote for a proposal that they were unhappy with anyway.

There was no hiding our disappointment when we discovered that we had come within 20 votes of victory, losing by only 217 to 237. But if we were disappointed the Tory whips were shocked. Seven Tories had voted with us and 29 abstained. Without the hereditary peers we would have won easily, as the Tory vote was comprised of 178 hereditary with only 59 life peers and no bishops. In contrast, over two-thirds of the opposition votes were life peers including seven bishops. The crossbenchers had split 40 to 22 in our favour.

While our lobbying team carried on the work of mobilization in the Lords, our public campaign really took off. Across London hundreds of anti-abolition meetings were held. A massive amount of work went into a petition which ended up with over a million and a quarter signatures, placing it in the same league as the great Chartist petitions of Victorian times. Requests for speakers were coming in not just from traditional Labour movement bodies but from professional associations, financial institutions and even local Tory parties.

The opinion polls now showed Labour pulling strongly ahead of the Tories in London. Although London had usually been a mirror image of national voting patterns, now for the first time a real gap opened up. By March 1984 Labour had a 10 per cent lead over the Tories in London compared with a Tory lead of two per cent nationally. By September 1984 the London lead had widened to 28 per cent while Labour was still four per cent behind the Tories nationally. Throughout the last two years of the Labour GLC we consistently ran 10 to 20 per cent ahead of Labour nationally in the polls.

Not all of this transferred to real support in the ballot box. When the European Parliament elections took place in June 1984 we tried to turn them into a mini-referendum on abolition, with only limited success. But even then the swing to Labour in London was twice the national average. As the results came in Roy Hattersley for once had nothing but praise for Labour's performance in London.

The polls also showed that the slow swing in our favour that had been registered by the MORI poll for the *Standard* in spring 1983 had accelerated. The *Standard* published another MORI poll on 23 March 1984. The number of Londoners satisfied with the way the GLC was running London had risen from 30 per cent to 53 per cent. Those dissatisfied had fallen from 49 per cent to 33 per cent. Those satisfied with the way I was doing my job had risen from 26 per cent to 43 per cent. Those dissatisfied had fallen from 58 per cent to 42 per cent. The poll showed that Londoners believed that after abolition rates would increase and services would get worse. With the change in the polls the National Labour Party's attitude changed. No longer were we a 'loony left' council to be kept at arm's length. Now our problem was avoiding being crushed to death in the rush of Labour MPs eager to associate themselves with the GLC by appearing at its public meetings and press conferences.

The Tories were becoming rattled by the success of our campaign. They were particularly annoyed at having to drive into work each day past vast numbers of prominent GLC posters after seeing the latest GLC advert in their morning paper. We had decided to concentrate our advertising in Tory papers (it would have been hard to do otherwise) as all the polls had shown virtually total support from Labour voters. I realized that at some point the Tories would move to stop our campaign, so in complete secrecy we entered into long-term contracts with our advertising agents, pollsters and lobbyists which would take us up to the end of 1985.

The week that began on Monday 25 June was the most hectic time since the dreadful month of October 1981 when we had the London bombings and SDP by-election gains. It started well with the long-awaited confrontation between Patrick Jenkin and me in a Capital Radio debate which was broadcast from the GLC Council chamber. Afterwards we could all understand why Patrick Jenkin had avoided debates. Capital Radio had tried to balance the audience but almost no one wanted to speak in support of abolition and Jenkin was fumbling and unsure of his facts. Later that night the local radio news said, 'Patrick Jenkin seemed to have trouble coping with the quick-witted Mr Livingstone.' It was a slaughter and it was also the first and last time Patrick Jenkin ever appeared in public debate with his opponents.

The following morning I was sitting at a committee meeting when I was summoned outside by my secretary. Bill Bush had just phoned from Rotten Row police station to say that he had been driving to work across Waterloo Bridge when a motorcyclist pulled in front of him and another car alongside forced him off the road. Several plain-clothes Special Branch police leapt out of their car, seized his keys and announced that he was under arrest in connection with stolen Cabinet documents. He had been questioned in his cell for two hours before being allowed to phone County Hall to ask for a lawyer. We immediately despatched Jeremy Smith, the legal adviser to the Labour Group, and I rushed round to the half-dozen people who had copies of the leaked Cabinet papers to ensure that they were burnt.

One councillor had unwisely left copies of the documents at home and had a strange conversation with their son. After being told where to find the documents and to tear them up before flushing them down the toilet, the child coyly asked, 'Have you been doing something you shouldn't? What do I get out of it?' I left the member concerned to continue negotiations with their son and went back to destroy my own copies. I found the Government's action so over the top that I wondered if the documents might contain some significance we had overlooked. My suspicions aroused, I was determined to keep a full set just in case. I contacted a friend who was due to go abroad later that day and asked him to deliver the documents to a friend in the country he was visiting, which was unlikely to be sympathetic to any legal action taken by the British Government aimed at recovering the documents.

Tony Banks had gone straight to the House of Commons to raise the issue as an emergency. In the Commons, Patrick Jenkin denied any knowledge of or involvement in the use of the snatch squad. Labour's deputy environment spokesperson Jack Straw said, 'Before Thatcherism and its authoritarian tendencies became rampant, there would not have been the climate in which the police could possibly have considered their powers to arrest and detain someone who worked for a leader of a Greater London Council. But a climate has been created by this government in which that is apparently a commonplace.'

Bill was released at lunchtime and came straight back to County Hall, which was by now crawling with reporters trying to find out what was going on. Before the inevitable press conference he explained that Special Branch had been trying to trace a different leak and had not mentioned the brothel papers. Thinking of the number of fires in wastepaper baskets, and my friend boarding his plane terrified that he was about to be arrested by security at the airport, we could not help laughing.

It took only a few minutes to find out what had happened and it raised a very disturbing issue of our own internal security. Bill Bush had recently been tipped off by a completely reliable source that Sir Keith Joseph was about to announce a reversal of Government policy towards the ILEA. The original intention had been that the ILEA should be retained but comprised of three or four members nominated from each of the local boroughs. After enormous public pressure, Sir Keith was going to concede Londoners the right directly to elect the members of the ILEA. Once we had been tipped off, we discussed how best to upstage the Government and decided to tell Frances Morrell (Leader of the ILEA) so that she could make the announcement. She had been out of London at the time and when Bill contacted her she asked that her deputy be given the task and that William Stubbs, the Chief Education Officer, be told before it happened.

I had clashed bitterly with Stubbs in the past over his attitude towards unofficial teachers' strikes, and had he been working for the GLC (instead of the ILEA over which I had no control) then he would have been at the head of my list for early removal. I had warned Bill that when he saw Stubbs he was on no account to reveal the source of his information. Bill had later reported to me that Stubbs had insisted on knowing the source of the information, and to save time he had said that he had a friend in the Cabinet Office.

Bill then promptly forgot about the issue until he was sitting in the cells at Rotten Row police station. The Special Branch officer conducting the interview had shown Bill copies of documents signed by Sir Keith and Patrick Jenkin to change policy and allow elections to the ILEA. Bill was then repeatedly pressed to reveal the name of anyone he knew who worked in the Cabinet Office. It was obvious that either the phones and offices at County Hall were bugged or that Stubbs had revealed his conversation with Bill to a third party. Whether or not information had been deliberately leaked to the Government was immaterial. I immediately saw Frances Morrell to brief her. What transpired I was never told. At the time of writing he remains Chief Education Officer.

Two days later, on Thursday 28 June, I spent the day travelling to and from Llandudno to address the NUR conference. I knew that the Lords were debating amendments to the Paving Bill and that the vote would be close. But as the train pulled into Paddington Station that evening I saw John McDonnell and Nita Clarke running alongside the train followed by television cameras and lights. I knew we must have won. What was stunning was the size of the victory. Nita and John were in a state of near ecstasy as they shouted that we had won by 191 to 143, a majority of 48, the biggest defeat a Tory Government had suffered in the Lords since the First World War. As I started the inevitable round of radio and television interviews I was able to claim, as I now believed, that we could win the struggle to save the GLC.

During the party in Lord Ponsonby's Opposition chief whips' office, Reg Race and Roland Freeman gave me a breakdown of the vote. The Government were claiming that they had lost because the vote clashed with the Wimbledon tennis championship and the first day of both the Henley Regatta and a cricket test match. This was only partly true. As Reg and Roland explained, out of the 94 peers who had voted with the Tories on 11 June at least 40 had been in the House of Lords during the vote but had chosen to abstain.

The amendment that had been carried was the same as that which Francis Pym had moved in the Commons. Its effect was that the 1985 elections could be cancelled only when the final, main Abolition Bill had become law. As this was not likely to happen before July 1985, this was unacceptable to the Government, who were now terrified of what might happen in such an election.

Patrick Jenkin was particularly bitter towards the peers. The following night he spoke to a group of business people in Bradford and described the debate in the Lords: 'One of my colleagues had a party of local constituents from a mental hospital in the public gallery and they watched with growing astonishment – and a growing sense of familiarity.' Such language was hardly likely to help him find a compromise but he had had a very rough day in the Commons fending off repeated calls for his resignation. There was now little doubt that one casualty of the Abolition struggle was going to be the political career of Patrick Jenkin.

Jenkin had made the fatal strategic error of trying to pretend that the abolition of the GLC and metropolitan counties was a purely administrative change, with no political motive at all. The fact that all seven councils just happened to be Labour-controlled was, according to him, pure coincidence. Not only did this mean that Jenkin was often interrupted by genuine laughter as he tried to explain it all away, but he was automatically denied the chance to attack us on all our controversial policies and he was never able to go on the offensive. Norman Tebbit, with his much surer sense of going for the jugular, had no such inhibitions. As far back as 14 March 1984 he had made a speech to the London Tory Party which completely upstaged Jenkin. He had said that there were 'some very dangerous people' at work in local government who were 'pursuing a policy of class warfare of which Karl Marx could only dream'. He said the Labour-led GLC had set out to impoverish London 'in the belief they will thrive in the resulting chaos'. While

the police stood in the front line of the war against crime, the GLC
had undermined the police.

> Leftwing committee after leftwing committee has been
> set up to harass the police force. The people of London
> have been twisted into paying the criminals by attacking
> the police. Of the 78 applications for money made to
> the GLC's police monitoring committee only one was
> rejected. While our police officers have been fighting
> crime, the GLC has been fighting the police. If this were
> not bad enough, Mr Livingstone has welcomed IRA
> supporters to London and he has deliberately encouraged
> the breaking of the law. Under Labour's leadership there
> has been a steady corruption of respect for law and order
> in London.

The politics of the GLC were, he said, to preach peace on earth
and to spread chaos in London. He went on:

> They are paying for an army of agitators to assault the
> Government and the people of London at every turn.
> They are trying to open a great gulf in London, between
> 'us' and 'them', between one side of the street and the
> other, between black and white, between man and woman,
> between one Londoner and another. The aim of Labour
> in London is the creation of poverty and despair, because
> it is among the poverty stricken and hopeless that they
> believe they will find support.

Tebbit said the GLC was deliberately exacerbating unemployment by increasing rates.

> While taxing industry to death – and weeping crocodile
> tears about the unemployed – they have also rejected
> Government money to help London. They have rejected
> rate support grant by disqualifying themselves through
> outrageous spending, which only serves to increase
> further the number of unemployed.

Tebbit finished his speech with one statement that spelt out the
Tories' motives with vivid clarity.

The Labour Party is the party of division. In its present form it represents a threat to the democratic values and institutions on which our parliamentary system is based. The Greater London Council is typical of this new, modern, divisive version of socialism. It must be defeated. So we shall abolish the Greater London Council.

The following morning the *Financial Times* headlined its coverage of the speech as 'TEBBIT IN OUTBURST' and stated that it was 'astonishing' and 'outspoken even by his standards'. If I had had to plan the Government's campaign for them, I would have been much more inclined to use Tebbit's line to rally the troops than Jenkin's waffle. The speech led to some speculation that Mrs Thatcher might replace Jenkin with Tebbit in order to try and regain the initiative. We relished the prospect.

After delivering such a shock to the Government the peers now seemed almost eager to let them off the hook. The Cabinet came to the conclusion that the best way to get the peers to back down was to extend the term of the existing administration until the final abolition of the GLC. This they did, and try as we might to mobilize a vote against, the proposal was carried. In an effort to prevent us from being obstructive, Jenkin also proposed a wide range of new controls as amendments to the Paving Bill. Announced on 12 July, they included a ban on the disposal of land without his consent and a requirement for prior ministerial consent before we could let any new contract worth over £100,000. He also established an anti-sabotage unit within the DOE to try to anticipate our moves in advance and block them.

Back in November 1983 Jenkin had asked to be allowed to set up a special information unit to counter our campaign but he was overruled by the Prime Minister. On 30 December 1983, however, Bernard Ingham, the Prime Minister's press secretary, recommended establishing an official Whitehall Committee to co-ordinate the Tory response to our campaign. This was agreed by a cabinet sub-committee on 18 January. Immediately, Tory newspapers were contacted and began to carry pro-abolition articles by Jenkin. The following month 'Aims of Industry' launched a propaganda campaign against our grants policy. In April the Tory leader of

Westminster Council, Lady Porter, launched 'Efficiency in London Ltd' to campaign for abolition and low rates.

None of these initiatives stemmed the flood of support for our campaign. Jenkin now intended to use his control over all contracts costing more than £100,000 to veto future GLC publicity. We kept secret the fact that I had anticipated just such a move and got the officers to sign contracts which would pay for all our campaigning for another eighteen months. It was entertaining to imagine Jenkin's officers pouring over our contracts looking for hidden publicity expenditure but never finding it. But the new controls would hit many of our other policies. The Government were making the new controls on land disposal effective from midnight on the day of the announcement and we therefore had officers meeting up to 11.59 pm to transfer the vital Thameside Coin Street development site to a consortium of local community groups.

For some reason Jenkin did not make the other controls effective from midnight on the 12th, giving us fourteen days before the Paving Bill became law to get everything else through. Reg Race was put in charge of this exercise and during those few days several hundred reports were rushed to dozens of special committee meetings to get approval for £40 million worth of contracts. The Tories and the press went mad but nothing could stop us. Once the bill became law we began sending 250 contracts a week to the DOE for Jenkin's approval. As the GLC was the bulk purchaser for goods and services on behalf of London boroughs this involved the DOE in a lot of work, vetting our contracts for everything from school equipment to baked beans. Highly paid civil servants pored over the contracts, looking for the ones dealing with publicity, and Tory MPs became even angrier with Patrick Jenkin because the advertising campaign was still in full swing.

With the bill's passage into law we began the detailed planning of the next stage of our campaign. We had by now assembled a mine of information on the House of Lords and its procedures; we had built up the most effective lobbying organization ever seen in the Lords; and we knew much more about the balance of forces. Tories claimed that they did not have a majority in the Lords, but on closer inspection this was untrue. There were 943 peers eligible to vote and only 413 took the Tory whip, but many of the peers never attended the House. In the 40 divisions on the Paving Act 627 peers voted. The breakdown was:

Tories	324			Labour	119
Tory cross-benchers	45	Independent crossbenchers	73	Alliance	66

369	73	185

	258	

This gave a 'real' Tory majority in the Lords of 111. The 45 crossbenchers in the Tory column were peers who, while claiming to be independent, had sided with the Government on every occasion on which they voted. It was apparent that the Government preferred to claim that the Lords was not Tory-dominated, thereby encouraging many real Tories not to take the Tory whip in order to maintain that fiction. The only factor that allowed the Tories occasionally to be defeated was the better attendance of the Opposition. If we deleted those peers who voted on less than seven occasions then the Tory majority dropped from 111 to 63.

These figures made clear that to win we needed a perfect machine geared to getting out the maximum vote as well as a sizeable Tory abstention. There was also the problem that the peers would not reject a policy which was contained in the winning party's election manifesto.

Leaving the GLC team to work out the strategy we would need in the Lords, I proposed that we get round the cancellation of the elections by causing four highly publicized by-elections.

We had been evolving the by-elections strategy for some months. Once the Lords had caved in to Government pressure and cancelled the elections, the only way of testing our support at the ballot box was in by-elections, as we had no legal power to hold a referendum. If we were to attract press interest the seats we chose for the by-elections could not be safe Labour seats. We decided to fight only where there was a Labour GLC member and a Tory MP representing the same constituency, and to fight in four constituencies so that if we lost, Labour would lose control of the GLC. We were giving the Tories the chance to end Labour rule of the GLC by winning in four seats in which they had won the parliamentary contest only fifteen months before. I believed we were making it impossible for them to sit the election out and if they took part the by-elections would become a referendum on abolition.

John McDonnell had been easily elected as deputy Leader at the Group AGM in April 1984. I proposed that as I would obviously have to be one of the four, he should take my place as Leader during the crucial seven weeks between my resignation and the election. But John would have none of it and insisted on joining me. This was particularly worrying given the near non-existent state of his local party in Hayes and Harlington, but I could not budge him. The other two seats were Lewisham West (Lewis Herbert) and Edmonton (Ken Little). The GLLP Executive, Neil Kinnock and Roy Hattersley had promised full support and we resigned our seats on 2 August, which allowed us to have the by-elections on 20 September. This was well before the Labour Party conference; I had no intention of trying to fight by-elections during the conference, which is always a potentially disastrous time with the press playing up endless stories of splits and rows.

The first thing to go wrong with our plan was that John Gummer, the chair of the Tory Party, took the decision not to fight the four by-elections. Although there were major objections to this strategy from local Tories in the areas concerned, Tory Central Office eventually got its way. The chair of the Paddington Tories was so annoyed by what he saw as an act of cowardice that he voted for me as his own private protest. But suddenly I was very worried. None of the four seats had a natural Labour majority and if the press did their usual 'red scare' stories and built up an Alliance bandwagon then we could all lose.

The second problem was totally unexpected. Early in the week following our resignation, Andy Harris came to see me to say that Labour Councillor XYZ had failed to declare a financial interest in a company bidding for a short lease on a small shop owned by the GLC. On further investigation it became obvious that Mr XYZ had put pressure on the chief officer concerned to prepare the report in a way which disguised XYZ's financial interest. The chief officer, who had been appointed by the Tories from private industry, did not seem to think the pressure was unusual. It was absolutely illegal in local government, however, even though the sum involved was only a few hundred pounds.

I would have been happy to see Mr XYZ go to prison for several years and felt particularly vindictive towards him since he had chosen to endanger all that we were fighting for at such a crucial stage. I had been proud that for all the political rows involving the 1981 administration no one had ever been able to suggest that any councillors had become part of that team in order to line their own pockets. Like Morrison's administration, our ambitions were to achieve change for others, not to pocket some for ourselves. The case was immediately reported to Maurice Stonefrost to investigate, but within two days the *Standard* had picked up rumours and was starting to ask questions. I left for a week's holiday to relax before the campaign started. However, the idea of the *Standard* running a corruption investigation throughout the campaign and the possible disaster of the Alliance taking some or all of our seats made it the worst holiday of my life. Far from relaxing, I just became very ratty.

I need not have worried. From the moment I returned to launch the campaign after the August Bank Holiday I knew from the mood on the streets that we were home and dry in Paddington. The other campaigns were also going well, except for John's in Hayes and Harlington, where the small number of activists had little experience of elections. I spoke to Bill Bush and asked him to find half a dozen bright young officers who would take three weeks out of their holidays in order to move in and turn the campaign round. It is an indication of the loyalty and enthusiasm of the staff working for us that John's campaign was immediately swamped with helpers.

Although the campaigns were going well the press had suddenly gone quiet. Even when Neil Kinnock turned up to our early-morning press conference almost no national press were there. Mark Hollingsworth analysed the coverage for his book *The Press and Political Dissent*. He found that in the four months before polling day *The Times* carried 16 GLC stories and the *Guardian* 19. All the tabloid papers put together managed a total of just 14 stories. There is no doubt in my mind that the Tory Party made known to editors its desire that coverage should be minimized: a reduced turnout would mean that results could be dismissed. In the absence of press coverage the usual Alliance bandwagon failed to roll, vividly revealing how dependent they are on sympathetic news coverage and phoney opinion polls.

Much more worrying for us was the fact that without press stories there was nothing much for radio and television to follow up. I started complaining to Nita Clarke, our press officer, that her ability to get me on to radio and television seemed to have taken a nose-dive just when we needed it most. Stung by this criticism she redoubled her efforts and returned after an hour. 'I've persuaded TV-AM to have you on tomorrow morning,' she proudly announced. 'But there's a problem. You can't be political because of by-election law so you're going to be Mad Lizzie's exercise partner!'

As I rolled around the floor puffing and panting at 7.30 the next morning, I was uncertain that this appearance could affect any voters, until I heard that my Liberal opponent had demanded equal time. In the days that followed dozens of people stopped me on the street to comment on my workout routine, but they were mainly too young to vote!

The final disaster came on polling day itself. From the moment the polls opened it poured with rain. At times it resembled a monsoon and there were so few people on the streets it was hard to believe this was a normal working day. Trying to get people out to vote when there is over one and three quarter inches of rain is something I never want to do again. In addition, most people had no doubts that we would win and did not believe that Mrs Thatcher would take any notice if we did. 'It won't make any difference: she doesn't listen to anyone,' was a frequent theme on the doorsteps.

The *Sun* newspaper's nerve finally broke. They could not follow Tory Central Office orders about ignoring the GLC completely. Just for old times sake they had to remind the voters of:

THE COST OF KEN
Today Red Ken Livingstone, with three of his Labour comrades, is standing in a by-election.

Does London really want him back?

Consider what he has done as GLC Leader.

In nine months, the Council has distributed £31 million to voluntary organizations.

Here are just some of the 2,073 groups which have received amounts ranging from £111 to £77,835.

Babies against the Bomb
Irish Women's Group
Rights of Women (ROW)
I Drum
Migrants Action Group
London Region Trade Union Campaign for Nuclear Disarmament
Union of Turkish Workers
Hackney Trades Council Trade Union Support Unit
Rastafarian Advisory Centre
Chile Democratic GB
Liberation Movement for Colonial Freedom
Police Accountability for Community Enlightenment
London Women's Liberation Newsletter Collective
Abyssinian Society
See Red Women's Workshop
Southwark Black Workers Group
Cultural Organization for Black Radical Achievement
Gay London Police Monitoring Group
Only Women Press
English Collective of Prostitutes
Lesbian Line

Cypriot Community Workers Action Group and Joint Council for the Welfare of Immigrants
London Region CND
National Peace Council
Unity of Afro-Caribbean People
Southall Black Sisters
Earth Resource Research
Hackney Black Women's Association
Black Amalgamated Self Help Co-op
Marx Memorial Library
Irish in Islington Project
Gay Switchboard
London Lesbian and Gay Centre
Medical Campaign against Nuclear Weapons
Black Trade Unionist Solidarity Movement
Jewish Socialists Group
Ecumenical Unit for Racism Awareness Programme
South East London Women for Life on Earth
Gay Bereavement Project
Campaign to Curb Police Powers
Women's Peace Bus
Spare Rib

Do you think this is the way ratepayers' money should be spent? If so, then Red Ken is your man. You deserve him!

With 12,414 votes to the Liberals' 2,729 the result was Labour's best ever in Paddington. The percentage split was 78.2 to 17.2 with the five other candidates sharing the remainder but the turnout was down to 30 per cent. Part of the problem was that the electoral registers in London are very inaccurate. In Paddington 25 per cent of the people on the voters list had moved or died. But no amount of statistics could hide the fact that the Tory press boycott had worked, and the press were able to ignore or rubbish the results. The other three results were similar. In Lewisham West, the seat which the Liberals had concentrated on, we had still won by 66.3 per cent to 29.9 per cent.

Fortunately, Tony Wilson had anticipated the low turnout and commissioned a MORI poll, and Thames TV asked the Harris Organization to sample London-wide opinion. The two polls were in close agreement. They asked how Londoners would have voted if it had been a full GLC election. The results compared with the actual result in 1981 were:

	May 1981	Harris Poll 1984	MORI 1984
Labour	42%	56%	55%
Tory	40%	28%	28%
Alliance	17%	15%	15%

Translated into an election result these figures would have given us a council of 84 Labour, 4 Tory and 4 Alliance. When Londoners were asked how they would vote at a General Election MORI gave Labour a 13 per cent lead and Harris 18 per cent. At a real election this would mean (based on the Harris figure) a loss of 33 Tory seats out of the 56 they held in London.

Thames TV's Harris poll had also found that 74 per cent of Londoners now opposed abolition. 61 per cent said that I had done a good job as Leader. It was exactly three years since I had been 'the most odious man in Britain'.

Following the elections we reviewed the position of the campaign. Maurice Stonefrost had been D-G since Sir James Swaffield's retirement at the beginning of the year, but had only been able to carry through a proportion of the reforms he would have liked to make because of the pressures of the anti-abolition campaign. After a year in his post, Reg Race had finally succeeded in assembling the team of officers he wanted in order to get control of the financial and information flows of the GLC. Together they were giving us the tighter management structure we wanted.

On the member side I chaired a weekly meeting to review the campaign. We received reports from three working groups: Tony Banks, on the parliamentary lobbying operation, Mike Ward, on the trade union campaign, and John McDonnell, on the publicity and public campaigns which gave him control of the newly enlarged outreach team. The internal structures were now working so smoothly that we decided that I should be used more widely, addressing more anti-abolition public meetings throughout the country and concentrating specifically on audiences which were not traditionally Labour.

It was a measure of the developing confidence and mutual trust of councillors and the smoother working of our collective leadership that I was able to spend more time out of the building campaigning. The mood of the public was so supportive that it carried me through the tremendous physical demands. I often bordered on exhaustion. I had been used to working a 70- to 74-hour week during the first half of the administration; now it crept up to 84 hours a week with lots of very tiring travel. On some Saturdays I would be whisked by Council car between up to five public meetings. Rather like an election campaign, the excitement and the adrenalin kept me going, but unlike an election we had already been campaigning for thirteen months with a good nine months still to go. Also, the more I was out of the building the greater the burden on John McDonnell, who was now carrying out the tasks of Finance chair, deputy leader, the bulk of the internal administration and preparation of the campaign, while also chairing the Irish Panel and coping with the important needs and demands of a young family.

The self-indulgence of Councillor XYZ, when contrasted with the tireless commitment of so many, made me more contemptuous and angry than anything else which had happened up to that point. The *Standard* had only run one lengthy piece on the story and this had been so complicated that few could understand it and no other media took it up. When I was re-elected Maurice came to see me to report that his investigation had revealed sufficient evidence to warrant reference to the police. He passed the papers to the Director of Public Prosecutions and I invited Councillor XYZ to come and see me.

He had been given a copy of Stonefrost's report and I told him that having read it there was no doubt in my mind that he had abused his position for financial gain. Although the sum of money involved was negligible, he had deliberately broken the law and risked damaging the reputation of the whole administration. I asked him to resign immediately from the Council. When he protested his innocence I said I would have no option but to propose his expulsion from the Group if he refused to go. Unfortunately, by this time Harvey Hinds had stepped down and the whole thing was then completely mishandled by the whips office and allowed to drag on so that by the time the Group met to reach a decision the DPP had told us that they did not intend to initiate a prosecution. They will often not proceed with a case because the sum involved is too small, and because the pressures on police time for other investigations take priority. Many members of the Labour Group were influenced by Councillor XYZ's generally pathetic nature, and some excused his behaviour on the grounds of a severe drink problem. In the end they voted to take no further action. The whole Group was opposed to allowing the police to investigate wrongdoing within their own ranks. I therefore thought it somewhat hypocritical that on the first occasion when we had to deal with one of our own number, we behaved exactly as the police usually do. We took no action at all.

While we were planning the final phase of our campaign, Mrs Thatcher was reviewing her own strategy. Patrick Jenkin was pushed to one side and Kenneth Baker, a Heath loyalist, was promoted to take charge of abolition with responsibility for steering the main bill through Parliament. Baker was much more intelligent than Jenkin and able to think and act quickly. His public image was that of a traditional, sensible and caring Tory who could just have easily been in the SDP, had it existed when Baker was deciding which party to join.

Lacking in any particularly strong ideological views, he chose not to make the sort of political attack we would have expected from Norman Tebbit, nor did he struggle to try and present the Government's case in the best possible light. His tactic was different and initially took me by surprise. Faced with an impossible position to defend he would simply look sincere, smile into the camera and be economical with the truth on such a scale as to be breathtaking.

Our first major debate took place on the LWT programme *The Battle for London* in October 1984. I had made the point that after abolition, instead of being devolved to the boroughs, most of the GLC's powers and responsibilities would come under the control of the Government. This statement was based on our analysis of the Government's bill, which showed GLC expenditure:

19%   London Transport. Under direct government control.

18%   Financial, legal and property services (London Residuary Body) under direct government control.

15%   Fire Brigade. A joint board with finances and staffing under direct government control.

7%   Arts, Sports, Thames barrier. Passed to government controlled quangos.

7%   Waste disposal. Joint borough arrangements.

31%   Grants policy and pensioners' travel direct to boroughs.

3%   To various other bodies.

Kenneth Baker simply announced that I was being alarmist and that the 'vast bulk of services would now be run by the boroughs'. Recordings of the programme show my complete surprise at this novel line of debate. There was a look on my face which was a mixture of disbelief and sheer amazement at his nerve as I lamely mumbled, 'But that's not true.' Although I was initially thrown by Baker's technique, it did not wash with the viewers. An opinion poll of those who had seen the programme showed that eight per cent out of the 21 per cent who were undecided before the programme made up their minds that the proposals were undemocratic. Only one per cent moved in the opposite direction. Having been caught once I did not let it happen again, and in future debates I prepared myself to deal with even the most imaginative fantasy.

As soon as Baker was appointed, one of our officers found an old pamphlet he had written in 1977 called 'Maybe it's because we are Londoners . . .' It contained wonderful statements such as:

In recent years there has been an increasing direction by central government over local government. Far from the

GLC being allowed greater independence, Whitehall has, quite wrongly, interfered more and more with the activities of County Hall ... It is impossible to have a proper strategic authority in Greater London without a change of attitude in Whitehall.

He went on to say that the GLC must become a 'proper strategic authority' and its role should be 'enhanced'. He called for a simplified fares policy (such as we had introduced), co-ordination with British Rail (which we had proposed and Norman Fowler had vetoed), a partial lorry ban (which we were struggling to introduce in the face of Government obstruction).

He also raised the issue of race.

Clear and constructive plans are required for promoting better race relations in Greater London. Improved life in a multi-racial society cannot come about without identifying and tackling the underlying causes of tension between the various communities ... There is no better way to improve race relations in London than to insist that equality of opportunity for the second generation of the coloured populaton is a reality ... Industry and commerce must ensure equality in recruitment, training and promotion, and in terms of conditions of employment. The GLC and the boroughs must set an example ... The role that education can play in promoting better race relations is of utmost importance.

Nine years later he was to lead the Opposition to just such policies when they were introduced by what he called 'Loony left' councils such as Brent, Haringey and Lambeth.

Similar examples occurred throughout the pamphlet, with Baker calling in 1977 for new initiatives which a decade later the Labour GLC had taken, only to find Baker in 1985 using all his powers to try and prevent us from carrying them out. I particularly liked his warning that:

It will be generally agreed that Greater London, an area of some 610 square miles containing seven million people,

must continue to be more than an agglomeration of 32
boroughs with different degrees of urban disease . . .

We immediately published highlights from this stirring defence of
the GLC and sent a copy to each member of Parliament.

When the Government finally published its bill, the effects of
our policy of non-co-operation were obvious by the great gaps
which occurred wherever the Tories had forgotten a particular
GLC service, such as the new town estate at Thamesmead or
Hampstead Heath. In many other areas they had still not made up
their minds about where a service should go, and the bill gave
Patrick Jenkin 68 separate new powers to deal with these by
Government diktat before or after the bill became law. It was just
what we wanted: a bill sloppy enough to waste hours of parliamentary time and set a wide range of new precedents which would
arouse concern in the Lords.

In the nine months that followed, Labour MPs and peers ground
away at the bill line by line, while we stomped the country maxim-
izing opposition to the proposals. We had already won all the
arguments about democracy and efficiency. Of the thousands of
responses to the Government's consultation exercise only one or
two per cent were in favour of abolition. Only the three Tory-
controlled boroughs of Kingston, Ealing and Bromley gave unqualified support to abolition. Independent financial studies had
ridiculed the Tory case and predicted that the cost of abolition
would be £225 million. A MORI poll of Tory MPs showed that
only 42 per cent thought abolition was a vote-winner, whereas 44
per cent saw the issue as a vote-loser. William Whitelaw at one
party had moaned, 'How do we get out of this mess without
appearing disloyal?'

John McDonnell's committee with Tony Wilson and Nita Clarke
present constantly devised new publicity gimmicks to attract television and radio, such as my parascending across the Thames. Ned
Sherrin was commissioned to write two hugely successful updates
of Gilbert and Sullivan's *Iolanthe* and the *Mikado*, and two dreadful
GLC staff pantomimes attracted wide media coverage. We were

lucky that during this period work finished on major projects which we could declare open, such as the world's most modern solid waste transfer station and the Battersea Peace Pagoda.

Nothing, however, matched the impact of the opening of the Thames Barrier. In the year before its completion we had begun to sound out various opinions on the best way to open it. The Labour Group initially wanted the longest-serving worker on the site, the chair of the GLC or a popular East End character to perform the opening. When the workforce heard of this, they made it quite clear that they expected the Queen to perform the opening. I went down to the site to meet them and they reiterated that if we tried to get anyone else they would strike and put a picket line across the ceremony. The building workers' union (UCATT) executive council voted to call on the GLC to ask the Queen, and their decision was supported by the TGWU. When the row spilt over into the press, Thames TV asked viewers to write in and vote between the Queen or the chair of the GLC performing the ceremony. The Queen won by a nose with over 14,000 votes to the chair of the GLC's 17.

After Mrs Thatcher's re-election I expected that the Queen would be advised by her officials that with abolition looming she should avoid the ceremony, but when we were informed that she would welcome an invitation I took the issue back to the Labour Group. Apart from bitter opposition by a small minority, the bulk of the Group recognized the public relations benefit of international attention focusing on our largest ever building project at the very time that the Tories were saying the GLC was of no value to London. Mair Garside made the most bitter attack on the idea and was joined by a strange collection of left- and rightwingers in opposition. I did not believe we had any real choice. The public relations disaster of trying to open the barrier while the workers who built it were on picket lines outside, and the likelihood that they might dump the chair of the Council into the Thames before he could reach the start button, made up my mind.

On the day itself I noticed that although the Queen had pressed the start button, two of the seven barrier gates had stuck in the mud. Fortunately they freed themselves just seconds before what would have been my fatal heart attack.

Public support continued to build. The Tory leader of Westminster Council, Lady Porter, decided to put herself in the vanguard of the abolition movement and wrote round to large firms to raise funds for her campaign.

> I am sure you understand – though many people do not – that we are in a revolutionary situation as far as local government is concerned.
>
> Regrettably the battle at the grass roots has so far been won by the left, which is highly organized. The GLC, for example, in 1983 has spent about £40 million in backing groups, many of them revolutionary. In addition, millions of pounds are being spent on expensive propaganda which is pouring through the letterboxes of ratepayers.
>
> A major campaign is, therefore, being set up ... Confidentially, the campaign has the full support of the Prime Minister and the Government, although the campaign itself will be non-party.
>
> As a major ratepayer, I very much hope you will support this campaign. Cheques should be sent to me for 'Efficiency in Local Government'.
>
> To give an indication of the importance of this campaign, the Prime Minister will be meeting a dozen or so of its business supporters towards the end of next month at 10 Downing Street. Because time is short and the matter is urgent, I hope you will forgive me for being blunt and saying that I very much hope you can come along to this meeting with the Prime Minister and that you will support us with a sum of at least four figures. We have already received donations of £5,000 and £2,000.

Fortunately, the rather brassy nature of Lady Porter's personality came through in most of her propaganda and stunts. Her inability to laugh at herself meant that her campaign was devoid of humour and failed to strike a chord with the public. The rest of London's Tory borough council leaders resented the initiative but were by now used to Lady Porter's pushy nature, and just ignored it. There was also considerable embarrassment when we got hold of a copy of the letter and gave it to the press. As soon as the story broke,

Mrs Thatcher had no option but to cancel the meeting referred to in the letter.

When her campaign failed to take off, Lady Porter's temper seemed to shorten. We had both been present at a meeting to open a Child Sports Centre and she took her leave before me. When I emerged, I found that she had launched into a long tirade against my driver, telling him to make the most of his job because he would be out of work after abolition. He had considerable pleasure telling her that he worked for a car-hire firm! On another occasion when Lady Porter and I were debating at the annual conference of local government chief executives, she condemned them for declining standards of objectivity after they had given me the obligatory round of applause. She then went on to berate them for being in their shirtsleeves, even though it was a hot and humid day.

The new Leader of the Tories at the GLC was little better. Alan Greengross could have led a strong Tory campaign against abolition but instead he seemed more concerned to hold back the Tory GLC Group from a full attack on the Government. When George Tremlett (his only serious rival) endorsed the Labour candidates in the four by-elections, Alan Greengross promptly expelled him from the Tory Group. The last three years of the GLC saw the Tories led by Greengross offering nothing more than a polite questioning of the government. In contrast, George Tremlett and Bernard Brook-Partridge became well known and respected because they were prepared to oppose their party when they knew it to be wrong. Shortly after abolition Greengross received his knighthood for political services for the Tories.

The Abolition Bill had been badly mauled in the first debates in the Commons but the Tory whips packed the committee dealing with the bill with 27 party loyalists and just a couple of token rebels. Even if the two rebels voted with Labour's 15 members and the three Liberals they could not win. Many of the Tories showed their contempt for Londoners by not even following the debate, reading their correspondence and raising their hands when required to do so by the whips. This contemptuous attitude only increased the bitterness of the Tory rebels, as was made clear by Edward Heath's reference to the 'pathetic image of a speech' from the Transport

Secretary, Nicholas Ridley, during the second reading debate, which the Government won by a majority of 132.

In the weeks that followed, our strategy was to overcome the peers' reluctance to ignore the precedent that they never reject Government legislation which implements a commitment from an election manifesto. We decided on a series of amendments to the bill which would retain London-wide services under separate bodies and then propose a new elected authority to be set up to co-ordinate them. The GLC would die but immediately be replaced by a new council doing most of the same things. A similar amendment was moved in the House of Commons by Tory MP Patrick Cormack on 14 December 1984 and was rejected by only 23 votes. Over 100 Tory MPs either voted against their Government or abstained.

When the bill arrived in the House of Lords, two Tory peers, including Baroness Faithful and former GLC Leader Desmond Plummer, joined independent peer Lord Hayter to propose setting up a new elected London-wide authority. By now the Opposition whipping system was better than at any time in living memory. A team of GLC officers working with Roland Freeman knew everything it was possible to know about the peers, individually or collectively. A fleet of hired cars brought them in to vote and took them home afterwards (an important consideration, given the frailty of many).

With the slow passage of the legislation we had had plenty of time to identify every conceivable vote against the Government. Many peers who were rumoured to have died or to be too ill to move were contacted, brought in and kept warm and comfortable until their votes were required. Unfortunately Bertie Denham, Tory chief whip in the Lords, was finally responding to our operation and overhauling the Tory machine, which had not been seriously challenged since the 1950s. Both sides put in a massive effort on 30 April, the day of the Hayter/Plummer/Faithful amendment.

As there was a full Council meeting in progress I was only able to visit the assembling peers at the beginning of the afternoon, and was quite moved by the determination of these frail old women and men. Day after day they were prepared to come in and wait around while the rather younger Tory peers prolonged things until they realized that the life peers were not going to give up and go home. Watching someone like 99-year-old Fenner Brockway, who had already given two lifetimes of service to the Labour movement before I even entered politics, firmly resolving to be present at every vote contrasted with the contempt I felt for younger, healthier peers who claimed their allowance and left before the vote took place.

When the result of the vote on the Hayter/Plummer/Faithful amendment was announced, we had lost by only 213 to 209 votes. The closeness of the vote made it clear that we could win and this had an electrifying effect on the last stages of the campaign. All over London people redoubled their efforts even though they had now been campaigning flat out for eighteen months.

As the Lords wound their way through the various clauses of the bill we began to win the key amendments on which our strategy was based. Between 7 and 13 May, the Tories suffered crucial defeats when the Lords passed amendments retaining London-wide waste disposal and highways organizations, and rejected the proposed reserve power in the bill to enable the Government to abolish the ILEA without further legislation.

These defeats were the final spur Bertie Denham needed to wring the last few extra votes out of the inbuilt Tory majority. Finally the Tories got their act together and their organization began to match ours. From mid-May, they began to win all the really crucial votes while continuing to lose those they could afford to do without.

The final day on which we had the chance to derail the bill was 20 June, when the Lords debated a joint amendment from Lords Barnett (Labour) and Diamond (Alliance), setting up an elected London Co-ordinating Authority. To Bertie Denham's horror and our good fortune we had been able to drag out the proceedings so that this last vital amendment was reached during Ladies' Day at Ascot. A large number of Tory peers promptly bunked off to drink champagne in the Royal Enclosure rather than sit through yet another debate on the GLC.

As the debate got underway the sky was blue and punters everywhere were delighted that the going was good to firm at Ascot for Gold Cup day. Denham was not so pleased. The Gold Cup race was at 3.45 followed by the King Edward VII Stakes and finally the King George V Handicap at 5.30. Denham knew that many peers would refuse to leave Ascot before the final race was over and he had to keep the debate going until seven o'clock to have any certainty of winning. Lord Whitelaw, Deputy Prime Minister and leader of the House of Lords, was despatched with a team of Government whips to prowl the paddocks at Ascot while Denham's small band of loyalists filibustered in the Lords. With only ten amendments before the Barnett/Diamond amendment this would be difficult. Four were to be moved by our supporters, Lords Rochester, Irving and Dean, and we intended to withdraw them so as to reach the Barnett/Diamond as early as possible.

While Lord Whitelaw hunted down the missing peers at Ascot, the deputy speaker called Lord Rochester's amendment. The scene was delightfully captured by Godfrey Barker, the *Daily Telegraph*'s correspondent:

> Lord Denham's face froze with horror as Lord Rochester intoned, 'Not moved.' Frowning tremendously, Lord Denham gazed over the thinned-out ranks of unsocial Tories behind. Lord Harmar-Nicholls staggered up. He announced he was disappointed that Lord Rochester was not moving. He was disappointed for 20 minutes.
>
> Lady Faithful rose next to the occasion. She seemed to think that the amendment had been moved. No one enlightened her. She made the speech she would have made if it had been.
>
> Lord Thorneycroft managed 10 minutes on the importance of amendments being important.
>
> The afternoon wore on. The air was as sepulchral as at Ascot it was rosy. The Earl of Gowrie, smooth talker, seized the Despatch Box at 4.20. He was helped through the King Edward VII Stakes by having to repeat a Commons statement to the Lords.
>
> At 4.55 Lord Gowrie was sent 3 extra pages at the Despatch Box for his speech to give him stamina in the Chesham Stakes. At 5.29 with the King George at the off, the last three amendments came up.
>
> '81B, Lord Irving?' called the Deputy Speaker. 'I withdraw,' replied that worthy.

'81b 2A, Lord Dean?' came next. 'Not moved,' his Lordship grunted, and ditto to 81B 2B. At 5.35 the tapes were up on Lord Barnett and the killer amendment on the GLC.

But Lord Denham is a man of the turf. At 6pm he was still looking as sick as a parrot. But as his men filibustered smoothly down the court through 6.30, then 7, his visage brightened.

At 7.20 we came to the awesome vote. One scanned Lord Denham's men: not a morning suit to be seen. But several lads in red ties never before seen in the Lords hove into view on the Government benches. Could his Lordship yet scrape home in the Denham Stakes?

'Content, 147,' intoned the Deputy Speaker for Lord Ponsonby's men: 'Not Content, 163.' The Opposition and the bookies were confounded.

There was a large element of farce in those last frantic whipping exercises. On one day an extremely aged peer approached a police officer to ask if the House of Lords was still in the same place. The last time he had attended was during the war, when the peers were temporarily moved to another site following a bombing raid. We were no better. After dispatching all our peers home by car after the 20 June vote, one driver phoned County Hall late that night from a public callbox. 'He can't remember where he lives. Can you look up his address for me, please?' he said. On people such as these hangs the defence of our unwritten constitution and the freedoms that flow from it.

From 20 June we knew we had no chance of winning. We could still win some amendments in the next twelve days. Aided by Wimbledon and the Second Test Match we could reduce the damage done by abolition. But we knew that we had lost and I began to draft a policy statement for the GLLP Executive on what could be done to protect and preserve as many of our services and staff as possible.

Although the Lords passed 100 amendments to the bill, there

305

were only two that the Government could not live with. Those were the ones that had established the London-wide waste disposal and highway authorities. When those amendments arrived at the Commons, the Government applied the guillotine after a mere seven hours of debate and mobilized their vast majority to reject them. Six days later, the Lords backed down and withdrew their amendments. The following day, on 16 July, the Royal Assent was granted and the Abolition Bill became law.

The Lords had sealed our fate but in so doing had undoubtedly sealed their own as well. The sole reason that has been used to justify the continuation of the hereditary chamber is that they could protect the people of Britain from undemocratic exercises by a House of Commons which was prepared to trample on democracy. In the absence of a written constitution it has been argued by the likes of Lord Hailsham that government in Britain is in reality an 'elected dictatorship'. Once a party has won a majority in the Commons it can technically do whatever it wants. The peers have argued that they provide a backstop to prevent any abuse of power, yet when faced with just such an abuse by the 'elected dictatorship' they failed to prevent the abolition of the democratic rights of Londoners to elect and sack the people who run the strategic services of their city. Overnight on 31 March 1986 Londoners would become the only residents of a capital city in Western Europe who were denied the right to elect their city government.

The peers faced a situation in which two-thirds of the citizens of London consistently, month after month, were shown by the opinion polls to be opposed to abolition. Every professional and academic body associated with London advised against abolition. The Government's case was flawed in most aspects and no independent opinion doubted that the new structures would be more bureaucratic, more expensive and more remote from the public. When faced with the four by-elections, the Government had to let them pass uncontested for fear of the likely scale of their defeat.

For the first time in over 150 years the progress of democracy had been reversed. In all previous legislation concerning people's rights to vote those rights had been extended: to middle-class men, to working-class men, to women over 30, to women over 21, to allow all to vote in local council elections, and finally to lower the voting age to 18. The Abolition Bill was the first law in 150 years which reversed that process. Instead of the 18 million residents of London and the other great cities being allowed to vote to determine how their cities and services should be run they would now be subject to rule by 62 new quangos.

If the Lords could not bring themselves to move against a Tory government on this issue then it is difficult to imagine on what issue they would ever be prepared to do so. Such deference is unlikely to be shown to a radical socialist government. The abolition campaign exposed the lie that the Tories no longer have a majority in the Lords. On paper this is true, but in the reality of the division lobbies there is a comfortable majority waiting to be used against the policies of a Labour government. Unless an incoming Labour government realizes this and abolishes the Lords, it will find that majority used to devastating effect precisely when that government is at its weakest.

If the people of Britain want a constitutional mechanism to prevent an 'elected dictatorship' then they will need to construct one based on a written constitution which cannot be changed by the House of Commons alone. We could then have either some form of elected second chamber to perform the task of revision, or provision for constitutional amendment by referendum. The fate of the GLC has shown that the House of Lords will never adequately perform the task of defending democratic rights against a Tory government.

9

The Rate-capping Fiasco

It was during the final days of the abolition campaign that we suffered our biggest setback since the Law Lords' decision on fares. The rate-capping fiasco had its origins in Mrs Thatcher's decision to include in the 1983 manifesto a commitment to make it illegal for some councils to increase their rates beyond a limit set by the Government. After all the defeats that Heseltine had suffered in trying to cut back local authority spending, this scheme looked foolproof. The Tories could apply it selectively to those councils that they did not like without affecting the others. It would be illegal to set a rate greater than the Government allowed; even if a council could muster the votes to pass an illegal rate, thereby risking penalties of surcharge and debarment from office, no one could be forced to pay a rate above the Government limit. Inevitably, councils would face the choice of cutting services and staff or going into a deficit, which was also illegal and carried the same penalties.

On Thursday mornings Ted Knight and I edited the following week's *Labour Herald*. We had discussed the matter and decided that when rate-capping became law we would have no alternative but to refuse to make the cuts required. Various Labour Party and local government conferences continued to discuss the issue, but the main debate was, as ever, whether or not it was morally or politically justified to break a bad law.

In June 1984 the matter was discussed further at a meeting of the twelve leaders of the Labour-controlled London boroughs. As the items discussed were usually of a financial nature, the GLC's representative at this regularly monthly meeting was John McDonnell. The topic arose of how to co-ordinate the Labour councils' response to rate-capping. As the financial situation of each council varied, the policy of refusing to make cuts and allowing a deficit to build up would mean each one coming into conflict with the Government at a different time. The following year, when I asked how the alternative 'don't set a rate' strategy came about, Margaret Hodge, who was chairing the meeting, claimed that it had been her idea.

During that summer Liverpool Council had refused to make a rate because the Tories had withheld much of their rate support grant. This tactic was quite new and had the Government worried. In contrast to the action taken against Liverpool and Lambeth the following year, the Government's response in the summer of 1984 showed signs of weakness. The fear of collapse of financial confidence in the City followed by bankruptcy and disorder at the same time as the Government was trying to defeat the miners caused Patrick Jenkin to make several concessions. Firstly, the Government continued to pay full rate support grant to the council without imposing any of the penalties for overspending. Secondly, they asked Jack Halligan, the retired treasurer of Lambeth Council, to visit the main banks and urge them to continue making loans to Liverpool.

It was against this background that the borough leaders hit on the idea of 10 to 20 Labour councils all refusing to set a rate at the same time. They believed that such a show of defiance might force the Government to back down, provided that trade unionists were prepared to support their councils with a campaign of industrial action. The strategy was set out by Ted Knight, John McDonnell and the leaders of Southwark, Lewisham and Greenwich Councils in a personal statement which appeared in *Labour Herald* on 22 June 1984.

> The point at which every Labour-controlled authority can be united is the end of one financial year and the beginning of the next.
>
> The common action to each is the levying of a rate or precept.
>
> A refusal to levy a rate or precept will unite each council in the same action, at the same time.
>
> In the face of such a challenge, the Tory Government

will have to evict every Labour councillor from town and county halls, or deal with a breakdown of local government.

The City of London, too, will face a crisis of confidence in the money market.

It is not that we are setting out to become law-breakers. The fact is that under the legislation it is no longer lawful for councils to carry out the policies on which they were elected.

Other tactics have been considered.

The call for deficit budgeting, whilst levying a modest or 'capped' rate does not provide the basis for unity because of differences in each authority's financial position.

The point at which each authority would run out of funds – if at all – would differ.

Confusion as to when this would happen would weaken the united action of workforces and the local community.

Similarly, calls for mass resignations of Labour councillors poses the dangers of temporary Tory control.

Even successful re-election does not alter the reality facing councillors, trade unionists or working-class communities.

Refusal to levy a rate or a precept in order to confront the Tory Government can only succeed with the support of the trade unions and the local communities.

Council workers know that a failure to fight will result in tens of thousands of jobs being lost.

My initial response was less than enthusiastic. Given the fact that the Labour Group had split 23 to 22 on the issue of breaking the law on fares, I saw no chance of doing much better on rate-capping. In my private discussions with Ted and John, as well as in my advice to the GLLP Executive, I pointed out than an immediate and spectacular defeat of the GLC on the issue would have an extremely damaging effect on the strategy as a whole. Ted replied, 'That won't be a problem. With a majority of four, no one expects you to win, but you must try to keep the GLC in the fight as long as possible.' Although I was unhappy I could not avoid the fact that the GLC was likely to be abolished. In May 1985 I would be out of office, whereas the Labour boroughs who supported this strategy would still be in power. I agreed to support the campaign.

The 'don't set a rate' option swept through the Party. Within a week of the joint statement appearing in *Labour Herald* the GLLP Executive had adopted it unanimously. Eight borough Labour parties agreed it at a joint meeting. The Lambeth Labour Group agreed it unanimously and in the Lewisham Labour Group there was only one vote against. By the time the Labour local government conference met in Sheffield on 6 and 7 July, the strategy had built up a considerable head of steam. Although the non-London councils were markedly less enthusiastic, the strategy seemed un-stoppable. By the end of the conference other leftwing councils had no real choice but to go along. At the Labour Party conference that autumn, it was broadly endorsed without any opposition from the party leadership.

By this time, we had defeated the Government over the Paving Bill and knew that the Labour GLC would be in office for at least a year after rate-capping. John and I knew that the GLC Labour Group would split as soon as it discussed the issue, so we decided to recommend to the Group that we should not discuss it until immediately before the final deadline in March 1985. This was agreed – only Mike Ward dissented – and from that day no internal Group discussion on the issue took place. It was also decided that no budget documents would be prepared for publication: accurate financial data would enable the Government to set a harsh rate limit. John and I agreed that he would take full charge of policy in this area as the anti-abolition campaign was making increased demands on my time.

The rate-capping campaign puttered along but was over-shadowed by the anti-abolition campaign. On Tuesday 11 December, Patrick Jenkin announced the rate limit for each of the rate-capped councils. I was voting in a full meeting of the ILEA when I was passed the information that our limit for 1985 was almost identical to the existing 1984 GLC rate of 36.5p. Since we had just lost control of London Transport, which had consumed 19 per cent of our budget, I was sure that we would be able to get by on such a figure without having to make any real cuts. Given the rate at which GLC programmes were expanding, however, we might not have enough funds for our growth programme. I made the point to John. 'No, you're wrong,' he replied. 'It means £140 million worth of cuts in our planned spending.' John was including our planned growth in that figure and was the only member dealing with the now confidential financial data. I was in no position to question his judgement, although I suspected that he was exaggerating the case somewhat.

John was due to answer questions to the Group the following Monday, but the right wing forced a long debate on Zionism. By the time we reached John's report it was too late to do it justice, so Mike Ward proposed a special Group meeting to discuss it on 7 January. I was out of the country at the time. On my return, Bill Bush reported that under close questioning John had stuck to the line of £140 million of cuts, and this had been accepted by the Group. They had instructed him to publish the full details for public consultation as the Government had no legal power to reduce the rate limit once it had been announced and we no longer needed secrecy.

A special London Labour Party conference took place on 19 January at which we restated the £140 million figure, as we did at Labour's local government conference in Birmingham on 1 and 2 February. At a General London Assembly of all trade unions, voluntary and community groups called to discuss rate-capping at Wembley Conference Centre on 23 February, John told me that we had run into legal problems in preparing the budget consultation document. However, he had circulated a letter in advance spelling out £138 million of cuts which would be required if we complied with rate-capping. At the assembly, every delegate was given a statement drafted by John.

> Rate-capping would mean crippling cuts in a whole range of everyday services. The amount the Government says the GLC can raise in rates this year is over £140 million LESS than the Council needs to continue maintaining its existing services. It could mean, for example . . .

- big cutbacks on free travel for London's million old people
- the end of the popular dial-a-ride service for those with disabilities
- the virtual end of the GLC's job creation programme. More people will go on the dole, including many GLC workers themselves who will be hit by the across-the-board cuts in services
- council tenants' rents up by at least £1.20 a week
- reductions in the fire service. Up to 1,400 fire-fighters' jobs at stake
- the virtual end of the GLC grants programme. These organizations will have to shut down, their workers made redundant and the people they help left stranded
- the end of road improvements and maintenance – more congestion, more potholes
- less money for flood prevention, controlling pollution and other hazards

A cuts package as severe as this (and these are only some examples) would hit every Londoner in some way or another.

At the Council meeting the week before on 12 February, the Tories had announced that they considered the government's 36.5p rate limit too generous. They would therefore be proposing a lower rate of 27p, and if this was rejected would vote against any higher rate if it was lawful to do so. I immediately turned to John and asked him to try and get from Roger Henderson (the barrister who had advised us on the second fares cut and was now advising us on rate-capping) a legal opinion which would allow the Tories to abstain or vote against. This would mean we could repeat the situation of the fares debate, where enough Tories had abstained to bring us within three votes of winning. With Tories actually voting against, we could win.

Suddenly, for the first time we faced the possibility that the GLC might really refuse to set a rate. This presented several problems, not the least of which was that as everyone had assumed that behind all the rhetoric there was no real possibility of this happening, none of us had even begun to explore the question of how to run a bankrupt Council. Certainly, no one had given any thought to how staff would react to no pay or how we could continue to provide essential services to the public. If we got it wrong we ran the risk of staff and public turning against us instead of the Tories.

There were also personal considerations. I was damned if I was going to allow the money I had saved to be seized by the District Auditor, so I arranged to cash it and give it to Bill Bush for safe-keeping. The parliamentary selection procedure was about to start in Brent East and if bankrupted I would be barred from standing as a candidate. I spoke to Paul Franklin and Bill Bush about how we could get around the problem. The only answer seemed to be a stand-in candidate, who would hold the seat for me until the next Labour Government removed the disqualifications and granted an amnesty for surcharged councillors. At that stage the stand-in would, one hoped, stand down.

It proved difficult to get Roger Henderson's opinion on the possibility of the Tories' abstention. It arrived in the building only 48 hours before the Council was due to meet. In the meantime, Barry Stead, centrist from Fulham, had written to John and me on 18 February regarding an undertaking John had given to the Group at its January meeting.

> I remain very anxious that a full range of options is available to the Group. Over a month ago, John agreed that a budget would be prepared on the basis of the legal maximum.
>
> Could you please therefore confirm that officers have been instructed to prepare a budget and draft rate precept resolution based on the legal maximum and these will be available for the Group in its budget discussions and for the relevant Council committees in time.

I asked John to draft a reply, which he did in his own handwriting. After I had signed it it was given to Barry Stead on 25 February.

> As you can see from Maurice Stonefrost's paper FGP 999, the Director-General has prepared a route through

the budget process which the officers are recommending. I will ensure that if the 'no rate' option falls in the Council chamber on budget day there will be a fallback proposal available which will put us as an administration in the best position to protect services and jobs in the coming year.

During the week of 25 February I began to pick up rumours from two Labour boroughs that they had been advised to change the strategy. Instead of voting to refuse to set a rate so that they maintained unity with the GLC and we all went illegal together, I was told that Camden and Lambeth were planning merely to defer the decision. This would leave the GLC and ILEA exposed to an immediate legal challenge as, unlike the boroughs, we were bound by law to make a rate by 10 March. It also completely negated the concept of the rate-capping struggle which had been spelt out in *Labour Herald* at the beginning: 'A refusal to levy a rate or precept will unite each council in the same action, at the same time.'

When I saw Ted Knight at our regular Thursday morning *Labour Herald* editorial board meeting, I raised the issue with him and this soon developed into an explosive row. He assured me that all that was involved was a change of wording. 'We will be going illegal with you on the day,' he said firmly. But for all his assurances I remained unconvinced. At one stage the discussions got so heated that I stormed out of the room. Ted followed me, his anger suddenly replaced by his most reassuring manner. Looking me straight in the eye and squeezing my arm, he said, 'Trust me, Ken. We're all going illegal together. I promise you, there's no backsliding. They can't fight us and the miners. We can bring Thatcher down and then anything is possible.'

I shook my head. 'Ted, I haven't got a cat in hell's chance of getting it through my Group if they think the boroughs are copping out. On top of that we might be able to get through the year without any real cuts and if that's the case enough of my Group will vote with the Alliance to set a rate.'

'Lambeth's in the same position,' he replied. 'We can get through the year. We've got £10 million unspent. But the other boroughs aren't in that position. If we don't give a lead they'll collapse. Then there will be real cuts right across London and we'll get screwed next year when they can pick us off one by one.'

I was unconvinced but was prepared to accept Ted's assurances until I saw evidence to the contrary. On my return to County Hall I briefed Bill Bush and asked him to find out what the truth was. As our representative at the meetings of the Local Government Campaign Unit (LGCU), John had not indicated any problem nor asked to make a report to the Policy Committee.

The day before, Wednesday 27 February, Reg Race had asked if he and Peter Brayshaw (Deputy D-G) could see me privately and I had agreed to a meeting late on Thursday afternoon. As they had specifically asked that John should not be present, I was expecting to hear about some personality clash arising over the preparations for the rate-making debate. They started by reporting that Maurice Stonefrost had finished his budget paper and it would be circulated to councillors and press on Friday evening. This I had expected as Maurice was under a legal obligation to give the Council his best advice. What shocked me was the news that the report would be recommending only £30 million of cuts, all of which were cosmetic. Reg then pointed out that simply by adjusting the borrowing figures we could actually propose a budget with £25 million worth of growth.

'Then why are we still pumping out propaganda saying £140 million cuts?' I asked.

'Because John instructed that no budget figures should be produced,' replied Race.

I was horrified. When the press got Maurice's paper they would say we had been lying all along. 'Why wasn't I told?'

'We thought John and you were working together on this,' said Brayshaw. 'We gave John a report on 20 December which showed you could have between two and four per cent growth. He told us to shred all copies,' said Race, who subsequently sent me a copy he had kept.

I still could not quite believe that John could have been so stupid as to assume figures like these could be kept secret. I asked Reg to prepare the amendments we would need to make to Maurice's paper to change its structure from a phoney cuts package to a growth budget. John was not available to see me until Friday afternoon, but that morning I spent a long time with Maurice, going over his proposals. He had included the cosmetic cuts in order to avoid any legal challenge made by the Tories or by a ratepayer who might be incensed that we were planning growth in the first year of rate-capping. Maurice explained that after a couple of months we could restructure the budget to reverse the cuts and go for real growth. I pointed out that any cuts package, however cosmetic, would be unacceptable to the Group, and asked him to work with Reg so that there was no disagreement about facts when we finally came to decide on which budget to adopt.

Before going to see John, I spoke briefly with Reg Race, who was able to give me the bare outline of his growth proposals. I met John in the corridor. When I asked him what he thought of Stonefrost's proposals, he simply said that they were wrong. I explained Reg Race's proposals; John dismissed them as inaccurate and continued to maintain the line of £140 million of cuts. We went round and round the figures for over half an hour as he repeatedly rejected my statement that it was unlikely that both Reg and Maurice were wrong and he was right. John claimed that it would all be clear at Monday's Finance Committee. I told him I was not convinced and had asked Race to prepare the growth package. He begged me to order Race to stop that work and I refused.

'If you don't stop Race you'll have destroyed the whole fucking campaign,' he said.

'And if these figures are right, we're going to look like the biggest fucking liars since Goebbels,' I replied.

As we returned to our respective offices I doubt if either of us realized the scale of bitterness that was to come or that we had just concluded the last conversation we were ever to have as friends. What had become the closest political relationship of my life was about to be consumed in an orgy of in-fighting and mutual loathing.

The most immediate problem I faced was how to get through the next two days of the GLLP Annual Meeting. I was certain that the figures on which the GLLP had based its policy were wildly wrong, but Reg Race would not have his own budget proposals in detail until Monday, and there was no way I could just throw all these new facts into the lap of the conference without causing chaos and derailing the entire anti-rate-capping campaign. Any figures I did produce were bound to be challenged by John, and it was impossible to expect the delegates to decide who to believe. Most councillors would have received Maurice Stonefrost's paper on the Friday before the conference and it took little intelligence to guess that they would be extremely worried and angry. If the left fell apart on this issue it could have devastating consequences for the fragile unity which held together the network of leftwing factions in London. It could open the way for the right wing to advance after a decade of retreat. I therefore had no doubt that I should do everything possible to avoid a split on the left.

When I arrived for the morning session, Bill Bush gave me a copy of the relevant minutes of the rate-capped councils' leaders meeting (LGCU). It confirmed my fears that the 'all go illegal together' strategy had been changed secretly at private meetings. At the LGCU meeting on 12 February the GLC was unrepresented due to a Finance meeting which had been called. After a brief discussion, the Liverpool representative had recognized that unity could only be achieved by a motion that meant deferral of the rate decision rather than an illegal refusal. This was agreed without dissent. The two metropolitan councils (South Yorkshire and Merseyside) made it clear that they had no majority for illegality and would vote to accept the rate-cap and go for a deficit budget. In Merseyside this policy was supported by Derek Hatton.

At the following LGCU meeting on 19 February, document MC(85)(11) was agreed without dissent. It stated that the form of words to be used in Council motions on 7 March should simply be that *'it will be impossible for the authority to make a rate'*. Lest there be any doubt, paragraph 7 spelt out the meaning of such wording:

> One thing an authority must not do is resolve in terms that it will not make a rate for 1985–6. The form of wording suggested above is to the effect that as at 7 March the authority considers that it will be impossible for it to make a rate, but that is not a declaration of a fixed intention not to make a rate, which would be unlawful.

Although John and Ted and other London Labour leaders had been present, none had opposed the switch, even though it was contrary to GLLP policy that we should all take 'the same action at the same time'. Neither Ted nor John had reported this change to the GLLP Executive.

When I confronted Ted with the document, he maintained that this still meant that the boroughs would be going illegal on the same day as the GLC. John just shrugged his shoulders and refused to talk to me.

One by one, members of the Labour Group sought me out at the conference. They were furious that the real financial position of the GLC had been hidden from them, and outraged that we appeared to have been 'set up' by the borough leaders so that they would be able to blame the GLC when the whole campaign collapsed. I was shortly due to introduce the GLC report, which would be followed by a general debate on rate-capping to which Ted and John would reply. I was under intense pressure from GLC members to read out the section in the confidential LGCU document (MC[85][11]) which revealed the boroughs' retreat from illegality. It would have been easy to use quotes from the document to make a savage attack on Ted and John and land all the blame on them, but I was determined to avoid doing so. The rate-capping campaign would have been destroyed and the coalition of leftwing forces torn apart. Instead, I called on Labour boroughs to beef up their resolutions from merely deferring to refusing to fix a rate. I avoided mentioning any details about the split in tactics which had emerged, and gave a pledge that there would be no cuts in service or loss of jobs while a Labour administration remained in office.

Far from continuing in the same vein, Ted launched a bitter attack on unnamed GLC members. 'Quite frankly,' he said, 'it's a bit late for some comrades to realize there are problems.' Given that the problems had arisen because of the borough leaders' change of policy, this speech caused fury amongst GLC members. They felt even more strongly than before that I should have nailed the borough leaders for their private change of tactics and focused the anger of the conference on them.

Unfortunately, John's speech made matters even worse. Without acknowledging that our dire financial predictions could be in any way wrong, he now made a new and even more audacious claim. 'This week, the Government made a private approach to Maurice Stonefrost,' he told the conference. 'They offered us a deal through him. If we agree to set a rate then they will change their financial controls so that we can get off the hook and require only a £30 million package of cuts.' By the time John had finished his speech, the bitterness amongst members was such that the Labour Group faced the prospect of disintegration. Later that weekend, I approached Ted and Margaret Hodge (chair of the Group of London Labour Boroughs) and asked them to convene a meeting of all London Labour councillors so that the GLC could appeal to them to take a firm decision not to set a rate. They both refused, even though I emphasized that they were making it almost impossible for me to hold the GLC Labour Group in line with party policy.

When the Labour Group meeting assembled on Monday night, I gave a full report on the latest financial position and the state of play with the boroughs. I proposed that irrespective of what had happened in the last seventy-two hours, we continue to stand by party policy and refuse to set a rate. Although the GLC could get by, many Labour boroughs had reported that they faced massive real cuts and I proposed that we should stand by them as an act of solidarity. Unfortunately, those GLC councillors who had felt the lash of Ted's tongue across their backs at the weekend were a bit short on solidarity.

In proposing that we continue to stand firm against rate-capping, I was also influenced by the principle that elected members should carry out their party's policy. I had argued for this since joining the party, and although the GLLP had decided its policy on the basis of false information, the principle of objection to rate-capping was still valid, even if the tactics were beginning to fall apart. The rest of the Group did not share my view. Mike Ward moved that we adopt the £25 million growth budget immediately, rather than, as I had suggested, keep it as a fallback position for when it became obvious that we could not prevent a rate being set.

After a long, acrimonious debate which revealed the incredible anger of those councillors who felt they had been led into an impossible position, the Group voted by 24 votes to 18 to accept

Mike Ward's proposal. Five councillors who had voted with me to defy the Law Lords' imposed fare increase voted to set a rate. Without the dissension caused by our financial position and the change of tactic by the boroughs, I would have won in the Group meeting and been able to mobilize 25 or 26 votes in the Council meeting. This would probably not have been enough to win in the Council even if the Tories had only abstained. In the event, the legal opinion we had asked for left the question of the Tories' legal immunity still in doubt.

That night I spent hours lying awake, going over in my own mind just how we had managed to screw up so effectively. Although I shared the anger of other Group members, I could see how we had got into this position. Ted and John had gone along with watering down the borough position, not because they wanted to expose the GLC but because they believed it was the only way to hold the boroughs together. Ted feared that if borough councillors were faced with the reality of going illegal on 8 March, then almost all of them would back down immediately and the campaign would never even get off the ground. The longer they could be kept going, the longer we had to build up a real campaign of public support which could keep them in line.

Equally I could understand how John had been trapped into this position. Only a few minutes after he had learned of the Government's rate-cap limit, I appeared, saying that it didn't look too bad. Shocked that the Tories had been infinitely more generous than he had anticipated, John had panicked and decided to maintain his original line. Because of our fear of leaks he was the only member with access to financial information and he was able to control its flow to all other members. This led him to assume he could continue to maintain what he believed to be true up to and beyond the rate-capping decision, just as Ted was able to do in Lambeth. John probably assumed I would go along with what he said. In fact, the closeness of our friendship in the preceding three years meant that I was prepared to turn a blind eye to what I believed to be his exaggeration; what I would not do was knowingly and deliberately proceed on figures which I believed to be inaccurate. John had made a grave error of judgement in assuming that I would go along with his figures.

In the end, the Group had to absorb too much new information too fast. The possibility of the Tories abstaining, our financial position and the change of tactic by the boroughs was just too much for councillors to absorb in seventy-two hours. Had we been honest about the finances of the Council when the Government announced our rate-cap limit, I might have had time to win over the crucial five votes. Seventy-two hours were not enough.

Fortunately, there was no rightwing challenge to my leadership in sight or I would have been in a vulnerable position. For the first time, I was opposed to the policy of the Group on an issue which mattered. After the meeting I spoke to my Paddington Labour party officers, who supported my decision to oppose the Group's policy. In the morning I would tell Maurice Stonefrost that until the budget debate was over he and his officers should work under the direction of Mike Ward, as I did not represent the majority view of the Group on this issue.

I felt no surprise and little anger towards Ted. We knew each other's strengths and weaknesses inside out, and neither of us suffered any illusions about the other's motives or ambitions. This was just another in a long line of bitter rows which would occasionally flare up between us. It had come at the end of a long period during which Ted had been particularly supportive and we had worked closely together, but it was wholly in character. It would not prevent us working together again in the future, after a decent pause for tempers to subside.

Towards John, however, I felt bitterness. We had worked so closely together that it had almost become a joint leadership, and we had each covered the other's back on many occasions when we were under attack. John was too competent and hard working for the Group to be able to afford to lose him. I knew, however, it would be difficult to persuade enough members of the dangers of a major split in time to prevent his sacking at the AGM in eight weeks' time.

In the morning as I was getting dressed, I listened to the LBC radio news and heard John being interviewed.

'Well, Ken is a friend and I don't want to say anything against him,' he said, 'but there is no doubt that he has betrayed the whole campaign in order to save his political career.' This was the theme that he warmed to as the day progressed. He was interviewed by the *Ham and High*.

> Ken and I may remain friends but I will never trust him again politically. I am resigning more in sorrow than in anger. We should stand firm and give a lead to the boroughs opposed to rate-capping.
>
> But we are selling the people out because those like Ken fear disqualification from office and are clinging to power no matter what. He is a Kinnock.
>
> He has dumped the boroughs in a way which is a betrayal of all we have campaigned for. Panic set in at the Labour Group meeting on Monday and Ken lost his bottle.
>
> When it came to the crunch he chickened out. I am resigning as deputy leader but I shall keep my seat on the GLC to do what I can to fight the cuts in jobs and services.

As the *Ham and High* pointed out, 'The outburst from Mr McDonnell was unprecedented and opens up a major split in the Labour left.'

There followed a flood of similar statements from John's office emphasizing that my cowardice and ambition had been the cause of our defeat in the Labour Group. Compounding the claim that we were doing a secret deal with the Government, John was soon able to announce that it was also part of a secret deal with Neil Kinnock. In exchange for destroying the rate-capping campaign, Kinnock would not use the NEC to block my selection as a parliamentary candidate, and it was also implied that a Cabinet job would soon follow my election to Parliament. Nowhere did John accept any responsibility for his part in the disaster.

I made no comment in response to his statements that morning, but as they continued throughout the day my anger boiled over and triggered a stupid decision to call a press conference to give my account of events. Acting with all the calmness and rationality of a bull elephant on heat, I made a long and bitter personal attack on

John. It was a disastrous decision which allowed the papers to divert attention from the real issues of rate-capping to the personal clash between John and me.

Tony Judge delivered the analysis of the Labour right in yet another press statement the following day:

> Ken Livingstone and John McDonnell between them have destroyed the credibility of Labour's campaign against the abolition of the GLC, rate-capping and the cuts.
>
> They have done this as part of their personal feud over the leadership of the Labour left in London. There is no precedent for the spectacle of the Leader of the GLC going on television with his deputy so that one can call the other a liar and the other call him a traitor.
>
> This is a squalid, phoney dispute in which we are seriously asked to believe that the Leader and deputy leader of the GLC did not know that County Hall has enough money to make a lawful rate.
>
> It has nothing at all to do with the real issue of democracy and the rates that ordinary people will pay to the GLC next year.
>
> It has everything to do with whether Mr Livingstone and his clique seize power in Brent East and whether Mr McDonnell grabs another seat in London.
>
> The best thing they can now do is resign. Really, there is nothing left for them to lead. It's a playground fight between two monitors over who is to be prefect.

By now all John's actions confirmed Tony Judge's view that behind the split was a struggle for the leadership of the London left. I have no doubt that was not John's original intention but with the collapse of the campaign he saw his opportunity and seized it. Several members of the anti-abolition Outreach Team (for which John had responsibility) were set to work to drum up support for John amongst the constituency activists and to try to get votes of censure through local Labour parties. By the time the Council meeting assembled on Friday the galleries were packed. I recognized a lot of people because I had clashed with them at some point in the previous ten years. Now they sat in the gallery with undisguised glee on their faces. I was in deep trouble and they had come to enjoy the spectacle.

As the meeting progressed the Tories' proposed 27p rate was rejected by 46 votes to 40. John then led a handful of members into the lobbies to vote with the Tories to reject my proposal to delete the £30 million worth of cuts from Maurice Stonefrost's proposed budget estimates. Then the £25 million growth budget was rejected by 59 votes (John's group and mine voting with the Tories) to 30 (Labour rightwingers and the centrists).

I had continued to vote not to set a rate, but by the time we reconvened on Sunday it had been made clear to me by the Labour right that they were not prepared to allow the no-rate position to win. As I had anticipated when I warned the Group of the consequences of a split, the Labour right would vote with the Tories to set a lower rate than the 36.5p if I could not persuade the Group to carry the £25 million growth budget. During an adjournment I explained the danger we now faced to the whole Group, and warned that unless we carried the growth budget we would end up with one lower than the Government's 36.5p limit.

The nine members voting with John agreed to convene on their own to discuss the situation, but I was not optimistic. John's bid to put himself in the leadership of the London left would flop if he voted at any stage to set a rate. Nita Clarke asked Larry Whitty, the new General Secretary of the Labour Party, to come in and help to keep the Labour right in line, while Labour NEC member Audrey Wise went to work on the McDonnell ten to explain the NEC view that the saving of jobs and services was more important than any short-term tactical considerations.

We went back into the Council chamber and the growth budget was again proposed, this time by John Carr. It was defeated by 54 votes to 34. Only four members had changed their vote. The right wing erupted in fury and walked out of the Group to form their own caucus. Larry Whitty arrived and went to work to persuade them not to vote for a Tory rate. He succeeded in getting them to agree to vote down the next Tory proposal for a 32.9p rate provided that we tried again to carry the growth budget. The Labour Group was now meeting in three parts: the right, John's group and those who had voted with me at each stage.

In a last attempt, Steve Bundred proposed the growth budget, but it was finally defeated by 53 votes to 36. It was the only time throughout the proceedings that I voted to set a rate. I had warned the McDonnell ten that if we failed to carry the growth budget we would be faced either with Maurice Stonefrost's original proposal of a 36.5p rate with £30 million of cosmetic cuts and no growth, or a compromise proposal from Barrie Stead of a 33.8p rate with £25 million of growth but £11 million of cuts. For different reasons both were unacceptable to me. The entire left united to oppose them but the patience of the right was exhausted, and by 60 votes to 26 Barrie Stead's budget was carried. The outside world was incredulous: we had managed to set a rate 6.5 per cent lower than the Government's limit and not maximize our spending.

The rate had been set at 8.00 pm on Sunday and the GLLP Executive was due to meet the next day on Monday 11th. John had enjoyed a week's clear run of propaganda which I had had no time to answer. There would now be a struggle within the party, so I set aside Monday to write a full report for that night's meeting. I expected to lose whatever vote of censure was moved against me but believed it would be vital to get on record a full account of what had happened and afterwards to circulate it throughout the party.

When the Executive met, however, it was obvious that the explanation of betrayal caused by my cowardice and ambition was not accepted. Too many people had been involved with me for too long and had watched my conduct throughout the media attacks and other pressures to accept John's simplistic charge that I had 'bottled out'. Militant supporter Eddie McPharland moved a motion of censure which effectively called on the Labour Party never to select for office anyone who had not voted with the McDonnell ten. To my surprise, John did not attend the meeting, and the critical parts of the motion were defeated by a vote of two to one, the minority being mainly *Militant*, *Socialist Organiser* and some but not all of the Labour *Briefing* supporters. In particular, Ted Knight, although he voted in favour of the motion, was very low key. He argued that we should 'bury the rotting corpse' and move on from the events of the last week. He clearly understood the dangers of widening the split into a permanent gulf on the left.

The following morning I went to a confidential meeting with a leading figure of the left to discuss the ramifications of the previous week. After long discussion we agreed that unless the rift was healed it could grow into a split which would weaken the left and open the way to a major advance by the right. We recognized that a witch-hunt to remove John from his post could be the trigger for a bitter civil war within the London left and should be avoided at all costs. I warned that it would not be easy but agreed to do what I could to prevent a purge of John and the nine who had voted with him.

When I returned to County Hall, the place was in uproar. Apparently, John had attended a meeting of the rate-capped authorities' leaders chaired by David Blunkett, at which the GLC was represented by Mike Ward. John had argued for the exclusion of the GLC from any further meetings and this was agreed. Councillors had also started to hear of censure motions being submitted to local Labour parties by staff employed in John McDonnell's Outreach Team. It now appeared that some of the workers in that team had been switched from anti-abolition work into campaigns aimed at undermining Labour councillors who had voted differently to John. John had also attended a meeting of London Labour Borough Council leaders and launched an unprecedented attack on the rest of us.

At the following morning's Policy Committee, I asked all officers to leave and then made several proposals to deal with the situation. In future, John would share control of the Outreach Team with Valerie Wise and John Carr. This was vital if I was to be able to head off demands from the right to sack those team workers who, on John's instruction, had been attacking Labour members. Secondly, whilst John would continue as Finance chair, with day-to-day control of the Council's finances, the control of the budget at broad policy level would pass to a new committee chaired by me. Until John had regained the trust of his colleagues it was essential that I had access to all financial data. Reg Race's team of officers would advise my new committee as an alternative source of guidance to the more traditional officers of the finance department.

This was the best compromise that I could hope to strike with those councillors who were demanding John's immediate sacking. If he played his cards right and did nothing provocative in the seven weeks remaining before the AGM, the situation might settle down enough for him to survive. None of the others who had voted with him were in any danger. Only John was in danger of being sacked. At the meeting John argued that things should be left as they were, but no one was prepared to take his word that the in-fighting would stop if we did not curtail his powers.

Sadly, John had no intention of trying to achieve any unity. He had seen the chance of building his 'lefter than thou' reputation for the future and was going to take it. A stream of letters flooded out of his office alleging a witch-hunt. Typical of many was one to the North Westminster Action Committee, which was based in my own constituency.

> Thank you for your letter dated 15 March 1985. I am very grateful for your committee's support.
>
> Things are pretty grim at County Hall. The new centre right realignment around Ken Livingstone has launched a purge to remove from positions of influence those councillors who stood firm on party policy.
>
> Rest assured however that we will stand firm to fight for the implementation of socialist policies at the GLC.

John refused to convene a meeting with John Carr and Valerie Wise to discuss future work for the Outreach Team. He was forcing the Group to remove him.

Any doubts about this were dispelled by the appearance of *London Labour Briefing* and a series of articles in the rest of the left press which alleged that a great witch-hunt was underway at County Hall. Relationships deteriorated further when it became known that John had met with a group of Brent East Labour Party members to discuss how to prevent my selection as their parliamentary candidate at the end of April. John had agreed to speak at a public meeting in Brent East the week before the final selection conference.

The stream of reports about a witch-hunt of the 'McDonnell

ten' continued to appear in *Briefing*. The position was in fact different. I had decided against calling an emergency meeting of the Group to discuss what to do now that we were faced with the consequences of our self-inflicted rate cut. I feared that in an early Group meeting there would be a move to sack John which would further widen the split on the left. The normal meeting was three weeks away and I was certain that tempers would cool if John would only lower his profile and ease up on his speeches, which equated the Labour rate-setters with scab miners in Nottingham. I also wanted to give Reg Race's team a chance to get control of the finance department so that we would have absolutely accurate figures about our financial position before the Group took any further spending decisions.

John had ceased the vital work of chasing the bureaucracy to ensure that grants got out to voluntary organizations, many of whom were on the point of issuing redundancy notices to their staff because of the delay in receiving GLC funds. I asked Valerie Wise to step in and take over progress-chasing in this area, and it was only due to her efforts that we narrowly avoided the collapse of several organizations.

John's campaign became increasingly bitter and personal. He attended a meeting of the Campaign Group of leftwing Labour MPs, and by the time he had finished his blood-curdling account of my role in the fiasco, the majority of the MPs were so disgusted that they rejected a proposal supported by Tony Benn that I be invited to put my side of the story at a subsequent meeting. Later that year they were still so bitter that they voted against my being allowed to attend their meeting for leftwing parliamentary candidates. Once again Tony Benn opposed the decision, but to no avail.

London Labour Briefing issued a statement under the headline 'REGROUP THE LEFT'.

> The betrayal of some council leaderships, in particular the GLC, who reneged on the collective decision to defy Government policy on rate-capping, and which followed on so rapidly after the defeat of the miners' strike, is another setback. That betrayal is all the more severe because it was carried out by leaders of whom we had

high expectations. Those that have fallen at this first
hurdle have shown themselves to be incapable of playing
a leadership role in these struggles to come.

Chris Knight and Graham Bash, who had remained friends and
supporters even when the *Socialist Organiser* element within *Briefing*
were baying for my blood, had accepted John's account in its
entirety. One member of the *Briefing* group reported that whenever
my name came up it unleashed a wave of bitterness and contempt,
'almost as though you had all been lovers and they came home to
find you in bed with somebody else'. It began to feel as though I
was the subject of a witch-hunt in which most of my old friends
were not even prepared to listen to my explanation of events.

Because of John's behaviour the bitterness within the Labour
Group showed no signs of subsiding. The Group had already
agreed to establish a new Policy and Resources committee (P & R)
to control the budget and it was vital that the left gain a majority
on this committee. The role that John played in the Group elections
to this committee removed any lingering doubts that he might be
an innocent victim in the bitterness which was tearing the left apart.
In spite of his statement to the *Ham and High* that he had resigned,
he stayed in office and behaved in a way which forced us to sack
him. He was then able to portray himself as the victim of a terrible
'centre–right' realignment, which was useful in both his campaign
for a parliamentary seat and his plans to 'regroup' the left of the
London Labour Party around his leadership.

With myself as chair of P & R and Alex McKay as vice-chair,
the PC/PCC had recommended to the Group that Mike Ward,
John Carr and Valerie Wise from the left, Simon Turney from the
centre and Tony McBrearty from the right comprise the seven
Labour members of the committee. A meeting of the McDonnell
ten decided to nominate four members, including John McDonnell
and Paul Boateng to P & R. The right also put up a slate.

During the voting, which was by secret ballot, it became obvious
that some of John's supporters were not following their agreed
slate. Although John Carr and I voted for Paul Boateng, his vote
was no higher than the other three names on the McDonnell slate:
some of them were clearly not voting for Paul. When McDonnell's

four nominees were eliminated, some simply stopped voting while others actually voted for the rightwing nominees in order to knock off Valerie, John Carr and Mike Ward. In the end, John Carr and Mike scraped on but Valerie was narrowly defeated by a rightwinger. Thus, by tactical voting John only just failed to ensure that the committee had a solid centre-right majority, a result which would have provided 'proof' of a deal between myself and the right. Instead, his plan had resulted in the election of an all-white, all-male committee, which was the next best thing from the viewpoint of his propaganda needs.

Articles immediately started to appear condemning the new committee. John's close associate Kevin Veness, writing in *Briefing* under the headline 'NOTHING LESS THAN A PURGE', said:

> The realignment of political control at County Hall is now well underway . . . It is a sad reflection on the Group that the new centre-left and right coalition were prepared to elect an all-male, all-white committee.

It was obvious that if such tactics were used at the AGM there would be a real danger of a shift to the right in the administration which was due to be elected on 29 April. I convened a meeting of the left (without the McDonnell ten) to discuss how to avoid this, and we decided to nominate for re-election to their positions all of the rebels, with the exception of McDonnell. On the question of who should run against John as deputy leader and Finance chair, we decided to split the two posts so as to avoid repeating the concentration of power that had existed under John. Alex McKay was the obvious choice for Finance chair but the deputy leadership was a problem. I wanted to avoid giving John the chance to continue his allegations that there had been a shift to the right. I was also determined to make it clear that we were sacking him because he had been prepared to damage the reputation of the GLC and split the left. I favoured running another one of John's 'ten' as his replacement so as to maintain the political balance in the Group, but recognized that it would be almost impossible for any of them to stand against him.

I approached both Dave Wetzel and Paul Boateng but as expected both declined, and by the time of the AGM Mike Ward was the only other candidate. Acting on John's behalf, Lesley Hammond had approached Tony McBrearty to ask him to stand for deputy leader so that some of the McDonnell ten could switch their votes to him in order to defeat Mike Ward. Tony had declined to be used in this way. I was amazed that John did not follow through the logic of his campaign and stand against me as Leader. It seemed to me remarkable that anyone would contest the deputy leadership and be prepared to serve under a man they had publicly condemned as a coward, and who had responded in like terms.

Any doubts about John's chances of survival were washed away at the meeting of the PCC/PC on Wednesday 24 April, just five days before the AGM. Reg Race presented a confidential report on the real state of GLC finances. Even those who had believed that John was wrong were stunned when Reg reported that without any deals or approach to the Government £120 million was immediately available for growth, with the chance of another £40 million if the more optimistic forecasts were confirmed. There was also the possibility of a further £150 million being available if we liquidated our capital fund once abolition became a certainty, although the Government might be able to prevent this.

The news was greeted with gasps of amazement which rapidly turned into embarrassed laughter. John was not present at the meeting but others of the McDonnell ten were. They asked a few questions to confirm, and then sat through the rest of the meeting looking more like sick parrots than any footballers ever will. Dave Wetzel, who arrived late, sat in a state of shock when he heard the news. Like most of the others, he had honestly believed John's claims and had voted with genuine integrity. I never heard how John managed to explain it all away to those who had followed him so loyally throughout the whole terrible period. I wish I had.

The PCC/PC recommended to the Labour Group that £62 million be used to restore the cuts in the Barrie Stead budget and to push ahead with a wide range of genuine growth proposals. We also agreed to give £58 million to the rate-capped boroughs so that no cuts would be required by any borough in order to survive within the Government's limits. We began to plan for an £80 million package of assistance to the ILEA and £20 million of forward funding for those voluntary organizations which might be forced to close in the event of GLC abolition. But even with such a range of schemes it still looked as though we would be physically unable to spend all the resources that Reg Race's team had found. We faced the embarrassing prospect that we would have to consult the boroughs to ask if they would like us to reduce the rate. When those Labour leaders who were still refusing to set a rate heard about this they were not amused.

The Group AGM was a foregone conclusion. While everyone else was re-elected to their positions unopposed, John was replaced as deputy leader by Mike Ward by 22 votes to 13 and as Finance chair by Alex McKay with a similar vote. Only a handful of CLPs had submitted motions supporting John; his attempt to realign the London left around his own leadership had failed. Most activists had not been taken in by the simple view that the rate-capping fiasco could be explained away by leadership betrayals. In my Paddington constituency, which was solidly on the left, only 14 delegates out of 45 present called on me to vote for John.

The closeness of our working relationship in the previous three years meant that the split between John and me was particularly painful and bitter. Night after night in the weeks running up to the AGM vote, I lay in bed endlessly going over where and why it had all gone wrong, never reaching a conclusion or finding the simple answer of personal ambition adequate. I was furious that John had managed to cloud the principled socialist record of the administration of which I had been so proud. I was also on the receiving end of equally personal hatred from many activists, including close friends. Chris Knight and Graham Bash, who had been in at the very beginning of the planning to take over the GLC, completely cut me out of their lives.

From the moment John was sacked by the Group, my feelings changed to remorse. Remembering Tony Judge's kindness to me in similar circumstances exactly a decade earlier, and the financial problems I had faced after my own sacking, I wrote to John asking him to continue as a full-time member with responsibility for our policies towards the Irish and disinvestment from South Africa. I received no response. I wrote again in July and invited him to lunch to explore the possibility of preventing the split within the London left widening still further. The reply I received perfectly captures the bitterness of the period. Although notionally from his Hayes and Harlington Party officers, it is very much in John's style.

> The left is defined within certain parameters of, among other things, the acceptance of class struggle, and a determination to fight in comradeship and solidarity . . .
>
> . . . When you were called upon to participate in this struggle in the rate-capping campaign and there was some personal risk involved, you stepped outside of these parameters of class struggle, determination, comradeship and solidarity. Representatives of this CLP were in attendance at every GLC Labour Group and Council meeting over rate-capping and judged your betrayal of the party as disgraceful.
>
> You have placed yourself permanently outside of the left and in our view therefore have no contribution to make in its development in struggle. We could never place any trust in your statements or rely upon you in struggle. For you to talk about 'doing something to heal the rifts on the left' plumbs the depth of hypocrisy when you eagerly pursued a McCarthyite witch-hunt against our GLC Councillor.
>
> On your offer to join McDonnell for a private talk over a free lunch you should know by now that we do not expect an elected delegate of this party to be engaged in private talks and secret deals which undermine and betray the principle of accountability. We do not consider there is anything that can be gained in the interests of socialism to have any discussions with someone who has done so much to undermine the struggle against this Tory Government.
>
> It gives us no pleasure to write this sort of letter but the Hayes and Harlington GMC meeting at which your correspondence was discussed was unanimous in the view that we should have no dealings with someone who has

scabbed on the movement and his former comrades for
personal political gain.

The frustration and impotence caused by the collapse of the
rate-capping campaign led to increasingly ultra-left attacks from
Militant, Briefing and *Socialist Organiser*, directed against the Labour
Group and myself. Both *Briefing* and *Labour Herald* started to call
for an immediate challenge to Neil Kinnock's leadership. This was
a position from which I dissociated myself. All these groups and
papers merely alienated more and more of their support amongst
the constituency activists as they went further over the top. They
made a considerable effort to get Mike Ward and Valerie Wise
defeated in the annual elections to the GLLP Executive, only to
see Mike and Valerie in the top two places, well ahead of the
Briefing-sponsored challengers. The bitterness worsened as the year
passed and *Briefing* declined to the point where it was happy to
reprint as fact the sexual smears about me that still occasionally
appeared in *Private Eye* and the *Standard.*
Given all the hysteria surrounding the issue of rate-capping both
in the press and the Labour Party, it is surprising that support for
the GLC and the Labour administration did not decline. The
whole affair had little impact on the public, although the campaign
dragged on, with Lambeth and Liverpool Councils not setting a
rate until July.
With increasing despair I watched many of my closest colleagues
and friends on individual boroughs continuing past the point of
illegality, even though the campaign was already effectively lost. No
London borough faced any cuts due to the availability of the 'newly
discovered' GLC funds. Immediately after the GLC finally set a
rate I urged the boroughs to review their tactics in the light of the
GLC's failure. My worry was that the boroughs would fall by the
wayside one by one, enabling the Government's District Auditor
to pick off a few councils as examples. The backlash of anger
against the GLC Group and myself, however, did not create the
sort of climate in which the borough leaders could re-evaluate their
tactics and switch to a deficit budget strategy. My fears were
confirmed with the surcharge and debarment of the Lambeth and
Liverpool councillors. More than two years later we are still in the

position that GLC funds and creative accounting have prevented any of the cuts we warned that rate-capping would bring. We must also accept that if Labour councils do finally face the crunch on rate-capping it will be difficult to persuade local people that 'this time we really mean it'.

Politics is not a game. Thousands of people's jobs and services depended on what the GLC did, and they expected us to do the best we could. Throughout the campaign, two factors determined my actions. Firstly, if at all possible I intended that the GLC should not set a rate. Secondly, if this was not possible, then our task had to be to protect jobs and services to the best of our ability. In contrast to GLC successes, the rate-capping campaign failed because it remained mired in the shadow-boxing of parliamentary and Council chamber politics, with the workforce being wheeled on as a stage army when required.

10

The Dandelion Effect

Throughout the months that followed the collapse of the rate-capping campaign and the final passage of the Abolition Act, all our efforts went into the task of trying to ensure that we preserved and defended as many of our policies and our staff as possible. It is not possible to go into the details of what we did to ensure that the bulk of surplus GLC funds went to those boroughs and voluntary organizations which were prepared to continue our work and employ our staff, as several legal challenges to our policy are still pending in the courts.

Having stayed at arm's length since the Law Lords' judgement on fares, the judges weighed in on the side of the Tories again in another political decision. Our barristers, Roger Henderson and Tony Gifford, had spent months refining our case on forward funding. It rested on Lord Denning's decision in the Court of Appeal, which had allowed the Tory-controlled Greater Manchester Council to pay for places at public schools for children living under the Labour-controlled Manchester City Council. Because the Tories knew that they would shortly lose control of Greater Manchester, they had set up a trust to continue paying for the children's education after the council had gone Labour. The Manchester City Council had gone to court but no one was surprised when Lord Denning ruled in favour of the council's forward funding of the children's education.

It was on the Greater Manchester precedent that we proposed to give each of the voluntary organizations we had been supporting another year's funds. We used the same principle to justify funding the completion of the Black Arts Centre at the Camden Round-house and to provide the ILEA with a sum to cover the initial costs of the disruption they would suffer as a result of taking on many GLC services and staff. As expected, Lady Porter's Westminster City Council took us to the High Court, where before Mr Justice MacPherson we won on every point of law and procedure. The judgement was so favourable that in normal circumstances no barrister would have advised their client to go to appeal. But the circumstances were not 'normal'. Mrs Thatcher and Lord Hailsham had had seven years in which to appoint a Court of Appeal which reflected their own political beliefs. From the moment Mrs Thatcher had appointed Lord Donaldson, a former Tory candidate, as successor to Lord Denning, we had avoided getting into the Court of Appeal at all costs.

Our fears were justified when we saw the nature of the Court of Appeal's judgements against us. The detailed and closely argued judgement of Mr Justice MacPherson was overturned in the most sweeping and superficial manner. One judge dismissed the High Court decision stating that he noted the decision but simply disagreed with it. With just a few days to go to abolition we knew that we had no more chance of success with Mrs Thatcher's Law Lords than we had in her Court of Appeal, so we switched £78 million into a scheme to carry on the GLC's housing modernization programme. Once again this was challenged in the High Court and Mr Justice MacPherson ruled solidly in our favour.

While the many court cases proceeded, we embarked on months of negotiations with the London boroughs and the Government-appointed quangos which were taking over GLC staff and services. As we had claimed throughout our long campaign, the GLC was not really being abolished. It was being split into several parts, and the right of Londoners to elect and dismiss the people running those services was being removed.

Each of the quangos took a different view of their responsibilities towards our staff. By far the most vicious was the Arts Council, who made two-thirds of the staff who ran the South Bank concert halls redundant while increasing senior management from 6 posts (paid £108,000) to 11 posts (paid £271,500).

The quango which was to take over the majority of our work, including all the financial, legal and property rights and responsibilities, was the London Residuary Body. The Tories had appointed

Sir Godfrey ('Tag') Taylor to run the LRB on a salary of £50,000 a year. Like all my colleagues, I had been earning £6,000 a year at County Hall, and we had to resist the temptation to submit back-dated claims for £220,000 to bring us up to Sir Godfrey's salary. While he was prepared to take on most GLC staff, Sir Godfrey was adamant that as he was 'neither racist nor sexist' he would not need our Women's or Ethnic Minority Units.

In the end we managed to persuade eight Labour boroughs to establish the London Strategic Policy Unit. This absorbed all the staff employed in our more controversial units and gave the boroughs a resource which would allow them to continue our campaigning work, if they had the imagination to do so.

By the time we reached the final weekend of the GLC's life, we had managed to find jobs for all of those staff who wanted them, although they were not always the jobs people wanted. A couple of hundred staff wished to be made redundant for personal reasons and over 2,000 jobs were lost by staff taking early retirement. Although we had avoided a disaster, the strain suffered by many people in the run-up to abolition took its toll in worry and insecurity. At least two members of staff committed suicide during that period.

We were able to preserve the bulk of our services for a short time. The financial arrangements we negotiated with the boroughs and the quangos ensured that there should be no need for any cutbacks within the first year or 18 months following abolition. We hoped that would be long enough to get us to the election and a change of government, but it could not stop those bodies which actually wanted to make cuts. The London Transport Quango (LRT) soon pressed ahead with fare increases and drastic cuts in bus services. The London Residuary Body rushed to dispose of as many GLC assets as possible – including County Hall itself – before a change of government.

Mrs Thatcher's real objective had never been simply to make a few more cuts in public spending. She had sought to destroy a form of politics which she considered a threat to her ideological dominance of British politics. With just 44 per cent of the vote in 1979 and 42 per cent in 1983, hers had always been a Government by default. It continued to exist only because of the lack of a really popular alternative on the Opposition benches in Parliament.

There was no doubting the popularity of our alternative. While the Labour Party seemed unable to break through the 40 per cent figure in national opinion polls, we surged forward from our low point of the mid-twenties in 1981 to reach and cross the 50 per cent barrier in 1984. By September 1984, the Labour GLC had reached levels of popular support in London which surpassed anything Labour had been able to achieve in the previous 84 years of its existence. A detailed analysis of the opinion polls conducted by the Harris organization is revealing.

Nationally, opposition to unilateral nuclear disarmament was running at 52 per cent, with 39 per cent in favour. After our peace year campaign the London figures showed 48 per cent opposed and 44 per cent in favour.

After four years' work by the GLC Police Committee, the view that crime should be dealt with by tackling the social problems that cause it was supported by 51 per cent of Londoners compared with only 46 per cent of people nationally.

The 19 per cent national majority in support of the Government's anti-trade union legislation was reduced to a mere 7 per cent lead in London.

Support for public transport subsidy was 10 per cent higher in London. A wide range of other progressive positions showed a consistent four to seven per cent higher level of support in London than in the rest of the country.

In London five per cent more people thought that the Labour Party would keep its promises than the national percentage who thought so. Six per cent more people gave their reason for supporting Labour in London as the fact that they liked Labour policies.

As well as this higher level of commitment in favour of our policies, the polls revealed higher levels of support for Labour in London amongst many traditionally Labour social groups, such as council tenants and trade unionists. There were also higher levels of support amongst pensioners and, most remarkably, amongst younger voters (aged 18 to 34) of social classes ABCI, who have recently become known as 'yuppies'. This vital group split nationally, with 40 per cent supporting the Alliance and only 29 per cent and 28 per cent for Tories and Labour respectively. In London, however, the split was 39 per cent Labour with only 30 per cent for the Alliance and 28 per cent for the Tories. Amongst the whole age range of the ABCI class, Labour was also 10 per cent up over the national figures but drawn more evenly from the other parties.

The conclusion of our pollsters was that 'you do not have to water down your policies in order to be popular, but they do have to be explained in a calm, rational way'. The Tory lead over Labour at the 1983 general election had been two per cent smaller in London than in the rest of the country, yet by December 1983 Labour was doing 12 per cent better in London than nationally. The difference remained in double figures in every poll taken for the remainder of the GLC's life, except for March 1984 when it slipped back to eight per cent. These figures are important because there are those who argue that the GLC's popularity was merely due to a slick advertising campaign. In fact, the advertising campaign did not start until March 1984, several months after the considerable gap opened up between support for Labour nationally and in London.

Equally, those who argue that Labour needs to blur its policies in order to win are ignoring the evidence of our polls, which showed that ABCI voters switched to support the Labour GLC precisely because of some specific policy that they supported. For some, it was our policies on transport or the environment; for others, our policies on women or lesbian and gay rights. But for all of them it was a specific vote *for* a policy, not simply a gut reaction against the Tories. If Labour is to win the support of this crucial group nationally it will need to sharpen its policy image. Merely relying on anti-Tory feelings means that voters have as much reason to vote for the Alliance as they have to vote Labour.

For the last week of the GLC we put on a vast array of arts and recreation events which drew hundreds of thousands of Londoners into our farewell festival. Perhaps because I was so busy over the last few months working to find jobs for our staff and protect our services, I had not had time to reflect on what I was feeling emotionally, but in the final four days I went through the draining and exhilarating experience of saying goodbye and thank you to

341

dozens of different audiences. As I did I could not help but wonder at how an unloved and boring bureaucracy on the South Bank had come to mean so much to so many. At midnight on Easter Monday there were still hundreds of thousands of people standing in the cold with tears streaming down their faces as the GLC flag was lowered to the sound of Nimrod, from Elgar's 'Enigma' Variations.

Through my own tears, I felt and shared the emotion of that crowd and knew how lucky I had been. Most politicians go through their whole lives without experiencing anything a tenth as fulfilling or rewarding as those five years had been to me. Even in the depths of October 1981 I had still been in love with every minute. People ask me which of my mistakes I would most want to go back and change, but that question overlooks the fact that we learn as much from our mistakes as our successes. All of it together stretched me to the limit. Nothing that had gone before could have prepared me for what I was to learn in those five years about the ability of ordinary women and men to become involved in the processes of government and change.

I had joined the Labour Party in the aftermath of the upheavals of 1968 because I believed that changing society requires an alliance: an alliance between progressive individuals and groups within the apparatus of the state, and the forces for change that exist outside the parliamentary system. The extent to which the GLC had touched the hearts and minds of Londoners, and the change it had undergone during that process, gave us a glimpse of our potential to transform our society, if we can ever persuade the leadership of the Labour movement to go down the road of a participatory democracy.

A state that removed the restrictions built up over generations to control and administer the people and chose instead to decentralize it, devolve and share power with those who have been excluded from it would create a power base that could bring irreversible change. It would have the power to override the forces of reaction and greed within our own society, whether in the senior reaches of the civil service, the judiciary and Fleet Street or in the unaccountable private and public corporations. It would have the power to resist the IMF, the World Bank, Washington, and NATO internationally.

Many of our critics claimed that it was easy for the GLC to become popular because we were not burdened with the problems of running unpopular housing, social service and education departments. That conveniently overlooks the unpopularity of those responsible for public transport in the 1970s. We were able to turn that situation around because we had worked out exactly what we wished to do before our election, realizing that people would rather provide enough subsidy for a good service than pay slightly less for a poor one. When planning the manifesto we still had responsibility for housing management. Had that not been removed from us by the Government, we intended to devolve control completely from County Hall and provide the funding necessary to bring about rapid improvements.

When I was on borough councils I never saw the personal services as a burden but as an instrument through which we could reach and empower local people. Those who now say that the GLC's task was relatively easy are usually the councillors who resist any moves towards genuine participation and power-sharing in their own authorities. They are those who resisted rate increases to develop services when they still had the freedom to go down that road. Where we were different from other Labour councils was in London's wealthy rate base and our ability to redistribute wealth on a scale normally reserved for governments. But so often in the past Labour governments have had that power in their hands and have declined to use it, leaving office with the balance of wealth and power in society unchanged.

In the months following abolition, it often seemed as though a concerted effort was being made to explain away the popularity of the GLC. People put it down to our publicity campaign, or to my coming over well on television. That is an insult to the intelligence of Londoners and the thousands of others who contributed to the success of the Labour administration. If our popularity had been due simply to our advertising campaign, the popularity of the GLC would have transferred to the Labour boroughs which were up for re-election five weeks after abolition. That did not happen. Londoners who had supported the GLC were never likely to vote automatically for Labour borough councils or a national Labour party which did not embrace the policies or working methods of the GLC.

343

Labour rapidly lost its GLC factor in the polls. Yet a year later, in the aftermath of the Greenwich by-election, the new *London Daily News* ran a Harris poll which asked several questions about the GLC before putting the standard voting intention question. In contrast to other polls, which showed Labour 10 per cent behind the Tories in London, the Harris poll registered a 4 per cent Labour lead. A powerful echo of the GLC's popularity even after eleven months without any publicity campaign.

The attempt to play down the lessons of the GLC is a vivid reminder that it represented a threat not only to the Tories but also to the bureaucratic traditions of labourism, which Richard Gott described so well in the *Guardian* of 17 June 1984.

> The party of Ramsay MacDonald and Lord George Brown, the party of the block vote and the fudged manifesto, the party of the tower block and the destroyed inner city, the party of the macho joke in the workingman's club, the party of ideas in opposition that fails to put them into practice in government, the party of the Bomb, of the Vietnam War. It is a party that has taken a long time to die. Its putrefying corpse still poisons the present and casts its baleful shadow over the future.
>
> Many of the most unsavoury elements have already gone off to join the SDP, but many of this ilk still remain. They had their chance to run the country in the Wilson and Callaghan years from 1966 to 1979, the years that the locust devoured. They had their moment in the sun, their chance to put their mark on history. And their failure was dismal to behold. Exhausted and without credibility, they virtually forced the votes into the Thatcher camp for lack of an alternative.
>
> Opportunities of the kind they were given then do not come round a second time, and, belatedly, most of that dreadful gang have agreed to slink soundlessly from the scene before a worse fate befalls them. But they have left a legacy behind them, they have sown the dragon's teeth.
>
> Must this go on forever?

The Labour GLC did not provide a ready-made alternative

344

model, only some important experiences from which we can draw lessons. Instead of trying to do everything for people, we broke away from Labour's client approach to politics and enabled some people to begin to do things for themselves. Contrary to the fears of authoritarians in the party, we were strengthened by that process, not weakened. We never asked to see someone's Labour Party card before we listened to them nor did we expect them to join the party because we had given assistance or access. And precisely because we did not do such things, so many did join us.

We recognized that the narrow definition of the working class as white skilled workers was no longer appropriate to describe the diversity we saw around us; I doubt that it ever was. We saw that the black youth who has never had a job, the mother working in the home harder than most men work outside it, and the gay couple whose lives are circumscribed by the ignorant fears of others, are all part of the working class as it exists in our city.

All strands of radical and socialist opinion came to work in the GLC's administrative melting pot. Orthodox and Eurocommunists, Trotskyists, anarchists, community activists, libertarians, feminists and liberals all seemed to be able to work together, to learn from each other and turn outwards into the community rather than look backwards into their old sectarian squabbles. Together these forces came to be seen as the denial of Mrs Thatcher's assertion that 'there is no alternative'. We demonstrated that voting can change things, and the Government found that so threatening that they set out to prove the truth of the old anarchist slogan which forms the title of this book.

Like Greenham Common, CND and Greenpeace, the GLC was unmistakably a product of the 1980s, and like them it grew out of the upheavals of the 1960s. The advance of the left in the sixties was part of an upsurge of creativity which affected the arts, popular culture, lifestyle and sex lives much more than it affected the party politics of the day. Racism, sexism, participation and ecology, issues which appeared on the agenda of the sixties, took over a decade to reach the attention of the political parties. It was only with the 1981 GLC administration that they finally took their rightful place alongside and integrated with the traditional agenda of the left. Significantly, Mrs Thatcher and Norman Tebbit never cease to identify the 1960s as the origin of so much that they perceive as rotten in today's society. In the aftermath of the 1981 riots, Mrs Thatcher was quick to point out that 'we are reaping what was sown in the 1960s'.

Unfortunately for the right, the GLC was merely the first intrusion of the 1960s generation into national politics. Both here and in the rest of Europe that generation will come into its own in the final decade of this century. It is a generation that grew up with and saw the limitations of a welfare state whose lack of democracy alienated those it was supposed to serve. It is that generation that faces the task of strengthening socialism's weakest flank by intertwining socialism and democracy so that the two become inseparable.

The abolition of the GLC has merely advanced that process. The attacks on us from the press, the judges and the media brought us to the attention of the world and enabled others to learn from our experiences. After abolition, the participants in the GLC at both councillor and officer level dispersed to other councils and to Parliament, to public and private institutions and to countries as diverse as Denmark, Spain and Australia. Those individuals will be applying what they learned at the GLC to their work in decades to come, and the results of that dispersal will be with us for the rest of our lives.

As the ideas and practices that made the GLC notorious start to sprout in other institutions and other countries, Mrs Thatcher may come to regret that she studied chemistry rather than botany. Even the dimmest gardener knows not to knock the head off a dandelion in its seed-bearing stage.

APPENDIX

LABOUR'S FIRST YEAR AND THE TORY RESPONSE

Paper submitted by Ken Livingstone on 11 January 1981 for discussion by Labour candidates.

The Tory Government's Options

Since the Local Government Act became law and Heseltine introduced his cuts in the Rate Support Grant and the new block grant there has been a wave of defeatism amongst councillors who are beginning to question the value of having Labour-controlled councils under the present conditions. This paper sets out the reasons why we must reject this defeatism and how we can move rapidly to implement our manifesto.

The GLC campaign will be fought against the background of massive rate increases in April caused by Tory Government policies. At the end of our first year the London borough elections will also be influenced by rate increases in April 1982 and by how effective our policies have been in improving the quality of life for Londoners. Unless we can show a measurable improvement in services rather than just another increase in the size of the bureaucracy, we could suffer a massive loss of support. Thus it is vital that all our key policies are started in the first three months following the election. Given the inertia within this building this will require a major time commitment from members.

This will also mean that expenditure rises above the budget left us by the outgoing Tory administration. The Tories may consider the abolition of the GLC and return to the idea of breaking up the ILEA, but it is likely that they will want to see how we react to their financial penalties before trying more drastic measures which would involve new legislation.

The 1981–2 GLC/ILEA Budgets

The new act gives the Government almost total control over all GLC/ILEA/London Transport capital spending. Unless a loophole is found then the Government has the power to prevent us building new housing, extending the tube, buying new buses or undertaking any works of improvement to housing or the environment. The new council will have no alternative but to lead a massive and continuing campaign to mobilize public opinion and force the reversal of these policies.

The GLC housing programme required a minimum allocation of £140

347

million from Government but has only received 95 million thus we need to find another £25 million to continue existing contracts.

The new council will inherit a GLC budget which is unlikely to cover even the outgoing Tories' commitments, London Transport will face an as yet unfunded deficit of between £35 to £55 million.

Revenue Expenditure

The new act does not prevent councils increasing the rates, indeed the Government's allocation to London will force many councils to increase them by over 50 per cent. The 1981–2 Tory GLC budget will be nearly £600 million but to qualify for the full RSG entitlement of £137 million will require the Tories to make a 9 per cent cut in the present level of spending. It is unlikely that even Cutler can do this and the Tories could end up with between £95 and £120 million if they fail to cut enough.

The Government has decided that the ILEA budget should only be £468 million and if we could cut spending by the 30 per cent required to reach this level then we would qualify for the full £141 million RSG. As the ILEA budget for 1981–2 will be between £680 million to £710 million the ILEA will lose at least £135 million, and possibly all of its RSG. This is because for each £1 we spend over the amount the Government believed we should spend they claw back the RSG we are entitled to as a penalty. Thus if we spend £100 million over the Government's target we lose about £60 million grant.

The GLC also will receive about £70 million Transport Supplementary Grant in addition to RSG. Thus the Government could withdraw grants which will total somewhere between £165 million and £214 million as Labour starts to implement its GLC/LT/ILEA policies. When the GLC increases the rate by 1p it gets in £20 million. Each 1p on the ILEA precept produces £11 million. The average domestic ratepayer has to pay another £2.50 a year with each 1p increase in the rate. The GLC rate base in 62 per cent commercial and 38 per cent domestic. The ILEA rate base is 75 per cent commercial and 25 per cent domestic. Each 1p increase in the rate produces £3 million from Westminster, £2.7 million from the City of London, £1 million from Camden and an average of just under £500,000 from each of the other 30 London boroughs.

The cost to the average ratepayer if the Government withdraws all grants would be between £20 and £25 next year. Thus the GLC is very close to being free of the Government penalties which can cripple individual boroughs. The ILEA having lost all its grant in this first budget under the system will be free of further revenue penalties unless the Government takes further powers. The Government can start to apply its clawback penalties as soon as they see projected overspending. They do not have to wait until the end of the financial year.

Appendix

Immediate Policy Changes

The working groups now being established by the GLLP executive will be drawing up detailed plans for the changes we need to make at County Hall in the period between the election and the August break. The decision of the ILEA Labour Group to implement the cut in school meal prices from 35p to 25p will take effect before the election and should help to build public support for our policies and show that we have a genuine commitment to the manifesto. We must ensure that our policies are implemented in a way that makes an immediate favourable impact on Londoners in the areas that affect their daily lives so that before the Government can move against us we have won popular support for our programme.

Transport

Clearly the fares cut will be the major issue. We need to have worked out the zonal fares scheme so that it is introduced at the same time as the fares cut and avoid the confusion that would be caused if it were introduced separately. The earliest date for introduction would be 1 August. We must be ready to offer British Rail subsidies for OAP free travel and a reduction in BR fares within GLC area in line with the 25 per cent LT cut.

Failure to do this would divide Londoners on the basis of which transport service they use. Any resistance from Government can be overcome by a campaign directed at Tory MPs in seats with large numbers of BR commuters.

We must negotiate wages and conditions of LT staff in order to get more from the existing bus and tube stock in order to provide the extra capacity needed when fares are cut. The bus lane programme must be the first priority of the Planning and Transport Committees to ensure that the increased service is not defeated by traffic congestion.

Unemployment

The level of unemployment will be a key factor in our campaign and I think we must introduce a 35-hour week for all manual staff as a firm policy for job creation. This will require agreement with the unions that the 35-hour week does not mean increased overtime for the existing workforce but a reduction in London's mounting unemployment figures. Camden Council introduced this policy in 1979 and if the GLC should become the second council to adopt this policy it will then reinforce those trade unions campaigning for a 35-hour week throughout the economy.

The Industry and Employment programme has been more fully detailed than the other manifesto areas and that working party should concentrate on bringing forward all the revenue-based aspects which can go ahead

349

quickly. Those areas subject to Government capital controls will be part of the campaign referred to elsewhere in this paper.

Housing Transfer

The remaining 95,000 properties in the eight resisting boroughs will not have been transferred before the election although it is likely that Parliament will have agreed a transfer order for a date such as August 1st. The incoming group must refuse to process the transfer and start an immediate major maintenance programme of revenue-funded improvements on these neglected estates whilst withdrawing the request for transfer. The manifesto proposals for district housing committees to run the estates without any central County Hall interference should be established at the first GLC meeting with tenant representatives comprising one third of the members. All revenue-funded improvements must be agreed in full consultation with tenants who would have a veto power over any particular scheme. Rents should be frozen.

Local Projects

Throughout London the GLC and other councils have been cutting back on grants to Law Centres, Community Relations Councils, tenants and other community organizations. The GLC should step in and take over the funding of these bodies. The decision of Ealing to stop funding its CCR because of CCR policy on the Southall riots is just a well publicized example of what has been happening throughout London. Many of these groups have a major local impact in terms of fighting on behalf of local people. We should be identified with that fight.

There are also a wide range of things a Labour GLC can do to fund local projects (such as recreational facilities in existing buildings) from revenue.

Often what people want is achievable for a small cost providing it remains under the control of a local community group and is not part of some vast long-term project involving capital expenditure. Local members should have access to GLC funds to finance these projects with the minimum of bureaucracy.

Police

The Police Committee we set up and the manifesto commitments to an effective unit monitoring racial and sexual discrimination, will need to have direct access to the Policy Committee and the Labour Group if their recommendations are to take effect in the short term. Too often similar bodies find that their recommendations are resisted at all levels within the system.

Civil Defence

The present group have committed us to ending the so-called civil defence programme and campaigning for unilateral nuclear disarmament. I would suggest that the funds available to this programme should be switched to help towards restoring the cuts in fire cover introduced by the present GLC.

Help to Boroughs

The Local Government Act 1963 gives the GLC power to provide massive help to those boroughs who have suffered the severest RSG cuts. For example, we could take over the housing maintenance organizations and costs of any boroughs whilst leaving them in effective control of the service and its standards. A Labour GLC could in this and other areas allow the boroughs to preserve their services in the face of RSG cuts.

Campaign

Whilst we will be able to press ahead with our revenue programmes we must campaign to explain why rates have risen so dramatically in London as a result of Tory policy and force the Government to release the funding required for our capital programme. Without capital spending the long-term decline of London will continue and negate the effects of our revenue programmes. This will mean the GLC becoming an active campaigning body which explains its policies in a sympathetic fashion which avoids jargon. We must start from the point of ordinary people's experience and build upwards from those. GLC members will have to be visible within their constituencies, explaining, helping and leading.

Those who have read 'Poplarism' or 'Red Bologna' will be aware of how local authorities were able to build up public support by adopting an open and participatory approach. Unfortunately, the GLC/ILEA/LT have since the 1930s existed on a basis of a strong, centralized, secretive method of organization. Unless we change this style we will be unable to carry the Labour Party with us, let alone the public.

Group Democracy

The leadership must operate on a basis of bringing to the Group informed options rather than the old style of 'leadership line' which has to be rammed through the Group under a threat of resignation by the leadership if that line is not supported. Instead of a vast number of committees pushing paper around the building we must have a small number of committees in which each Labour member is given a specific area of policy to push through the machine or investigate.

One committee chair and vice-chair cannot hope to ensure that our policies are carried out.

The use of 'Chairman's Action' should be ended. In future, items that do not need full committee approval should be agreed by three members acting as an executive sub-committee. All such items should be reported to the full committee.

All committees must have a Labour Group which meets once to discuss the committee agenda and once in each cycle to review the progress of policy implementation and receive reports from the individual members about their area of delegation.

Each CLP and TU should be invited to send an observer to each full Group meeting. Recorded votes should be introduced to be taken if 10 per cent of members request one. It will be vital that we carry the staff with us in our policy changes and this will require the co-option of staff representatives to all committees and a regular series of meetings between the Group and the staff unions. Similar meetings should take place between departmental staff and the relevant committee membership.

The GLC must produce a free newspaper for distribution to each London household at least every other month and organize a public meeting in each constituency at least twice a year so that members can report back to constituents. One member should be elected to co-ordinate the above activities and the work of the press department.

Full council meetings should start in the morning to enable evening press coverage.

All meetings should end in time for members to be free for public campaigning. We should offer facilities for a press agency within the building and full council meetings should take place on Monday to ensure local press coverage in the week of the meetings.

The GLLP will have to maintain a continuing campaign beyond the election throughout 1981–2 as the emphasis switches to the borough elections. If we have established both credibility and respect amongst Londoners this will be of major assistance in the borough elections. It is important that in our campaign to get the resources London needs and to roll back Government policy, we avoid the issue being seen as either the GLC looking for a fight or simply as a personality clash between the Leader and Heseltine. We must keep the focus of attention on our policies.

Because we will have an honest mandate there is no need for defeatism about our ability to carry out the programme but we must avoid an apocalyptic approach that hinges the whole campaign on one issue or one date. We are in a long and bitter struggle with the Government, the outcome of which will be determined as much by the unforeseen miscalculations of the Tories as by our positive actions. But our campaign can play a major role in speeding the defeat of the Government and in winning respect for the Labour Party and support for socialist policies.

EVENTS 1965–86

1965

Apr: GLC created from the LCC.

1967

Apr: Conservatives capture GLC.

1968 Lab Govt introduces Act to prevent black British entering UK.

May: Lab lose Lambeth to Tories.

1969 Apr: Troops to N. Ireland to defend Catholics.

First Draft of Greater London Development Plan (GLDP).
Mar: KL joins Lab Party.

1970 Feb: Special Public Order Act for N. Ireland.
Jun: Heath wins Gen Election.

Tories hold on to GLC control in elections with reduced majority.
Jun: Govt ends restrictions on sale of council houses.

1971 Feb: Rolls Royce goes bankrupt.
Immigration act.
Aug: Introduction of internment without trial in N. Ireland.
Clydeside shipbuilders occupy yards.

May: KL becomes councillor in Lambeth, vice-chair of Housing cte.

1972 Jan: Miners' strike.
'Bloody Sunday' in Derry.
Jul: National dock strike.
Nov: Govt introduces wage controls.

Aug: Housing Finance Act (90% of costs of building, restoring council houses to be born by Govt).

1973 Jan: Britain joins EEC.
Oil crisis.
Dec: The 'three-day week'.

Apr: Lab regains control of GLC. Sir Reg Goodwin's administration begins.

353

KL wins seat,
vice-chair of Film
Viewing Board.

1974   Ulster Assembly takes rule
of N. Ireland.
Feb: Miners' strike.
    Gen Election,
    minority Lab Govt
    takes office.
May: Protestant workers
    strike, Assembly
    suspended,
    resumption
    of direct rule from
    Westminster.
Oct: Lab wins majority in
    Gen Election.

Mar: KL elected to exec of
    GLLP.
May: Borough elections in
    Lambeth.
    KL becomes
    vice-chair of
    Housing
    Management.
    Crisis over GLC
    finances begins.
Nov: Strategic Housing
    Plan.

1975   Feb: Thatcher becomes
    leader of Tories.
    Collapse of British
    Leyland.
Jul: '£6-a-week' formula for
    pay restraint.
Oct: Unemployment
    reaches 1m for first time
    since war.
Nov: Oil flows from North
    Sea.

Collapse of Labour's
'Housing Strategy Plan'.

1976   Layfield report on local govt
financing recommends
preservation of local govt
autonomy.
Apr: Callaghan becomes
    Prime Minister.
Aug: Grunwick dispute in
    Brent East.
IMF loan to Lab Govt.
'Peace' movement in N.
Ireland.

Mar: Left fail to win
    majority on GLLP
    exec but exec drafts
    radical manifesto
    GLC report on Major
    Technical Problems
    on GLC housing
    estates.

1977   Mar: Lib/Lab Pact.
Govt rescue of British
Leyland.

Feb: Right wing on GLLP
    reverse plans for
    radical manifesto.

Aug: Grunwick dispute ends.

Mar: Attacks on left by Goodwin, Keys and Mellish.
May: Conservative victory in GLC elections. Sir Horace Cutler becomes leader. KL wins seat for Hackney North.

1978 Nov: Publication of *The Times* suspended for a year.

May: Ted Knight becomes leader of Lambeth Council.
KL stands for Camden council, chair of Housing.

1979 'Winter of Discontent'.
Feb: NUPE go on strike.
May: Mrs Thatcher becomes Prime Minister.
Nov: 'Red Robbo' sacked by BL.

May: KL chair of GLC Transport working party.
79–81 unity of left behind drive to capture GLC. Massive rent and fare increases by Cutler.

1980 Apr: Rioting in St Paul's, Bristol.
Sep: Local Govt Planning Act.
Housing Act: council tenants can buy their houses at a discount.
Nov: Govt introduces 6% ceiling on pay increases in public sector.
Michael Foot becomes Leader of Lab Party.

Feb: *London Labour Briefing* launched.
Apr: Sir Reg Goodwin resigns as leader of Lab Group, Andrew McIntosh takes over.
Jul: London Transport on verge of bankruptcy.

1981 Jan: Deptford fire, 13 killed, racist motivation suspected.
Wembley conference, Lab introduces its Electoral College.
Gang of Four

Jan: Govt plans to surcharge Camden councillors begin.
May: Labour victory in GLC elections under McIntosh, then left win vital vote of Lab

'Limehouse Declaration'.
Feb: Murdoch buys *The Times*.
Mar: SDP launched.
Apr: Rioting in Brixton.
May: Death of Bobby Sands.
Jul: Rioting in Toxteth, Moss Side, Wood Green.
Sep: Healey retains deputy leadership beating Benn by 0.8%.
Dec: Scargill elected leader of NUM.

Group and KL becomes Leader. Press hysteria begins. Left take control of ILEA. March for jobs.
Sept: GLC funds *City Limits*.
Oct: Govt legislation to control local council expenditure introduced. 'Fares Fair' introduced, cutting LT fares, Bromley Council takes GLC to court over policy.
Dec: Heseltine forced to withdraw legislation to limit rate increases. Ethnic Minorities cte anti-racist programme. Lesbian and Gay Men's working party established.

1982   Jan: Unemployment reaches 3m.
Feb: Local Govt Finance Act.
Apr–Jun: Falklands War.
Jun: Lab plan action against *Militant*.
Jul: Succession of strikes by ASLEF.

Jan: 'Keep Fares Fair' campaign.
Feb: 'Can't Pay, Won't Pay' campaign.
May: John McDonnell chair of Finance. Women's Committee founded.

1983   Jan: Opening of Sizwell inquiry.
Jun: Tories win Gen Election.
Oct: Kinnock elected Leader of Lab party, Hattersley deputy leader.

Jan: 'Peace Year' and exposure of Govt's plans. High court action over GLC fares policy.
Feb: Dialogue with Sinn Fein

Nov: First cruise missiles arrive at Greenham Common.

May: Govt plans to abolish GLC.
Second fare reduction.

1984
Mar: Miners' strike begins.
Sarah Tisdall gaoled.
Jul: High court rules that Govt ban on unions at GCHQ illegal.
Oct: Sequestration of NUM assets.

Govt prepares Paving Bill.
Mar: 'Say No to No Say' campaign.
Jun: House of Lords victory for GLC over amendments to Paving Bill.
House of Lords finally passes Paving Bill.
Jul: Plans to refuse to set a new rate, despite rate-capping.
Sep: By-elections held.
Nov: Abolition Bill published.

1985
Mar: Miners call off strike.
Jun: Govt proposals for social security reforms.
Sep: Riots in Handsworth and Brixton.
Oct: Riots in Tottenham.
Dec: Westland crisis begins.

Mar: KL/McDonnell split.
16 July Abolition Bill becomes law.

1986
Jan: Wapping dispute begins.
Mar: Massive demonstrations at Wapping.

31 March GLC abolished.

BIBLIOGRAPHY

Carvel, John, *Citizen Ken* (The Hogarth Press, 1984)
Cockburn, Cynthia, *The Local State* (Pluto Press, 1977)
Forrester, Lansley and Pauley, *Beyond Our Ken* (Fourth Estate, 1985)
Griffiths, J. A. G., *The Politics of the Judiciary* (Fontana, 1985)
Hollingsworth, Mark, *The Press and Political Dissent* (Pluto Press, 1986)

INDEX

359

Index

Index

Hatch, Stephen, 74
Hatfield, Richard, 273
Hattersley, Roy, 179, 260, 280, 289
Hatton, Derek, 263, 318
Havers, Sir Michael, Attorney-General, 217
Hayes and Harlington: GLC by-election (1984), 289, 290; Labour Party, 334
Hayter, Lord, 311, 302–3
Haywood, Ron, 179
Healey, Denis, 114
Heath, Edward, 18, 26, 27, 41–2, 251, 254, 270, 276–7, 301
Henderson, Roger, QC, 218, 219, 220, 221, 313, 314, 337
Herbert Commission (Sir Edwin Herbert), 249, 250
Herbert, Lewis, 109, 112, 261, 289
Heseltine, Michael, 130, 181–3, 189, 190, 191, 251, 252, 254, 308
Hillman, Ellis, 61, 92, 118
Hinds, Harvey, 50, 60, 107, 109–10, 113, 114, 115, 118, 119, 122, 137, 138, 139, 144, 172, 175, 205, 206, 214, 244–5, 295
Hodge, Margaret, 309, 320
Hollamby, Ted, 30
Holland, Stuart, 148
Holliday, Richard, 157, 158, 159, 161, 164, 167
Hollingsworth, Mark, *The Press and Political Dissent*, 157, 163, 164, 290–1
Hollocks, John, 235
homeless people, homelessness, 23, 31, 36–7, 41, 98; single and young people, 98–9
Home Rule for Ireland (1886), 247
homosexuality *see* lesbians and gay men
Hornchurch, 136, 203, 204
Horstead, Elsie, 36
House of Commons, 306, 307; Abolition Bill debates, 302; Paving Bill debates, 276–7, 278
House of Lords, 271, 287–8; Abolition Bill debates, 301–7; Paving Bill debates, 277–9, 283–4, 286, 288
Housing Associations, 23
Housing Commissioner, 26, 27
Housing Finance Act (1972), 26, 27, 28, 40, 47, 51, 183
housing programmes, 81, 87; allocation of housing, 32, 234; bed and breakfast hotels for homeless, 37; Camden Council, 95, 96–103, 142; cuts in, 63–4, 67, 70–1, 72, 76; GLC, 32, 41, 47, 51, 55, 57, 58, 63–5, 70, 76, 81, 338; halfway homes, 23, 32–3; house-building, 81, 186, 189; Lambeth, 11, 14–15, 17, 21–3, 27, 29–33, 34, 36–9, 40, 41, 58; modernization programmes, 338; municipalization, 41, 48, 57, 64, 97; sale of council houses, 76, 186–9, 210; Strategic Housing Plan, 64
Howell, David, 199, 200, 207, 210, 216–17, 221

ILEA (Inner London Education Authority), 48, 66, 72, 92–3, 108, 140, 150, 241, 251, 303; election of members, 282–3; GLC forward funding of, 337–8; Labour Group AGMs, 44, 140–1; Left take control of (1981), 180; price of school meals, 149; and rate-capping, 315, 333

immigration legislation, 11
inflation, 58, 60, 62, 218
Ingham, Bernard, 286
inner-city areas, gentrification of, 31
International Monetary Fund, 62
IRA, 157, 165, 166–8
Irving, Lord, 304, 305
Isaman, Gerald, 155
Islington Council, 26

Jacobs, David, 244
Jay, Douglas, 208–9, 210
Jenkin, Patrick, 259, 266, 269, 270–3, 275, 281, 282, 283, 284, 286, 287, 295, 309, 311
Jenkins, Marie, 48, 49
job/employment, 148–9, 151, 313; cuts, 70, 72, 104, 181–2; equal opportunities in, 233, 234–8, 297–8; People's March for Jobs (1981), 151–2
Joseph, Sir Keith, 282, 283
Judge, Tony, 57, 58, 68–9, 74, 80, 82, 92, 119, 143, 324, 333
judges/judiciary: Bromley Council's action against GLC's cheap fares policy (1981), 193–203; Camden surcharge case, 100–3, 219–20; Court of Appeal, 193–6, 197, 202; fiduciary duty concept, 197–8, 202, 218–19; GLC court action against LTE (1982–3), 222; Greater Manchester Council forward funding case, 337; GUS v. Merseyside County Council, 217; Kensington and Chelsea Council challenges GLC budget in courts, 218–19; Law Lords, 194, 195, 196–8, 199, 200, 201, 202–3, 206, 214, 217; political role of, 202–3, 338; sale of council houses, 186, 188–9; Westminster Council's High Court action against GLC, 338

'Keep Fares Fair' campaign, 201, 203–4, 209–10, 216–17, 233; public meeting (January 1982), 205–6
'Keep London Free Campaign', 183–4, 256
Keith, Lord, 196
Kennedy, Robert, 12
Kerr, Lord Justice, 222
Keys, John, 20–1, 59, 69, 72, 73, 76, 77, 78, 79, 90, 139
Kensington and Chelsea Council, 184, 219–20, 256
King, Martin Luther, 12
King, Mike, 107, 135
King, Tom, 252, 253, 254, 258, 259, 271
Kinnock, Neil, 260, 267, 289, 290, 324, 335
Kirwan, Patricia, 134
Kissinger, Henry, 12
Knapp, Jimmy, 221
Knight, Chris, 93, 210, 225, 226–8, 330, 334
Knight, Rev. David, 171
Knight, Ted, 18, 26–8, 33, 35, 36, 40, 42, 90, 106, 114, 122, 130, 133, 138–9, 142, 156, 161–2, 182, 216, 217, 218, 257; defeated in Norwood GLC election (1981), 137; elected Leader of Lambeth Council (1978), 39, 86, 89, 124–5; and rate-capping, 308, 309, 310, 315–16, 319, 320, 321, 324, 326–7; spending cuts crisis (1980–1), 130–1

Index

McNeill, Mr Justice, 218–19, 220, 221, 223
McParland, Eddie, 326
MacPherson, Mr Justice, 338
Mail on Sunday, 277
Manchester City Council, 337
Manson, Charles, 55
Marsh, Richard, 189, 190
Masefield, Sir Peter, Chairman of LTE, 146–8, 190–1, 199, 200–1, 214, 224
Matthews, Lord, 135
Megarry, Sir Robert, 186, 188–9
Mellish, Bob, 59, 69, 72, 73, 77, 78, 85, 86
Merseyside County Council, 217, 318
Metropolitan Board of Works, 247, 248
Metropolitan County Councils, 251; abolition of, 246, 252–3, 284
Militant, 326, 335
Militant Tendency, 18, 42, 229, 326
Miller, Millie, 95
Mills, John, 95, 103
miners' strike, 163, 225, 270, 329
Mitcham and Morden by-election (1982), 87
Moore, Paul, 36, 131, 148, 190
Morgan, Margaret, 180, 239
MORI polls, 255, 258, 280, 293, 298
Morrell, Frances, 173, 180, 282
Morrison, Herbert, 125, 249, 251, 290
motorways, 41, 42, 51, 116; Archway inquiry (1976), 42
municipalization programme, 41, 48, 57, 64, 97

NALGO, 38, 98, 178, 236, 265
National Front, 15, 203
National Health Service, 11, 249
National Union of Students, 250
NEC (Labour National Executive), 43, 46, 83, 106, 324; women's section of, 243
neighbourhood councils, 17, 22, 23, 29, 30–1, 37
Newsnight (BBC TV), 259
News of the World, 160
New Statesman, 166
Nicholas, David, 87
Nicholson, Brian, 88
Nicholson, District Auditor, 101
Nicholson, George, 261
Nine O'Clock News (BBC TV), 264–5
Nixon, President Richard, 12
Noble, Malcolm, 38, 39
Nolan, Mr Justice, 222
northern Ireland, 27, 106, 165, 166–8, 175, 185
North Sea oil, 84
North Westminster Action Committee, 328
Norwood, 74; 1973 GLC election campaign, 40, 42; 1981 GLC election defeat, 137
Norwood Labour Party, 13, 16–18, 40, 49, 72–3, 74; Livingstone joins (1969), 11, 13–14, 16
Norwood Young Socialists, 13, 71
Nuclear Free Zones movement, 233
nuclear weapons *see* Civil Defence
NUPE, 99
NUR Conference (1984), 283

Observer, 81–2
O'Connor, Paddy, 47, 61

Oliver, Lord Justice, 194, 195–6, 197
O'Mahony, John, 89–90, 211, 215, 226
opinion polls, 18, 83, 132, 133, 158, 162, 166, 168–70, 174, 177–8, 181, 185, 209, 245, 254–6, 257–8, 275, 276, 279–80, 293–4, 299, 307, 340–1, 344; telephone, 168, 169, 257
Opinion Research Centre polls, 169–70
Ormrod, Lord Justice, 220, 221
Ouseley, Herman, 234, 237
Owen, Dr David, 232, 265, 266

Pacter, Trudi, 163
Paddington, 184, 187, 188, 242; Livingstone elected GLC Councillor for (1981), 133–4, 136, 137; by-election (1984), 289, 290, 292
Paddington CLP, 133, 322, 333
Page, George, 90, 138, 139, 181
Parkinson affair, 274
Parliamentary Labour Party (PLP), 177, 179; dissociation from GLC Labour administration of, 177–8
Paving Bill (1984), 275–9, 283–4, 286–7, 288, 310
PC/PCC Committee (Policy and Policy Co-ordinating Committees), 126, 141–4, 150, 166, 173, 196, 206, 240, 261, 330, 332
'Peace Year' (1983), 233, 340
pensioners, 341; free travel for, 16, 17, 22, 73, 86, 148, 151, 191, 201, 216
People's March for Jobs (May 1981), 151–2
Perkins, Bernard, 14, 15
Petrou, Mike, 22, 29
Phillips, Mr Justice, 193
Phipp, Ken, 42
Pickwell, I., District Auditor, 100–1, 219, 220
Pitt, Bill, 38–9, 178–9, 210
Pitt, Lord David, 74
Plummer, Sir Desmond, 41–2, 81, 263, 302, 303
Police Federation Journal, 58
Ponsonby, Lord, 283, 305
Porter, Lady, 287, 300–1, 338
Powell, David, 171
Prentice, Reg, 45, 46, 66
Prescott v. Birmingham Corporation case (1955), 198
Press Association, 167
Press Council, 162
press/media, 121, 127–8, 134–6, 152–3, 201, 203, 204, 207, 238, 274; abolition of GLC, 246, 267, 277–8, 290–3; attacks against Labour GLC administration, 154–77, 179, 184–5, 192, 238, 239, 241, 242; cartoons, 157–8; 'creative' and inventive reporting, 159–61
Price, Chris, 263
Private Eye, 160, 161–2, 263, 335
Profumo affair, 274
Protect and Survive (government civil defence booklet), 232, 233
Putney, 137
Pym, Francis, 277, 284

quangos, government-appointed, 338–9

Race, Reg, 278, 283–4, 287, 293, 316, 317, 327, 329, 332, 333

365